Developmental Disabilities

Developmental Disabilities

A Handbook for Best Practices

Edited by

Phillip J. McLaughlin, Ed.D.

University of Georgia
Athens, Georgia

Paul Wehman, Ph.D.

Virginia Commonwealth University
Richmond, Virginia

Andover Medical Publishers
Boston   London   Oxford   Singapore   Sydney   Toronto   Wellington

Andover Medical Publishers is an imprint of Butterworth–Heinemann.

⊗ Recognizing the importance of preserving what has been written, it is the policy of Butterworth–Heinemann to have the books it publishes printed on acid-free paper, and we exert our best efforts to that end.

Library of Congress Cataloging-in-Publication Data

Developmental disabilities : a handbook for best practices / edited by
   Phillip J. McLaughlin, Paul Wehman.
      p.   cm.
   Includes bibliographical references and index.
   ISBN 1-56372-023-X (alk. paper) :
    1. Developmentally disabled—Handbooks, manuals, etc.
I. McLaughlin, Phillip J. II. Wehman, Paul.
   [DNLM: 1. Handicapped. 2. Mental Retardation—rehabilitation.
3. Social Adjustment. 4. Vocational Education. WB 320 D489]
HV1570.D48 1992
362,1'966—dc20
DNLM/DLC
for Library of Congress   91-41192
                                                CIP

Butterworth–Heinemann
80 Montvale Avenue
Stoneham, MA 02180

10 9 8 7 6 5 4 3 2 1

Printed in the United States of America

For K.B.
Thank you for showing the way.

Contents

Contributors

Rebecca J. Anderson, M.S., is on the faculty at George Mason University, Fairfax, Virginia. She is the coordinator for the Early Childhood Special Education Technical Assistance Center for northern Virginia. This technical assistance center provides workshops, library services, and direct consultations to personnel serving young children with disabilities. These services are funded by grants to the Center for Human Disabilities at George Mason University from the Department of Education.

Beth A. Bader has spent the past seven years of her career learning "what works" and "what doesn't work" in the provision of case management from hands-on experience as a case manager, supervisor, administrator, and consultant. Having a combined educational background of social work and physical therapy, she has had the opportunity for a continuously changing perspective in working with consumers who have developmental disabilities and with their families. Ms. Bader is currently a Program Support Consultant in the Virginia Department of Mental Health, Mental Retardation and Substance Abuse Services and is pursuing part-time doctoral studies at Virginia Commonwealth University.

William N. Bender, Ph.D., is an Associate Professor of Special Education at the University of Georgia. His current research interests include behavioral and social–emotional functioning of children and adolescents with learning disabilities, as well as instructional strategies for students with learning disabilities in mainstream classrooms. Currently, Dr. Bender is writing a text, *Introduction to Learning Disabilities: Identification, Assessment and Instructional Practices*, with Allyn and Bacon, for publication in 1992.

Kathryn A. Blake was Alumni Foundation Distinguished Professor of Special Education at the University of Georgia. She had extensive experience in programs for handicapped people both in the public schools and in higher education. Her teaching and research interests included mental retardation, physical and multiple handicaps, and research, development, and evaluation methodology. She published numerous books, monographs, chapters, and articles on topics within these specialty areas as well as on more general aspects of special education. Dr. Blake died in July of 1991.

Elaine Clark, Ph.D., is an Associate Professor of Educational Psychology and the

Director of School Psychology at the University of Utah in Salt Lake City. Dr. Clark conducts research on children and adults with neurologic and psychiatric disorders and provides consultations at the Western Institute of Neuropsychiatry and Primary Children's Medical Center in Salt Lake City.

Tom Clees, Ph.D., is an Assistant Professor of Special Education at the University of Georgia. His research reflects a commitment to community-based programs for persons with severe developmental disabilities. Tom has also worked at the University of Wisconsin on several projects relating to the habilitation of seriously emotionally disturbed individuals.

Ronald C. Eaves, Ph.D., is a Professor of Special Education, Auburn University. His career research interests have followed two main themes: emotional disturbance (particularly autism) and measurement issues in special education. He has authored the *Pervasive Development Disorder Rating Scale* and has co-authored the *Cognitive Levels Test* with Bob Algozzine, Lester Mann, and H. Robert Vance. Dr. Eaves has served as Editor-in-Chief of *Diagnostique*, the official journal of the Council for Educational Diagnostic Services, since 1980.

Trudie Hughes, M.Ed., is a Training Associate of the Rehabilitation Research and Training Center on Severe Traumatic Brain Injury at the Medical College of Virginia.

Katherine J. Inge, O.T.R., M.Ed., is a Training Associate at the Rehabilitation Research and Training Center on Supported Employment at Virginia Commonwealth University. She has been the coordinator of several demonstration projects that served individuals with severe disabilities and is currently the co-director of the Vocational Options Project for Youth with Severe Disabilities.

William R. Jenson, Ph.D., is a Professor of Educational Psychology and Chair of the Department of Educational Psychology at the University of Utah in Salt Lake City. Dr. Jenson's research focuses on interventions with behaviorally disturbed children and adolescents. He conducts parent and teacher training workshops across the nation. Dr. Jenson consults for Primary Children's Medical Center and the Children's Behavior Therapy Unit in Salt Lake City.

John Kregel, Ed.D., began his career as a classroom special education instructor for students with severe and multiple handicaps. After completing doctoral training, he received an appointment to Virginia Commonwealth University (VCU) in Educational Services. Since 1986, he has been the Research Director for the Rehabilitation Research and Training Center (RRTC) at VCU, and was recently appointed Associate Director. Dr. Kregel's areas of specialization include supported employment for persons with developmental and other severe disabilities, analysis of federal and state policies affecting the community and vocation integration of persons with severe disabilities, and career development and transition for exceptional students.

John Langone, Ph.D., is currently an Associate Professor in the Department of Special Education at the University of Georgia. He is the author of three books in the field as well as a number of articles in professional journals. His major research and academic interests center around the application of microcomputer technology in special education and the development of community-based instructional programs for individuals with mild to moderate and severe handicaps.

David C. Littman, Ph.D., is an assistant professor of computer science at George Mason University, Fairfax, Virginia. He also consults privately on numerous topics. He provides specific assistance in the area of early intervention with program evaluation, design of instruments and surveys, computer assistance, and statistics.

Michael Malone is the Training Coordinator for the Georgia University-Affiliated Program (UAP) for Persons with Developmental Disabilities and an Adjunct Assistant Professor in the Department of Child and Family Development at the University of Georgia. He coordinates the Georgia UAP's interdisciplinary masters and doctoral programs in aging and developmental disabilities. He has published in *Gerontology Review* and made numerous presentations on the demographics of aging and developmental disabilities.

JoAnn M. Marchant, M.Ed., is Principal of Virginia Randolph School in Henrico County, Virginia. Her interests include community-based, functional programming and behavior management techniques for students with severe or multiple disabilities.

Phillip J. McLaughlin, Ed.D., is an Associate Professor at the University of Georgia in the Department of Special Education. He is a leader in teacher training and career education for youth with mild mental retardation. Dr. McLaughlin has published a number of articles and books and has made numerous national presentations to audiences in the mental retardation field. He is currently working on a new book, *Advances in Special Education and Rehabilitation.*

Susan H. Neal is currently Director of Training at the Virginia Institute for Developmental Disabilities, the university-affiliated program at Virginia Commonwealth University. As a faculty member, Ms. Neal has developed preservice and inservice case management curricula aimed at promoting best practice throughout the Commonwealth's developmental disabilities service system. Ms. Neal's prior experience in case management includes serving as the Chair of the Statewide Case Management Task Force, which set policies and procedures for case management in Virginia, certifying and evaluating case management programs as a State Mental Retardation Consultant, and working in administrative and direct service positions in local mental retardation services.

Linda M. Nutt is a doctoral student in social work at the University of Alabama. She has worked with developmentally disabled adults and children in educational and institutional settings. Her current research focuses on social support, life satisfaction, and integration of elderly individuals with mental retardation in communities.

Susan O'Mara has extensive experience in developing and implementing supported employment programs for persons with severe developmental disabilities. For the past four years, she has been a consultant for the Virginia Office of Supported Employment, providing training and technical assistance to rehabilitation professionals. Ms. O'Mara is a specialist in the area of Social Security benefits.

David Pitonyak is an adjunct faculty member at the University-Affiliated Program (UAP) of New Jersey and a private human services consultant. David believes that challenging behaviors, such as self-injury, can be viewed as "messages" that can tell us important things about a person and the quality of his or her life. He believes that understanding the "meaning" of behavior is the first step in supporting a person (and everyone else) to change. David received his doctorate from Virginia Commonwealth University in 1990.

H. Kenton Reavis, Ed.D., is a Specialist in the Comprehensive System of Personnel Development and Behavior Disorders, Utah State Office of Education.

William R. Sharpton, Ph.D., is an Associate Professor on the faculty of the Department of Special Education and Habilitative Services at the University of New Orleans. Dr. Sharpton is the director of the Louisiana Institute on Developmental Disabilities and coordinates a graduate-level personnel preparation program focusing on the needs of individuals with severe disabilities. His research interests include the design of effective instructional programs that result in integrated opportunities for individuals with severe disabilities, including employment in community settings.

Richard E. Talbot, Ph.D., is currently Chair of the Communication Disorders Program at the University of Virginia. Previously he was Chair of the Division for Exceptional Children at the University of Georgia, which included the Departments of Special Education and Communication Disorders and the Developmental Disabilities Program. Dr. Talbot also served as the Executive Director of the University Affiliated Program at the University of Georgia. His doctorate is from the University of Oklahoma Health Science Center in Audiology.

Paul Wehman, Ph.D., is Professor at the Department of Rehabilitation Medicine, Medical College of Virginia, and Director of the Rehabilitation Research and Training Center, Virginia Commonwealth University. Internationally recognized for his service and scholarly contributions in the field of vocational rehabilitation, Dr. Wehman is the recipient of the 1990 Joseph P. Kennedy, Jr. Foundation Award in Mental Retardation. He is the author of numerous books, research monographs, journal articles, and chapters in the areas of traumatic brain injury, mental retardation, supported employment, and special education.

Michael D. West, M.Ed., is a Research Associate at the Rehabilitation Research and Training Center on Supported Employment and on Severe Traumatic Brain Injury at Virginia Commonwealth University and a doctoral candidate in the Virginia Commonwealth University School of Education's Urban Services Leadership Program. His research and policy analysis interests are predominantly in supported employment services for persons with severe disabilities, particularly for persons with severe mental retardation and severe traumatic brain injury.

Pamela S. Wolfe is an Assistant Professor in the Department of Educational and School Psychology and Special Education at The Pennsylvania State University. Her interests include transition, instructional methodology, and advocacy for individuals with severe disabilities.

Preface

The decade of the 1980s witnessed tremendous advances in services for people with developmental disabilities. These advances were characterized by a greater public awareness of needs, by a broader range of services being provided locally, by innovations in services (for example, supported employment, assistive technology) and, most importantly, by a greater flow of persons with developmental disabilities into the mainstream of American life.

There has also been an explosion of information in this field, with increasing numbers of books and journals being devoted to specialized topics. With this increasing specialization has come a wider network of university developmental disability training programs and expanded university-affiliated program (UAP) activities. New federal legislation provides support for an expanded range of developmental disability activities, including planning, education, and service delivery programs.

The purpose of this book is straightforward: to provide a basic, introductory reference text for students and professionals *beginning* their careers in or *expanding* their careers to include developmental disabilities. As noted previously, many publications are devoted to specialized topics, which usually do not provide the "big pic-

ture" of services. In this book we not only present best practices but also try to show a comprehensive view of different disabilities and the range of services necessary to work with people who have such disabilities. The goal of this book is to present current material that appeals to a wide range of people working in many disciplines within the field of developmental disabilities.

To achieve this goal, we have assembled a number of experts in developmental disabilities. Some of the authors are academicians and some are practitioners who work daily with people with developmental disabilities. Each chapter includes multiple case studies. A brief overview of each chapter follows.

The first chapter, Mild to Moderate Mental Retardation, by John Langone, gives an overview of the major cognitive, learning, and affective characteristics exhibited by individuals with developmental disabilities. Topics such as self-care, language development, learning and cognition, mobility, and self-direction are developed along practical lines that provide readers with suggestions for implementing program options in these areas. In addition, sections on transition from school to work and on independent living skills include preferred strategies for developing activities to assist learners with mild to moderate cognitive deficits in becoming productive members of society.

Chapter 2, Severe and Profound Mental Retardation, by William West and Michael Sharpton, illustrates competencies developed by individuals with severe or profound retardation and their abilities to learn and perform complex tasks in a variety of integrated settings. The key to success in this area has been the manner in which service providers train and support persons with disabilities and the commitment of service providers to achieving meaningful outcomes and community integration and participation. A framework for services for this population is presented, involving training, adaptation, and support of tasks and activities.

Katherine Inge's chapter, Cerebral Palsy, provides a solid foundation on cerebral palsy and implications for diagnosis and treatment. The problems in identifying good community services are also discussed.

In the chapter written by Elaine Clark, Kenton Reavis, and William Jenson, Emotional Impairments, the authors describe areas of dysfunction that are typically seen in individuals with emotional and behavior disturbances. Although some areas of daily living remain relatively intact, others are devastated. As the authors point out, learning deficits that are related to emotional problems contribute heavily to the general dysfunction, especially the capacity for independent living and economic self-sufficiency. The authors analyze frequently used interventions and provide suggestions for best practices for intervention. Important resources for parents, teachers, and professionals are recommended.

In Ronald Eaves' chapter on Autism, the reader is provided with four important components of dealing with autistic individuals. First, a brief history is presented to explain the many competing terms that have been applied to the autistic person. Second, the problem of differential diagnosis is addressed. A functional description of autistic characteristics is presented in the third component. Finally, the bulk of the chapter details treatments for the more common behaviors displayed by autistic individuals (that is, self-injurious behavior, aggression, and aberrant speech and language development).

William Bender follows with an excellent chapter on Learning Disabilities in which he emphasizes how service delivery for this population—ranging from assessment to instruction—has changed radically within the last two decades. Despite this constant change, similarities among children with learning disabilities can be identified, including academic problems that are not attributable to identifiable handicapping conditions, difficulties in social–emotional–behavioral functioning, difficulties in expressive language—particularly pragmatic use of language—and poor attention and memory skills. Despite these difficulties, the prognosis for most children and adolescents with learning disabilities is positive.

The chapter, Communication Disorders, by Richard Talbot emphasizes the need for early assessment and remediation of the communication status of all individuals with developmental disabilities. The importance of establishing a communication base as a prerequisite to all other intervention is also discussed. The chapter provides the reader with an overview of the many types of and treatments for communication disorders that may be encountered by professionals working with developmentally disabled individuals. In addition, a discussion of the application, both current and future, of technology on behalf of individuals with communication disorders is presented.

JoAnn Marchant's chapter on Deaf–Blind Handicapping Conditions details strategies for teaching students with dual sensory disabilities. It also presents an historic perspective of how services have been provided for these students. Case studies are cited and concrete suggestions are offered for classroom teachers, parents, and care givers.

Pamela Wolfe has developed an excellent chapter that outlines the Challenges for Service Providers in the community. She provides an extensive discussion of community services and ways to access these services.

The chapter by Rebecca Anderson and David Littman on Early Intervention offers practical tools for working with young children and their families. Information is organized around a service delivery cycle. The components of this cycle include assessment, program design, delivery, and evaluation, the evaluation being utilized for the subsequent trip around the cycle. Individualized family service plan components are addressed. Assessment and intervention checklists are included.

In the chapter on Special Education, Kathryn Blake considers how best to deliver instruction to developmentally disabled youngsters. First, she discusses special education and related services as they are defined in the Education of All Handicapped Children Act. Then, she describes components of instructional programs and how they are used with developmentally disabled youngsters. Finally, she presents information about how our work is organized within special education law. Throughout, she emphasizes the importance of coordination among services as well as the need to apply the principle of normalization as frequently as possible when working with developmentally disabled youngsters.

Case Management is described in the chapter by Susan O'Neal and Beth Bader. It is an exciting time for case management services. Everything about this service is being questioned, reviewed, and revised, as its importance is documented in legislation, research, literature, and programming. This chapter, using a set of values as a framework for responsive case management, addresses what case management has been, is now, and can be. Topics in case management that are addressed include components of service coordination,

role of the supervisor, inservice and preservice training needs, and quality assurance. Examples of interventions with consumers and their families provide the reader with a practical approach to enhancing case management services.

Supported Employment is the topic of the chapter by Trudie Hughes and Paul Wehman. The impact of supported employment is discussed; several case studies portray supported employment implementation.

Behavior Management, especially the treatment of self-injury, is discussed in depth by David Pitonyak. This is a specialized area, but one in which tremendous abuses have taken place over the years against persons with developmental disabilities. Pitonyak discusses nonaversive interventions.

Tom Clees, in the chapter on Community Living, discusses the degree to which people with disabilities obtain and maintain independence from restrictive settings, including institutions, nursing homes, group homes, workshops, and other segregated settings. The current continuum-of-services model restricts individuals with disabilities by allocating the vast majority of fiscal, direct, and related service supports to segregated living arrangements and places of employment. This chapter describes alternatives to current service models, most notably supported living models, and provides procedures for identifying and teaching relevant independent living skills. In addition, the importance of collaboration and advocacy within and between schools, agencies, and postschool support programs is discussed. Finally, a collaborative model for assisting individuals with disabilities to make transitions to, and maintain independent living status within, integrated community settings is offered.

Susan O'Mara and John Kregel tackle one of the toughest areas in the field today: Social Security. The complicated regulations and their far-ranging implications are discussed.

Linda Nutt and Michael Malone, in the final chapter, Gerontology, discuss the fact that individuals with lifelong disabilities are living longer than ever before. As a result, the individual, their families, and service providers are facing a host of situations that challenge each of them to respond in an enlightened manner. The mission of service providers is to help the elderly individual with developmental disabilities create a meaningful set of life resources that enables him or her to enjoy a high quality of life.

This book is comprehensive in scope. Although it is impossible to cover all topics in the area of developmental disabilities, we believe that this book will be an excellent core reference for providers in most of the helping disciplines. Extensive use of case studies brings the information to life.

Chapter 1
Mild to Moderate Mental Retardation

John Langone

Functional Description

By definition, people who have mild to moderate mental retardation are differentiated from people without cognitive disabilities using two criteria: intellectual capacity and adaptive behavior. Intellectual capacity and adaptive behavior are the two major components of the American Association on Mental Retardation's (AAMR) definition, the one most used by educators. This definition has evolved over the years, with the latest revision occurring in 1983.

In the 1983 revision of its *Manual on Terminology and Clarification in Mental Retardation*, the AAMR defined mental retardation as "significantly subaverage general intellectual functioning existing concurrently with deficits in adaptive behavior and manifested during the developmental period" (Grossman 1983). For the purposes of this definition, the developmental period includes birth through age 18 and is characterized by slow, arrested, or incomplete development of a person's intellectual functioning. Significantly subaverage intellectual functioning is described by severity levels (mild, moderate, severe, and profound) in terms of how far an individual's measured intelligence deviates from the norm.

The concept of adaptive behavior has been the definitional component that has caused the most controversy among professionals. Adaptive behavior is defined as an individual's ability to meet ". . . the standards of maturation, learning, personal independence, and/or social responsibility" (Grossman 1983) one would normally demonstrate at each of life's stages. Many professionals believe that one's ability to function in society, regardless of intellectual capacity, is the best measure of competence. Although this view may be true, the concept of adaptive behavior has not been universally accepted. This lack of acceptance may be the result of the preconceived lack of objectivity involved in measuring what constitutes successful adaptation to society.

Accurate measurement of adaptive behavior is important. This fact is especially crucial for those individuals who fall in the borderline range of mental retardation. For example, a person who falls below a score of approximately 70 on an individually administered intelligence test would not be considered to have mental retardation if he or she did not demonstrate concurrent deficits in adaptive behavior. The importance of an accurate measurement of adaptive behavior is obvious when one considers that the outcome of this evaluation may be all that stands between an individual and the label "mentally handicapped."

Measures of adaptive behavior can be subjective, and the ratings of the same person can vary from rater to rater. Professionals who remain cognizant of this fact can decrease the probability of mislabeling individuals by obtaining a number of adaptive behavior ratings from a variety of sources. Parents, teachers, neighbors, and relatives should all be consulted, and the information gathered from these sources should be used to formulate a more thorough profile of a person's ability to function in his or her environment.

Mild Mental Retardation

People with mild mental handicaps demonstrate cognitive abilities at the top end of the continuum from mild to profound. The most recent AAMR definition identifies an IQ range of between 50 to 55 and approximately 70 as the intellectual functioning criterion for individuals who would fall in this category (Grossman 1983). An individual can be classified as having mild mental retardation only if this range of intellectual functioning exists concurrently with deficits in adaptive behavior.

For example, Will was referred for testing by his teacher because of Will's poor academic achievement and lack of social skills that the teacher deemed appropriate for individuals in Will's age group. Further testing revealed that Will achieved a Binet IQ of 68, with a range of four testing levels, and a Vineland score of 78. His adaptive behavior scores were within the normal range; therefore, he did not meet one of the criteria for mild mental retardation. His performance, however, indicated that he needed additional assistance, so the psychologist, referring teachers, and remedial specialists worked together to develop strategies that could be used with Will in the regular class.

Individuals with mild cognitive deficits differ greatly from one another. Over the years the number of these persons identified and labeled as needing special education services has decreased considerably (Patton et al., 1990). This decrease is the result of a number of variables, including a lack of clear evidence that special education has helped these individuals make significant academic and social gains and the identification of inappropriate testing practices that labeled a disproportionate number of minority students as having mild mental handicaps.

In any event, the population of individuals identified as having mild cognitive disabilities is smaller and demonstrates more intense academic and social skills deficits than those of individuals enrolled in special education programs in the 1970s (Polloway and Smith 1987). Individuals with mild cognitive disabilities still constitute the greatest number within the category of mental retardation. The causes of mild mental retardation are the least understood. Heredity is certainly an important factor in the onset of mild mental retardation; however, medical researchers are currently unable to pinpoint identifiable organic causes for most cases. Other variables such as environmental pollution (for example, lead emissions in the air), lack of environmental stimulation, little or no pre- and postnatal health care, and poor nutrition all affect the cognitive deficits experienced by some individuals. This complex interaction of heredity and environment (nature versus nurture) results in a disproportionate number of individuals with mild mental retardation coming from families at the lower socioeconomic level of society.

Children with mild cognitive deficits develop social, motor, and language skills at a slower rate than their peers. These developmental delays, however, often go unnoticed during the preschool years (Thurman and Widerstrom 1990). When these children enter school, their disabilities become more pronounced, and a combination of academic as well as behavioral deficits causes teachers to begin the referral process (Ysseldyke and Algozzine

1990). La Tonia's parents stated that she was always "slower" than her siblings. She began walking later than her brothers and sisters and had trouble communicating her needs until she was 3 years old. Her parents felt that these delays were normal because La Tonia was "born early" and that she would "catch up" to the other children in time. When La Tonia entered school her teachers noticed that she exhibited deficits in preacademic readiness skills. They also estimated that her maturity level was delayed by about one to two years. After La Tonia repeated a second year of developmental kindergarten, during which she made small improvements, her teachers referred her for additional assessment and potential special education services.

Moderate Mental Retardation

Those children who function at a level lower than that of mild mental retardation are usually identified earlier, often at birth. The most recent AAMR definition identifies individuals with moderate mental retardation as those who function intellectually within a range of 30 to 35 and 50 to 55 on standardized intelligence measures and who exhibit significant deficits in adaptive behavior (Grossman 1983). For example, Martin's Binet IQ was 38 and he demonstrated significant developmental delays (approximately two years) in learning to sit, crawl, and walk. He is currently 8 years old and requires help dressing and feeding himself more difficult foods such as spaghetti or soups. Martin's language continues to be delayed. He has good receptive language, but his ability to express himself verbally is limited to single words or short phrases.

A variety of clinical syndromes have observable physical characteristics (for example, Down's syndrome) that are associated with moderate mental impairments. Many individuals with moderate cognitive disabilities also have additional handicap-

ping conditions (for example, cerebral palsy). The disabilities associated with moderate mental handicaps are more likely to be directly linked to a genetic or biochemical problem that manifested itself during the prenatal period.

In the past, the common outcome for individuals with moderate mental retardation was institutionalization. Today, we realize that the prognosis for community placement of these individuals is excellent. With early and continual support to families and innovative educational programs, these learners can become independent, productive citizens.

☐ Case 1-1: Carrie

Carrie is an 18-year-old high school student with Down's syndrome. She enjoys attending after-school activities such as football games and occasionally attends movies with a boy from her special education class. Carrie attends a self-contained special education class that emphasizes community-based instruction (Langone 1986, 1990). Carrie spends most of her day in community settings learning to work, shop, and live as independently as possible. She attends some classes with her regular education peers, such as physical education, and eats lunch with neighborhood friends. The goal for Carrie is eventually to live in a supervised apartment in the community and to work in a local library. Her transition plan, currently being developed, indicates that, in addition to the preceding goals, Carrie will be helped to participate in a regular bowling league whose members are not handicapped and in a support group composed of individuals with handicaps.

Mild to Moderate Mental Retardation

In reality, individuals with mild to moderate cognitive deficits have the same needs and desires as anyone in the general population. As a group, people with mild to moderate mental retardation are more alike than different in terms of the program goals set by parents and professionals and the instructional strategies designed to help them reach those goals.

The main differences among people with mild to moderate mental retardation are not between subgroups (for example, mild compared with moderate mental retardation), but between each individual and the distance to his or her life goals (Grey 1981). All individuals have differing needs regardless of the severity level of their handicapping conditions. The common denominator is that all people have the right to live as independently as possible. To achieve this goal, professionals must take into account the life goals of *each* individual when developing programs to teach academic, social, or vocational skills (Langone 1990). Activities should be offered in an environment in which the individual is expected to use the targeted skills. For example, Bobby, a student with mild cognitive deficits, may have problems choosing the appropriate clothing for work or leisure settings. Sam, a student with moderate mental retardation, may have difficulty dressing himself as well as choosing appropriate clothing. Both students require assistance learning self-care skills, each one differing only in the distance to his life goal of independently working and living in the community.

Mere labels cannot predict what individuals need to learn in relation to their life goals. Regardless of whether an individual is labeled as having mild or moderate mental retardation, he or she will need help learning the same skills. The level of skills ultimately learned and the intensity of the strategies used to teach them are dependent on each individual's needs and the distance to one's life goals. The remainder of this chapter describes a variety of curricular areas that relate to the needs of all learners with mild and moderate mental retardation. Each section includes a general description of characteristics that in-

dividuals with these disabilities often exhibit and suggestions for program development and instructional strategies.

Self-Care

The ability to take care of one's own personal needs is a vital component of independent living. For individuals with mild to moderate mental retardation, deficits in caring for these needs are evident. In most cases, these individuals can learn to care for their personal needs at least as well as the general population who do not have handicaps. Because of the heterogeneity of this group, self-care needs and the intensity of training required to help them master the related skills vary tremendously. For example, one student with mild cognitive disabilities might need to learn more appropriate table manners at a local restaurant. Another student with moderate mental handicaps might need to learn to use eating utensils properly when faced with a variety of foods.

Generally, self-care skills are grouped into two categories: eating and dressing/ grooming. A variety of skills can be clustered under these two categories:

Eating

1. Chooses foods of proper nutritional value.
2. Shows appropriate eating habits, such as table manners and clearing his or her place.
3. Orders and eats food appropriately in different community restaurants.

Dressing/Grooming

1. Uses a variety of electrical self-care appliances appropriately and safely (for example, razors).
2. Showers or bathes independently as needed and does so in variety of environments (for example, YMCA and home).

3. Matches clothing for color, style, or design.

4. Matches clothing to a variety of conditions (for example, weather, work environment).

The preceding self-care skills are a small sample of those that might be targeted for instruction in an educational program for students with mild to moderate cognitive deficits. Regardless of the age of the learners, professionals would first determine what self-care skills the students need in their current and future environments by implementing a community needs assessment process (Langone 1986). This approach, accomplished through interviews and observations, provides information that allows professionals to determine the level at which students currently function.

Because of the heterogeneity of the group categorized as mild to moderate cognitively impaired, the range of skills addressed is broad and based on the age of the learner. A 5- or 6-year-old child with moderate cognitive delays may not be completely toilet trained or may demonstrate inappropriate toileting skills (for example, refusal to wipe him- or herself after defecating). In such cases, instructional strategies can be designed to omit the inappropriate responses and teach the appropriate alternative behaviors.

The literature is replete with examples of interventions designed to teach basic self-care skills to younger individuals who have mild to moderate mental retardation such as toilet training (Foxx and Azrin 1973), dressing (Nutter and Reid 1978), and eating (Riordan et al. 1984). In addition, more advanced self-care behaviors such as restaurant skills are being taught with great success (Marholin et al. 1979).

□ Case 1-2: Carmen

Carmen, a high school student with mild mental retardation, often comes to school dressed in clothes that are both provoca-tive and of loud colors that often do not match. During the community needs assessment process, the teacher learns that Carmen's mother also dresses in this fashion. During the needs assessment process, the teacher gathers information about the types and styles of dress appropriate for potential employment outcomes.

At this point, the teacher develops an instructional program designed to help Carmen discriminate and use appropriate dress for certain environments. The teacher attempts to do this without attaching a value judgment on Carmen's current style. Knowing that Carmen's mother also dresses in this fashion helps the teacher avoid alienating the mother and eventually Carmen. The goal is to help Carmen learn to discriminate among the environments in which specific types of clothing can be worn. The teacher does this by exposing her to many appropriate role models in the community.

Receptive and Expressive Language

MacMillan (1982) states that speech and language deficiencies occur at a significantly greater frequency among learners with mild to moderate mental retardation than might be expected in the general population. This observation appears to be the result of three factors. First, more individuals with moderate mental retardation may have associated physiologic problems that adversely affect their ability to produce clear speech. Second, individuals with mild mental retardation who come from lower socioeconomic groups may not be exposed to as many good role models (for example, their parents may not be able to talk to them as often as parents in higher socioeconomic groups). Finally, cognitive ability and language development are linked, and a decrease in cognitive ability may lead to language deficits (Patton et al. 1990).

Receptive and expressive language difficulties range in severity from problems with articulation of sounds or pronunciation of words to a significant delay in language development (Spradlin 1968). For many individuals with mild cognitive impairments, speech and language problems can be a secondary handicapping condition. Epstein and colleagues (1989) found that, in a sample of 107 individuals with mild mental retardation, over half were eligible for speech pathology services. As mentioned previously, this high incidence can be attributed partly to the poor environments where these children reside. Speech and language problems in this group can also be attributed to cultural differences (Patton et al. 1990). Researchers and government statistics have demonstrated that a disproportionate number of students labeled as mildly retarded come from minority groups. The cultural differences and language barriers working in tandem with environmental influences possibly contribute to the language delays experienced by many of these individuals.

In addition, individuals with more moderate cognitive deficits run the risk of having secondary physical impairments that can adversely affect their speech and language development (Thurman and Widerstrom 1990). Motor development problems and physiologic anomalies may decrease the individual's ability to produce intelligible speech. For example, a protruding tongue, a characteristic found in many individuals with Down's syndrome, adversely affects the pronunciation of words (MacMillan 1982).

Hearing problems are more common in learners with moderate cognitive deficits (Patton et al. 1990). These problems may be directly linked to language delays and poor speech production (Thurman and Widerstrom 1990). Regardless of the cause, the presence of deficits or delays in speech and language development is increased for individuals with mild to moderate cognitive disabilities.

A variety of annual goals can be developed to improve both the receptive and expressive language skills of learners who are mildly or moderately mentally handicapped. Table 1-1 provides a list of speech and language goals common found in an Individualized Education Program (IEP).

As with all other areas of the curriculum, the best place to teach appropriate use of receptive and expressive language is in a natural setting. Over the years, researchers and educators have found that language skills learned in isolated classroom activities do not automatically generalize to other daily living activities. Younger chil-

Table 1-1. Typical Language Goals for Students with Mild to Moderate Cognitive Deficits.

Demonstrates understanding of common sounds.

Imitates simple sentences.

Discriminates between singular and plural nouns.

Says phrases that have correct noun–verb agreement.

Discriminates present tense verbs from other tenses.

Completes tasks when orally directed.

Answers oral questions with correctly spoken sentences.

Gives oral directions involving places and task completion.

Asks for directions or help.

Converses in social situations.

Converses in consumer situations.

Demonstrates the ability to decode the nonverbal behavior of others.

Uses appropriate nonverbal behavior to communicate intent or mood.

Uses appropriate skills in conversation such as opening and closing, turn taking, appropriateness of topics, and staying with a topic.

Tells a story and shares events.

From Langone, J. (1990). *Teaching Students with Mild to Moderate Learning Problems*. Boston: Allyn & Bacon. With permission.

dren require more traditional language-training designed to help them master basic verbal behaviors and verbal prerequisites (Bricker, 1983). These children, however, still need assistance with generalizing newly acquired language skills to play groups, family functions, and other community-based activities.

The best time to assist mild to moderately handicapped children to obtain language skills is during their early years (Thurman and Widerstrom 1990). Language training by an early-intervention specialist should include both direct service to the child and assistance to the parents designed to help them teach and foster these skills in their children.

Early instruction involves systematically teaching and reinforcing a learner's ability to imitate and discriminate gestures or vocalizations. The teacher accomplishes these objectives by using both chaining and shaping strategies. Initially, the teacher reinforces all vocalizations, thereby increasing the overall number. Gradually, only those vocalizations that more closely resemble the final objective are reinforced until the learner can reliably produce the sound or word. Eventually, the teacher reinforces only more complex vocalizations such as a statement (for example, "say, I want a drink").

The most important component of a language and communication program and the one most often overlooked is the promotion of the generalization of these skills. As with all skills, a systematic program designed to enhance generalization is necessary because these students do not transfer learned skills easily. As the student initially acquires language and communication skills, the teacher simply increases the number of stimuli the student is exposed to during the course of instruction. For example, when teaching the student to respond to the request "Put the can in the box," the teacher can use boxes and cans of different sizes and weights or cans with different labels.

Teaching students to generalize more advanced language and communication skills requires increasing their exposure to naturally occurring events. Students with mild to moderate cognitive deficits appear to learn more advanced communication skills when they are in the setting where the communication demands have real life value. Teaching advanced language skills in community and school environments helps learners to see that language is a way to control the environment, thus motivating them to master these skills. For example, Wendi might be learning to remember and repeat orally five important criteria for renting an apartment. Once she can state the five points, the teacher might ask her, onsite in a model apartment, to repeat each point orally for the group and note its significance. A final activity or test for Wendi would be to call or visit apartment managers and ask them the questions related to the criteria (for example, how many bedrooms does the apartment have?). Generalization of Wendi's advanced communication skills continues to improve as she practices these activities in more apartments and in the presence of more apartment managers. A variety of instructional strategies are used to teach language to learners with mild to moderate cognitive handicaps. All of these individuals can learn to control their environments and communicate with people using language. The extent to which they advance their skills is dependent upon the types and numbers of innovative social and other community activities developed for them by their teachers.

Learning and Cognition

Individuals with mild to moderate mental retardation have pervasive limited cognitive ability (Keogh 1988). This pervasive limited cognitive ability is not as inconsistent, in terms of intelligence versus achievement, as one might expect from students accurately identified as having learning disabilities or behavior disorders. These students have frequent "peaks and valleys" in terms of their ability to grasp new concepts and apply new skills.

All comparisons are relevant. Although students with mild to moderate mental retardation show much less of a discrepancy between their measured intelligence and their achievement compared with non-handicapped students, they differ considerably within their own group (Edgar 1987; MacMillan 1982). The major characteristic shared by all categories of learners with mild to moderate handicaps is that they fall significantly behind their general education peers in tasks that require learning and using academic skills. Deshler and Schumaker (1986) found that by high school many learners categorized as having mild handicaps had fallen *at least* six years behind their general education peers in academic achievement. If this is true for those students with mild handicaps, the differences for those with moderate mental retardation are great enough that comparisons lose their meaning.

Two basic theories have been used to describe the cognitive development of individuals with mild to moderate mental retardation. The developmental theory, best described by Zigler (1969), postulates that individuals progress through the same developmental levels as those who do not have handicaps, but they do so at a much slower rate. Adherents to the developmental approach also postulate that the highest developmental levels reached by individuals with cognitive deficits are much lower than the highest levels reached by their peers without handicaps.

The difference theorists postulate that the mental capabilities of individuals with mental retardation are qualitatively different from those of their nonhandicapped peers (Zigler, 1969). These theorists contend that differences exist in the ability of people with cognitive deficits to process learned information.

Research supporting or refuting each theory is equivocal. Regardless of one's theoretical point of view, the results of these studies underscore the fact that individuals with mental retardation are slow to learn new skills, do not grasp concepts well at symbolic or abstract levels, are inefficient learners, and do not readily transfer learned skills to new settings or when different materials are required (Langone 1986). Therefore, more recent research has focused on finding the most effective and efficient instructional strategies to use in helping these individuals overcome the deficits resulting from mental retardation.

Learning Skills

For many reasons, individuals with cognitive deficits may learn facts and lists by intensive drill, but they fail to master higher-order learning skills. Abstract concepts such as numerical reasoning, time, measurement, and money use may be difficult skills for them to master (Langone 1990).

Part of the question that has not adequately been answered is whether these learners cannot master advanced learning skills or whether professionals have not adequately identified and taught these skills because they overemphasize drilling basic facts. The trend toward improving the learning skills of individuals with cognitive deficits is to teach more advanced skills in environments where these skills have a high probability of being used.

For example, high school students with mild mental handicaps may have a great deal of trouble learning to add, subtract, and generally use fractions in classroom activities involving a blackboard and paper and pencil tasks. These same students may be able to master the use of fractions when they are taught in cooking exercises conducted in hospital kitchens or in building trade exercises conducted at an office remodeling project.

Having acknowledged that individuals with mental retardation have varying deficits in memory, attention, organization of material, ability to model others, and language, researchers have turned their attention to identifying and testing strategies to accommodate for these deficits. Effective teachers instruct learners how to pay close attention to the relevant parts of any task by color coding the important components of reading, mathematic, or vocational tasks. This approach helps students discriminate between what is important and what is not, thus minimizing their memory problems and improving the quality of their work.

Many other examples exist of instructional strategies that can be used to help learners with mild to moderate mental retardation minimize their weaknesses in cognition. Memory improvement devices (mnemonics) as mediators help learners with poor memories complete a variety of advanced tasks.

□ Case 1-3: Paul

Paul, a high-school-age student with moderate mental retardation, has been taught to remember the word "state" as a mnemonic device when he goes to a restaurant. This device helps Paul remember skills he has learned in his community-based instructional activities.

*s*ay hello to the waitress (waiter)

*t*ell him/her what you want

*a*sk for help when needed

*t*ake your time eating

*e*mploy good manners

Paul has learned a variety of words he uses in different situations. His teacher reinforces Paul socially for verbally modeling her by saying each letter and statement aloud at appropriate points (depending on the task). Over subsequent trials, Paul is encouraged

and reinforced for repeating the statements in an increasingly softer voice until he eventually repeats them silently to himself. The teacher judges the use of the mnemonic by the accuracy of Paul's task completion. At some point, it becomes difficult to judge whether Paul uses the mnemonic device or completes the task because he has learned the chain of steps. The mnemonic is merely a backup device that Paul can refer to if, for some reason, the chain of skills is interrupted. Mnemonic devices are especially useful for learners who are confronted by social situations because these devices help them remember what actions are appropriate for the conditions.

Generalization of Skills

Individuals with mild to moderate cognitive impairments have trouble generalizing skills they have learned in one setting to other settings that involve different materials, different people, and different time (Langone and Westling 1979; Wehman et al. 1977). This problem also exists among persons in the general population; however, it appears more pronounced among individuals with mental retardation.

A number of behaviorally oriented strategies have been developed to assist these learners in overcoming most deficits they have in generalizing learned skills. Varying the settings, the time of day, the materials, and the people working with a student appears to facilitate generalization (Stokes and Baer 1977). These seem like common sense suggestions. Unfortunately, many educational programs that provide services to learners with cognitive deficits do not take these issues into account. Community-based instruction (Langone 1986, 1990) allows learners to minimize their problems with generalization by practicing skills in environments where they are expected to use them.

Mr. Cedar may want his middle-school-age students with mild mental retardation to apply math skills to everyday problems such as cost-comparison shopping. He has attempted to accomplish this task over many weeks using only classroom-based activities. On a field trip to a local grocery store, Mr. Cedar was dismayed to discover that most of his students became confused and were unable to complete their assigned problems.

At the time Mr. Cedar did not realize that the root of the problem was the students' inability to generalize. His alternative was to teach and practice some of the skills using classroom-based activities and concurrently allow the students frequent practice applying these skills in a variety of grocery stores in the community.

Teachers of students with moderate cognitive deficits are more frequently using these strategies to teach independent living skills. For example, when teachers want their students to order, pay for, and eat in fast-food restaurants, they teach the skills in a variety of community-based locations.

Mobility

Mobility for individuals with mild to moderate mental impairments is not a crucial issue. Most individuals who fall into this category do not have long-term physical problems that impede their ability to move from one place to another. This statement is, however, relative. For example, many children with mild deficits develop motor skills at a slower rate than do their peers (Patton et al. 1990). Similarly, most children with moderate cognitive disabilities develop motor skills (for example, crawling and walking) at a slower rate than their peers with mild mental handicaps (Thurman and Widerstrom 1990).

The same relationship across categorical areas is true for multiple disabling conditions. Based on the variety of biomedical conditions associated with moderate mental retardation, one would expect a higher percentage of these individuals to have physical impairments compared with their peers with mild cognitive delays.

In any case, the number of individuals with mild to moderate mental retardation who have mobility problems as a result of physical impairments is small compared with people with more severe mental retardation. Those students who have additional mobility problems should work with physical and occupational therapists who assist the primary program providers. For example, occupational therapists can locate and train the students to use devices that allow them to overcome the physical inability to type, thus allowing them to use microcomputers to complete their school work.

Self-Direction

The ability to direct one's self can be defined in many ways by different professionals. In the context of this chapter, self-direction is defined as one's ability to control the events that ultimately effect his or her life and one's belief that the control of such events is possible. Historically, individuals with mild to moderate cognitive deficits have not fared well in becoming self-directed. Seen as a variety of personality characteristics, these skills were thought to be deficient in persons with mental retardation and directly linked to their cognitive deficits (Zigler 1966).

Many educators today tend to view these personality variables in a different light and to approach the problems that students have with self-directed behavior from a behavioral viewpoint. The reinforcement history of persons with mild to moderate mental retardation is often considerably different from that of their peers without handicaps. Because of their intensive history of failure over long periods of time, many of these individuals begin to lose confidence in their abilities, causing them to over-rely on the leadership and skills of others. Therefore, personality disorders exhibited by people with cognitive deficits may be the result of the complex inter-relations among these individuals, their families, and the social system that provides them services (Balla and Zigler 1979). Betsy, who was born with moderate mental handicaps, was not born with personality problems. Her birth caused her family to react adversely to the increased stress placed on it by Betsy's disability and resulted in a decrease in the quality of parenting and sibling interaction she received. Over the years her reaction to an overprotective environment caused her to demonstrate less desirable behavior such as overdependency on others and her belief that she could never do anything right.

A protracted history of failure with a variety of experiences may cause some individuals with cognitive deficits to distrust their own abilities and become overdependent on others to direct them. Thus, individuals with mental retardation may show more outer-directed behavior than one might expect. When individuals exhibit outer-directedness they tend to rely on external cues rather than to trust their own problem-solving skills (Zigler 1966).

Another characteristic of self-direction involves a person's ability to see the cause and effect relationship between his or her behavior and subsequent events. Locus of control is essentially a personality characteristic that causes people to judge whether or not they control many of life's events that directly affect them. People who believe they control their own lives and many of the events that surround them seem to be more intrinsically motivated and have what theorists believe is an internal locus of control (Bialer 1961). Conversely, those people who feel they have little or no control over their lives demonstrate an external locus of control and seem to be more extrinsically motivated.

The more classical research literature provided results that supported the theory that individuals with mental retardation tend to be more dependent on others, less trusting of their own abilities, and more motivated by extrinsic reinforcers. Obviously, within the group of individuals with

mild to moderate mental retardation, the variability of these characteristics is great. When one is developing educational programs, it makes sense to view these characteristics as a behavioral paradigm rather than as intrinsic to mental retardation.

Because of their significant cognitive delays, individuals with mental retardation may be treated differently by significant others and professionals, thus affecting their reinforcement histories and experience with failure. For example, children with mild mental retardation placed in regular education classes from kindergarten may face repeated failure trying to grasp increasingly more difficult academic content. Even after a relatively short period (kindergarten and first grade), these children may have experienced many situations of failure that over time cause them to doubt their own abilities.

One example of how reinforcement history can be affected can be traced to the overuse of tangible reinforcers (for example, food, toys, extra play time) by professionals and family members. Because children with mental retardation are delayed developmentally, caregivers frequently reward small gains in behavior with large amounts of primary or tangible reinforcers. Over time this practice tends to teach children that one (the learner) works only when the rewards are large enough.

The tendency of individuals with mild to moderate cognitive deficits to be less self-directed can be minimized if caregivers practice common sense strategies. For example, by gradually fading prompts and cues, teachers assist students in relying more on their own problem-solving skills. This approach, paired with a systematic and gradual fading of tangible reinforcers, allows learners to become less reliant on external motivations. Asking students if they are proud of themselves when they accurately complete tasks while *showing* them you are proud of their efforts (using smiles, pats on the back) helps them "internalize" reinforcers.

Task analysis, that is, breaking a task down into smaller parts, helps learners deal with more manageable tasks and allows them greater chance for success. Applying task analysis to the range of academic, vocational, and leisure and recreation skills has become the most successful curricular and instructional tool available to special educators. Breaking tasks (skills) into component parts reduces student avoidance behavior and anxiety that often accompany the presentation of activities that they perceive as being beyond their abilities.

Capacity for Independent Living

The word *independence* is one that, in daily use, has many different meanings. Most professionals would agree that the major goal of all special education programs is to help people with handicaps become as independent as possible. For individuals with mild to moderate mental retardation, the definition of independence has been defined in a narrow fashion.

People who have mental impairments have often been relegated to positions of dependence, having continually to look to others to meet their needs. Most individuals with mild mental retardation are assimilated into society as part of the underclass, at the lowest socioeconomic level. Individuals with moderate cognitive disabilities lead dependent or semi-dependent lives, with the smallest proportion living in group homes or semi-independent apartments managed by state agencies. Most of these citizens are cared for by their families or relegated to residential/institutional settings.

In either case, the quality of life for these citizens, in terms of the number of independent living activities they are taught, does not compare to what their peers without handicaps learn. This situation can be traced to the emphasis placed on academic training in school programs. People without handicaps usually learn independent living skills outside of school in the context of extracurricular clubs and groups (for example, 4-H, Scouting),

through instruction in their homes, or simply through trial and error resulting from modeling the behaviors of others.

Individuals with mental retardation are included less often in extracurricular activities, come from homes less likely to provide this training, and do not have the same ability to learn through trial and error by modeling the behaviors of others. Therefore, their continued exposure to out-of-context, academically based activities or, at best, to simulations of independent living skills hinders any successful transition to community living.

During the 1980s, special educators became increasingly more interested in teaching independent living skills to students with moderate mental retardation in environments where they ultimately will be required to use these skills. Programs were designed to teach independent shopping skills in community grocery stores, restaurant skills in fast-food establishments, and leisure skills in a variety of community-based sites (Langone 1986).

Unfortunately, programs emphasizing independent living skills have not been a top priority in classes for students with mild mental retardation (Smith 1989). The case for teaching community-based independent living skills to all learners with mild to moderate disabilities is receiving increased emphasis in the literature (for example, Langone 1990; Polloway et al. 1989; Schuler and Perez 1988; Smith and Edelen 1990).

The importance of teaching independent living skills is obvious when one considers that the major goal of special education is to assist learners in becoming independent. Students with mild to moderate mental retardation often have deficits in social skills, and these deficits can severely affect their successful integration into both the community and other school environments. Teaching social skills appears to be most effective when it is done in context with actual daily living activities (Foxx et al. 1986). In addition, the broader area, or independent living skills (for example, home management, family care, leisure, consumer skills) can provide realistic opportunities for developing activities that help these students apply a variety of general cognitive, academic, and language skills.

Economic Self-Sufficiency

A person's worth, both in his or her own perception and the perception of others, is often judged by his or her ability to earn a living. Status is often placed on the type of job one does, and this status may affect the individual's overall quality of life. Because of the status that society places on work, it is important for individuals with mild to moderate mental handicaps to enhance and increase their status by finding and maintaining employment (Langone 1990).

The potential for economic self-sufficiency of individuals with mild to moderate cognitive deficits is excellent. Many published research studies, project reports, and program guidelines outline successful vocationally related programs for learners with mental handicaps (for example, Hill and Wehman 1983; Szmanski and King 1989; Wehman et al. 1988).

The programs that have been successful are, unfortunately, too few and have not had the most desired national impact. Rusch and Phelps (1987) cited a 1986 Senate subcommittee report indicating that at least 67% of Americans with handicaps are not working. Those people with handicaps who are employed are more likely to be employed only in part-time jobs. Finally, for those Americans with handicaps who are not working, 67% indicate they want to work. These data, although dated, do not appear to have changed much in 1991.

Transition from School to Work

Developing program options that help individuals with handicaps make successful transitions from school to all aspects of life has received national emphasis over the past five years. Previously, only those activities that dealt with movement from school to the world of work were stressed. Professionals are now emphasizing consideration of an individual's successful transition at every important life juncture (Ianacone and Stodden, 1987). For example, children with handicaps who move from one program to another (for example, preschool to elementary, elementary to middle school) should have transition plans developed that allow for more meaningful movement with little lost ground between programs. Transition plans should assist individuals with handicaps whenever a major program change is initiated.

The employability potential of learners with mild to moderate cognitive deficits is dependent on the quality of their entire school program, not just their educational opportunities in high school. The amount and quality of time students with handicaps spend participating in tasks related to work (for example, vocational education classes or community-based worksites) appears to determine their eventual success in competitive employment (Edgar 1987; Hasazi et al. 1985). Unfortunately, there does not appear to be a relationship between these data and what actually is taught in special education classes (Edgar 1987). The importance of restructuring special education curricula with more emphasis on work-related and independent living skills is evident.

The emphasis on appropriate work-related skills begins in elementary school and continues throughout one's life. For example, to minimize or eliminate poor work attitudes, students beginning in elementary school can spend time in the community with their teachers learning work-related skills through job samples simplified for their needs (Langone, 1990). This process allows students to learn about the world of work in actual community settings and allows them to observe community members doing their jobs. Teachers can choose good work role models for the students to observe and talk to and generally help them see the positive side to employment.

As students progress through middle and high school programs, the amount and sophistication of the activities increase. Students accompanied by their teachers can participate in a variety of job sites that represent a cross section of their community's employment possibilities. These activities allow the students to learn work-related behaviors (for example, social and community skills, task behavior, and assertiveness) and allow teachers to teach academic skills related to each job.

References

1. Balla D, Zigler E. Personality development in retarded persons. In: Ellis N. ed. Handbook of Mental Deficiency, Psychological Theory and Research. 2nd ed. Hillsdale, NJ, Lawrence Erlbaum, 1979, pp 143–168.
2. Bialer I: Conceptualization of success and failure in mentally retarded and normal children. J Pers 29:301–333, 1961.
3. Bricker D: Early communication development and training. In: Snell M. ed. Systematic Instruction for the Moderately and Severely Handicapped. Columbus, OH, Charles E. Merrill, 1983, pp 269–288.
4. Deshler D, Schumaker JB: Learning strategies: An instructional alternative for low-achieving students. Except Child 52:583–590, 1986.
5. Edgar E: Secondary programs in special education: Are many of them justifiable? Except Child 53:555–56, 1987.
6. Epstein MH, Polloway EA, Patton JR, Foley R: Mild retardation: Student characteristics and services. Education & Training of the Mentally Retarded, 24:7–16, 1989.
7. Foxx RM, Azrin NH: Toilet Training the Retarded. Champaign, IL, Research Press, 1973.
8. Foxx RM, McMorrow MJ, Bittle RG, Ness J: An analysis of social skills generalization in two natural settings. J Appl Behav Anal 19:299–305, 1986.
9. Grey RA: Services for the LD adult: A working paper. Learning Disability Quarterly 4: 426–434, 1981.
10. Grossman HJ. ed. Manual on terminology and classification in mental retardation. Rev ed. Washington, DC, American Association on Mental Deficiency (now called American Association on Mental Retardation), 1983.
11. Hasazi SB, Gordon LR, Roe C: Factors associated with the employment status of handicapped youth exiting from high school from 1979–1983. Except Child 51:455–469, 1985.
12. Hill M, Wehman P: Cost benefit analysis of placing moderately and severely handicapped individuals into competitive employment. Journal of the Association for the Severely Handicapped 8:30–38, 1983.
13. Ianacone RN, Stodden RA: Transition issues and directions for individuals who are mentally retarded. In: Iannacone RN, Stodden RA. eds. Transition Issues and Directions. Reston, VA, The Council for Exceptional Children, 1987, pp 1–9.
14. Keogh BK: Improving services for problem learners: Rethinking and restructuring. Journal of Learning Disabilities 21:19–22, 1988.
15. Langone, J: Teaching Retarded Learners: Curriculum and Methods for Improving Instruction. Boston, Allyn & Bacon, 1986.
16. Langone, J: Teaching Students with Mild and Moderate Learning Problems. Boston, Allyn & Bacon, 1990.
17. Langone J, Westling DL: Generalization of prevocational and vocational skills: Some practical tactics. Education and Training of the Mentally Retarded 14:216–221, 1979.
18. MacMillan DL: Mental Retardation in School and Society. 2nd ed. Boston, Little, Brown, 1982.
19. Marholin D II, O'Toole KM, Touchette PE, Berger PL, Doyle DA: "I'll have a Big Mac, large fries, large coke, and apple pie," . . . or teaching adaptive community skills. Behav Ther 10:236–248, 1979.
20. Nutter D, Reid DH: Teaching retarded women a cloth selection skill using community rooms. J Appl Behav Anal 11:475–487, 1978.
21. Patton JR, Beirne-Smith M, Payne JS: Mental Retardation. 3rd ed. Columbus, OH, Merrill Publishing, 1990.
22. Polloway EA, Patton JR, Payne JS, Payne RA: Strategies for Teaching Learners with Special Needs. 4th ed. Columbus OH, Charles E. Merrill, 1989.
23. Polloway EA, Smith JD: Current status of the mild mental retardation construct: Identification, placement, and programs. In: Wang MC, Reynold MC, Walberg HJ. eds. Handbook of Special Education Research and Practice. Volume 2: Mildly Handicapped Conditions. Oxford, Pergamon Press, 1987.
24. Riordan M, Iwata B, Finney J, Wohl M, Stanley A: Behavioral assessment and treatment of chronic food refusal in handicapped children. J Appl Behav Anal 17:327–342, 1984.
25. Rusch FR, Phelps LA. Secondary special education and transition from school to work: A national priority. Except Child 53:487–492, 1987.
26. Schuler, AL, Perez L: The role of social interaction in the development of thinking skills. In: Meyen

E, Vergason GA, Whelan RJ. eds. Effective Instructional Strategies for Exceptional Children Denver, Love Publishing, 1988, pp 259–275.

27. Smith DD: Teaching Students with Learning and Behavior Problems. 2nd ed. Englewood Cliffs, NJ, Prentice-Hall, 1989.

28. Smith GJ, Edelen-Smith PJ: A commencement model of secondary education and training in mild mental retardation. Education and Training on Mental Retardation, 25:15–24, 1990.

29. Spradlin JE: Environmental factors and the language development of retarded children. In: Rosenberg S, Koplin JH. eds. Developments in Applied Psycholinguistic Research. New York, Macmillan, 1968.

30. Stokes TF, Baer DM: An implicit technology of generalization. J Appl Behav Anal 10:349–367, 1977.

31. Szmanski EM, King J: Rehabilitation counseling in transition planning and preparation. Career Development for Exceptional Individuals 12:3–10, 1989.

32. Thurman SK, Widerstrom AH: Infants and Young Children with Special Needs: A Developmental and Ecological Approach. 2nd ed. Baltimore, Paul H. Brookes, 1990.

33. Wehman P, Abramson M, Norman C: Transfer of training in behavior modification: An evaluative review. The Journal of Special Education 11:127–131, 1977.

34. Wehman P, Moon MS, Everson JM, Wood W, Barcus JM: Transition from School to Work. Baltimore, Paul H. Brooks, 1988.

35. Ysseldyke JE, Algozzine B: Introduction to Special Education. 2nd ed. Boston, Houghton Mifflin, 1990.

36. Zigler E: Research on personality structure in the retardate. In: Ellis NR. ed. International Review of Research in Mental Retardation. Volume 1. New York, Academic Press, 1966.

37. Zigler E: Development versus difference theories of mental retardation and problems of motivation. American Journal of Mental Deficiency 73: 536–556, 1969.

Chapter 2
Severe and Profound Mental Retardation

William R. Sharpton
Michael D. West

Reference works on persons with different degrees of mental retardation typically describe expectations of their abilities, capacities, and potential for development. For persons with severe and profound mental retardation, however, one is more likely to find a description of *in*ability, *in*capacity, and little or no expectation for growth and development. Descriptions such as these are common:

> . . . unlikely to achieve any measure of productivity . . .

> . . . unable to enter into relationships . . .

> . . . total dependency on family or support agencies . . .

> . . . potential limited to self-help skills . . .

> . . . require lifelong supervised care . . .

Instructional Options

This chapter takes a different approach: It illustrates competencies developed by individuals with severe or profound retardation. The key to their success has been the manner in which service providers train and support persons with disabilities,

which may be summarized in the following framework:

> If a task can be taught, teach it.

> If it can't be taught, adapt it.

> If it can't be adapted, support it.

Table 2-1 illustrates this framework, along with decision rules for the use of each option. This service delivery model can be used to assist persons with severe and profound mental retardation in performing meaningful, rewarding, and socially valued activities in a variety of real-life settings. Case examples presented throughout this chapter illustrate the use of these options in varying combinations and degrees, based on the individual characteristics, needs, and preferences of the learners.

Option 1: Teach the Skill

Skills can be systematically taught to be performed in the same manner that a typical learner would perform them. The key to effective instruction is to provide only the level of assistance needed by the learner to complete the task successfully, a determination that must be supported by collecting training data. Ideally, the learner will be able to complete the task without any assistance other than that provided in

Table 2-1. Model for Selection of Instructional Options

Instructional Options	Decision Questions
Option 1: Teach the task	1. Can the task be divided into smaller steps that are easier to master? 2. Does the learner have the capacity to complete the task as it is typically performed?
Option 2: Adapt the task	1. Will adaptation of the environment facilitate task completion? 2. Will adaptation of the steps facilitate task completion? 3. Will adaptations to the learner (prosthetics) facilitate task completion?
Option 3: Support the task	1. Have all other options been considered? 2. Will support be provided in the least intrusive environment?

the natural setting. For example, in the laundromat, there are signs that explain how to operate the machines. This kind of information is called a *natural cue*. The information is not always written, however, as in the example of an electric door. The rubber mat in front of the door is the cue for its operation.

In most cases learners with severe intellectual impairment need instructional assistance if the task is to be performed correctly. This instructional assistance is known as a *prompt*. Prompts vary in type and intensity, and the prompt selected for successful instruction should offer sufficient information for correct task completion but not so much assistance that the learner is not challenged. Instructional data can be used to assist the trainer in making decisions about what types of prompts to provide. Detailed descriptions of systematic training procedures are beyond the scope of this chapter. Interested readers are referred to these excellent sources: Falvey et al. 1980; Guess and Helmstetter 1986; Haney and Falvey 1989.

Option 2: Adapt the Task

Adaptations can be designed to make the task easier or to assist an individual in task performance. Most adaptations have to be developed by the trainer; therefore, the trainers must know how to determine whether an adaptation is appropriate for the individual. Service providers should ask the following types of questions about the adaptive devices and techniques they develop to address specific tasks:

1. Is the adaptation effective? That is, does the use of the adaptation result in correct task completion?

2. Does the adaptation maintain the dignity of the individual? It is important that service providers remember their roles as advocates for the people they serve. Therefore, adaptations should be developed so that they are appropriate to the age of the individual and do not draw negative attention to him or her.

3. Is the adaptation durable? Can it be used as it was intended without quickly becoming unusable because of wear and tear? Nothing is more frustrating for the learner than to fail in the performance of a task because an adaptation is not working.

4. Is the adaptation portable? The adaptation should be designed so that it can be easily taken by the learner to the place where it is needed. Adaptations are particularly useful if they can be used in a variety of settings.

Option 3: Support the Task

Service personnel can support the learner by assisting the difficult steps while allowing the learner to perform those that are within his or her abilities. The concept of allowing people with mental retardation to perform part of a task even though they cannot complete all of the task independently is known as *partial participation* (Baumgart et al. 1982). The alternative to partial participation is exclusion from the task until the individual has learned all of the prerequisite skills. The requirement of learning all prerequisite skills often results in the instruction of isolated skills over long periods of time, with the learner still waiting to perform tasks or engage in activities that could very well enrich his or her life.

The person providing the support or assistance ideally should be a part of the setting in which the task naturally occurs. For example, store clerks are available to provide assistance to all shoppers, including those who have disabilities. There are, of course, cases where sufficient support is not available in the natural environment, and instructional programs must be designed to provide support. In these cases, it is important for service providers to develop a plan to transfer support as soon as possible to individuals present in the natural setting or to make external supports as unobtrusive as possible.

Functional Description

There has historically been disagreement over definitions of mental retardation. The most widely accepted definition, put forth by the American Association on Mental Deficiency (Grossman 1973), is "significant subaverage general intellectual functioning existing concurrently with deficits in adaptive behavior and manifested during the developmental period." This definition recognizes the interplay and occasional incongruity between measured intelligence levels and an individual's ability to function relatively unhindered within social and cultural environments. Many individuals may score in the range of

retardation on intelligence tests, but be able to function adequately within the social norms of their own families, schools, neighborhoods, and other immediate environments. They are not "retarded" because no one suspects that they are, and labeling them mentally retarded would cause tremendous stigma and potential harm.

For individuals with severe or profound retardation, inconsistency between measured intelligence and social adaptation is rarely an issue. From birth or early childhood, many of these individuals show outward signs of an organic pathologic condition, such as a genetic syndrome or brain damage, to account for the presence of impairment in mental functioning. Diagnosis is dependent upon formal assessment of general intellectual capabilities, typically deriving an intelligence quotient or a mental age level. A person scoring at least four standard deviations below the mean on a standardized intelligence test is termed severely retarded, and those scoring at least five standard deviations below the mean are termed profoundly retarded. Persons with severe and profound mental retardation together comprise no more than 3% to 4% of all persons with mental retardation (Scheerenberger 1983).

According to Carr (1984), reduced intellectual capacity generally is manifested (1) by limitations in the range of cognitive skills that the individual can master and (2) by limitations in the individual's capacity to respond to environmental cues. Persons with severe intellectual impairment have significant delays or complete interruptions in the development of motor skills, language abilities, problem-solving abilities, and other aspects of learning. Their inability to respond to environmental cues may result in lack of affect or in the presence of self-stimulatory, repetitious, and socially immature or inappropriate behaviors.

Persons with severe or profound mental retardation are more likely to have other disabling conditions as well. For example, the incidence rates for visual and hearing impairments, physical handicaps, epilepsy, and psychiatric impairment increase with level of retardation (Kelleher and Mulcahy 1986). These secondary problems probably result from the pathologic condition that contributed to retardation.

Self-Care

Individuals with severe and profound mental retardation do not typically develop many of the self-care skills through the maturational process. However, with intensive training, adaptation, and support, all can participate to some degree in dressing, feeding, toileting, grooming, and other self-care responsibilities.

To effectively train and involve their clients, it is important for service providers to view self-care not as the sole focus of an instructional program, but as a part of the normal routine of life. Thus, self-care skills should be taught when they naturally occur and within natural context of preparation for school, work, or bed. Too often, self-care skills are taught during therapeutic encounters, apart from the natural routines, resulting in ineffective, pointless instruction.

☐ Case 2-1: Mary

Mary is a young woman in her late twenties with severe mental retardation who lives in a group home with three other young adults. Her active treatment plan includes an intensive training program for building self-help skills. When the training program was first designed, the staff decided to provide instruction during the evening hours after dinner because they could spend more time with Mary on an individual basis. Despite this instuction, Mary's ability to prepare herself in the morning when she was getting ready to go to work did not improve significantly.

The group home support staff decided to change the instructional program for Mary. First, they decided that it made more sense to provide instruction on these tasks twice daily: once during the morning when she was preparing for work and once in the evening when she was preparing for bed. Next, they identified all of the tasks involved during her morning and evening routines. For each task, the critical steps were identified, and for each step, the staff decided whether to teach a typical performance, design an adaptation, or provide support. Where possible, the tasks that required the most assistance were grouped so that the staff could provide needed support for one "cluster" of tasks, leaving Mary to complete the remaining tasks more independently. Thus, it was easier for the staff to schedule their instruction and to provide support to the other household residents.

Problems still remained with Mary as she moved from one self-help task to the next. The staff designed a checklist that included a picture of each critical task in the order in which it should be performed. The checklist was laminated and a grease pen attached so that Mary could mark each task as it was performed. Of course, Mary did not learn to use this adaptation independently. The support staff used prompts systematically to teach Mary to perform the critical tasks. Careful collection of instructional data over a six-week period showed that Mary had significantly improved her ability to prepare herself for work and bed. She still requires support for some steps, but the staff have noticed that it is much easier to provide assistance to Mary.

Receptive and Expressive Language

Because cognition and language development are interrelated, it is not surprising that persons with severe or profound mental retardation generally have more severe communicative disorders than persons with lesser degrees of retardation (Schiefel-busch 1972). In fact, Grossman (1983) indicated that these individuals typically develop only minimal communication skills even with intensive training. He notes, however, that some members of this group may develop complex verbal skills, grammar, and sight word recognition.

Impaired receptive and expressive language abilities of people with severe or profound retardation originate from a number of sources, including abnormal speech mechanisms, physiologic problems, potential hearing loss, poor language learning environments, and impaired cognitive processes (Dodd and Leahy 1989). In recent years, however, tremendous advances have been made in providing members of this population with functional communication skills (Reichle et al. 1988). This is accomplished by conducting an ecologic examination of the functions that communication serves across natural environments and providing the learner with training in communication skills or with an adaptive communication system that enables him or her to fulfill those functions. Adaptive communication systems include the use of pointing, gesturing, signing, or a graphic system, such as symbols, picture cards, or communication boards or electronic system, or any combination of any of these methods. In providing speech or language intervention, service providers need to remember that communication is a function of environment. When communication is deficient, environments should be examined and enriched where needed to promote effective communication.

Too often, language and communication are taught during prescribed times in therapeutic environments, with the expectation that the individual will transfer these skills to real-life encounters. To be effective, communication training, as all training activities, should occur at natural times and places and in natural contexts (Halle 1988).

The goal of communication training is for the learner to gain some control over his or her immediate environment. Success toward that goal can be *reduced* in two ways:

1. Service providers teach the learner to use a single form of communication with the expectation that it will work in all settings. It is rare that a single communication board, set of picture cards, gestural language, or other communication system can be developed that the learner can master and that will work effectively in all environments in which he or she is expected to function. To attempt to do so invites frustration and failure.

2. Control over communication systems or communication opportunities is maintained by the service provider and not the learner. A classic example is the communication board that the student is taught to use during "speech class," but that is locked up or unavailable during other school activities or when the learner is at home.

☐ *Case 2-2: Laura*

Laura is a 13-year-old girl who is severely mentally retarded and attends a middle school near her neighborhood. Because she is nonverbal, her teacher, in cooperation with the speech therapist, developed a communication board and taught her to use it to express a variety of concepts. This year, her Individualized Education Program (IEP) has been expanded to include instruction in community settings. In particular, her parents want Laura to learn to order a meal in a fast-food restaurant, because the family eats in a variety of these establishments.

Her teacher initially decided to let Laura use her regular communication board to order food at the restaurant. Unfortunately, Laura became confused by the large number of symbols on the board, and the restaurant personnel were unable to understand what Laura wanted to eat. After carefully analyzing the problems, the instructional team created a special communication board just for the fast-food restaurant. The board was organized so that the items of food were presented within "categories" of food types (for example, beverages). Laura was taught to identify a choice in each of the three categories, thus ordering a complete meal.

Through systematic instruction in the use of this adapted strategy for communication, Laura now independently orders her food in three fast-food settings. In fact, she uses separate boards for each restaurant; the boards were designed to reflect the menu of each establishment. Laura's participation in this task has been expanded to include selecting the correct order card before leaving for the restaurant. She is now able to participate much more independently with her family when they eat out.

□ Case 2-3: Charles

Charles recently entered his first year of high school on a regular campus; however, he had little experience in performing functional tasks in community settings. In fact, instructional personnel always set fairly low expectations for Charles because of his severe mental retardation and dual sensory impairments. His new teacher wanted to involve him in functional activities but was concerned that he attempted to communicate only with grunting noises or by reaching out with his arms. Based on his mother's report that Charles liked soft drinks, the instructional team decided to teach him to purchase a drink from a vending machine. The communication specialist used a pop top as an object cue for Charles. At first, he was given the pop top each time he was taken to the vending machine to purchase a drink. Later, the pop top was placed in a calendar box that was divided into compartments. By follow-

ing a left-to-right sequence, Charles knew which activity should be performed by the object the staff had placed in the compartment. The instructional team was particularly excited the day that Charles went to the calendar box and, instead of following the sequence in the set order, searched until he found the pop top, which he held out toward the teacher. In essence, Charles was saying, "I want to buy a drink." In this case, his language had moved from a receptive to an expressive mode.

Learning and Cognition

Impaired learning ability and capacity is, of course, the embodiment of mental retardation. According to Owens (1989), problems with learning and problem solving originate with impairments in the following cognitive processes:

1. Identifying salient stimuli and attending to them for sufficient periods of time.

2. Organizing and encoding incoming sensory information into categorical groupings.

3. Storing and retrieving information in both short- and long-term memory.

4. Transferring learning to new tasks or settings.

Persons with severe or profound mental retardation typically have significant difficulties in each of these cognitive areas.

In times past, these problems were used to justify segregated, lifelong custodial care for these individuals. Now, more and more people who provide assistance to this population recognize that these deficits point to the need for specialized and individualized instruction, adaptation, and support. A major evolutionary change is occurring in research and application of instructional technology to the needs of persons with severe and profound retardation. Past efforts have demonstrated the ability of all

individuals, regardless of their level of retardation, to learn isolated tasks through
competent instruction. More recently, emphasis is being placed on teaching functional skills that lead to an enhanced life-
style for these individuals (Homer 1989).

☐ Case 2-4: Gerald

Gerald is a young man with severe mental
retardation who is involved in a high
school vocational training program. His
mother expressed her concern to the instructional team during the IEP conference
that her son is not involved in household
routines. In fact, he is very dependent
upon family members for most activities of
daily living such as selecting clothing,
grooming, preparing meals, and maintaining his bedroom. Gerald can count to five,
but has not mastered many academic skills
such as color identification, reading, and
typical readiness skills.

Gerald recently began training at a new
work site that requires employees to wear
uniforms. The instructional staff noticed
immediately that Gerald was highly motivated to wear the uniform. In fact, his
mother had problems with Gerald wanting
to wear his uniform every day rather than
on Tuesdays and Thursdays when he reports to the training site. The instructional
team worked with the family to incorporate this new-found motivation in critical
home routines. The teacher adapted a calendar by placing large green dots on Tuesdays and Thursdays and attaching a red
marker on a string (see Figure 2-1). Now
when Gerald gets up in the morning, he
goes to the refrigerator with his mother to
look at the calendar. He locates the current
day to determine whether or not it is a
uniform day. After making this decision,
he takes the marker and places an X on the
day so that he will know where to look for
the next day. Now he is ready to assist in
the selection of clothing. The instructional
team also decided to teach Gerald to par-

ticipate in washing the uniform. This has
now become a Saturday chore in the home.
At this time, Gerald is not able to perform
all of the steps, but he does load and un-
load the machine as well as operate the controls, which are adapted with colored tape.

Even though Gerald is still not independent in the performance of household
tasks, he is certainly more involved than he
was before. Not only are his parents
pleased with his progress, but his younger
siblings have begun to comment about
their older brother going to work.

Mobility

Functional mobility may be assessed along
two interrelated parameters: (1) as the individual's capacity for physical movement
within the specific environments in which
he or she functions (for example, the workplace, the home) and (2) as the capacity to
move from one environment to the next or
through the community at large.

As mentioned previously, persons with
severe or profound mental retardation

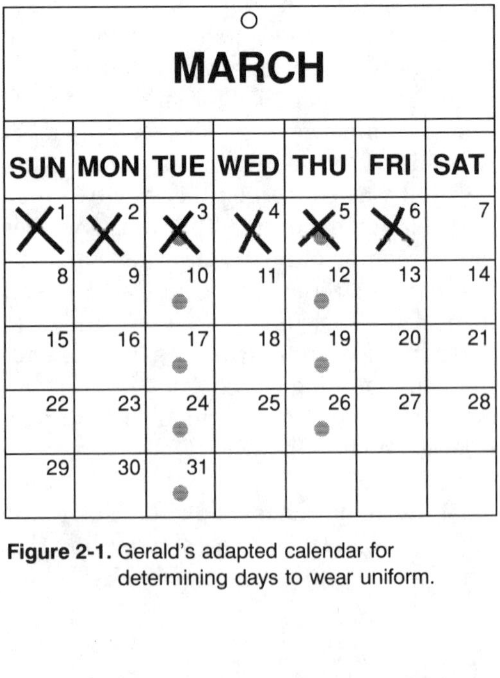

Figure 2-1. Gerald's adapted calendar for
determining days to wear uniform.

frequently have physiologic or neurologic impairments that impair physical movement. These impairments, as well as learning deficits, result in limited functional mobility both within and among environments.

Mobility is emerging as a critical issue for enhancing the physical integration and participation of persons with severe handicaps in work and social activities, particularly as the field progresses from center- and school-based services to community-based models of instruction and support. Independent ambulation may be taught or adapted using wheelchairs, walkers, handrails, and other aids. Community movement may be facilitated through adaptation and training to use a variety of transportation modes, including family vehicle, public transit, and independent movement by foot, bicycle, and so forth. Community movement can also be supported by carpooling and other ride-sharing options.

☐ Case 2-5: Kesha

Kesha is 25 years old and had been waiting for an integrated employment opportunity for approximately 6 months. A suitable job became available in a laundry facility within a large urban hospital. However, the job coach had concerns about Kesha's safety because she is severely mentally retarded and blind. The concern centered around the fact that, to reach the locker rooms and the cafeteria, Kesha had to walk down a busy corridor that is used by forklifts.

Kesha does not need assistance at the folding table because all of the work takes place there. The task is typically structured so that two workers fold clothes at the same station and retrieve clothes from a large bin approximately 20 feet away when all clothes on the table have been folded. The job coach worked with management to slightly alter the task to accommodate Kesha's presenting needs. Kesha's coworker retrieved all of the clothes from the bin; however, Kesha folded a greater number of

the smaller items because she did not have to interrupt her work to walk over to the bin.

Through careful planning, the job coach designed a strategy to afford Kesha maximum independence in negotiating the corridor, yet insuring her safety. Kesha typically crossed the corridor only three times daily: during her morning and afternoon breaks to get to the bathroom and during lunch to reach the cafeteria. The job coach decided that support was necessary for Kesha to walk safely down the corridor. The job coach also felt that the most important issue besides Kesha's safety was for support to be provided in as natural a way as possible without compromising Kesha's dignity. Two coworkers were identified who act as sighted guides for Kesha when it is time to go on break or to lunch. They walk over to Kesha, sign "break" into her hand, and offer their arm so that she can accept their assistance. Because these workers have the same schedule as Kesha, there is no interruption of the work flow.

☐ Case 2-6: Jeremy

Jeremy attends a middle school and has been learning to participate in shopping for groceries in a neighborhood supermarket. Because he uses a walker for support, he has been paired with a peer for the shopping activity. Typically, Jeremy identifies the correct item and the peer pushes the cart.

For the past year, the school occupational therapist has become increasingly discouraged with the use of an isolated therapy model. She works with Jeremy in the occupational therapy room twice a week and is concerned that he may or may not use newly learned skills in natural settings. When she expressed these feelings to Jeremy's teacher, they decided to incorporate the occupational therapy objective of transferring to and from the walker with the grocery shopping activity.

The therapist developed a program to teach Jeremy to leave his walker at the front of the store, transfer to the grocery cart, and use the cart as support while he shopped. At first, this task was difficult for Jeremy because the cart would roll as he attempted to transfer. Another concern was the fact that Jeremy could not let go of the cart when retrieving an item or he would lose his balance. Thus, they taught him to move through an aisle of the store selecting items only on the right-hand side. At the end of the aisle, he makes a U-turn so that he can pass down the aisle again to select items on the left side.

Although he still shops occasionally with a peer, Jeremy is especially proud that he can go through the store alone while his teacher waits at the front of the store or his mother completes her own shopping.

Self-Direction

Most people cherish their ability to make decisions and choices about the many facets of their lives: where they will live, work, and play and with whom; the types of social and leisure activities in which they will engage; what to have for dinner; which skills are important to have in one's repertoire; what clothes to wear today. For many persons with mental retardation, these choices and many others are usually made for them, with the likelihood of imposed choices increasing with the severity of the retardation. Freedom of choice and decision making have only recently been proposed as viable and essential components in the lives of persons with severe and profound retardation (Guess et al. 1985; Shevin and Klein 1984).

Persons with significant retardation are highly unlikely to develop sufficient abilities to achieve complete self-direction and autonomy. However, the complete absence of self-direction is undignified and frequently leads to "learned helplessness" and total dependence on others (Guess et al. 1985). Therefore, a central theme of each treatment or educational program

should be that persons with significant retardation be allowed to show preferences, make choices and decisions, and exhibit some control over their own day-to-day activities and long-term goals. Service providers can foster self-direction in several ways:

1. Individuals with significant retardation can be trained to discover their preferences and to make choices and decisions. In areas where independent choice making is not feasible or safe, choice making can be adapted or supported. Individuals with severe and profound mental retardation can partially participate in self-direction by exerting control over specific situations or life choices.

2. Opportunities for expressing preferences and making choices and decisions should be available in all areas of service. Learning to make good decisions requires experience with the process of decision making, with alternatives, and with consequences of decisions.

3. Service providers should respect the decisions that people with significant mental retardation make, even if they do not necessarily agree with the end result. They should keep in mind that making choices is a means of establishing one's own identity and individuality, not that of the service provider. They should also keep in mind that it is part of the human condition sometimes to make bad decisions and to learn from mistakes.

□ *Case 2-7: Ms. Kindricks*

Ms. Kindricks decided to incorporate choice making with the shopping activity that her elementary students perform on Wednesdays and Fridays. To assist the children in preparing for the shopping trip to a convenience store, she developed a picture sequence board that paced the children through using the rest room, getting their coats, selecting a dollar bill, and performing the other tasks associated with "getting ready."

She then added a component to the sequence that assists the children in making a selection of what they want to buy at the store. She designed a "choice board" by hanging cards representing the items that the parents reported were their children's favorites. Each item is actually a wrapper affixed to a small piece of laminated cardboard, which is attached to the board with Velcro. As the children decide what they want to purchase, they remove the choice card from the board and take it to the store so that they will know what to purchase. Ms. Kindricks has made duplicate copies of each choice so that each child can select from the full range of options.

☐ Case 2-8: Jane

Jane is a young adult with severe mental retardation who has been working with support for over one year. Unfortunately, she does not appear to participate in many leisure activities even though she is now earning money. The support staff in her group home have noticed that Jane likes certain types of clothing, particularly scarves of bright colors.

The staff decided to teach Jane to shop for clothing items as a leisure activity. At first, she required a great deal of assistance in making a selection. However, by preselecting stores that have clothing in Jane's price range, teaching Jane to find the areas of the store with her favorite items, and allowing her multiple opportunities to go shopping, Jane's group home staff have enabled her to select and purchase clothing of her choice. Jane also keeps a catalog at home to get ideas of what to purchase when she goes shopping.

Capacity for Independent Living

There is universal consensus that persons with severe or profound mental retardation, because of their cognitive impairments, re-

quire some form of domestic support. This support typically includes assistance with such activities as meal preparation, shopping, money management, self-care, transportation, and other day-to-day needs. Whereas most persons with severe or profound retardation receive this assistance from their immediate families, these individuals also comprise disproportionately large segments of the populations of residential services, especially institutions (Seltzer and Seltzer 1983).

Recent trends in residential placement for persons with severe and profound mental retardation have generally mirrored those of the field as a whole: away from large congregate living facilities and toward small group living or individual placement options, such as specialized foster care, adoption, or supported apartment living (Lakin et al. 1988). More progressive programs are shifting focus away from funding residential services to supporting *individuals* with all levels of retardation wherever, however, and with whomever they choose to live, thereby promoting a greater degree of independence, integration, and "sense of home" (Walker and Salon 1987). In addition, there is growing commitment by service providers and state funding agencies to provide needed and desired support to families who have a member with severe disabilities, to allow the family to remain intact and prevent or delay out-of-home placement (Cohen et al. 1989).

☐ Case 2-9: David

After David had lived in a state institution for people with severe retardation, his family decided that they wanted him to live in the community. The case worker from the Division of Mental Retardation and Developmental Disabilities informed the family that David had two options: a group home for six residents or a supported apartment for David and one other individual.

The family thought a great deal about the two options and the impact of each on David's life-style. Their major concern was that, because David is very outgoing and enjoys being with other people, they did not want him to be isolated without opportunities for social interactions. After great consideration, they selected the group home option even though many professionals advised them that it is the more restrictive residential option. They felt that, because David is used to living with many people, the group home would require less of an adjustment.

David now lives in the group home, which is located in a suburban neighborhood, with five other housemates. He enjoys participating in household tasks and is involved in numerous activities sponsored by a community church. Additionally, he is known by many of the residents throughout the neighborhood because he walks a mile and a half every evening as part of an exercise program.

□ Case 2-10: Tina

Tina lived at home throughout her school years and after she first became employed as an office worker. When Tina reached age 24, her parents began to look for an alternative residential option; however, they were not pleased with the concept of a group home. They felt that it would be too much of an intrusion of her life-style for Tina to learn to live with a large number of people in one household. In fact, they became frustrated with the case worker from the Division of Mental Retardation and Developmental Disabilities because she seemed to feel that Tina did not have sufficient skills to live in a less restrictive setting.

The family was fortunate in that Tina qualified for a new residential initiative for persons with disabilities that allowed for monies to be used more flexibly than in the past. Tina now resides with a nondisabled roommate in an apartment that is convenient to the bus that she takes to work. She pays for her portion of the rent with human services funds and uses part of her salary to contribute to living expenses. Her family has assisted her in decorating the apartment, a leisure activity that Tina really enjoys.

Economic Self-Sufficiency

Persons with severe and profound mental retardation historically have not been economically self-sufficient; they have relied on financial support from family members, public and private agencies, and income assistance programs such as Supplemental Security Income, food stamps, and the like. In addition, vocational training and employment programs for increasing economic self-sufficiency have historically excluded members of this population or placed them in nonremunerative, therapeutic activities, from which they were expected to progress to paying jobs when they were "ready."

Research and demonstration projects of the late 1970s and early 1980s established that persons with severe and profound mental retardation, generally thought to be unemployable outside of the sheltered workshop or activity center, could achieve success in competitive work through a combination of intensive training and post-placement follow-along efforts (Bellamy et al. 1979; Rusch and Mithaug 1980; Wehman 1981; Wehman et al. 1979). A central theme to each of these efforts was the abandonment of the "readiness" model of vocational preparation, in which people were endlessly preparing to work, and the adoption of a job placement method, "place first, then train and support." The vocational strategy that emerged from those early efforts, known as supported employment, has since grown in acceptance, funding, and scope, and is now a Vocational Rehabilitation service option for persons with severe disabilities in every state.

Supported employment became a service option through the 1986 Amendments to the Rehabilitation Act. The final regulations for the Amendments define supported employment as paid work for persons with severe disabilities in integrated settings with ongoing support services, such as job skills reinforcement and continuing monitoring and assessment (52 *Federal Register* 30546). Supported employment has dramatically improved the vocational outlook for members of a number of disability groups, including persons with severe and profound mental retardation (Wehman and Kregel 1990). This new service delivery option also affects the curriculum used in many educational programs at state and local levels. Federal initiatives and funding have also made competitive work available to more students with severe disabilities (Wehman et al. 1988).

☐ Case 2-11: Michael and Sara

Mr. Clarkson is a vocational rehabilitation counselor who is responsible for identifying individuals in need of supported employment services. Although he would like all persons with severe disabilities to access supported employment services, he often must select from among many individuals because a limited number of supported employment opportunities are available at one time. He has been directed to include some individuals who are exiting public school and has just received two descriptions of exiting students in two community school districts.

The first description is approximately one-half page long and states that the student, Michael, has been involved in 2 years of work adjustment training. Additionally, he has participated in an intensive prevocational program that involved assembly, sorting, and packaging a variety of items in a classroom converted into a simulated sheltered workshop. The report describes Michael's fine and gross motor skills and his ability to follow one-step, two-step, and multiple-step directions. Finally, there is a checklist that describes his ability to count, sort, recite his name, address, and telephone number, and perform other basic skills.

The second report is written as a resumé. Over a 5-year period, the student, Sara, participated in vocational training in ten community business sites. Each of the ten sites represents a different occupational cluster such as food service or office/clerical work. For each cluster, there is a description of the duties Sara performed and of her work accuracy and speed at the beginning and end of the training period. During her last year of school, Sara worked part-time in a bakery.

A second part of the resumé describes the adaptations and strategies used to assist Sara in completing vocational tasks. In fact, she is able to follow complex sequences through the use of a picture-prompting system. The resumé also describes her ability to perform or participate in essential activities such as shopping, using the telephone, crossing the street, and using the public transit system. Finally, references are provided so that supervisors and coworkers who are familiar with Sara can be contacted.

It is not hard to understand why Mr. Clarkson decided to provide supported employment services to Sara first. Of course, he is charged with the responsibility of providing services to all individuals who meet the eligibility requirements. The case for serving Sara was stronger, however, because her resumé clearly attested to her employability.

☐ Case 2-12: Jason

Jason is 26 years old and has worked in a sheltered workshop for 5 years prior to taking his new job in a spice factory. Although some adult service personnel wanted to find Jason an integrated employment opportunity earlier, the fact that he was severely retarded influenced the decision to allow him to remain in the sheltered workshop. Just this year, his parents felt secure enough about the success of the supported employment program operated by the center to allow Jason to participate.

While in the sheltered workshop, Jason worked approximately 32 hours a week and earned an average of $40 per month. He was not entitled to any benefits such as health care or paid vacation time. At this time, Jason is working 30 hours a week at his new job and earns $105 a week. He accrues 2 weeks vacation annually and is eligible for health care benefits.

Jason has also decided to join the company bowling league. In fact, he travels to the bowling alley with a neighbor who is employed at the same company. His parents are beginning to realize the variety of opportunities available to Jason because of his entry into a typical employment setting.

Conclusions

We began this chapter by stating that the manner in which service providers operate helps their clients achieve success. This observation is not intended to discount or detract from the efforts of the learners, for indeed they also have to put forth a great deal of work and enthusiasm for learning to occur. Our closing comments concern the unifying attitudes, beliefs, and practices of the trainers described in the case studies.

First, the service providers recognized the importance of integrated opportunities for their clients in fostering normative behavior and in setting expectations of families, staff members, clients themselves, and other significant individuals with whom the clients worked, lived, and socialized. These providers began with the belief that their clients not only *could* participate meaningfully in integrated settings and activities but that they *should* partici-

pate as well. The service providers also recognized the value of the individual needs and preferences of their clients and their clients' families in selecting activities and settings for the instructional programs, which also contributed to their success.

Second, these service providers achieved success because they perceived that their clients' problems and failures resulted from problems with the task or the environment rather than from problems with the client. Thus, the focus of training became how to creatively manipulate those factors to meet the presenting needs of the learners. This manipulation involved training, adapting, or supporting new behavior and was firmly rooted in (1) a foundation of empirical and theoretical support, (2) a demand that outcomes be meaningful for clients and contribute to a more normal and enriched life-style, and (3) a respect for the dignity of the learner.

Finally, service providers did not succumb to an "all or nothing" approach to inclusion in normalizing, integrated activities. That is, meaningful activities were not disregarded simply because the learner would not be able to achieve complete independence or to engage in the particular activity in the same manner as persons without disabilities. Participation in normalizing, integrated activities, even if it must be adapted or supported, is more dignified, opens more opportunities, and enhances the dignity and quality of life for persons with significant mental retardation.

References

1. Baumgart D, Brown L, Pumpian I, Nisbet J, Ford A, Sweet M, et al. Principle of partial participation in educational programs for severely handicapped students. Journal of the Association for the Severely Handicapped, 7: 17–27, 1982.
2. Bellamy GT, Horner RH, Inman DP. Vocational Habilitation of Severely Retarded Adults: A Direct Service Technology. Baltimore, University Park Press, 1979.

3. Carr TH. Attention, skill, and intelligence: Some speculations on extreme individual differences in human performance. In: Brooks PH, R Sperber, C McCauley. eds. Learning and Cognition in the Mentally Retarded. Hillsdale, NJ, Lawrence Erlbaum, 1984, pp 189–215.

4. Cohen S, Agosta J, Cohen J, Warren R. Supporting families of children with severe disabilities. Journal of the Association for Persons with Severe Handicaps 14: 155–162, 1989.

5. Dodd B, Leahy J. Phonological disorders and mental handicap. In: Beveridge M, Conti-Ramsden G, Leudar I. eds. Language and Communication in Mentally Handicapped People. London, Chapman and Hall, 1989, pp 33–56.

6. Falvey M, Brown L, Lyon S, Baumgart D, Schroeder J. Strategies for using cues and correction procedures. In Sailor W, Wilcox B, Brown L. eds. Methods of Instruction for Severely Handicapped Students. Baltimore, Paul H. Brookes, 1980, pp 109–133.

7. *Federal Register.* Final regulations. August 14, 1987; 52: 30546–30552.

8. Grossman H. ed. Manual on Terminology and Classification in Mental Retardation. Washington, DC, American Association on Mental Deficiency, 1973.

9. Grossman H. ed. Classification in Mental Retardation. Washington, DC, American Association on Mental Deficiency, 1983.

10. Guess D, Benson HA, Siegel-Causey E. Concepts and issues related to choice-making and autonomy among persons with severe disabilities. Journal of the Association for Persons with Severe Handicaps 10: 79–86, 1985.

11. Guess D, Helmstetter E. Skill cluster instruction and the individualized curriculum sequencing model. In: Homer RH, Meyer LH, Fredericks HD. eds. Education of Learners with Severe Handicaps. Baltimore, Paul H. Brookes, 1986, pp 221–248.

12. Halle J. Adopting the natural environment as the context of training. In: Calculator SN, Bedrosian JL. eds. Communication Assessment and Intervention for Adults with Mental Retardation. Boston, College Hill, 1988, pp 155–185.

13. Haney M, Falvey MA. Instructional strategies. In: Falvey MA. ed. Community-Based Curriculum. Baltimore, Paul H. Brookes, pp 63–90.

14. Horner RH. Editorial farewell. Journal of the Association for Persons with Severe Handicaps 14: 253, 1989.

15. Kelleher A, Mulcahy M. Patterns of disability in the mentally handicapped. In Berg JM. ed. Science and Service in Mental Retardation. New York, Muthuen, 1986, pp 15–22.

16. Lakin KC, Hill BK, Bruinicks RH. Trends and issues in the growth of community residential services. In: Janicki MP, Krauss MW, Seltzer MM. eds. Community Residences for Persons with Developmental Disabilities: Here to Stay. Baltimore, Paul H. Brooks, 1988, pp 25–42.

17. Owens R. Cognition and language in the mentally retarded population. In: Beveridge M, Conti-Ramsden G, Leudar I. eds. Language and Communication in Mentally Handicapped People. London, Chapman and Hall, 1989, pp 112–142.

18. Reichle J, Piche'-Cragoe L, Sigafoos J, Doss S. Optimizing functional communication for persons with severe handicaps. In: Calculator SN, Bedrosian JL. eds. Communication Assessment and Intervention for Adults with Mental Retardation. Boston, College-Hill, 1988, pp 239–264.

19. Rusch FR, Mithaug DE. Vocational Training for Mentally Retarded Adults: A Behavioral Analytic Approach. Champaign, IL, Research Press, 1980.

20. Scheerenberger RC. A History of Mental Retardation. Baltimore, Paul H. Brookes, 1983.

21. Schiefelbusch RL. Language disabilities of cognitively involved children. In: Irwin JV, Marge M. eds. Principles of Childhood Language Disabilities. New York, Appleton-Century-Crofts, 1972, pp 209–234.

22. Seltzer MS, Seltzer GB. Classification and social status. In: Matson JL, Mulick JA. eds. Handbook of Mental Retardation. New York, Pergamon Press, 1983, pp 185–198.

23. Shevin M, Klein NK. The importance of choice-making skills for students with severe disabilities. Journal of the Association for Persons with Severe Handicaps 9: 159–166, 1984.

24. Walker P, Salon R. Creating residential supports: Centennial Development Services, Inc., a community-centered board serving Weld County, Colorado. TASH Newsletter. August: 8-9, 1987.

25. Wehman P. Competitive Employment: New Horizons for Severely Disabled Individuals. Baltimore, Paul H. Brookes, 1981.

26. Wehman P, Hill JW, Koehler F. Helping severely handicapped persons enter competitive employment. AAESPH Review 4: 274–290, 1979.

27. Wehman P, Kregel J. Supported employment for persons with severe and profound mental retardation: A critical analysis. Int J Rehabil Res 13: 93–107, 1990.

28. Wehman P, Moon MS, Everson JM, Wood W, Barcus JM. Transition from School to Work: New Challenges for Youth with Severe Disabilities. Baltimore, Paul H. Brookes, 1988.

Chapter 3
Cerebral Palsy

Katherine J. Inge

Functional Description

Approximately two children per 1,000 live births are affected by some type of cerebral palsy resulting in problems with movement and posture (Copeland and Kimmel, 1989). Cerebral palsy is a nonprogressive disorder caused by a lesion or defect to the brain occurring prior to birth, during the birth process, or during the first four years of life (Bleck and Nagel 1983; Copeland and Kimmel 1989; Inge 1987). Nonprogressive refers to the fact that the actual damage to the individual's brain does not worsen over time. However, if proper programming and treatment are not provided, the individual's ability to move and perform functional activities can decrease.

Different types of cerebral palsy are identified based on the individual's resulting movement disorder and the portion of the body involved (Tables 3-1, 3-2). Information about the classification and location of the disability is helpful in program planning. Professionals are, however, cautioned not to limit individuals based on their medical diagnoses.

Mobility

The foundation for all movement is postural muscle tone, which allows an individual to have postural stability while moving to complete a motor action (Campbell 1987). For example, a person can sit upright with the arm in a stable position while writing with a pen or typing on a keyboard. He or she is able to make adjustments in the position, that is, move the hand from left to right across the page without losing balance in sitting. The individual with cerebral palsy, however, usually has atypical muscle tone that can be excessive (spasticity/hypertonicity) or insufficient (hypotonia) or that fluctuates between the two (Copeland and Kimmel 1989).

In addition to problems with atypical muscle tone, the individual with cerebral palsy may have persistent primitive reflexes that would normally disappear as an infant matures (Copeland and Kimmel 1989; Inge 1987). For instance, the individual whose movements are affected by the symmetric tonic neck reflex may have difficulty straightening his or her arm to reach for an object if the head is flexed (bent) forward. Another individual may have difficulty combing his or her hair if movement is affected by the asymmetric tonic neck reflex. This causes extension of one arm and flexion of the other upon head turning.

It is not the intent of this chapter to describe fully the influences of abnormal muscle tone and reflex movement. The following case studies, however, are provided

Table 3-1. Cerebral Palsy: Classification by Type

Type	Characteristics
Spasticity	Increased muscle tone (hypertonicity) Increased stretch reflex Muscle tone that varies in response to movement, stimulation, or effort Voluntary movement may be slow or impossible
Athetosis	Involuntary, uncontrolled movements Fluctuating muscle tone that increases upon purposeful activity Difficulty maintaining a stable position
Dystonia	Distorted movement Muscle tone that fluctuates between hypotonic and hypertonic, particularly in the trunk and proximal parts of the extremities (limbs)
Rigidity	"Lead pipe" movement Invariable muscle tone
Hypotonia	Floppy or low muscle tone
Mixed	Characterized by more than one type, that is, spasticity and athetosis One type usually predominates.

(Adapted from Bigge 1882; Copeland and Kimmel 1989; Inge 1987)

Table 3-2. Cerebral Palsy: Classification by Distribution

Monoplegia	Only one extremity (limb) involved Usually rare in children with cerebral palsy
Hemiplegia	One side of the body involved, including the arm and leg on the same side
Triplegia	Three limbs of the body involved Usually one arm and both legs
Paraplegia	Only the lower extremities (legs) involved Very rare in cerebral palsy May be person with diplegia who has mild upper extremity involvement
Diplegia	All limbs involved, but legs more involved than arms and hands Usually associated with spasticity
Quadriplegia	Whole-body involvement, including the trunk and four limbs Arms may be more involved than the legs

(Adapted from Copeland and Kimmel 1989; Inge 1987)

to describe the different types of cerebral palsy and the resulting effects on movement and posture. The reader should refer to the texts listed in the reference section as well as consult with physical and occupational therapists to obtain additional information. Remember, two individuals with cerebral palsy can have the same classification and body part involvement, but have very different abilities. Review and assessment through a team approach can identify each individual's strengths and limitations.

□ Case 3-1: Bill and Mary (Part 1)

Bill is physically challenged by spastic cerebral palsy with right hemiplegia. This information reveals that he has increased muscle tone, or hypertonicity, on the right side of his body that includes his arm and leg. His involvement is mild, which means that he can walk with a cane and use his right arm as an assist to the left. For instance, when working on table-top activities, Bill can hold down a piece of paper while writing with his left hand. He cannot, however, use his right hand to complete fine motor activities such as buttoning or opening packages.

Mary, Bill's friend, also has spastic cerebral palsy with right hemiplegia. Mary, however, is severely affected by her disability and is unable to walk. She uses a wheelchair that she propels using a left, one-arm manual drive. Because she had limited programming as a young child, Mary can no longer straighten her right arm, which is held close to her body with the elbow and wrist flexed (bent). The term used for this immobility is contracture. Mary is unable to use her hand or fingers for any functional tasks; however, her left arm has normal muscle tone and movement.

☐ Case 3-2: Sarah (Part 1)

Sarah is a young woman with athetoid cerebral palsy that affects her ability to perform motorically. Movements throughout her body are characterized by flailing, involuntary motions with extensor tone predominating. She is able to sit independently when positioned on the floor as well as scoot about on her buttocks. Sarah can bear weight on her legs momentarily when supported by another person, but she is unable to stand independently or walk because of fluctuating muscle tone. Sarah uses an electric wheelchair with a joystick that she pushes with her right fist.

Fine motor activities are problematic, because Sarah has difficulty stabilizing her arm at the shoulder joint. Involuntary movements are noted at her elbows, wrists, and fingers. Speech is also limited because

of athetosis; however, Sarah has learned to communicate by typing messages on a communication device using a head pointer.

☐ Case 3-3: Keith

Keith's ability to move independently is affected by spastic cerebral palsy, quadriplegia. This information reveals that he has hypertonicity (increased muscle tone) throughout his head, trunk, and limbs. Keith has difficulty moving any part of his body for purposeful activity. His muscles always appear to be very stiff, and any movement he makes is slow and labored. Keith uses a manual wheelchair that has knobs on the rims of each wheel. He pushes the knobs with the heel of each hand, since he is unable to adequately grasp the wheel rims. His parents are currently saving funds to purchase an electric wheelchair to improve his mobility skills.

Mobility out of his wheelchair is limited to rolling over from his stomach to his back on a mat and sitting independently once someone has assisted him to that position. He loses his balance easily and falls to one side, unable to return to sitting. The effort to complete any gross motor task can be seen throughout his body with increased extensor tone.

Fine motor tasks are also completed slowly with noted spasticity. Keith is able to use his hands for activities such as self-feeding using a built-up handled spoon, typing on a typewriter using the index finger of his right hand, and completing leisure recreation tasks such as playing checkers with his friends. He is able to speak, but this is labored and difficult to understand because of spasticity.

Handling and Positioning Considerations

Individuals with cerebral palsy often require lifting, handling, and positioning assistance from the many professionals who interact with them on a daily basis. It is critical that these professionals learn to provide this assistance properly to prevent injury to themselves and to the individuals being lifted and positioned. The use of proper "body mechanics" ensures that back strain and injury do not occur when one is moving an individual with cerebral palsy. Table 3-3 provides a list of precautions for lifting and positioning.

The presence of hypertonicity, hypotonicity, or fluctuating muscle tone usually results in atypical movements and postures that limit skill development for individuals with cerebral palsy (Campbell 1987; Inge 1987; Rainforth and York 1987). Knowledge of proper positioning and handling techniques can assist the individual in completing an activity that he or she may otherwise be unable to perform. In addition, if an individual is allowed to persist in using abnormal movement patterns and positions, he or she may eventually be unable to move in a more normalized fashion.

The goals of proper positioning include normalizing muscle tone, maintaining proper body alignment, stabilizing the body, and promoting participation in activities (Rainforth and York 1987). For instance, a young child with cerebral palsy who is unable to stand independently may be positioned in a prone stander that stabilizes the hip joint and allows him or her to stand while performing an activity. Some suggestions include making a sandwich on the kitchen counter, drying dishes at the sink, brushing or combing hair in front of the bathroom mirror, or brushing teeth.

Many different positioning devices can be purchased or built, including wedges, side-lyers, corner chairs, bolsters, and adaptive wheelchairs. It is critical that each individual's abilities are assessed and that adaptive equipment is selected for optimal functioning. Occupational and physical therapists usually assume this responsibility in program planning. The reader is directed to Finnie (1976); Sobsey (1987); and Copeland and Kimmel (1989) for de-

Table 3-3. Safety Precautions for Lifting and Handling

- Never try to life someone by yourself if the person is over ¼ of your total body weight. **If in doubt, seek assistance!**
- Keep the weight you are lifting as close to your body as possible. The further away the person is, the "heavier" he or she will be.
- Always keep your knees bent when lifting and your back straight. *Never* lift using your back. The leg muscles are much stronger, and will allow you to lift the maximum amount of weight.
- Never twist or rotate at the waist when lifting. Move your body as one unit. To change directions, step around and turn your body without twisting at the waist or lower back.
- Never lift an individual with cerebral palsy by taking an arm and leg while someone else takes an arm and leg. This is especially true of an individual with hemiplegia because weight and tone will be different on the two sides of the person's body.
- Always lock the wheelchair brakes prior to moving an individual to and from a wheelchair.
- Make sure all seatbelts and straps have been unfastened prior to lifting.
- Detach removable armrests and legrests from the wheelchair and get them out of the way.
- Clear the environment of all extraneous materials, i.e., toys that you may trip over during lifting.
- If the individual has more involvement on one side of the body than the other, make the transfer in the direction of the stronger side. For example, if the person has left hemiplegia, transfer him or her to the right whenever possible.
- Always require the individual to assist based on his or her capabilities.
- Movements should be slow and smooth. The individual being lifted should be aware of what is going to occur and what is expected of him or her.
- If you do injure your back, be sure to have it checked by a physician.

(Adapted from Copeland et al. 1976; Copeland and Kimmel 1990; Rainforth and York 1987)

tailed instructions on positioning and handling techniques. Table 3-4 provides basic guidelines in this area.

Associated Problems and Cognition

Many individuals with cerebral palsy are not affected by any other disability; however, approximately two thirds have associated problems (Prensky and Palkes 1982). These additional disabilities can include mental retardation, seizures, visual impairments, hearing loss, speech and language disorders, and learning disabilities. It is possible for an individual to be severely limited motorically yet have normal intelligence. For instance, one would assume that a child with limited mobility who is unable to speak would be severely mentally retarded. Professionals are cautioned not to make these assumptions and to assess thoroughly an individual's capabilities. A review of the case studies already presented may be useful in understanding the varying abilities of individuals with cerebral palsy.

Bill (Case 3-1), the young man with spastic hemiplegia, also has a learning disability. This disability became evident when he had difficulty learning to read and spell; however, math never seemed to be a problem for him. In fact, Bill usually earned As and Bs in math. Testing revealed that he had a learning disability but was of normal intelligence. With assistance from a resource teacher, Bill was able to stay in a regular education classroom throughout his school years and receive a high school diploma.

Mary (Case 3-1) also has a diagnosis of spastic hemiplegia; however, she is severely mentally retarded. Her disability was identified early because Mary did not show an interest in people or toys as an infant. Psychologic testing revealed that she has an IQ of 27, which places her in the severe range of mental retardation. Mary's school years have been spent in a program for students with severe disabilities where she receives intensive instruction in do-

Table 3-4. Positioning and Handling Guidelines

- Never leave individuals positioned indefinitely in adaptive equipment. Check them frequently and correct body alignment as needed. Remember, many of these individuals cannot move themselves and may develop pressure sores if left in the same position for extended periods of time.
- Select adaptive equipment that assists the individual in completing an activity in as normal a position as possible.
- Identify a "menu" of positioning options and rotate among them during a day's activities.
- Modify the environment to eliminate excessive noise and distractions. Overly stimulating environments can increase muscle tone and facilitate abnormal movement patterns.
- Learn to feel muscle tone changes. **Stop** if you are increasing abnormal patterns.
- Avoid quick movements when positioning and handling individuals with hypertonicity because rapid or jerky movement can stimulate spasticity. Slow, steady movement is important.
- Learn the key points of body control: the head, trunk, shoulders, hips, and pelvis.
- Never pull on a body part that is flexed. This will increase spasticity.
- Never carry the child like an infant because this limits his or her visual field and he or she will never learn head or body control.
- Increase muscle tone in individuals with low tone (hypotonicity) by bouncing or tapping a body part in the direction of the required movement.
- Provide the least amount of assistance and encourage the individual to participate whenever possible. Providing too much support or control does not allow the individual to develop motor control. Assess needs often and change as indicated.

(Adapted from Copeland and Kimmel 1989; Finnie 1976; Sobsey 1987).

mestic, leisure-recreation, vocational, and community skills. Her school days include community-based instruction as well as opportunities to interact with her age-appropriate nonhandicapped peers.

Although Sarah (Case 3-2) is severely physically disabled with athetoid cerebral palsy, she has normal intelligence. As an infant she was unable to learn to speak, but Sarah was fortunate to have a speech therapist and teacher who quickly recognized her intellectual abilities. She attended regular classes but, because of her physical limitations, she received assistance with personal care and with classwork. With individualized attention, Sarah was quickly able to learn to read and type on a typewriter using a head pointer. Currently she is an avid reader of mystery novels and is enrolled in a computer programmer course at her local university.

Receptive and Expressive Language

Individuals with cerebral palsy, as in any area of functioning, may have normal to severe receptive and expressive language difficulties. Abnormal muscle tone limits not only gross and fine motor abilities but also the muscles that control facial and tongue movements. This can result in difficulty with articulation, speech production, and breath control (Copeland and Kimmel 1989).

Fortunately major advancements have been made in the area of communication for individuals with severe disabilities (Coots and Falvey 1989; Miller and Allaire 1987; Reichle and Karlan 1985; Reichle and Keogh 1986; Reichle et al. 1989; Sobsey 1987). Many options are available, depending on the abilities of the individual in need of speech and language programming. Speech therapy may be indicated for those individuals who have difficulty with articulation, or an alternative system may be appropriate for individuals unable to develop speech.

Augmentive communication systems can be as simple as a picture or word board or as complicated as a computerized electronic device. Electronic boards are available with synthesized voices or message printouts that can be accessed with a variety of special input devices. Examples include head pointers, light beams, and pressure-sensitive switches that respond with the touch of any body part. The complexity of the system is matched to the individual's intellectual and physical abilities.

The design of a communication program for an individual with cerebral palsy can include input from the speech pathologist, parents, teacher, and occupational and physical therapists. Together, these professionals can determine whether the individual has the ability to develop speech or if an alternative device is needed. If the team determines that speech is not a functional option, physical and occupational therapists can help determine the optimal position and body part to be involved in using a communication system as well as determine the input device that should be utilized. The speech pathologist is most familiar with the systems available commercially and the level of abilities required to operate the device. Parents and teachers can provide information on the individual's communicative intent, which is crucial for matching skill level to an augmentative system.

In any case, language programming should occur in the natural environment during naturally occurring times of the day. For instance, the speech pathologist may accompany a student into the community to learn how to use a communication board for ordering a meal at the local fast-food restaurant. The following case studies may be useful in understanding the communication needs of individuals with cerebral palsy.

☐ Case 3-4: Mary (Part 2)

Mary had difficulty developing speech and language due to her combined problems of cerebral palsy and severe mental retardation. As a young child, she made several sounds that were understood by her parents to indicate that she was happy, uncomfortable, or hungry. When she began school, however, her teacher, speech pathologist, and occupational and physical therapists determined that Mary would need an alternative communication system.

Because Mary had full use of her left arm, it was decided that she could point directly to pictures on a communication board. Initially, only three picture symbols were put on her board to indicate eat, drink, and bathroom. Instructional sessions were scheduled during mealtime, snacks, and toileting time rather than set up as special sessions for language instruction. Mary's teacher designed a program using a time-delay procedure with a physical prompt to teach her to use the pictures on the board (Halle et al. 1979; Snell and Gast 1981). Initially 25 trials were implemented at a 0-second delay. For instance, during snack time, the teacher would hold up Mary's cup and say "Mary, what do you want?" At the same time (0-second delay) that the teacher asked the question, she physically prompted Mary to point to the picture of drink. Mary was then given the opportunity to drink from the cup.

After the first 25 trials, the teacher gradually began to delay the physical prompt, giving Mary an opportunity to respond independently. This was done systematically by implementing 25 trials at 2 seconds, 25 trials at 4 seconds, and so forth until Mary met her program objective of pointing to the picture independently. During the training procedure, the teacher designed an error correction procedure to use if Mary made more than three errors in a row during delay levels greater than 0. When this occurred, the teacher dropped back to 5 consecutive trials at 0-second delay before returning to a higher delay level.

☐ Case 3-5: Sarah (Part 2)

Sarah, the young woman with athetoid cerebral palsy, never developed speech because of fluctuating muscle tone in her facial muscles and tongue. Sarah was able to make sounds and "talk" in complete sentences, but only people who were familiar with her could understand these vocalizations. Speech therapy was attempted when she was a young child but with little improvement in oral communication.

Initially, a picture communication board was developed that was replaced with an alphabet board when Sarah learned to read and spell. Because she was unable to use her hands consistently to point to the symbols or letter, Sarah used a head pointer to spell what she wanted to say. Sarah recently received an augmentative communication device that has a synthesized female voice as well as a printout strip. Sarah uses a head pointer to type what she wants to say, and the computer "talks" for her. This particular device can be programmed to respond to commonly asked questions using codes that Sarah easily learned how to use. The code system increases her speed, since every word no longer needs to be typed. With the help of this device, Sarah is able to communicate effectively in complete sentences at a good conversational pace.

Self-Care

Completion of self-care tasks is often difficult for individuals with cerebral palsy because of the sophisticated and coordinated movements required to perform even the most simple tasks (Sobsey 1987). Motor responses that most people take for granted such as sitting or standing without support while dressing are problematic for the individual whose movements are influenced by spasticity or athetosis. The child with a severe asymmetric tonic neck reflex may not be able to take a spoon to his or her mouth because head turning to look at the spoon causes the arm to extend. Another individual may have difficulty with toileting due to a spastic bladder. In frustration, many care-providers resort to completing self-care activities for a person who is physically disabled because they assume that it is easier and faster to do it themselves.

This tendency to complete self-care activities for individuals with cerebral palsy can be referred to as the "all or none" philosophy. In other words, if a person cannot complete all of an activity, he or she should not receive instruction on that task. The result is increased dependency and the exclusion of many skills from a training curriculum that an individual could at least partially learn to complete.

Baumgart et al. (1982) advocate individualized adaptations to enhance the performance of skills using material adaptations, adapting the environment, adapting skill sequences, and using personal assistance. If care-takers implement these strategies, the individual with a physical disability can partially participate in age-appropriate, functional activities. Table 3-5 suggests material and environmental modifications to increase participation in self-care activities.

Material Adaptations

Rainforth and York (1987) define an adaptation as any device or material that is used to accomplish a task more efficiently. Adaptations for individuals with cerebral palsy are usually designed to decrease the physical demands of an activity. For instance, Sarah's (Case 3-2) involuntary movements in her hands, which are related to athetoid cerebral palsy, make it impossible for her to grasp a spoon. She uses a self-feeder designed for individuals with this problem. Keith (Case 3-3), the young man with spastic cerebral palsy, has difficulty grasping small objects. He is successful in self-feeding using a spoon with an enlarged handle.

Both of these individuals required an assistive device for the same activity; however, two different solutions were identified. It is important to remember that not

Table 3-5. Using the Principle of Partial Participation for Self-care Activities

Material Adaptations

- Utensils or swivel utensils with built-up handles
- Adaptive hand splints for holding utensils
- High-sided dishes, scoop bowls, and plate guards
- "Nosey" cutout cups
- Cup holders, two-handled drinking cups, adaptive straws
- Suction cups and nonslip mats
- Velcro closures, button hooks, and zipper pulls
- Dressing sticks, reachers, shoehorn aides, and stocking aids
- Toothbrushes, weighted, with built-up handles
- Dispenser handles on toothpaste pump containers
- Razor holders
- Deodorant and shaving cream dispenser handles to depress nozzles
- Long-handled combs and brushes
- Built-up handles or velcro-handled combs and brushes
- Bathing mitts and bath brushes
- Soap-holder mitts and sponges
- Hand-held urinals and toileting aids

Environmental Adaptations

- Removing architectural barriers
- Lowering light switches, checking counter heights
- Re-arranging furniture
- Ramps
- Doorknob extensions
- Grab bars
- Bed rails
- Tub-transfer bench, bath-support chair, shower chair
- Elevated toilet seat or toilet chair

all individuals with cerebral palsy can use the same adaptations. When selecting and designing materials, several things should be taken into consideration (Copeland et al. 1976; York et al. 1985; Rainforth and

York 1987): First, an adaptation should not be used if the person has the potential for learning a task without one. Second, professionals should work in teams that include the teacher, the occupational therapist, and the physical therapist. Together, they can assess the movement required to perform the task and evaluate the individual's abilities. They should then decide what type of assistive device is needed, and if it must be made or is available commercially.

The final selection should be made based upon the least intrusive design that allows the person to be as independent as possible. Keith, for example, is unable to perform fine motor prehension tasks due to spastic quadriplegia. One activity that he is unable to complete is turning on a lamp switch. At first, his teacher thought she should attach a microswitch to the lamp in Keith's bedroom so that he would perform this task independently. After some thought, it was determined that Keith could learn to use a commercially available lamp that turns on when the base is touched. With instruction, he learned to tap the lamp with his forearm and thus turn it on. The adaptation selected was more normalizing, since many homes have this type of lamp. It should be noted, however, that use of the microswitch would be acceptable for those individuals who could not learn to operate the lamp in any other fashion.

Adapting Skill Sequences

Often the sequence or manner in which a task is completed can be altered in order for the person with cerebral palsy to be successful in skill completion (Baumgart et al. 1982; Sobsey 1987). For instance, a person with limited range of motion of the arms may not be able to reach his or her hands under the faucets of a sink. Therefore, the task of handwashing could be modified by positioning a basin of water, soap, and towel within the individual's reach.

Dressing is another self-care area that can be modified for individuals with severe physical disabilities. To complete dressing and undressing tasks, a person usually needs to be able to maintain a stable base of support; shift body weight when leaning forward, backward, or side to side; reach and grasp clothing; and move arms and legs (Copeland and Kimmel 1989). Many of these movements are problematic or impossible for the individual with severe cerebral palsy. However, modifying the way the task is completed, such as by providing an external base of support in sitting, may make it possible for a person successfully to complete a dressing or undressing task.

The first step in determining if a task should be altered is to assess the physical capabilities of the individual and the demands of the activity. It is not necessary for a person to be able to stand or sit independently to complete dressing tasks without assistance or at least to participate partially. However, it is important to ensure that abnormal movement patterns are not facilitated when asking a person with cerebral palsy to participate in dressing and undressing activities (Campbell 1987). It is recommended that the teacher, careproviders, and therapists work together as a team when designing self-care programs to determine carefully which movements can be utilized that do not promote atypical patterns. Table 3-6 provides information that can serve as a guide for conducting an assessment for dressing and undressing activities.

The simplest way to modify a task for a person with a physical disability is to write a task analysis for that skill based on the person's mobility. After completing an assessment of the person's skills and comparing this to the activity demands, the team is ready to design a task analysis. The following two case studies demonstrate how this can be accomplished.

The process for modifying a task using a team assessment and program planning strategy can be applied to any instructional activity. This is true for skills in all program domains, including domestic, vocational,

Table 3-6. Assessing Physical Abilities for Dressing Activities

Evaluate the Person's Upper Body Control

Can the person . . .

Sit in a straight chair without support?

Lean forward away from the back of the chair without losing his/her balance?

Sit in a chair with arms and pull himself/ herself forward away from the back of the chair using one hand?

Reach with one or both hands overhead?

Reach with one or both hands to the back of the neck, waist, and feet?

Grasp with one or both hands?

Do "push-ups" using the armrests in his/her wheelchair to lift the buttocks off the seat?

Lean back in the wheelchair and lift buttocks off the seat? (May be contraindicated for an individual with total body extension.)

Evaluate the Person's Mobility on the Floor

Can the person . . .

Roll from side to side?

Lie on his/her back and independently lift buttocks off mat?

Lift his/her buttocks off the mat by pushing with the feet against a stable surface such as a wall?

Reach with both or one hand overhead?

Place one or both hands on the back of the neck, waist, and feet?

Grasp with one or both hands?

Sit up from supine (back) or prone (stomach position)?

Get to a kneeling position independently?

Use a chair or grab bar to pull himself/herself to a kneeling position?

Evaluate the Person's Ability to Stand

Can the person . . .

Stand momentarily without support?

Use a chair or grab bar to pull himself/herself to standing position momentarily?

Reach with one or both hands while standing to his/her neck, waist, knees?

Grasp with one or both hands while standing?

leisure-recreation, or community. In fact, it is critical for individuals with cerebral palsy to become as independent as possible.

☐ Case 3-1: Mary (Part 3)

Mary's mother has always been overprotective of her and assumed that Mary would never learn dressing and undressing tasks because of her severe mental retardation and spastic cerebral palsy. The teacher and occupational therapist at her school evaluated Mary's capabilities for dressing and identified the following physical characteristics:

- Mary uses a wheelchair for mobility.
- She can lean forward away from the back of the chair for approximately 5 seconds.
- Mary cannot use her right arm, which is usually flexed tightly at the elbow and hand. She can, however, raise it to shoulder height.
- Her left arm and hand have normal motor functioning.

After they discussed the findings, the teacher and therapist decided that putting on a buttoned shirt or sweater would be a good first objective. They developed the following task analysis based on Mary's abilities.

An important point to note in this task analysis is that Mary was taught to put her

Task Analysis for Putting on a Buttoned Shirt or Sweater

1. Lay sweater face up on lap (neck at knees).
2. Grasp sweater at armhold (using left hand).
3. Pull sleeve over (right) hand.
4. Pull sleeve over (right) elbow.
5. Pull sweater onto shoulder.
6. Grasp neck of sweater.
7. Lean forward from wheelchair.
8. Pull sweater across back.
9. Lean back in wheelchair.
10. Grasp neck of sweater.
11. Lean forward in wheelchair.
12. Shake sweater into position.
13. Lean back in wheelchair.
14. Put (left) arm into sleeve.
15. Straighten front of sweater.

right arm into the sweater sleeve before her left. Dressing the arm or leg first that is more affected by cerebral palsy makes the task easier (Payne and Reyder 1983). This is true whether the person is attempting to dress himself/herself or the care giver is providing assistance.

The other consideration in developing a dressing task analysis for Mary was her ability to lean away from the back of her wheelchair for only 5 seconds. It was necessary to have several steps in the task analysis that allowed her to lean forward, complete a portion of the activity, rest, and then lean forward again for another step in the task. Time for rest may be a necessary consideration for many individuals with cerebral palsy who have physical limitations that prohibit them from completing a task in a more typical way.

☐ Case 3-7: David

David is a classmate of Mary with severe athetoid cerebral palsy and severe mental retardation. He is dependent on his family for all daily living activities. No one has ever worked on dressing tasks with him before, because he is mentally retarded and is not able to sit in his wheelchair without trunk supports and a seat belt. His teacher and occupational therapist decided that David should be able to complete some dressing activities with skill sequence adaptations and systematic instruction. The assessment of his physical capabilities revealed the following information:

- Rolls from side to side freely when placed on a mat.
- Can reach his feet in side-lying and grasp with both hands.
- Rolls to his back and lifts his hips off the mat.
- Cannot sit unsupported.

Based on these findings, a pants-off program was selected as David's first dressing goal. Because David had good mobility on

the mat, the team felt that David could easily learn to take off a pair of stretch pull-on pants that did not have fasteners. Undressing was selected as an easier initial task to master than dressing (Snell 1987).

The next step in the process was to develop a task analysis for use during instruction. The team members decided that each step should be written as a verbal prompt to ensure program consistency from one trainer to another. Regardless of whether the teacher, occupational therapist, physical therapist, or teacher's aide was providing instruction, the verbal prompts would remain the same. This was an important point to consider, because David was also severely mentally retarded. Consistency of instruction would be crucial for skill acquisition. The following task analysis was developed:

Task Analysis for Taking off Pants

Note: The trainer positions student on the mat for instruction.

1. Grasp waistband of pants with both hands.
2. Push pants down to hips.
3. Lift hips off mat.
4. Push pants below hips.
5. Lower hips to mat.
6. Roll onto side.
7. Grasp pants at waistband with both hands.
8. Push pants down onto thighs.
9. Bend leg up to chest.
10. Push pants off leg.
11. Roll onto other side.
12. Bend leg up to chest.
13. Push pants off leg.
14. Straighten out leg.
15. Roll onto back.

Once the task analysis was completed, the teacher decided to use a modified version of Azrin's "Rapid Method" of teaching dressing skills to individuals with severe and profound mental retardation (Azrin et al. 1976; Snell 1987). The teacher or therapist initially provided a verbal prompt for

David to initiate the first step in the task analysis. If no response occurred, the teacher or therapist would point to the part of the garment involved in that step of the task. After several more seconds, the teacher or therapist molded David's hands around the pants and repeated the verbal instruction. Finally, if no response were initiated, physical guidance was provided to complete the step correctly. A 5-second latency was allowed between each prompt to give David time to respond independently. Continuous use of praise and touch for any attempt to complete the task comprised the reinforcement strategy. Because his care givers utilized a team approach, David began to learn skills for independence.

Personal Assistance for Partial Participation

Personal assistance can be an effective strategy for enabling individuals with severe physical disabilities to perform tasks they could not otherwise manage. A person with cerebral palsy, for instance, may not be able to open a drawer to remove clothing articles; however, if given a choice of two garments to wear, the person could point to the preferred item. Another individual may require assistance transferring to and from a shower chair for bathing, assistance washing his or her feet, and assistance towel drying the lower part of his or her body. However, the remainder of the bathing activities might be completed independently using adapted bathing mitts, long-handled brushes, soap dispensers, and over-sized bath towels. Personal assistance should be the last resort to ensure partial participation in any activity. Modifying the task and supplying adaptive devices often makes human assistance unnecessary for the individual with a physical disability.

Feeding Concerns

Mealtime is often problematic because abnormal muscle tone results in poor feeding positions; in inadequate oral motor control leading to drooling, choking, and gagging; and in lack of motor control for self-feeding. In most cases, the occupational or speech therapist assumes the lead in designing feeding programs. As in all other programmatic areas for individuals with cerebral palsy, however, a team approach is recommended.

There are many excellent resources available for professionals responsible for planning and implementing feeding programs (Copeland and Kimmel 1989; Finnie 1975; Fraser et al. 1990; Morris and Klein 1987; Sobsey 1987). Specific program management encompasses many different aspects including gross motor and positioning considerations, the presence of primitive postural reflexes, oral-motor reflexes, and abnormalities (Fraser et al. 1990). A brief overview of specific feeding problems and considerations is discussed below for each of these areas.

Gross Motor Concerns and Positioning Considerations

Individuals with cerebral palsy often have abnormal postural reflexes that interfere with gross motor development and successful feeding (Fraser et al. 1990; Copeland and Kimmel 1989; Morris and Klein 1987). The first reflex to consider that has an influence on feeding is the asymmetric tonic neck reflex. Individuals with this reflex have difficulty in total body reactions as well as oral motor functions. For instance, this reflex can be noted when the person turns his or her head to one side. The arm on that side of the body extends while the other arm flexes. Some individuals are so affected by this reflex that voluntary positioning of the head in midline is inhibited. This reflex makes it difficult for the care giver to get food into the individual's mouth, and it interferes with normal oral-motor control and self-feeding (Sobsey 1987).

Another reflex that affects feeding is the tonic labyrinthine reflex. This reflex influences the positioning of the individual's head, often resulting in excessive head extension or flexion. Extreme flexion or extension of the head affects the person's ability to swallow in a controlled manner (Fraser et al. 1990). Neck extension is especially problematic, because it may result in food aspiration, limited respiration, and inhibition of swallowing.

Another problem that may affect gross motor movement and positioning is muscle tone. Increased muscle tone, or spasticity, can result in head hyperextension and shoulder elevation. As stated previously, this head positioning causes difficulty in swallowing and in some instances may be life threatening to the individual who aspirates food.

A person with hypotonia, or low muscle tone, can also have poor trunk and head control. In this instance, the individual may not have the ability to lift his or her head from a flexed position. Excessive head flexion is just as problematic to the feeder as is head extension for proper swallowing (Fraser et al. 1990). Finally, the person with athetosis may be difficult to feed because of excessive involuntary movements of the head, neck, and trunk. Athetosis can result in difficulty with mouth closure as well as with involuntary tongue movements.

Morris and Klein (1987) suggest that a total-body assessment be completed to determine the individual's postural strengths and needs, to include observation of total-body posture, trunk mobility and stability, shoulder position, and head control. None of these can be looked at in isolation, because one body part influences the position of another. For instance, the person who has inadequate trunk control and stability may posture in an asymmetric seated position with more weight shifted to one hip than another. This position results in total-body compensations that make it difficult for the person to eat properly. An-

other example of posture compensation is seen in the person who does not have adequate foot support in a seated position. This individual may experience an increase of postural muscle tone that is evident even in the oral-motor musculature.

Hip and pelvis placement during mealtimes should also be assessed when determining feeding problems. Forward and backward tilting of the pelvis can result in problems with head control, breathing, and mouth control (Morris and Klein 1987). A forward or anterior tilt of the pelvis causes postural compensations throughout the body. The shoulders counterbalance the hips by pulling backward into retraction, which tightens the neck muscles, decreases jaw mobility, and inhibits swallowing. Retraction of the shoulder girdle also causes a tension that can pull the neck into hyperextension.

Fraser et al. (1990) state that mealtime is not the time to emphasize developing gross motor skills such as head and trunk control. Finnie (1975) stresses the need to provide proper positioning control to the "whole" person; if this is not done, the person becomes more spastic or has increased involuntary movements. Appropriate positioning allows the individual to concentrate on eating skills without attempting to maintain the stability and support of other body parts necessary for eating (Fraser et al. 1990). This approach translates into positioning provided manually by the feeder or by adaptive equipment until the individual develops better total-body control.

Head support varies based on the abilities of the individual being fed. For instance, individuals like Beth may need support from the care giver whereas others may benefit from a commercially available headrest on the wheelchair. Still others with severe involvement may find sidelying a functional alternative in a sidelyer or on a wedge (Fraser et al. 1990). Morris and Klein (1987) as well as Finnie (1975) provide excellent diagrams as guidelines for assessment and selection of proper feeding positions.

In any case, positioning should be a team decision made by the teacher and the occupational and physical therapists. Proper positioning helps break up abnormal muscle tone and movement and allows for isolated movements of the head, jaw, tongue, and lips. A positioning assessment determines the problems that can be addressed and minimized through adaptive devices or care-giver control (Copeland and Kimmel 1989).

☐ Case 3-8: Beth

Beth has severe spastic quadriplegia and requires chest and hip supports to maintain a seated position. Prior to mealtime she is positioned in her wheelchair using external support to ensure that her hips are flexed to the back of the chair and that she is upright rather than leaning to one side. Beth's feet are strapped to the footplates of her chair to provide increased total-body stability.

Beth also has difficulty with head control and usually holds her head in hyperextension. As previously discussed, neck extension leads to aspiration and difficulty in swallowing. Therefore, the person assisting Beth during mealtime uses manual jaw control to maintain her head slightly flexed 5 to 15 degrees. This assistance reduces extensor hypertonus (Fraser et al. 1990). The care giver is careful not to flex Beth's head flexion greater than 15 degrees, because this can inhibit swallowing.

Oral-Motor Concerns

Tonic Bite

A number of oral-motor problems interfere with successful mealtime experiences for individuals with cerebral palsy. One is the tonic bite pattern, which is an obligatory closure of the jaw upon tactile stimu-

lation of the teeth and gums (Fraser et al. 1990). Several factors stimulate a tonic bite in a person with cerebral palsy: poor positioning with too much hip flexion or extension, posterior pelvic tilt, an overstimulating environment, and oral hypersensitivity (Morris and Klein 1987).

Tom is a young child with a tonic bite associated with severe spastic cerebral palsy. His treatment team identified that poor positioning with excessive hip extension facilitated Tom's tonic bite reflex. Proper placement of his wheelchair lap strap kept Tom's hips flexed during mealtimes if the feeder checked periodically to make sure that Tom's hips had not moved into extension. If a tonic bite occurred during feeding, the care giver learned to wait until Tom relaxed to take the spoon out of his mouth. Pulling on the spoon only served to stimulate Tom's tonic bite problem (Fraser et al. 1990). Finally, the team designed a program to decrease Tom's oral hypersensitivity. Morris and Klein (1987) provide a detailed description of oral-motor desensitization exercises that can be utilized based on each individual's treatment needs.

Hyperactive Gag Reflex

Individuals who have a hyperactive gag, which is stimulated by input to areas of the mouth other than the posterior tongue or soft palate, have difficulty eating. Several treatment approaches are used to assist the person in dealing with this problem (Morris and Klein 1987). For example, Mary's mother has been shown how to use applesauce as a "binder food" to assist Mary with forming a bolus of food for swallowing. Her mother alternates a bite of hard, lumpy food with a spoonful of applesauce to bind the remaining loose pieces into a bolus. Mary then is less likely to choke on small pieces of food that she has difficulty swallowing. Her mother also learned that flexing Mary's head forward when she gags during feeding stops the response.

Next, Mary's occupational therapist designed an oral-motor program to decrease her hypersensitive gag. Firm downward pressure on the tongue was applied with a spoon or tongue depressor carefully working to the point of Mary's tolerance. When this program was initiated, Mary would gag when even the tip of her tongue was stimulated. Over time, the therapist gradually was able to "walk" the spoon further back into her mouth without stimulating a gag response. This approach may be useful with other individuals who have a hypersensitive gag; however, each individual should have a program designed for his or her specific needs.

Jaw and Tongue Thrust

Jaw thrust is characterized by an abnormally strong downward extension of the lower jaw and is associated with head extension or total body extension patterns (Fraser et al. 1990). Poor positioning with too much hip extension and posterior pelvic tilt contributes to an increase in jaw thrust (Morris and Klein 1987). Therefore, program plans that include working on better sitting are indicated. The trunk and pelvis should be in alignment with the shoulder girdle forward and abduction of the scapulae. Manual jaw control during feeding to maintain jaw closure and promote stability is also indicated. Illustrations can be found in Finnie (1975) and in Morris and Klein (1987).

Tongue thrust is an abnormally strong protrusion of the tongue that is characterized by a swallow of anterior and posterior movement (Fraser et al. 1990). Tongue thrust makes it difficult to insert a spoon into the individual's mouth and results in expulsion of food. Increased extensor tone, neck hyperextension, and shoulder retraction also create extensor patterns in the mouth. Therefore, it is critical to assess the person's positioning during mealtime and make adjustments as needed. Manual jaw control is indicated for some individuals (Finnie 1975).

It is not uncommon for an individual with cerebral palsy to have difficulty with both jaw and tongue thrust. For instance, Jimmy is a youngster who is unable to successfully feed himself because his jaw and tongue thrust are so severe. When Jimmy attempts to place food in his mouth, the combined force of these two problems causes food to be pushed forward instead of back for swallowing. An assessment of Jimmy's physical abilities revealed that he has spastic quadriplegia; however, he is able to walk with a walker and sit in a chair independently. Because Jimmy is not dependent on a wheelchair for mobility and support, it was assumed that positioning was not an issue for feeding. Upon closer observation, however, it was noted that Jimmy had limited trunk control and that his positioning was influenced by extensor tone and spasticity. He often sat in a cafeteria chair with shoulders slumped forward, pelvis tilted backward, and legs extended at the hips. This position created increased tone in the facial muscles and tongue resulting in increased tongue and jaw thrust during mealtime. A chair was designed for him to use for meals that ensured that his feet were supported and hips flexed. Increased support through his lower body decreased the excessive tone resulting in decreased oral-motor problems. In addition, the care giver assisted Jimmy with manual jaw control to inhibit both tongue and jaw thrust.

Lip Closure

A lack of lip closure often is associated with feeding problems for individuals with cerebral palsy and may be caused by low muscle tone or spasticity. Severe spasticity associated with increased extensor tone can cause lip retraction, which is a pulling back of the lips from the teeth. Poor lip closure causes difficulty in taking food from a spoon and problems with swallowing (Fraser et al. 1990). Treatment procedures for lack of lip closure are based on whether it is caused by increased or low muscle tone. Tapping around the mouth may be indicated for the individual with low muscle tone but contraindicated for the person with increased tone. Positioning for feeding should be assessed to decrease spasticity and extensor tone as much as possible. In addition, the feeder should use a shallow spoon and be careful not to scrape the food on the individual's teeth. Feeding should be slow, allowing the person to use his or her lips to remove the food from the spoon. Manual jaw control may be indicated (Finnie 1975).

Tongue Lateralization

The final oral-motor problem to be considered is lack of tongue lateralization, which inhibits the development of chewing and is identified by predominating in-and-out movements of the tongue. This problem may be caused by oral hypersensitivity, hypotonicity, or insufficient jaw stability (Morris and Klein 1987). Positioning to reduce abnormal muscle tone should be the first consideration. Increased sensory input to the tongue should include manual stimulation as well as placement of food directly on the biting surfaces of the teeth. Foods that dissolve easily and are relatively soft such as graham crackers, pieces of cheese, and cereal are the items of choice for this activity. One should gradually change the types of food for chewing as the individual's ability to lateralize the tongue improves.

The oral-motor problems discussed in this chapter are only a few of those faced by individuals with cerebral palsy. An attempt has been made to provide a representative sample that will serve as an initial guide to assessment and program planning. Table 3-7 provides an overview of feeding concerns and techniques for remediation. The reader is directed to Morris and Klein (1987) for additional treatment techniques.

☐ Case 3-9: Genny

Genny has decreased muscle tone, or hypotonia, which is noted throughout her body as well as in the oral musculature. Because she does not use her upper lip to remove food from the spoon during mealtime or attempt to chew, her mother has always fed her baby foods. This practice has only made the problem worse, because Genny has not had any experiences that would stimulate oral-motor development. Since Genny's problems centered around low tone, the occupational therapist designed a program to stimulate muscle tone. The mother and teacher were taught to tap the muscles for lip closure and chewing prior to mealtime. In addition, they were shown how to avoid scraping food on Genny's teeth by stimulating the upper lip to move using firm pressure upon spoon removal. The next step was to introduce soft foods for chewing such as oranges wrapped in cheesecloth, graham crackers, and cheese by placing the food directly on Genny's molars. Tongue lateralization for this activity was encouraged by stroking the side of her tongue with a spoon or tongue depressor. The texture of Genny's food was gradually changed to replace the baby food with chopped table food. Her mother is happy to have Genny eating the same food as the other family members.

Dressing Concerns

The principle of partial participation related to dressing skills for individuals with cerebral palsy was discussed earlier in this chapter. However, it may be necessary to provide total assistance to some individuals who have severe to profound motor involvement. There are a number of positioning and handling strategies that make assisted dressing easier for the care giver. Finne (1976) and Copeland and Kimmel (1989) are excellent sources for this information. Table 3-8 provides some basic ideas for dressing the individual with severe motor limitations.

Table 3-7. Feeding Concerns and Treatments

Problem	Description	Intervention
Spasticity	An abnormal increase in muscle tone resulting in a stiffness or lack of mobility that interferes with normal patterns of movement. Jaw thrust may be a problem in individuals influenced by severe extension. A bite reflex is sometimes seen when the person's movements are domainted by flexion.	Good Positioning 1. Person should be positioned securely so that he/she is supported and relaxed. 2. If possible, positioning should be upright or slightly reclined. 3. Head and trunk should be in midline. 4. Hips should be to the back of the chair with protective seat belt. 5. Trunk should be aligned over the pelvis with feet on firm foot rest. 6. Check positioning during mealtimes and correct as needed.

Oral Motor Problems Associated with Spasticity

Problem	Description	Intervention
Lip retraction	Tone is increased in upper lip so it is drawn over the teeth. The person is unable to relax and pull the lips together.	1. Manual jaw control. 2. Use firm pressure starting at the bridge of the nose to draw the upper lip over the teeth. 3. Use total body relaxation exercises prior to mealtime. 4. Encourage the person to swallow prior to giving a bite of food. 5. Do not scrape the spoon on the person's teeth.
Poor jaw gradation	Tone is increased in facial muscles, often resulting in either exaggerated mouth opening or inability to open mouth wide enough for food presentation.	1. Manual jaw control. 2. Encourage the person to watch the feeder so he/she will correctly anticipate when to open the mouth. 3. Use relaxation techniques.
Tongue thrust	Food is pushed out of the mouth by the tongue instead of moving it to the rear of the mouth for swallowing. This is especially aggravated by improper positioning, especially head hyperextension.	1. Minimize through positioning. 2. Avoid holding spoonful of food in front of the person. 3. Provide inward/downward pressure on the tongue with spoon. 4. Jaw control, applying firm pressure to the base of tongue.
Bite reflex	A touch around or inside the mouth triggers the jaw to clamp down. Aggravated by an increase in flexor tone.	1. Minimize reflex with positioning. 2. Use oral motor exercises to desensitize oral cavity. 3. Use rubber-coated spoon. 4. If person clamps on the spoon, allow him/her to relax. Do not pull spoon out of mouth before person relaxes.
Oral hypersensitivity	Adverse response to tactile stimulation that may be seen as anxiety, discomfort, or withdrawal. Can be seen in individuals with hypertonia or hypotonia.	1. Use oral motor exercises for oral desensitization. 2. Wipe the mouth area by moving toward the mouth with firm pressure.

Table 3-7. *Continued*

Problem	Description	Intervention
Hypotonia	An abnormal decrease in muscle tone resulting in decreased posture and movement.	Good positioning: 1. Person should be positioned securely so that he/she is supported. 2. If possible, positioning should be upright or slightly reclined. 3. Head and trunk alignment should be in midline. 4. Check positioning during mealtimes and correct as needed.
	Oral Motor Problems Associated with Hypotonia:	
Lip immobility	Low tone in lips results in inability to remove food from the spoon or make an adequate lip seal.	1. Use manual jaw control. 2. Stimulate lip closure with oral-motor stimulation: a. Tap around the lips. b. Stretch upper lip.
Tongue immobility	Low tone in the tongue results in inability to get the food back to the molars where it can be chewed or swallowed.	1. Oral-motor exercises: a. Tap the base of the tongue. b. Stroke the side of the tongue prior to chewing. 2. Place food on the molars to stimulate chewing and tongue lateralization.
Low tone in facial muscles	Results in reduced ability to chew.	1. Oral motor exercises: a. Tapping b. Stimulate masseter muscle 2. Work on chewing during feeding.
Hypotonic gag	Absence of gag reflex, often resulting in aspiration of food.	1. Oral-motor exercise. 2. Careful feeding to prevent aspiration.

Capacity for Independent Living

One of the most serious barriers to community living for individuals with cerebral palsy is the lack of living options and support services. A recent survey conducted in Virginia (Community Needs Survey 1989) reported the following barriers to independent living for individuals with physical disabilities:

- Housing is too expensive.
- Nothing is available in the desired locations.
- The waiting list is too long.
- Housing is not accessible.
- Home modifications are needed.
- Assistance is needed with household responsibilities.
- Personal care assistance is needed.

Personal assistance services are perhaps the most crucial needs on the list for independent living. These services make it possible for individuals who are unable to care for their daily living needs such as personal hygiene, dressing, eating, toileting, mobility, and household maintenance to live in community rather than institutional settings. For example, John is 35 years old and a law school graduate; however, he has severe physical limitations because of spastic cerebral palsy. John

Table 3-8. Positioning and Handling Strategies for Dressing

- Dress and undress a young child or infant with extensor muscle tone prone (on the stomach) across the lap of the care giver and diaper him or her on the stomach rather than on his or her back.
- Bend or flex the individual's hips, knees, and ankles to reduce excessive extensor muscle tone.
- Decrease abnormal movement patterns by side-lying. Roll the individual from side to side while dressing and undressing him or her. This slow rolling movement reduces excessive muscle tone.
- Use side-lying to lessen the individual's tendency to push back into extension, making it easier for the care giver to bring the head, shoulders, and arms forward for dressing. The individual's feet and legs are also easier to bend.
- Use slow movement with firm pressure when moving an individual for dressing and undressing.
- Put clothes on the arm or leg that is more involved first.
- Straighten the individual's arm prior to putting on clothing. Do not try to pull by the hand through the sleeve an arm that is bent.
- Bend the individual's leg before putting on socks and shoes. Extended legs make the ankle and foot stiffer, and the toes are more likely to be flexed.
- Use fuller cut clothing with front openings, elastic waistbands, or Velcro closures when necessary.

would not be able to have his own apartment and work in the community if it were not for his full-time assistant, Mike. Mike provides assistance with dressing, feeding, toileting, household maintenance, and transportation. In addition, Mike accompanies John to work and provides physical assistance as needed.

John can afford to hire a personal assistant because he works fulltime as a lawyer. However, many individuals with cerebral palsy are not as fortunate and must reside in more restrictive housing situations.

Cindy, who is also 35 years old, has severe spastic cerebral palsy. She has been living in a nursing home since the age of 22. At that time, her parents felt that Cindy must leave home, because they were elderly and could no longer care for her physical needs. Because they could not afford to hire an attendant to assist with her care, their only choice was to select a nursing home as her living arrangement.

Because most of Cindy's education took place through a homebound program, she has limited work skills. In addition her community does not have a program to assist individuals with severe physical disabilities enter employment. Cindy relies on Medicaid to pay her nursing home expenses and to provide her with a $30-a-month allowance. In addition, Cindy lives in a state that does not have a Medicaid waiver program, so she cannot use Medicaid funds to pay for a personal-care attendant to assist her in independent living. Unfortunately, at this time, Cindy's chances for independent living appear slim. The following issues are critical in improving the independent living options for individuals with physical disabilities (Volunteers Disability Service Planners Work Group 1990):

- Development of family-like environments in community neighborhoods with nondisabled individuals
- Development of stipend programs or financial assistance for families to purchase or obtain needed services, home modifications, and adaptive equipment within the home environment
- Development of incentive programs to access federal and state financial resources to increase the number of accessible and affordable housing options
- Improvement of accessible and efficient transportation services
- Identification of potential funding sources to expand personal assistance services.

Economic Self-Sufficiency

Supported employment has made a difference in the vocational lives of many individuals with severe disabilities. To date, however, only 10% of the consumers placed nationally through the supported employment initiative have had physical or sensory disabilities (Wehman et al. 1989). This may be due to a perceived lack of vocational competence for this group as well as their varied physical abilities and limitations.

In addition, many professionals lack the skills to identify the physical barriers to employment and to utilize assistive technology to eliminate the problems. Franklin (1990) states that, in the 1990s, assistive technology in combination with supported employment will redefine employability for individuals with disabilities. The passing of P.L. 100-407, the Technology-Related Assistance for Individuals with Disabilities Act in 1988, has provided support and direction for the development of model programs designed to promote employability for individuals with severe disabilities.

Assistive technology for employment may include both high- and low-tech devices as defined by Congress. For instance, a low-tech device may be blocks to raise the work area of an individual who is seated in a wheelchair. A high-tech device, on the other hand, is usually designed by a rehabilitation engineer or therapist or purchased commercially (for example, a device for inputing information into a computer). An individual's need for technology should be carefully assessed, and adaptive equipment provided only if a person cannot function without its use. Professionals are also cautioned to assess thoroughly an individual's capabilities and utilize supported employment strategies to match them to appropriate job types. Assistive technology cannot provide solutions for all limitations. For instance, it may be unwise to place a person with severe fine motor limitations in a high-production assembly job even if adaptive devices can be made to assist in task completion. Table 3-9 provides a list of resources in the area of assistive technology. The following case studies demonstrate the use of supported employment and assistive technology to assist individuals with cerebral palsy in the world of work.

□ Case 3-10: Ginny

Ginny is a young woman who has spastic cerebral palsy, quadriplegia. She recently began work at a parts store as an office worker. The job was identified for her by a supported employment program using a consumer-assessment, job-analysis, and job-compatibility-analysis process (Moon et al. 1986). Her employment specialist identified that Ginny had many of the basic skills to complete the job duties, which included answering the telephone, processing invoices, and filing. She was able to communicate effectively and could read in order to complete the invoice and filing tasks. At first, however, her physical limitations seemed to interfere with the completion of her job duties. Ginny was unable to raise her arms higher than shoulder height, and she tired easily from using her hands for activities. Her electric wheelchair did not fit under a standard desk, and Ginny was unable to access the file cabinets because she could not maneuver her chair close enough to open the bottom as well as top drawers.

After reviewing the situation, the employment specialist and an occupational therapist determined that a number of low-tech devices could be used that would aid Ginny in carrying out her job duties. The employer was willing to have the office area arranged to fit Ginny's needs as well as assign a coworker to provide additional physical assistance as indicated. The following modifications were developed:

Table 3-9. Assistive Technology Information Centers

ABLENET
Cerebral Palsy Center
Griggs-Midway Building
1821 University Avenue
St. Paul, MN 55104

Association for Retarded Citizens
Bioengineering Program
2501 Avenue J
Arlington, TX 76011

AT&T National Special Needs Center
2001 Route 46, Suite 310
Parsippany, NJ 07054-1315

Center for Special Education Technology
Information Exchange
c/o The Council for Exceptional Children
1920 Association Drive
Reston, VA 22091

IBM National Support Center for Persons with
Disabilities
P.O. Box 2150
2500 Windy Ridge Parkway
Marietta, GA 30067

Materials Development Center
Stout Vocational Rehabilitation Institute
University of Wisconsin-Stout
Menomonie, WI 54751

National Information Center for Handicapped
Youth and Children (NICHCY)
7926 Jones Branch Drive
Suite 1100
McLean, VA 22102

National Information Center on Deafness,
Gallaudet College
800 Florida Avenue NE
Washington, DC 20002

National Organization on Disability
2100 Pennsylvania Avenue NW
Suite 234
Washington, DC 20039

National Rehabilitation Information Center
8455 Colesville Road
Suite 935
Silver Spring, MD 20910-3319

National Resource Library on Youth with
Disabilities
National Center for Youth with Disabilities
Adolescent Health Program
University of Minnesota
Box 721-UHMC
Harvard Street at East River Road
Minneapolis, MN 55455

United Cerebral Palsy Association
66 East 34th Street
New York, NY 10016

(Adapted from the *Assistive Technology Sourcebook*, RESNA 1990)

- Blocks were used to raise the desk to a comfortable work height.
- A head set was placed on the phone to eliminate the need to constantly pick up the receiver.
- A temporary hanging file was placed next to Ginny's desk for use during a day's worth of filing. A coworker assisted her by placing the files in the office cabinets at the end of the work day.
- An electric stapler was purchased for stapling invoices together.
- An electric typewriter was used to take office messages and orders rather

than to write on a note pad. The employment specialist designed a form for Ginny to use that made her note taking easier.

☐ Case 3-11: Susan

Susan is currently in a special education program for students with severe mental retardation and physical disabilities. Because she is 20 years old, her teacher is concerned about transition from school to work and has referred Susan to a grant program designed to work with students who have similar disabilities. Project staff identified a job at the local university library stamping identification numbers on the spines of new books. This job is typically performed daily by graduate assistantship students in a large room of the library (Renzaglia and Hutchins 1990). After assessing her physical strengths and limitations, the following characteristics were identified:

- Susan uses a wheelchair for mobility and requires personal assistance for movement from one place to another.
- She has limited movements in both arms because of hypertonicity throughout her head, trunk, and limbs.
- Lateral wheelchair supports and a seat belt are necessary to assist Susan in sitting upright in her chair. She also requires foot support and straps.
- Susan can raise her right arm at the shoulder joint so that her forearm is parallel to and 6 inches above her wheelchair lap tray.
- She does not have any functional mobility in her fingers, which are usually tightly fisted into the palms of both hands.
- She is visually attentive and can turn her head from side to side.
- Susan is severely mentally retarded.

Given that she had these physical characteristics, it was obvious that Susan would need assistive technology to complete the job of stamping books with the library identification number. Project staff worked closely with a rehabilitation engineer, and a spring-loaded device was designed to assist Susan in completing the task. The first step in the job required personal assistance from a coworker or project staff member to load the equipment with ten books for stamping. At that point, Susan was responsible for pressing a switch to drop a book into position. She then would touch another plate that held the heat stamp in order to apply heat to the spine of the book. Susan kept this in place for 10 seconds, finally touching another switch to move the book off the work surface. Intensive systematic instruction was provided by a trainer to assist Susan in learning her job.

Susan's community-based work experience highlights several critical issues in the area of vocational programming for individuals with severe disabilities. First, her instruction is taking place outside of the classroom setting. Typically, students with Susan's characteristics have been limited to "classroom only" programs that have failed to assist students in making the transition from school to work (Moon et al. 1990). Professionals **must** be creative in providing functional, age-appropriate vocational experiences for this group of individuals.

Second, Susan is being given an opportunity to interact with nonhandicapped peers. Integration, that is, physical proximity and the opportunity to interact socially with others, is a primary value of supported employment (Moon et al. 1990). It is a work characteristic that most people take for granted in their everyday lives. For individuals such as Susan, however, work usually translates into sheltered workshop and activity center settings where minimal access to real daily environments is provided. Expectations for individuals with severe disabilities will remain low as long as professionals continue to place them in segregated environments.

Individuals with cerebral palsy can be contributing members of America's work force. For some, it may mean the traditional route from college to employment. Others may require assistive technology and transitional employment services to locate and perform a job. Still others, like Susan, may require job modifications, supported employment, and intensive on-site support to become employed.

Summary

The real issue for the 1990s is consumer empowerment and involvement in program planning. Empowerment means that human service professionals must work with individuals who have disabilities rather than do something to or for them (Nichols 1990). An individual with cerebral palsy, regardless of the severity of disability, has the same rights to live and work in the community as his or her nonhandicapped peers. It is the professionals' responsibility to identify the barriers to successful living and provide assistance in overcoming these obstacles.

References

1. Azrin NH, Schaeffer RM, Wesolowski MD. A rapid method of teaching profoundly retarded persons to dress by a reinforcement-guidance method. Ment Retard 14(6): 29–33, 1976.
2. Baumgart D, Brown L, Pumpian I, Nisbet J, Ford A, Sweet M, et al. Principle of partial participation and individualized adaptations in educational programs for severely handicapped students. Journal of the Association for the Severely Handicapped 1: 17–27, 1982.
3. Bigge JL. Teaching Individuals with Physical and Multiple Disabilities. 2nd ed. Columbus, OH, Charles E. Merrill, 1989.
4. Bleck EE, Nagel DA. Physically Handicapped Children: A Medical Atlas for Teachers. 2nd ed. New York, Grune & Stratton, 1983.
5. Campbell PH. Physical management and handling procedures with students with movement dysfunction. In: Snell ME. ed. Systematic Instruction of Persons with Severe Handicaps. Columbus, OH, Charles E. Merrill, 1987, pp 174–187.
6. Community Services Assistance Center. Results of the Board for the Rights of the Disabled Survey of Virginians with Disabilities. Richmond, Virginia Commonwealth University, Virginia Institute for Developmental Disabilities, 1989.
7. Coots J, Falvey MA. Communication skills. In: Falvey M. ed. Community-based Curriculum: Instructional Strategies for Students with Severe Handicaps. Baltimore, Paul H. Brookes, 1989, pp 255–285.
8. Copeland M, Ford L, Solon N. Occupational Therapy for Mentally Retarded Children. Baltimore, University Park Press, 1976.
9. Copeland ME, Kimmel JR. Evaluation and Management of Infants and Young Children with Developmental Disabilities. Baltimore, Paul H. Brookes, 1989.
10. Enders A, Hall M. Assistive Technology Sourcebook. Washington, DC, RESNA Press, 1990.
11. Franklin K. Rehabilitation engineering and assistive technology. In: Griffin SL, Revell WG. eds. Rehabilitation Counselor Desktop Guide to Supported Employment. Richmond, Virginia Commonwealth University, Rehabilitation Research and Training Center, 1990, pp 99–117.
12. Fraser BA, Hensinger RN, Phelps JA. Physical Management of Multiple Handicaps: A Professional's Guide. Baltimore, Paul H. Brookes, 1990.
13. Finnie NR. Handling the Young Cerebral Palsied Child at Home. 2nd ed. New York, E.P. Dutton, 1975.
14. Halle JW, Marshall AM, Spradlin JE. Time delay: A technique to increase language use and facilitate generalization in retarded children. J Appl Behav Anal 121: 431–439, 1979.
15. Inge KJ. Atypical motor development and cerebral palsy. In: Orelove F, Sobsey D. eds. Educating Children with Multiple Disabilities: A Transdisciplinary Approach. Baltimore, Paul H. Brookes, 1987, pp 43–65.
16. Miller J, Allaire J. Augmentative communication. In: Snell ME. ed. Systematic Instruction of Persons with Severe Handicaps. Columbus, Charles E. Merrill, 1987, pp 273–298.
17. Moon MS, Goodall P, Barcus M, Brooke V. The Supported Work Model of Competitive Employment for Citizens with Severe Handicaps: A Guide for Job Trainers. Rev. ed. Richmond, Virginia Commonwealth University, Rehabilitation Research and Training Center, 1986.
18. Moon MS, Inge KJ, Wehman P, Brooke V, Barcus J. Helping Persons with Severe Mental Retardation Get and Keep Employment: Supported Employment Issues and Strategies. Baltimore, Paul H. Brookes, 1990.
19. Morris SE, Klein MD. Pre-feeding Skills: A Comprehensive Resource for Therapists. Tucson, AZ, Therapy Skill Builders, 1987.
20. Nichols JL. The new decade dawns: The search for quality and consumer empowerment converge. Journal of Rehabilitation Administration 14(3): 69–70, 1990.
21. Payne JW, Reder RD. Occupational and Physical Therapy Home Instruction Manual. Cincinnati, Children's Hospital Medical Center, 1983.
22. Prensky AL, Palkes HS. Care of the Neurologically Handicapped Child: A Book for Parents and Professionals. New York, Oxford University Press, 1982.
23. Rainforth B, York J. Handling and positioning. In: Orelove F, Sobsey D. eds. Educating Children with Multiple Disabilities: A Transdisciplinary Approach. Baltimore, Paul H. Brookes, 1987, pp 183–218.
24. Reichle J, Karlan G. The selection of an augmentative system in communication intervention: A

critique of decision rules. Journal of the Association for Persons with Severe Handicaps 10: 146–156, 1985.

25. Reichle J, Keogh WJ. Communication instruction for learners with severe handicaps: Some unresolved issues. In: Horner R, Meyer L, Fredericks HD. eds. Education of Learners with Severe Handicaps: Exemplary Service Strategies. Baltimore, Paul H. Brookes, 1986.

26. Reichle J, York J, Eynon D. Influence of indicating preferences for initiating, maintaining, and terminating interactions. In: Brown F, Lehr D. eds. Persons with Profound Disabilities: Issues and Practices. Baltimore, Paul H. Brookes, 1989, pp 191–212.

27. Renzaglia A, Hutchins M. Supported Employment for Individuals with Severe Disabilities. Presentation at the Virginia Commonwealth University, Rehabilitation Research and Training Center Symposium on Supported Employment, Virginia Beach, October, 1990.

28. Snell ME. Basic self-care instruction for students without motor impairments. In: Snell ME. ed. Systematic Instruction of Persons with Severe Handicaps. Columbus, Charles E. Merrill, 1987, pp 334–389.

29. Snell ME, Gast DL. Applying delay procedures to the instruction of the severely handicapped. Journal of the Association of the Severely Handicapped 5(4): 3–14, 1981.

30. Sobsey D. Mealtime skills. In: Orelove F, Sobsey D. eds. Educating Children with Multiple Disabilities: A Transdisciplinary Approach. Baltimore, Paul H. Brookes, 1987, pp 219–252.

31. Volunteer Disability Service Planners Work Group. Issue papers on the service needs for persons with physical and sensory disabilities. Richmond, Virginia Commonwealth University, Virginia Institute for Developmental Disabilities, 1990.

32. Wehman P, Kregel J, Shafer M. Emerging Trends in the National Supported Employment Initiative: A Preliminary Analysis of Twenty-seven States. Richmond, Virginia Commonwealth University, Rehabilitation Research and Training Center, 1989.

33. York J, Nietupski J, Hamre-Nietupski S. A decision making process for using microswitches. Journal of the Association for Persons with Severe Handicaps 10(4): 214–223, 1985.

Chapter 4
Emotional Impairments

Elaine Clark
H. Kenton Reavis
William Jenson

Considerable differences of opinion exist about how certain developmental disorders should be defined and treated. This is especially true of emotional and behavioral disorders. As Kazdin (1985) points out, beyond agreement that these impairments need to be conceptualized from a developmental and contextual framework, there is little consensus. In this chapter, we make no attempt to arrive at a consensus; rather, we have sought to describe what is generally meant by "emotional impairment," what areas of function are impaired, and what are considered to be the best practices for intervening.

Functional Description

Special Education Definition

More emotionally impaired, or behaviorally disordered, children and adolescents are classified according to special educational classification systems than any other type of system. The federal definition of a severe emotional disturbance, according to Public Law 94-142, is:

(i) The term means a condition exhibiting one or more of the following characteristics over a long peirod of time and to marked degree, which adversely affects educational performance:

(a) An inability to learn which cannot be explained by intellectual, sensory, or health factors;

(b) An inability to build or maintain satisfactory interpersonal relationships with peers and teachers;

(c) Inappropriate types of behaviors or feelings under normal circumstances;

(d) A general pervasive mood of unhappiness or depression;

(e) A tendency to develop physical symptoms or fears associated with personal or school problems.

(ii) The term includes children who are schizophrenic. The term does not include children who are socially maladjusted, unless it is determined they are seriously emotionally disturbed (Education for All Handicapped Children Act of 1975, Section 121a.5).

As a direct result of funding requirements, the federal definition generally serves as a model for state classifications. State classifications are defined by state boards of education and used primarily by local school districts to assure proper funding for educational programs. Because funding to schools is tied to the number of children classified with a particular disability, state definitions are generally broad in coverage and include disorders of emotion and behavior, interpersonal difficulties, and learning and achievement problems (Cullinan et al. 1986). For example, according to the special education rules in the State of Utah, "behavioral disordered" is used as a generic term to describe behavioral difficulties that adversely affect academic performance (State Board of Education Special Education Rules 1988). Like the federal definition, this definition includes individuals who are severely emotionally disturbed, whereas those who are socially maladjusted are excluded unless they are determined to be behavior disordered.

The breadth of the definition of emotionally impaired, or behavior disordered, has led to accusations that the definition is too vague and leads to inadequate interrater agreement (Walker et al. 1985). Further, because both the federal and state definitions exclude "socially maladjusted" children and adolescents unless there are demonstrated emotional or behavioral impairments, the definitions virtually ignore the fact that most emotionally disturbed, or behaviorally disordered, children referred for special education are socially maladjusted. Despite the definitional problems, many children with serious conduct problems manage to qualify for special education services. Recent studies have shown that 29% of the children placed in special education programs for emotional and behavioral disturbances behave aggressively one or more times a week (Ruhl and Hughes 1985). Whereas the special education definition will, by necessity, continue to be used in school settings, other classification systems, such as the *Diagnostic and Statistical Manual of Mental Disorders, Third Edition–Revised* (DSM III-R; American Psychiatric Association, 1987), are preferred by many professionals.

Clinically Derived Classification Systems

The DSM III-R is a widely accepted, and often used, classification system. As an atheoretical approach that places emphasis on symptoms rather than on cause, the DSM III-R is a radical departure from previous classification systems derived from clinical observations and expert opinion. The fact that the DSM III-R lends itself to the assessment of the context of the problem as well as of the problem itself makes it particularly well suited to the diagnosis of children and adolescents. Disorders such as the ones listed in Table 4-1 are defined in a descriptive manner, with specific criteria for diagnosis provided. Further, as a multiaxial system, the DSM III-R affords the opportunity to not only make multiple diagnoses (something that is clearly needed when identifying childhood psychopathologic conditions, but also to determine the severity of situational stress and the highest functional level of the individual for a period of one year previously.

Despite a number of strengths, the DSM III-R has been a frequent target of criticism. Perhaps the most common criticism pertains to its reliability. Whereas diagnostic agreement across the broader categories of disorders (for example, disruptive versus anxiety disorders) is generally adequate, agreement within these categories is not (Werry et al. 1983). The same is true for the validity of the DSM III-R; as finer discriminations are called for, validity suffers (Fernando et al. 1986).

Empirically Derived Diagnostic Systems

The psychometric shortcomings of the DSM III-R have been attributed by some to the manner in which the categories were derived (Achenbach 1982). That is, instead of empirically identifying diagnostic categories, expert opinion and consensus were used. Multivariate procedures, on the other hand, have used sophisticated statistical techniques to empirically define behavioral patterns of interrelated characteristics of emotional impairments. Like that of the previously discussed diagnostic systems, the goal of the multivariate technique is to identify a syndrome using a dimensional

Table 4-1. DSM III-R Classification: Axes I and II: Disorders Usually First Evident in Infancy, Childhood, or Adolescence

Disruptive behavior disorders
  Attention-deficit hyperactivity disorder
  Conduct disorder
    Group type
    Solitary aggressive type
    Undifferentiated type
  Oppositional defiant disorder
Anxiety disorders of childhood or adolescence
  Separation anxiety disorder
  Avoidant disorder of childhood or
    adolescence
  Overanxious disorder
Eating disorders
  Anorexia nervosa
  Bulimia nervosa
  Pica
  Rumination disorder of infancy
Gender identity disorders
  Transsexualism
  Gender identity disorder of adolescence or
    adulthood
Tic disorders
  Tourette's disorder
  Chronic motor or vocal tic disorder
  Transient tic disorder
Elimination disorders
  Functional encopresis
  Functional enuresis
Speech disorders not elsewhere classified
  Cluttering
  Stuttering

Other disorders of infancy, childhood, or
  adolescence
  Elective mutism
  Identity disorder
  Reactive attachment disorder of infancy or
    early childhood
  Stereotypy/habit disorder
  Undifferentiated attention-deficit disorder
DEVELOPMENTAL DISORDERS
(Note: These are coded on Axis II)
Mental retardation
  Mild mental retardation
  Moderate mental retardation
  Severe mental retardation
  Profound mental retardation
Pervasive developmental disorders
  Autistic disorder
  Pervasive developmental disorder, not
    otherwise specified
Specific developmental disorder
  Academic skills disorders
  Developmental arithmetic disorder
  Developmental expressive writing disorder
  Developmental reading disorder
  Language and speech disorders
  Development articulation disorder
  Developmental expressive language disorder
  Development receptive language disorder
  Motor skills disorder
  Developmental coordination disorder
  Specific developmental disorder NOS

approach rather than a categoric one. Instead of assessing the presence or absence of a disorder, the degree and severity of demonstrable symptoms are quantified along a behavioral gradient (Kazdin 1985). If desired, classification is possible. Cluster analytic techniques have often been used to achieve the goal of classifying individuals according to similar patterns of symptoms. The most extensive research of this type has been conducted by Achenbach and Edelbrock (Achenbach and Edelbrock 1978; 1979). Factor analytic studies of children with, and without, referral concerns for emotional and behavioral problems have yielded two broad factors, externalizing and internalizing behavior problems.

Whereas the former typically reflects behavioral excesses that are directed outwardly toward the environment, such as noncompliance, cruelty, hyperactivity, delinquent behaviors, and aggression, the latter often involves behavioral deficits, or problems that are inwardly directed, such as anxiety, phobias, social withdrawal, depression, immaturity, and obsessive-compulsive behaviors (Edelbrock and Achenbach 1980).

Multidimensional classification systems have a number of advantages, including the capability of covering multiple behavioral characteristics and empirically determining the salience of particular areas of dysfunction; however, they too have weaknesses. One of the greatest limitations has to do with the fact that low-frequency problem behaviors are likely to be overlooked because empirically derived systems rely on data that comprise items and subjects that reflect the more common behavior problems. Regardless of which diagnostic system is used, that is, an empirically or clinically derived system, there are flaws in these grossly underdeveloped systems (Kazdin 1985). Nonetheless, diagnosis is central to understanding the multiple facets of a disorder, including the cause(s) and the course.

The remainder of this chapter addresses the functional limitations of individuals with emotional and behavioral impairments. Although, as with other developmentally disabled persons, these individuals may not demonstrate impairment in all areas of functioning defined by the Developmental Disabilities Act, each of the following areas covered by the Act will be discussed: self-care, language, learning, mobility, self-direction, capacity for independent living, and economic sufficiency.

Self-Care

Individuals with emotional impairments typically possess the necessary cognitive and motor skills to care for their personal needs. As a result of the emotional difficulties, however, these persons often are unable to care properly for themselves. The problem is frequently one of neglect. Compliance with medical regimen is poor, and preventive health care is often nonexistent. This is especially disturbing given the fact that individuals with emotional impairments are often more susceptible to disease (for example, infection) and injury than their "mentally healthy" counterparts (Barkley 1985; Shanok and Lewis 1981). At other times, however, the problem of self-care has more to do with the problem of complying with prescribed medical treatments such as medication.

Pharmacologic agents have been used to treat emotional and behavioral problems of children and adolescents since the 1930s; the first was a stimulant, amphetamine, followed 15 years later by antipsychotics, chlorpromazine, and thioridazine. Antidepressants and anxiolytic medications were added later, but the search for proper medications to modify behavior continues. Although psychotropic medications have been used successfully to treat some of the behavioral concomitants of emotional impairments, the underlying disturbance is typically not changed (Cepeda 1989).

Depending on which medication is used, that is, tranquilizer, antidepressant, stimulant, or anticonvulsant, and the person's age, the greater the qualitative difference in medication response. Research has shown that the younger the person (that is, under 10 years), the greater is the variability of response to medication (Gualtieri et al. 1983; Minde 1977) and the greater the difference in side effects.

Although all medications have side effects, that is, pharmacologic actions that occur in addition to the intended action for relieving target symptoms, some side effects can seriously interfere with a person's functioning, in particular, the ability to care for his or her own needs. For example, sedation is a common side effect of many psychotropic medications. Although sedation is more often associated with initial use, it is also a frequent complaint of those on higher dosages. Other side effects that are not uncommon yet that have the potential to influence self-care, include impaired visual-motor coordination, blurred vision, dizziness, appetite disturbance, and tremors. Even side effects such as dry mouth and constipation can affect a person's functional capacity. Despite the fact that children generally adapt to medications rather quickly, it is important to insure that prescribed medications are of sufficient benefit to risk the potential adverse side effects. Especially when one is treating children, one should use as an adjunctive treatment with nonmedication therapies, such as behavioral therapy (Gualtieri et al. 1983; Ross and Ross 1982; see Hutchens 1987 for a review).

In addition to the problems they have with prescribed medications, individuals with emotional difficulties also have problems associated with using nonprescribed substances such as alcohol and other drugs. Whereas many individuals, especially younger persons, only experiment with alcohol and drugs, many others are repeat users. Persons with emotional problems tend to be at greater risk for engaging in a pattern of continued use and abuse (Millman and Botvin 1983). Chronic drug use not only poses health risks from the drugs themselves, but often leads to other serious health concerns that have the potential to interfere with a person's ability to care for personal needs. Some of the effects from commonly abused drugs like alcohol, stimulants, opiates, cannabis, psychedelics, and inhalants include stimulated or depressed central nervous system function; depressed cardiac and respiratory activity; insomnia; nausea and vomiting; hyperactivity; seizures; and unconsciousness (Forman and Randolph 1987). Further, alcohol and drug use have been associated with increased risk of accident-related injuries, some fatal (Cohen 1981). For adolescent populations, alcohol consumption has been shown to contribute to death rates as high as 45% for motor vehicle accidents (Mayer 1983).

Although school-based prevention programs that stress the development of adaptive coping skills hold the greatest promise in attacking the problem, targeting potential abusers and gaining their cooperation in treatment is difficult. Therefore, a variety of outpatient and residential treatment programs exist. Although these programs all stress the importance of associated problem behaviors in addition to the substance abuse itself, many have different philosophies and approaches to treat-

ment (for example, total abstinence versus controlled use). Austin and Prendergast (1984) reviewed research literature on such treatments for substance use and abuse by adolescents. Further, the National Institute of Drug Abuse published an excellent review of prevention and early intervention programs (Glynn et al. 1983).

Suicide is another serious concern among individuals with emotional impairments. Whereas studies have shown that 40% of suicides by adolescents are alcohol-related (Forrest 1983), data also show that the majority of adolescents who committed suicide had serious conduct disorders (Shaffer 1974). Many individuals with internalizing disorders, such as depression and schizophrenia, also complete suicides (Hahn 1987). Obviously, prevention is the only treatment of choice. The rates for suicide among adolescents have more than doubled over the past several decades (Smith and Crawford 1986), and it is unclear whether the rate has plateaued. Cantor (1986) suggested some reasonable means to work toward the goal of prevention, such as reducing the prescribed dosages of medications and limiting the availability of lethal weapons. To be effective, however, prevention efforts must focus on improving the mental health atmosphere of the school as well as the home and must be implemented as early as possible. The Fairfax County Public Schools have developed an excellent prevention program aimed at the adolescent. For information about the program, contact the Fairfax County School District in Fairfax, Virginia. For a comprehensive volume on child suicide, Pfeffer's *The Suicidal Child* is recommended reading (1986).

☐ Case 4-1: Jamie

Jamie is a 17-year-old boy with a history of physical problems. Beginning in early childhood, he was frequently taken to the emergency room for injuries that his brothers never seemed to have. On more than one occasion, Jamie had a broken leg set and his head sewn up for cuts he sustained during falls. To his parents' dismay, Jamie did not take care of himself any better when he became an adolescent. In fact, in many ways things got worse. When he learned to drive, his impulsive nature resulted in a number of accidents with the family car. Jamie wanted friends so badly that he took dares and needless risks to impress them. For instance, he took alcohol from the bar in his own home and rifled through medicine cabinets in the homes of friends and relatives looking for drugs. Although he gave a lot away, he also began abusing drugs and alcohol himself. His last admission to the emergency room was for a drug overdose.

Receptive and Expressive Language

A number of problems can put an individual at risk for self-destructive behavior. Perceived incompetence is one. Studies of children with speech and language problems indicate a high incidence of other emotional and behavioral impairments, including anxious and avoidant disorders, oppositional defiant behaviors, conduct disorders, and attention-deficit disorders (Beitchman et al. 1986). Regardless of whether a language problem is primary, or secondary to an emotional impairment, it places an individual at risk for developing other problems. Whereas some individuals overcome their language problems with little residual effects, many continue to experience language difficulties that further compound their situation (Wolpaw et al. 1977). Language problems not only have the potential to disrupt interpersonal communication, affecting social functioning, but can also cause problems with a person's capacity to function independently, including financial self-sufficiency.

The disturbance of language is frequently seen in some of the more pervasive developmental disorders such as autism (DeMyer et al. 1981). In fact, many children with autism who are verbal exhibit pronominal reversals, immature grammar, and difficulties with abstract language. The language of the child with autism clearly distinguishes him or her from other seriously disturbed children with language disorders, such as children with schizophrenia. The structure of language for those with schizophrenia may be normal but the content is not. Often the inappropriateness of logic and oddities of thought are reflected in the expressive language (American Psychiatric Association 1987). Although it is beyond the scope of this chapter to describe remediation techniques, perhaps a reminder is in order that intervening with language problems from a social context perspective may reap the greatest benefit for this population (Kretschmer 1986). Conant et al. (1983) devised materials and activities for this purpose, that closely adhere to rules of discourse. Individuals who limit their verbalizations or who do not respond in self-selected situations (for example, electively mute) may be more likely to benefit from interventions based on social learning theory. For example, in the electively mute child, increases in verbalization have been achieved using self-modeling techniques (Kehle et al. 1990).

☐ Case 4-2: Seth

Seth, a third grade student, has always had trouble in school. His parents were aware of his problems, most notably with peers, even before he entered kindergarten. The other children often made fun of the way Seth talked. The more he struggled to express himself, the more he was ridiculed. The speech therapist recently informed Seth's parents that he has a serious speech articulation, and language, problem. Seth has resisted working on his problems; in fact, he becomes angry when others offer to help. This response has seriously impaired his interactions with his teachers and with the other children. Seth is a loner. He is the last to be asked to participate in games or to be invited to sleep over at another child's house. He has recently begun complaining about stomach pains and headaches and is having problems sleeping. The school psychologist who evaluated Seth is worried that Seth might be depressed. The psychologist plans to meet individually with Seth and to involve him in a social skills training group.

Learning and Cognition

Academic skill deficits, especially in the area of reading (Wells and Forehand 1985), have been shown to be one of the strongest correlates with emotional and behavioral disorders in children and adolescents (Rutter and Yule 1978). Studies have shown that learning problems are correlated with a lack of participation because of truancy and school phobia. Learning problems have also been associated with higher rates of aggression (Lewis et al. 1980). These findings do not, however, mean that emotional and behavioral problems inevitably lead to learning problems; it is just as likely that the reverse is true. Rutter and Yule (1978) suggested that learning problems and academic failure may lead to the emotional and behavioral problems of this population. In this case, the focus of intervention needs to be on improved learning.

Although pharmacologic therapy aimed at improving learning has been tried, especially with children who have attention deficit disorders, its effectiveness in improving learning has not been demonstrated (Chase and Clement 1985). Instead, direct behaviorally oriented interventions have been shown to be most effective in improving academic performance (Elliott and Shapiro 1990; Kesler 1987). These interventions have the advantage of potentially reducing some of the disruptive behavior problems while enhancing learning. Hoge and Andrews (1987) reviewed a number of studies examining the effectiveness of modifying academic performance and of managing specific classroom behaviors to improve learning. Attempts to modify academic performance typically are made by increasing the amount of work completed, whereas modifying classroom behavior is affected by manipulating behaviors that might facilitate or detract from learning (for example, on- or off-task behaviors). Hoge and Andrews (1987) concluded that manipulating academic performance compared with modifying classroom behavior resulted in far greater improvement in learning. Although attempts at modifying classroom behavior were successful, that is, the behaviors changed in the desired direction, this change did not have the anticipated effect on achievement.

Shapiro (1986) drew similar conclusions from his review of this research. He found that academic achievement was most improved by increasing the content mastered and the amount of time engaged in academic tasks. Although the diverse learning styles of individuals should not be overlooked (see Polce, 1987 for a review), it is widely known that "time on task" serves as a good predictor of how much is learned. In fact, it is unlikely that increases in the amount of content learned will occur if time engaged in academic tasks is not increased. As Walberg (1984) pointed out, homework extends this time. Although many expect homework to yield academic benefits, research has shown that much of the homework that is assigned is not only inconsistent with validated instructional techniques (McDermott et al. 1984; Keith 1986), but also improperly implemented (Walberg 1984; Walberg et al. 1985). Regularly scheduled, appropriate homework is an important intervention with individuals who have learning problems (see Jenson et al. [in press], for a review). To conform to the best teaching practice, homework assignments should be (1) designed to parallel classroom curriculum and instruction; (2) properly introduced; (3) allowed sufficient time for mastery of a given instructional step; and (4) graded immediately for feedback. In fact, performance feedback alone is effective in improving academic performance (Van Houten and Lai Fatt 1981). Anesko and Levine's (1987) *Winning the Homework War* provides excellent suggestions for assessing homework difficulties and developing proper homework habits. *Homework Without Tears* by Canter and Hausner (1987) is also a good resource because it can be used with assertive discipline classroom techniques used in the schools.

In addition to assigning homework, a number of other methods are used to enhance academic performance. Although it is beyond the scope of this chapter to provide a comprehensive analysis of these techniques, a brief description is warranted. Many researchers have examined the effectiveness of self-management, that is, the application of contingencies to one's own behavior. This typically involves self-monitoring, self-evaluation, and self-reinforcement (Kanfer 1971). Self-management is an extremely effective method for improving academic skills (Childs 1983; McLaughlin et al. 1981; Shapiro 1986). This method not only has the advantage of being more efficient (the reinforcer is always present), but also has been shown to increase generalization in a variety of settings (Rhode et al. 1983). Self-management also has the unique feature of having the potential to increase independent learning. Self-management uses techniques for contingency control and involves the use of self-instruction, a strategy that has been documented as effective in improving learning (Fox and Kendall 1983).

Manipulating group contingencies is another useful method. Several studies have shown that group control of contingencies can be an effective means of improving academic achievement (Shapiro and Goldberg 1986). Other effective techniques include cooperative learning (Slavin et al. 1984); peer tutoring (Greenwood et al. 1984); and parent training (O'Leary et al. 1976).

Elliott and Shapiro (1990) believe that one component underlying the various methods that have been effective in improving academic performance is contingent reinforcement. It is, therefore, critical that opportunities for reinforcement be made available, regardless of the method selected (Johnston and McLaughlin 1982; Lieberman 1984). Even with this approach, there are some individuals with emotional and behavioral impairments who will not benefit. When emotional impairment is the primary deterrent to learning (for example, depression, anxiety, or psychosis), the most effective interventions are those aimed directly at improving the emotional status of the individual. For example, in cases in which anxiety plays the key role, counterconditioning procedures (for example, relaxation training, anxiety hierarchy construction, systematic desensitization, and forced exposure), modeling, operant procedures (for example, shaping and positive reinforcement) and self-control procedures (for example, self-monitoring, relaxation, self-reinforcement and self-punishment, self-instruction, and stimulus control) have been shown to be most effective (see Siegel and Ridley-Johnson 1985).

☐ Case 4-3: Doug

Basic reading and arithmetic have been problems for Doug for several years. Being in junior high school has not changed things. He will not follow the teacher's directions and argues when required to complete his work. Even when Doug does his homework, he often fails to turn it in. The teacher really cares about Doug and works hard to teach him basic academic skills. She even works after school for several hours each week teaching him reading and arithmetic skills. Unfortunately, Doug seems to forget these the next day. He is extremely frustrated and has begun referring to himself as a "retard." Over the past several weeks, Doug has started to skip school. He is often found riding his skateboard around mall parking lots.

Mobility

Individuals with emotional impairments rarely experience mobility problems. These individuals generally have no difficulty ambulating unless gross motor impairment exists in addition to the emotional problems. Problems with ambulation that are related to emotional impairment may, however, be the result of medication side effects. Emotional problems rarely immobilize a person, but immobilization is seen with a catatonic-type schizophrenic disorder (American Psychiatric Association 1987). In either case, medication adjustment may relieve the problem. There is little doubt that psychotropic agents can affect motor capacity (Nicholson and Ward 1984). Even with individuals who elect not to ambulate (for example, phobias and anxiety disorders), medication therapy may have positive effects, especially when used in conjunction with nonmedication, or behavioral, therapy techniques (Hutchens 1987).

Self-Direction

Lack of self-direction, which plagues many individuals with emotional impairments, is rarely the primary referral concern, but it can have serious ramifications for learning and daily functioning. Although most individuals display dependency during development, a fact that is considered a crucial stepping-stone for normal, independent behavior later in life (Ainsworth 1979), most eventually assume responsibility for their own lives. Some people, however, passively allow others to assume

this responsibility. These individuals not only show excessive reliance, or dependence, on the environment for direction, but show a lack of self-initiated motivation. Children may have difficulty starting or finishing academic tasks without a great deal of assistance. This behavior, of course, has the potential to become avoidant or manipulative. These problems tend to cluster with other problems that reflect internalizing disorders such as anxiety, withdrawal, poor peer relations (may show a tendency to interact with persons younger than themselves), and fearfulness (Achenbach and Edelbrock 1978). Other associated behaviors include lack of self-confidence, avoidance and manipulative behavior, poor independent work habits, and basic skill deficits (McBride and McFarland 1987). The lack of independent decision-making behavior may, therefore, be a function of any of these deficits.

It is important to assess the actual deficit, whether it is a cognitive or a learning deficit, a social skill deficit, or a behavioral problem. Interventions that focus on the deficiency area will be most effective. *Skillstreaming the Elementary School Child* by McGinnis and Goldstein (1984) and Swift and Spivak's (1978) *Alternative Teaching Strategies* may be helpful for dealing with skill deficiencies, but they do not present the proper intervention for individuals whose lack of self-direction is rooted in a lack of secure attachment or is fostered by parent behaviors that encourage dependency and discourage self-initiative (Schaefer and Millman 1981).

Capacity for Independent Living

Deficits in what Barkley (1985) refers to as "rule-governed behavior" make it difficult for these individuals to live independently. They respond more readily to the immediately available reinforcers in the environment and are what Skinner (1954) called "contingency governed." They show greater concern for what will happen to themselves, than for how their behavior affects others. According to Patterson (1976), they are "retarded in the development of many of the basic social skills." Such persons are not only uncooperative, but are also extremely competitive and are rejected by peers. Whereas they are not necessarily disliked by peers, even individuals who do not show "retarded development" in basic social skills are often neglected socially. The fact that individuals with emotional and behavioral problems have serious social skills problems (either skill or performance deficits) means that they often have no significant, or meaningful, relationships. This situation, combined with a lack of basic academic skills, can easily lead to decreased independence.

Traditional approaches to therapy, such as catharsis and insight-oriented treatments, have not been particularly effective in improving the social deficits (Kazdin 1985). Whereas deficits in rule-governed behavior are difficult to remedy, programs have been developed that emphasize problem solving, conflict negotiation, aggression control, and social skills training (Goldstein et al. 1987; Morgan and Jenson 1988). Behavioral therapy that modifies both parent and child behaviors within the context of the home and community have shown the greatest effects (Wells and Forehand 1985). In general, the social learning and behavioral approaches (for example, time out, point systems, reinforcement, and precision request making) are most promising (Forehand and McMahon 1981; Gelfand et al. 1988).

The capacity for independence, however, is not only determined in the social arena. In addition to lacking the basic academic skills, many of these individuals lack the capacity to learn independently. Learning how to learn is a critical element to success, regardless of academic ability (Davenport 1984). Research has shown that these skills are not acquired naturally nor are they specifically taught in schools

(Gettinger and Knopik 1987). Helpful guidelines for teaching study skills have been published (see Bragstad and Stumpf 1982; Brown et al. 1981; Graham and Robinson 1984). Although these materials have been written with the teacher in mind, others are specifically written for parents (see Cohn 1979; Duckett 1983).

Economic Self-Sufficiency

As mentioned previously, individuals with emotional and behavior problems often lack the requisite academic skills necessary for employment as an adult. Not only have they failed to develop the proper study skills to facilitate independence in learning, but they have serious deficits in basic subject matter areas. Reading difficulties are particularly noteworthy because reading is critical for employment and for other daily activities (Gelfand et al. 1988). As discussed in an earlier section (learning and cognition), direct behavioral treatment programs are likely to be most effective in improving these academic skill deficits.

☐ Case 4-4: Jonathan

Jonathan is a disappointment to his parents. Although he tests well, he has never applied himself in school. Most family members are also bright, but high achievers. His parents are both physicians, and his sister is a law student. Jonathan has never lived up to family expectations. He lived at home until he was 23 years old. Jonathan probably would not have moved out then, but his father insisted that he get his own apartment. One of Jonathan's basic problems is that he cannot keep a job. Just as he had difficulty with his teachers' and parents' requests, he has had difficulty taking orders from his employers. Although he does not talk back to the boss, he often insults customers with curt comments. Jonathan was fired from his last job. He was suspected of stealing tires out of the back warehouse. Just last week, Jonathan made a near fatal suicide attempt with a hand gun. Jonathan's parents deny that he is depressed, but admit that their son does not have any present, or future, goals.

Conclusions

More than two decades ago, in a survey for the Joint Commission on the Mental Health of Children, Glidewell and Swallow (1969) concluded that one out of every three school-age children have adjustment difficulties and one tenth require professional service. It has been estimated that only 2% of the population needing service could obtain it if professionals continue to provide such services on a one-to-one basis (Jason 1983). Not only does the service delivery mode need to be consultative, but also preventive. It has become increasingly apparent since the development of the Primary Mental Health Project (Cowen et al. 1975) that an orientation toward remediation is not sufficient.

Individuals must be taught the skills that have the potential to facilitate their adjustment. Perhaps the most obvious conclusion that can be drawn from this chapter is that one of the greatest handicaps of individuals with emotional impairments is their deficits in learning. Many of the problems with self-direction, independent living, and economic self-sufficiency can be solved by improving basic academic skills. Another major handicap is the deficit in social relationships. If service providers are to have any chance to comply with legislative mandates to provide the "least restrictive environment," and to meet the needs of exceptional clients, it is imperative that special instruction be designed to meet the special educational needs of developmentally disabled populations such as those with emotional and behavioral impairments.

References

1. Achenbach TM. Developmental Psychopathology. 2nd ed. New York, Wiley, 1982.
2. Achenbach TM, Edelbrock CS. The classification of child psychopathology: A review and analysis of empirical efforts. J Consult Clin Psychol. 78:1275–1301, 1978.
3. Achenbach TM, Edelbrock CS. The Child Behavior Profile: II. Boys aged 12–16 and girls 6–11 and 12–16. J Consult Clin Psychol. 47:223–233, 1979.
4. Ainsworth MDS. Infant-mother attachment. Am Psychol. 34:932–937, 1979.
5. American Psychiatric Association. The Diagnostic and Statistical Manual of Mental Disorders—III—Revised. Washington, DC, The American Psychiatric Association, 1987.
6. Anesko KM, Levine FM. Winning the Homework War. New York, Simon and Schuster, 1987.
7. Austin GA, Prendergast ML. Drug Use and Abuse: A Guide to Research Findings. Vol. 2, Denver, ABC-Clio Information Services, 1984.
8. Barkley RA. Attention deficit disorders. In: Bornstein PH, Kazdin AE. eds. Handbook of Clinical Behavior Therapy with Children. Homewood, IL, Dorsey Press, 1985, pp 158–217.
9. Beitchman JH, Nair R, Clegg M, Ferguson B, Patel PG. Prevalence of psychiatric disorders in children with speech and language disorders. Journal of the American Academy of Child Psychiatry. 25:528–535, 1986.
10. Bragstad BJ, Stumpf SM. A Guidebook for Teaching Study Skills and Motivation. Boston, Allyn & Bacon, 1982.
11. Brown AL, Campione JC, Day JD. Learning to learn: On training students to learn from texts. Educational Researcher. 10:14–21, 1981.
12. Canter L, Hausner M. Homework Without Tears. New York, Harper and Row, 1987.
13. Cantor P. Prevention, Intervention, and Postvention: National trends. Paper presented at Suicide in the Schools. Pittsburgh, PA, May 1986.
14. Cepeda ML. Nonstimulant psychotropic medication: Side effects of children's cognition and behavior. In: Reynolds CR, Fletcher-Janzen E. eds. Handbook of Clinical Child Neuropsychology. New York, Plenum Press, 1989, pp 475–485.
15. Chase SN, Clement PW. Effects of self-reinforcement and stimulants on academic performance in children with attention deficit disorder. Journal of Clinical Child Psychology. 14:323–333, 1985.
16. Childs RE. Teaching rehearsal strategies for spelling to mentally retarded children. Education and Training of the Mentally Retarded. 18:318–320, 1983.
17. Cohen S. The Substance Abuse Problem. New York, Haworth, 1981.

18. Cohn M. Helping Your Teen-age Student: What Parents Can Do To Improve Reading and Study Skills. New York, Dutton, 1979.

19. Conant S, Budoff M, Hecht B. Teaching Language-disabled Children: A Communication Games Intervention. Cambridge, MA, Brookline, 1983.

20. Cowen EL, Trost MA, Lorion RP, Dorr D, Izzo LD, Isaacson RV. New Ways in School Mental Health: Early Detection and Prevention of School Maladaptation. New York, Human Sciences Press, 1975.

21. Cullinan D, Epstein MH, McLinden D. Status and change in state administrative definitions of behavior disorder. School Psychology Review. 15:383–392, 1986.

22. Davenport E. Study skills: Tools of the trade to make studying easier and more efficient. Early Years. 15:43–44, 1984.

23. DeMyer MK, Hingtgen JN, Jackson RK. Infantile autism reviewed: A decade of research. Schizophr Bull. 7:388–451, 1981.

24. Duckett JC. Helping Children Develop Good Study Habits: A Parent's Guide. Washington, DC, National Institute of Education, 1983.

25. Edelbrock CS, Achenbach TM. A typology of Child Behavior Profile patterns: Distribution and correlates for disturbed children aged 6–16. J Abnorm Child Psychol. 8:441–470, 1980.

26. Education for All Handicapped Children Act of 1975. Public Law 94-142. November 1975. 20 USC 1401.

27. Education of the Handicapped Act Amendments of 1986. Public Law 99-457.

28. Elliott SN, Shapiro ES. Intervention techniques and programs for academic performance problems. In: Gutkin TB, Reynolds CR. eds. The Handbook of School Psychology. New York, Wiley, 1990, pp. 635–660.

29. Fernando T, Mellsop G, Nelson K, Peace K, Wilson J. The reliability of Axis V of the DSM-III. Am J Psychiatry. 143:752–755, 1986.

30. Forehand R, McMahon RJ. Helping the Noncompliant Child: A Clinician's Guide to Parent Training. New York, Guilford Press, 1981.

31. Forman SG, Randolph MK. Children and drug abuse. In: Thomas A, Grimes J. eds. Children's Needs: Psychological Perspectives. Washington, DC, National Association of School Psychologists, 1987, pp 182–189.

32. Forrest GG. How To Cope with a Teenage Drinker. New York, Atheneum, 1983.

33. Fox DEC, Kendall PC. Thinking through academic problems: Applications of cognitive behavior therapy to learning. In: Kratochwill TR. ed. Advances in School Psychology. Vol. 3. Hillsdale, NJ, Lawrence Erlbaum, 1983, pp 269–301.

34. Gelfand DM, Jenson WR, Drew CJ. Understanding Child Behavior Disorders. New York, Holt, Rinehart and Winston, 1988.

35. Gettinger M, Knopik SN. Children and study skills. In: Thomas A, Grimes J. eds. Children's Needs: Psychological Perspectives. Washington, DC, National Association of School Psychologists, 1987, pp 594–602.

36. Glidewell JC, Swallow CS. The Prevalence for Maladjustment in Elementary Schools: A Report Prepared for the Joint Commission on the Mental Health of Children. Chicago, University of Chicago Press, 1969.

37. Glynn TJ, Leukefeld CG, Ludford JP. Preventing Adolescent Drug Abuse: Intervention Strategies. Rockville, MD, National Institute of Drug Abuse, 1983.

38. Goldstein AP, Glick B, Reiner S, Zimmerman D, Coultry TM. Aggression Replacement Training: A Comprehensive Intervention for Aggressive Youth. Champaign, IL, Research Press, 1987.

39. Graham KG, Robinson HA. Study Skills Handbook: A Guide for All Teachers. Newark, DE, International Reading Association, 1984.

40. Greenwood CR, Dinwiddie G, Terry B, Wade L, Stanley SO, Thibadeau S, Delquadri JC. Teacher versus peer-mediated instruction: An ecobehavioral analysis of achievement outcomes. J Appl Behav Anal. 17:521–538, 1984.

41. Gualtieri CT, Golden RN, Fahs JJ. New developments in pediatric psychopharmacology. Dev Behav Pediatr. 4:202–209, 1983.

42. Hahn J. Children and suicide. In: Thomas A, Grimes J. eds. Children's Needs: Psychological Perspectives. Washington, DC, National Association of School Psychologists, 1987, pp 602–610.

43. Hoge RD, ANdrews DA. Enhancing academic performance: Issues in target selection. School Psychology Review. 16:228–238, 1987.

44. Hutchens TA. Children and medication. In: Thomas A, Grimes J. eds. Children's Needs: Psychological Perspectives. Washington, DC, National Association of School Psychologists, 1987, pp 356–364.

45. Jason LA. Preventive behavioral interventions. In: Felner RD, Jason LA, Moritsugu J, Farber SS. eds. Preventive Psychology: Theory, Research and Practice. New York, Pergamon Press, 1983.

46. Jenson WR, Olympia D, Clark E, Sheridan S. Homework: A natural link between home and school. In: Christiansen S, Close-Conoley J. eds. Home-School Collaboration: Building a Fundamental Educational Resource. Washington, DC, National Association of School Psychologists, [in press].

47. Johnston RJ, McLaughlin TF. The effects of free time on assignment completion and accuracy in arithmetic: A case study. Education and Treatment of children. 5(1):33–40, 1982.

48. Kanfer FH. The maintenance of behavior by self-generated stimuli and reinforcement. In: Jacobs A,

Sachs LB. eds. The Psychology of Private Events. New York, Academic Press, 1971, pp 39–58.

49. Kazdin AE. Alternative approaches to the diagnosis of childhood disorders. In: Bornstein PH, Kazdin AE. eds. Handbook of Clinical Behavior Therapy with Children. Homewood, IL, Dorsey Press, 1985, pp 3–43.

50. Kehle TJ, Cressy ET, Owen SV. The use of self-modeling as an intervention in school psychology: A case study of an elective mute. School Psychology Review. 19:115–121, 1990.

51. Keith TZ. Homework. Kappa Delta Phi Classroom Practice Series. West Lafayette, IN, Kappa Delta Phi, 1986.

52. Kesler J. Corrective reading: A method for changing the learning rate of behavior disordered children. University of Utah, 1987. Master's thesis.

53. Kretschmer R. Language as a communication process: Implications for assessment and programming. Paper presented at the National Association of School Psychologists Convention, Hollywood, Florida, April, 1986.

54. Lewis DO, Shanok SS, Balla DA, Bard B. Psychiatric correlates of severe reading disabilities in an incarcerated delinquent population. Journal of the American Academy of Child Psychiatry. 19:611–622, 1980.

55. Lieberman L. The homework solution. Journal of Learning Disabilities. 16(7):435, 1984.

56. Mayer W. Alcohol abuse and alcoholism: The psychologist's role in prevention, research, and treatment. Am Psychol. 38:1116–1121, 1983.

57. McBride CK, McFarland MA. Children and dependency. In: Thomas A, Grimes J. eds. Children's Needs: Psychological Perspectives. Washington, DC, National Association of School Psychologists, 1987, pp 151–156.

58. McDermott RP, Goldman SV, Verenne H. When school goes home: Problems in the organization of homework. Teachers College Record. 85(3):391–405, 1984.

59. McGinnis E, Goldstein AP. Skillstreaming the Elementary School Child. Champaign, IL, Research Press, 1984.

60. McLaughlin TF, Burgess N, Sackville-West L. Effects on self-recording and self-recording + matching on academic performance. Child Behavior Therapy. 3:17–27, 1981.

61. Millman RB, Botvin GJ. Substance use, abuse and dependence. In: Levin MD, Carey WB, Crocker AC, Gross RT. eds. Developmental Behavioral Pediatrics. New York, Saunders, 1983, pp 683–708.

62. Minde K. The role of drugs in the treatment of disturbed children. In: Steinhauer PO, Rae-Grant Q. eds. Psychological Problems of the Child and His Family. Toronto, Gage, 1977, pp 413–426.

63. Morgan D, Jenson WR. Teaching Behaviorally Disordered Children: Preferred Practices. Columbus, OH, Charles E. Merrill, 1988.

64. Nicholson AN, Ward J. Psychotropic drugs and performance. Br J Clin Pharmacol 18(Suppl 1): 1984.

65. O'Leary DK, Pelham WE, Rosenbaum A, Price GH. Behavioral treatment of hyperkinetic children. Clin Pediatr (Phila), 15:510–515, 1976.

66. Patterson GR. The aggressive child: Victim and architect of a coercive system. In: Mash EJ, Hamerlynck LA, Handy LC. eds. Behavior Modification and Families. New York, Brunner/Mazel, 1976.

67. Pfeffer CR. The Suicidal Child. New York, Guilford, 1986.

68. Polce ME. Children and learning styles. In: Thomas A, Grimes J. eds. Children's Needs: Psychological Perspectives. Washington, DC, National Association of School Psychologists, 1987, pp 325–335.

69. Rhode G, Morgan DP, Young KR. Generalization and maintenance of treatment gains of behaviorally handicapped students from resource rooms to regular classrooms using self-evaluation procedures. J Appl Behav Anal. 16:171–188, 1983.

70. Ross DM, Ross SA. Hyperactivity: Current Issues, Research, and Theory. New York, Wiley, 1982.

71. Ruhl KL, Hughes CA. The nature and extent of aggression in special education settings serving behaviorally disordered students. Behavioral Disorders, pp 95–104, February, 1985.

72. Rutter M, Yule W. Reading difficulties. In: Rutter M, Hersov L. eds. Child Psychiatry: Modern Perspectives. Oxford, Blackwell Scientific Publications, 1978.

73. Schaefer CE, Millman HL. How To Help Children with Common Problems. New York, Van Nostrand Reinhold, 1981.

74. Shaffer D. Suicide in childhood and early adolescence. J Child Psychol Psychiatry. 15:275–291, 1974.

75. Shanock SS, Lewis DO. Medical histories of female delinquents: Clinical and epidemiological findings. Arch Gen Psychiatry. 38:211–213, 1981.

76. Shapiro ES. Behavior modification: Self-control and cognitive procedures. In: Barrett RP. ed. Severe Behavior Disorders in the Mentally Retarded. New York, Plenum Press, 1986, pp 61–97.

77. Shapiro ES, Goldberg R. A comparison of group contingencies in increased spelling performances among sixth grade students. School Psychology Review. 15:546–559, 1986.

78. Siegel LJ, Ridley-Johnson R. In: Bornstein PH, Kazdin AE. eds. Handbook of Clinical Behavior Therapy with Children. Homewood, IL, Dorsey Press, 1985, pp 266–308.

79. Skinner BF. Science and Human Behavior. New York, Macmillan, 1954.

80. Slavin RE, Madden NA, Leavey M. Effects of team assisted individualization on the mathematics achievement of academically handicapped and nonhandicapped students. Journal of Educational Psychology. 76:813–819, 1984.

81. Smith K, Crawford S. Suicidal behavior among "normal" high school students. Social & Life Threatening Behavior. 16:313–325, 1986.

82. State Board of Education Special Education Rules. Utah State Office of Education, Salt Lake City, UT, April 1988.

83. Swift MS, Spivack G. Alternative Teaching Strategies. Champaign, IL, Research Press, 1978.

84. Van Houten R, Lai Fatt D. The effects of public posting on high school biology test performance. Education and Treatment of Children. 4:217–226, 1981.

85. Walberg HJ. Families as partners in educational productivity. Phi Delta Kappan. 65(6):397–400, 1984.

86. Walberg HJ, Paschal RA, Weinstein T. Homework's powerful effects on learning. Educational Leadership. (9):76–79, 1985.

87. Walker HM, Reavis HK, Rhode G, Jenson WR. A conceptual model for delivery of behavioral services to behavior disordered children in a continuum of educational settings. In: Kazdin A, Bornstein P. eds. Handbook of Clinical Behavior Therapy with Children. Homewood, IL, Dorsey Press, 1985, pp 700–741.

88. Wells KC, Forehand R. Conduct and oppositional disorders. In: Bornstein PH, Kazdin AE. eds. Handbook of Clinical Behavior Therapy with Children. Homewood, IL, Dorsey Press, 1985, pp 218–265.

89. Werry JS, Methven RJ, Fitzpatrick J, Dixon H. The interrater reliability of DSM III in children. J Abnorm Child Psychol. 11:341–354, 1983.

90. Wolpaw T, Nation J, Aram D. Developmental language disorders: A follow-up study. In: Burns MS, Andrews JR. eds. Selected Papers in Language and Phonology. Vol. 1. Evanston, IL, Institute for Continuing Professional Education, 1977.

Chapter 5
Autism

Ronald C. Eaves

Functional Description

Terms

Although autism has had a relatively brief history, it has nonetheless been marked by confusion, controversy, and change. Less than 50 years ago, when Kanner first described it, autism was considered a rare type of childhood psychosis. Today, it represents the only specific severe or profound emotional disorder of childhood.

Many different terms have been used to describe individuals who are now commonly diagnosed as autistic. Kanner (1943) argued originally that autism represented no more than 10% of children then broadly considered to be suffering from childhood psychosis. At the time, the most common form of childhood psychosis was termed childhood schizophrenia. Through the years, other terms were suggested, sometimes offering a unique classification system (for example, primary and secondary autism), but often simply fractionating the population into smaller segments (for example, atypical personality development [Rank 1949], and symbiotic psychosis [Mahler 1952]). Autism gradually became a more popular and, therefore, a more commonplace label, ultimately supplanting alternative rubrics. Because many of the terms are

still in use, or may be encountered in the files of older individuals, the reader should familiarize him- or herself with them. It is fairly safe to assume that the particular label applied is as much a function of the date of diagnosis and the age of the diagnostician as of the symptomatology of the subject.

Today, classification is largely governed by the categories and criteria of the revised third edition of the *Diagnostic and Statistical Manual of Mental Disorders* (American Psychiatric Association 1987). In this system, autism is one of two pervasive developmental disorders (PDD); the other is pervasive developmental disorder not otherwise specified (NOS). Historically more common diagnoses (for example, schizophrenia) may still be made, but only if the individual meets adult criteria.

Differential Diagnosis

Autism represents a reasonably distinct gestalt to those who have actually worked with an array of autistic individuals over a long period of time. Yet, there are at least four reasons why the disorder is often misdiagnosed.

1. Because the condition is rare (roughly 6 to 10 per 10,000 in the population), few professionals have extensive experience with it.

2. Autism shares a number of characteristics with other disorders; in fact, Wing and Attwood (1987) offered reasons for confusing autism with 16 other conditions. For instance, most autistic and all mentally retarded people exhibit low IQs, and both may manifest stereotypic body movements. The autistic person may appear to be hearing impaired and thus may be confused with that population. Speech and language disorders (including mutism) are common among autistic individuals.

3. Because they usually demonstrate severe disorders in more than one domain, autistic children are often simply labeled multihandicapped. The placement in multihandicapped facilities is, however, frequently motivated by a lack of an appropriate alternative placement rather than by ignorance of the actual condition.

4. The inability of the professional community to establish a stable classification system has undoubtedly caused confusion among practitioners with little or no personal experience with the autistic population.

Characteristics

Eaves and Hooper (1987–88) and Eaves (1990) completed two factor analyses of behavior commonly ascribed to autistic children. They found evidence to suggest five primary factors: affective and cognitive indifference; expressive affect; passive affect; anxiety/fear; and cognition.

Affective and Cognitive Indifference

According to Eaves (1990), this was the primary feature of subjects who clearly met the diagnostic criteria of autism in his studies. For instance, subjects labeled *atypical*—a label assigned to those who share some of the features of autism but who differ in important ways from it—or simply, pervasive developmental disorder, generally received lower scores on the affective and cognitive indifference factor.

Eaves (1990) speculated that this factor might reflect lower-order behavior controlled by the brain stem and the cerebellum.

Among the dimensions and behavior contributing to the affective and cognitive indifference factor were:

1. Autism—avoids eye contact, blank expression, emotionless, prefers to be left alone, dislike for hugging
2. Hand and body movements—finger flicking, hand shaking, rocking, head banging, stares at hands close up
3. Sensory stimulation—spins jar lids and plates, plays with spinning tops, fascination for rushing air and "crinkly" sounds
4. Bizarre compulsive behavior I—unusual interest in texture, inappropriate toy play, enjoys "dangling" objects, mouthing

It should be mentioned that the majority of these symptoms involve motor behavior and four of the five senses, vision, hearing, touching, and tasting.

Expressive Affect

This factor characterized autistic individuals who were relatively outgoing and who readily interacted with the environment, but in distorted ways. It was related more closely to the affective and cognitive indifference factor than to any other. Among the dimensions and behavior contributing to the expressive affect factor were:

1. Distorted affect—cries on "happy" occasions; cries without vocalizing; hits, bites, or scratches others; unwarranted whining, crying, and screaming when desires are unmet; smiles or laughs without reason, no response to pain
2. Hallucinations/superstitions—sees or hears things not present, picks up objects with the backs of hands, makes peculiar sounds inside the mouth
3. Masturbation/howling
4. Sensitivity to certain smells

Passive Affect

Subjects with high scores on this factor tended to be self-involved and more aloof from living things than those with high scores on the expressive affect factor. Instead, their interests tended toward inanimate objects. Among the dimensions and behavior contributing to the passive affect factor were:

1. Collecting/hoarding—saves or hoards items of no value, carries a special object with him
2. Meticulosity—exaggerated interest in cleanliness, has special locations for objects
3. Bizarre compulsive behavior II—walks on tiptoes; spins and whirls body; over-reacts to environmental changes; rarely stacks objects, usually lines them up

Anxiety/Fear

This factor was one of two positively skewed distributions that resulted from the factor analysis (Eaves, 1990). Eaves hypothesized that, although autistic individuals may manifest anxiety and fear reactions, the factor may not be primary evidence of autism in general. In any case, it was clear from the results that relatively few autistic subjects exhibited extreme fears or anxieties. Among the behaviors contributing to the anxiety/fear factor were (1) believing harmless entities to be dangerous; (2) excessive fear of loud noises; (3) anxiety around water; and (4) fear in crowds.

Cognition

This factor also exhibited a positively skewed distribution among the subjects in Eaves' (1990) sample. This result is consistent with the common finding that most, but not all, autistic people exhibit low levels of cognitive ability. Among the dimensions and behavior contributing to the cognition factor were:

1. Savant behavior—extreme skill in one area, memorizes commercials and advertisements
2. Speech—misuses pronouns, monotonal or "wooden" speech, echolalia, switches from normal to monotonal or glottal speech, loud speech
3. Skill development—spontaneous use of skill lags behind elicited use of skill, uneven skill development, exhibits surprising skill at times

The factors of autism reflect the three major human attributes: the motor, emotional, and cognitive domains. Unlike many other disabilities, the condition is not characterized by slow development that mirrors the usual developmental sequence. Instead, the autistic individual displays a unique behavioral topography that may be fairly described as strange, distorted, even bizarre. No autistic person demonstrates the full range of the behavioral topography; indeed, it is the individual who exhibits only a few of the relevant symptoms who continues to be difficult to diagnose accurately. Among those properly labeled as autistic, however, there are some rough rules of thumb regarding prognosis. First, the individual who shows more social and emotional contact has a better prognosis than one who shows little or no inclination to interact with others. Second, the person who has relatively good cognitive ability has the best prognosis among the autistic population.

The remainder of this chapter is a description of treatment approaches for three autistic individuals. Their characteristics place them in the levels briefly defined above. The first youngster, John, is operating at a fundamental autistic level. His behavior may be characterized as manifesting little affective and cognitive content. The second case, Shaka, displays a more emotional nature, but one that is socially unacceptable because of extreme aggression. Finally, there is Rodney, whose relatively high intelligence marks him as a good bet for a happy future in the mainstream of society.

☐ Case 5-1: John—Affective and Cognitive Indifference

John's unusual development was noticed at an early age by his parents. Almost from birth he seemed remote and uninvolved with the world around him. His mother, Barbara, became concerned when John failed to engage in the bonding characteristics she had so enjoyed when nurturing his two older siblings. For instance, he was an indifferent eater, often nursing only a few moments at a time; sometimes he rejected his mother's breast entirely, even when he should have been hungry. In addition, when he was picked up by one or the other of his parents, he showed neither the usual anticipatory response nor the infant smile familiar to every parent. Instead, he seemed entirely content to be left alone in his cradle.

Other early signs of emotional development were also absent. Both Barbara and her husband, Tom, agreed that their son seldom made eye contact with either of them. Even when they positioned themselves directly in front of his gaze, they had the chilling sensation that John was looking "through" them rather than at them. His lack of interest in social contact with his parents—indeed, with all human contact—was manifest in many other ways. His usual facial expression was described by his family as "unconcerned" or "just a blank." Although he did not usually resist hugging and cuddling by his family, there was no mistaking that such expressions of affection held little attraction for him. At other times, particularly when some solitary activity was interrupted, John showed displeasure by resisting; on rare occasions, he displayed true emotion through crying and temper tantrums when an activity was interrupted. Although he had considerable contact with age peers, as well as with his two siblings, John showed no interest in them, preferring his solitary activity to cooperative play.

As John grew into childhood, peculiar physical symptoms came to characterize his behavior. He spent long periods staring intently at the palm of one hand. Gradually, he would become agitated and, with a wide-eyed, hysterical look in his face, begin shaking both hands up and down rapidly. He often held his fingers and hands in a stiff, distorted posture; such behavior was frequently accompanied an odd flicking motion of his index finger. Other common physical activities included rocking back and forth or side to side, mouthing unfamiliar objects, and an activity that his family members referred to as "dangling." John usually dangled his mother's hair, which was often worn in a "pony-tail" style, but he was attracted to any similar hanging material. For instance, he often grasped a venetian blind cord, jerking it up and down, causing it to bounce or "dance."

Objects had always captured John's attention more readily than people. Yet, he seldom manipulated objects in expected ways (for example, toy cars and dolls were held upside down as often as right side up). Also, the objects that John cherished most were often far outside the realm of usual childhood playthings. For John, the opportunity to listen to the sound made by a piece of cellophane was the equivalent of a day in the park to most children. Further, he generally showed far more interest in the texture of objects than do most children. In fact, he spent a significant proportion of time touching materials or rubbing them against his cheek. A favorite texture was that of pencil erasers and other rubbery objects, but soft, cloth fabrics were also favored. It was a rare occasion when he did not have either an eraser or a piece of cloth within easy reach.

Although John's physical appearance was normal, even attractive, and people attributed him an "intelligent look," as he grew older it became all too obvious that his cognitive development was severely diminished compared with that of his age peers. For instance, he never developed speech; he was entirely mute. Nor did he show any real interest in activities demanding cognition at any level. For instance, magazines, books, movies, and television rarely engaged his attention more than momentarily.

A more troubling attribute was John's increasingly severe self-injurious behavior. As a child of 4 or 5 years of age, he developed a tendency to strike his chin with a closed fist. At first, the blows carried little force and were not alarming. By the time he was 9 years of age, his repertoire of self-destructive behavior had grown to a shocking extent. He continued to hit himself in the chin (and other parts of his face and head), but the force of the blows had become much more severe. Further, he now frequently banged his head against any available stationary object. Beyond that, he bit the back of his right hand so often that he had developed a thick callus.

Observation revealed that John's self-injurious behavior was most often displayed when his parents or his teacher asked him to engage in behavior that he disliked. Examples of requests that marked occasions of self-injury included (1) cleaning up around his desk at school; (2) making eye contact with an adult; (3) eating with appropriate utensils; (4) changing an activity; and (5) bedtime preparations. The list of occasions was extensive; the common thread seemed to be John's (usually successful) attempt to gain control over others in his environment by exhibiting alarming self-injurious behavior.

□ Treatment of Self-Injurious Behavior

Preliminary Considerations

Before planning a treatment strategy for self-injurious behavior, it is important to investigate several factors known or presumed to stimulate self-injury. Carr (1982b) developed a screening sequence for this purpose. First, the subject should undergo genetic screening to determine whether or not an anomaly exists. For instance, Lesch-Nyhan and de Lange syndromes have been strongly associated with lip, finger, and tongue biting. In the case of Lesch-Nyhan syndrome, drug treatment using L-5 hy-droxytryptophan and carbidopa was reported to show promising results (Nyhan, 1976). Screening for other biophysical abnormalities should also be conducted. For example, chronic otitis media has been associated with relatively high levels of head banging (de Lissovoy, 1963).

In addition to organic causes, three environmental explanations have been postulated for self-injury and other unwanted behavior: positive reinforcement; negative reinforcement; and self-stimulation. In terms of screening, one should first look for evidence that self-injury serves to obtain positive reinforcement from the environment. Most commonly, the more extreme behavior results in attention from others, particularly when milder, less extreme behavior produces little attention for the subject. In such circumstances, it is anticipated that self-injurious behavior will occur at higher rates in the presence of significant others but may be nonexistent when the subject is alone.

Negative reinforcement occurs when an aversive stimulus is removed as a consequence of the subject's self-injurious behavior. In this instance, self-injury serves to avoid aversive demands that are placed upon the subject (for example, demands to complete work, attend a task, make eye contact). Given the extreme nature of self-injury and its obvious connection to the demand stimulus, the timid parent or practitioner usually quickly withdraws the demand. Thus, the subject is negatively reinforced for the self-injurious behavior and the probability of its repetition on similar, future occasions is increased. This certainly appeared to be the explanation for John's behavior.

Finally, some theorists believe that self-injurious behavior serves as its own reinforcer by providing the subject with sensory stimulation. Cogent parallels have been drawn by Carr (1982b) between self-injury in autistic individuals and similar behavior observed in other mammals raised in isolation (compare Harlow and Harlow 1962). Indeed, studies of both normal and handicapped subjects indicate that self-injury is elevated under conditions of environmental deprivation. For instance, Levy (1944) reported that head banging disappeared among institutionalized orphans confined to their cribs after toys were introduced. Likewise, Collins (1965) reduced the head banging of a restrained adult retardate by introducing stimulation in the forms of toys, activities, and a radio.

Selecting Treatment Variables

The treatment of choice depends upon the practitioner's ability to identify the causes underlying self-injurious behavior. As mentioned previously, genetically determined self-injury may best be treated through drug therapy. The primary objective regarding self-injury associated with disease states (for example, otitis media) is to gain control over the disease medically. Self-injury associated with both positive and negative reinforcement has been modified environmentally through a variety of operant conditioning approaches such as extinction; time out; differential reinforcement of other (DRO) behavior; differential reinforcement of incompatible (DRI) behavior; positive punishment; and response cost. Finally, alternative sources of stimulation have most often been used to gain control over self-injury considered to be motivated by self-stimulation.

Several considerations led to our selection of differential reinforcement of incompatible behavior and response cost as procedures to gain control over John's self-injury. Extinction was eliminated as a primary strategy because it works slowly and often results in temporarily elevated levels of the behavior to be modified. Because we planned to train John's parents and teacher to implement the intervention, we wanted a procedure that could plausibly demonstrate early positive results.

Time out is a mild punitive procedure in which the subject is removed from a setting following an inappropriate behavior such as head slapping. The opportunity to gain reinforcers (for example, adult at-tention) available in the setting is also removed. Time out has often been used effectively to reduce self-injurious behavior, but it was not chosen in this case because it would serve to reinforce the very behavior we sought to eliminate. If our judgment was correct, John used self-injurious behavior to avoid aversive demands placed upon him. Presumably, time out would provide him with a guaranteed avoidance mechanism.

Positive punishment was not eliminated entirely as a method because it often obtains dramatic results quickly (Lovaas 1969). It was, however, selected as a last resort for three reasons. First, other, milder forms of intervention had not been systematically attempted; consequently, we hoped that the use of positive punishment would prove unnecessary. Second, although John's behavior was initially alarming to see, we knew that he had engaged in the activity for at least three years without serious mutilation or permanent damage. Therefore, we doubted that there existed a significant risk of such damage during the intervention. Third, since we knew John's parents were uncomfortable with the idea of punishing their severely handicapped child, we doubted that they could apply any punitive procedure consistently. To the extent that they and his teacher applied the intervention inconsistently, we knew there would be little hope for success.

Finally, we preferred the use of DRI over DRO because the former offered John a specific, reinforceable, alternative behavior in which to engage that prevented the display of self-injurious behavior. In addition, some research (Tarpley and Schroeder 1979) has indicated the superiority of DRI over DRO schedules, though both have proven effective in decreasing this target behavior.

Defining Treatment Procedures

Although it is highly desirable to design a treatment plan that is explicit, simple, and clear, that objective is usually met only after a period of trial and error. It is during this early phase that an awareness of alternative procedures is valuable. Although we knew that an overall goal of the intervention was to remove John's control over the environment and to place that control back in the hands of his parents and teacher, selecting the specific technique within a particular situation was an ongoing determination.

We began by placing arbitrary demands upon John that we expected might normally precipitate self-injurious behavior. Initially, we chose tasks that we knew John could perform easily because we would also be demanding that he not physically abuse himself during the activity. We also kept the time periods short (30 seconds) for the same reason. Had we demanded more challenging and therefore more aversive activities from John, we could not seriously expect him to control his self-injury. Early attempts to reinforce John with crackers for playing catch with a volley ball (and no self-injury) failed rather miserably. Although he sometimes managed to complete a 30-second session and obtain a reinforcer, it remained clear that John was in control of the environmental contingencies. As expected, attempts to extinguish John's self-abusive tantrums had no apparent effect.

At this point we hit upon the idea of removing a highly desirable object from John's possession for 5 minutes whenever he injured himself. The procedure is called response cost. The primary object we removed was John's eraser or cloth, whichever he had with him at the time. It will be recalled that he relished the texture of these objects and seldom went anywhere without them. At first he demonstrated an uncanny ability to find substitute materials (for example, rubber ball, wash cloth), but we soon managed to remove all conceivable substitutes from the setting. Under this added contingency, John learned to control his inappropriate self-injurious behavior, ultimately replacing it with a variety of previously aversive behaviors (such

as counting to ten, picking up toys in a messy room, brushing his teeth). After experiencing success in controlling John's behavior under highly structured circumstances, his parents and teacher were able to transfer the principles they had learned to a wide variety of situations.

☐ Case 5-2: Shaka— Expressive Affect

Little information could be gleaned from the records regarding this 23-year-old girl's history. Aside from scant demographic data, all that was known was that she was given up for adoption by her natural mother at birth. Shaka had spent her entire life in state facilities, moving from one mental hospital to another as she grew older. She developed good language skills, though her communication was often disconnected, self-centered, and riddled with profanity.

Like many autistic individuals, Shaka maintained only a tenuous contact with her surroundings. Often, she appeared not to hear when spoken to, but clearly did hear sounds within the speech range at other times. Her primary physical manifestation of autism was persistent pacing; usually she wandered in wide circles at a very brisk pace. Other physical symptoms, such as hand gazing, finger posturing, and rocking, were not in evidence.

Unlike John, Shaka was not remote and indifferent to others. Indeed, she displayed a wide variety of facial expressions, which covered the spectrum from happiness to deep sorrow and violent rage. Yet, her emotions tended to be distorted, frequently failing to conform to environmental circumstances. For instance, during a party when others were decidedly enjoying themselves, Shaka broke into tears. In contrast, Shaka once closed a car door on her hand, breaking two fingers in the process, but neither cried nor even grimaced. Similar events indicated that Shaka felt little physical pain.

Shaka's most problematic behavioral displays were gross and socially unacceptable as well as unhygienic. For instance, she was prone to remove her clothes and masturbate at odd times and places throughout the day. Attempts by hospital staff to interfere with this behavior nearly always resulted in violent physical rejoinders from Shaka. Her physical violence was accompanied by shouted profanities. Indeed, profane language was Shaka's medium; she used it like a painter uses oils. Most of the staff were convinced that Shaka enjoyed the reaction of mortification she frequently received when she undressed, masturbated, and shouted profane epithets at anyone nearby.

During her circular pacing, everyone in the vicinity soon learned to keep an eye on Shaka's location. It was her practice to walk up behind a person and, upon passing the individual, to turn swiftly and try to scratch the person in the eyes. She never attacked an individual from the front; apparently, the element of surprise was a key to her tactic. Shaka also howled frequently, as if in pain, without apparent reason. Her howling was so common (some 50 to 100 times each day) that staff and patients alike soon learned to discriminate Shaka's howl from those signaling genuine emergencies. Finally, Shaka exhibited a deep attraction to odors, most particularly the odor of feces. One of her less endearing habits was to enter a bathroom and wipe her hand around every toilet seat. She also used her hand to gouge her own anal area. Following such behavior, Shaka spent considerable time sniffing the hand that was covered with the scent of fecal matter.

□ Treatment of Aggression, Noncompliance, and Profanity

Preliminary Considerations

Our decision to begin by improving Shaka's social conduct hinged on four facts. First, some of the targets we identi-

fied represented a physical danger to other patients and staff members. Second, even when no one was physically hurt as a result, her episodes of aggression, noncompliance, and profanity were very disruptive to ongoing programs, not to mention the emotional equanimity of those around her. Third, extreme behavior such as Shaka's prevented her from making much progress in other areas. For instance, she had never been seriously considered as a candidate for a vocational skills program because of her inappropriate social responses. Last, but important in its own right, we believed the staff would benefit by learning a procedure that would ultimately place Shaka under their verbal control, thus greatly reducing the need to use violent, physical intervention.

Selecting Treatment Variables

Psychobiologic research (Restak 1979) has demonstrated that emotional behavior is under the control of an elaborate neurologic system interconnecting all four major units of the brain (that is, the brain stem, cerebellum, limbic system, and cerebrum). It is currently widely assumed that behavior such as Shaka's is caused by anomalous neurologic pathways or chemical aberrations within the system. Like many other patients in her institution, Shaka received drug therapy in the form of Haldol (haloperidol), a neuroleptic designed to reduce psychotic symptoms.

Our analysis of Shaka's behavior led us to believe that she used aggression, noncompliance, and profanity to gain control over her surroundings. For instance, she seemed to take pleasure in asserting her dominance, often placing her face inches away from a staff member while shouting at him or her in an intimidating manner. Also, since we could identify no eliciting antecedent events that stimulated her behavior, we concluded that most disruptive episodes were provoked by Shaka herself. To be sure, she often sought out groups of people prior to these episodes even though she could have remained apart from the group. As such, we believed her behavior to be a source of positive reinforcement.

Based on our conclusion that Shaka gained gratification from her inappropriate social behavior, we selected time out as the procedure to reduce its occurrence. Because she rarely spent time alone, we hoped that isolation would motivate her to comply with our requests in order to rejoin the group. At the same time it was important that we teach Shaka that there were other, more gratifying ways to obtain reinforcement.

Defining Treatment Procedures

In keeping with our desire to develop an explicit, simple, and clear treatment plan, we first drew up a list of aggressive acts, instances of noncompliance, and profane terms that would lead to Shaka's immediate isolation from the group. Next, we established a set of alternative (DRO) behaviors that would be expected and systematically reinforced by the staff. The alternative behaviors were designed to reflect standard rules of comportment: approaching others from the front; saying please to make a request; saying thank you when a request was granted; using appropriate salutations when joining and leaving a group; and rapid compliance to reasonable requests from the staff. Finally, we selected a set of activities in which we knew Shaka often participated (for example, singing, eating, simple board games, building with Duplo blocks) that we intended to use as the forum for our intervention.

Time out requires an area (usually a room) with particular characteristics. We felt we needed a relatively barren, but clean environment that would produce no reinforcement to its occupant. In addition, the room had to be structurally able to withstand considerable physical violence without falling apart. At the same time we wished to be able to observe and interact with Shaka at all times when she was placed in time out. Because only one room with the necessary characteristics was available for our use, we could not implement the treatment program throughout the institutional environment. This limitation meant that we might have to make special arrangements to ensure that Shaka transferred gains observed in the treatment location to other sites within the institution. On the other hand, by conducting the treatment in a single, well-designed location, we were able to control the treatment variables much more effectively.

Intervention began with a series of activities in the treatment room with participation from Shaka, two well-behaved patients, and three staff members. Each patient was prompted to use the standard rules of comportment outlined above, and each instance of their use was reinforced verbally by one or more of the staff. If a staff member perceived that Shaka was about to exhibit any of the undesirable behaviors, he or she warned Shaka about the consequences of such behavior. When Shaka actually manifested any one of the unacceptable behaviors included in the list, she was immediately told, "Shaka, you're going to time out for (explication of the misdeed)." Upon being placed quickly and efficiently in the time out room, she was told, "You can come out when you've calmed down."

Rather than specify an exact amount of time during which Shaka remained calm (that is, no kicking, howling) as the contingency for rejoining the group, we varied the required duration from 30 seconds to up to 10 minutes. The criterion for the period of calm behavior for any given instance of time out was based on the staff's estimate of the degree of violence exhibited by Shaka on that occasion. More violent reactions led to longer required periods of calm.

Following these procedures Shaka showed a marked decrease in the target behaviors and a parallel increase in good comportment. As the treatment progressed, a new, and as it turned out, important activity was spontaneously added to the sessions: the Good Behavior Game, which emphasized the rules of comportment outlined above. It consisted of role playing situations invented by the staff and patients with the object of determining what would be the "correct" thing to do in the given situation. It was the feeling of the staff that the inclusion of this game added significantly to the success of the treatment. Practitioners should be alert to such serendipitous events. They often significantly strengthen well-designed programs.

Transfer of Shaka's new behavioral repertoire to other locations on the institutional campus did not occur automatically. It is often the case that the learner must be specifically schooled to recognize the similarities between the treatment setting conditions and those in other locations that call for the same behavior. After the treatment program was well under way and significant improvements had occurred, we made jaunts to other settings that Shaka habitually frequented: the cafeteria, gymnasium, dormitory, and so on. Although an ideal room for time out was usually not available, we made the best of the facilities we had (for example, the gymnasium equipment room, an empty dorm room). Happily, Shaka quickly transferred her new social comportment skills as soon as she discovered that similar contingencies were applied across all settings.

Of course, Shaka continued to exhibit bizarre behavior that was not specifically addressed in our treatment plan. For instance, her fascination with the smell of feces required a unique program to obtain substantial gains. She was allowed to maintain her pacing since it was not considered a danger and seemed to fulfill a need to expend energy. However, all staff agreed that subsequent treatment programs owed much of their success to elimination of Shaka's aggression, noncompliance, and profanity.

□ Case 5-3: Rodney— Cognitive Behavior

Perhaps because Rodney had always been a handsome, physically healthy child, and one with extremely good fine-motor coordination, Rodney's parents, Anne and Bob, failed to attach much significance to his delayed speech and language development. He seldom cried as an infant and rarely produced the cooing, gurgling, and babbling sounds familiar to the parents of normal children. Because he was their first child, neither parent had much prior experience to guide them, and Rodney's pediatrician seemed to think that his lack of vocabulary would eventually be reversed.

As time passed, Anne became more concerned. Not only did Rodney's language skills continue to lag (his speech vocabulary contained some 15 words at age 4 years), his other behavior seemed odd as well. Still, Anne could convince neither Bob nor Rodney's pediatrician that he had any genuine problems. They both admonished Anne not to smother the child, but to let him develop in his own good time. Anne eventually became so exasperated that she gathered Rodney's dishes, jar lids, and pot covers and arrived at the physician's office demanding to see the doctor. When he entered the examination room, what he saw convinced him that, indeed, Rodney was not a simple case of developmental delay. For there on the floor, Rodney kept seven jar lids, pot covers, and dishes all spinning simultaneously! His dexterity was amazingly advanced for a child of any age, much less one of 4 years.

Although family physicians often fail to detect the telltale signs of autism, professionals considerably experienced with this population usually have little difficulty in making the correct diagnosis. Such was the case when Rodney was seen by the director of a nearby school that specialized in working with autistic children. Along with his language delay and spinning ability, Rodney exhibited many of the symptoms of classic autism. For instance, he was fascinated by water play and rushing air (whether generated by wind, fan, or air conditioning). He rarely stacked his blocks; instead he placed them in horizontal lines. He spent considerable time whirling his body, and he tended to walk on his toes. Finally, he exhibited approach–avoidance behavior toward several objects: fans, elevators, escalators, soft-drink machines, and food. One moment he would seem to be attracted to these objects; the next, he would run away as if frightened by them. Later, when he became interested in drawing, the mechanical objects maintained a central position in his artwork.

A nonverbal intelligence test administered at the school indicated an IQ of 81—low by general population standards, but high among autistic individuals. This news was presented with enthusiasm by the director because fully 75% of autistic children have IQs in the retarded range. Further, low IQs are associated with a failure to develop speech; in fact, about 50% of all autistic people do not develop communicative speech (Rimland 1964). Poor language skills are associated with a poor prognosis and, all too frequently, with lifelong institutionalization. Given encouragement by the director and the staff they met, Bob and Anne immediately enrolled Rodney in the school.

□ Speech and Language Acquisition

Preliminary Considerations

Many approaches have been used to help autistic people acquire speech and language skills. The most common broad method employed has been operant conditioning. Lovaas' (1977) work is probably the most widely disseminated and best documented of the operant methods, but many others have contributed to the literature. Used in isolation, operant techniques have attained mixed results. Although many children make significant gains when this approach is used, many others either fail to learn usable speech or make only minimal gains (Carr 1982a). In addition, transfer of skills to settings in the general environment and maintenance of skills across time have both been problematic. Although there are many indications that these problems can be addressed within the behavioral approach, others have been led to search for alternative methods.

Perhaps the most common alternative used during the 1970s and 1980s was sign language. The rationale stemmed from evidence that a significant number of autistic children exhibit auditory dysfunctions in the central nervous system (Paul 1987). It seemed to follow that, because autistic visual processing tended to be a relative strength for many individuals, the use of visual cues (that is, signs) would enhance the development of communication. Several researchers (for example, Barrera et al. 1980; Clarke et al. 1988; Konstantareas, 1987) have debated the virtue of using simultaneous communication, in which the instructor presents both speech and signs together, or sign-alone procedures. At present, empirical results favor the simultaneous approach, at least for higher functioning individuals, but both approaches are widely used. As happened with operant approaches, the use of sign language has gotten mixed results; that is, communication skills are sometimes acquired using sign language and sometimes they are not. Also as occurs with operant technology, autistic individuals often fail to transfer and maintain the skills that they do acquire. Finally, they usually fail to use spontaneously the communication skills they acquire, and there is often an absence of generative signing (that is, the creation of sign combinations that have not been specifically taught).

There has recently been heightened interest in the *pragmatics* of both signs and speech among autistic individuals (Carr 1982a). Pragmatics refers to the way one *uses* language and communication skills, in contrast to static estimates of vocabulary size and ability to construct appropriate syntax. An emphasis in this approach has been incidental teaching, which occurs throughout the environment, in contrast to structured teaching, which occurs primarily in the classroom. The approach has stirred excitement among those who work with autistic people because it addresses some of the most nettlesome problems so far encountered with this population: the transfer of acquired skills, the maintenance of those skills, and the development of generative communication.

Selecting Treatment Variables

As might be evident from the preceding discussion, the three methods in common use are not mutually exclusive. Rather, they represent an historic progression over the past 25 to 30 years that, it is hoped, will culminate in an effective but complex systematic program for the improvement of the communication skills of autistic individuals.

The school staff, being well trained, experienced, and familiar with the research literature regarding their charges, have developed a long-term speech and language program that includes all three approaches. Given his young age, his modest, but nonetheless existent, speech vocabulary, and his relatively good cognitive ability, Rodney was a perfect candidate for the program.

Defining Treatment Procedures

The development of speech and language in autistic youngsters is a long, involved process. Therefore, practitioners (and family members) must learn to appreciate very small gains over relatively long periods. For instance, Lovaas and colleagues (1966) noted that 84 instructional hours were required to teach the first two words to one of their subjects. However, as an individual's vocabulary grows, the acquisition of new words rapidly increases.

Staff at Rodney's school adopted the procedure reported by Koegel and Traphagen (1982) to select the initial words for Rodney's speech training. The procedure first required the collection of a 30-minute sample of Rodney's spontaneous vocalizations. The vocalizations were then transcribed using the International Phonetic Alphabet. Next, Rodney was given a consonant imitation test and a vowel imitation test. By combining these assessment data, staff identified phonemes that occurred frequently in Rodney's spontaneous and tested vocalizations. From these phonemes, words were constructed that would also meet the criterion of having a high degree of functional use in the home and school environment.

The structured teaching component of Rodney's initial program consisted of operant methods. In Step One, he was taught to attend to task on request. In Step Two, he learned to imitate, first, large motor movements and, later, fine motor movements of the mouth and tongue. In Step Three, verbal imitation was taught using modeling and a series of graded physical and visual prompts. In this step Rodney's vocalizations were shaped by reinforcing him for successive approximations of the modeled vocalization. All prompts were faded gradually. In Step 4, Rodney moved from imitative speech to functional speech, in which he learned to label actual objects (and later, actions) in the environment. Of course, Rodney's successful attempts throughout these steps were consistently reinforced to maintain a high level of motivation.

After four weeks of training, the staff discussed Rodney's achievement of speech and language objectives through the oral medium alone. Children who display difficulty using the auditory model are introduced to a simultaneous communication approach that combines oral presentations and responses with signed presentations and responses. In Rodney's case, the discussion was brief. Their optimistic prognosis was supported by the progress he had made during the early weeks of his program.

Nevertheless, the staff continued to meet at intervals to consider his progress and to make any adjustment they deemed necessary.

As soon as Rodney developed a working speech vocabulary, the staff began to emphasize the pragmatics of his communication. An important component of this part of his program was the training of Anne and Bob. It was important for Rodney to use his newly developed skills both at school and at home. Because the words he had learned were selected to be highly functional, it was not difficult to identify everyday situations to promote their use. In this component of the program, two principles were applied as often as possible. First, Rodney was encouraged to *initiate* communication rather than to depend on others to initiate interactions. This procedure tended to promote spontaneous speech. Second, Rodney was encouraged to *broaden* his use of speech beyond the restricted stimulus—response arrangement used in structured teaching. For instance, he had learned to discriminate the concepts "big" and "little" using a limited number of objects in the structured classroom. By prompting his application of the same concepts to a wide variety of environmental objects, he learned to transfer the narrow skill learned in the classroom to the environment at large. Also, Rodney was prompted to combine words he had learned in as many unique ways as possible. Thus, he was reinforced strongly when he first combined the words "big" and "ball" because he had never been taught that particular sequence of words in the classroom. Combining words to form multiple-word communication and generating combinations of words not specifically taught both work against a common characteristic of autistic speech: the tendency to telegraph communication by reducing, rather than embellishing, the words used to communicate.

Unfortunately, a fuller description of Rodney's program cannot be presented in this space. It may be said, however, that Rodney was one of the lucky youngsters who, because of the effort of competent practitioners, caring parents, and his own hard work, has succeeded in making the transition to a normal life. Today, he is a solid "B" student in a regular classroom in his home community. The reader is encouraged to refer to the contributions by Koegel and Traphagen and by Carr in *Educating and Understanding Autistic Children* (Koegel et al. 1982) for a comprehensive description of this general approach.

Conclusions

There has been tremendous progress in the development of treatment programs for the autistic population during the last 25 years. Although treatment outcomes continue to fall short of cures for the majority of those who suffer from this condition, it seems safe to assert that carefully implemented programs now result in happier, more fulfilled individuals. Such improvement has been the consequence of the work of a growing band of professionals and lay people who are dedicated to improving the lives of autistic people. Through their efforts, we now have a bona fide technology to guide decision making and program planning.

On the darker side, it must be noted that the available technology is not being implemented uniformly across the nation. Too few parents and service delivery personnel have information and training that allows them to maximize the outcomes of their work. It was the purpose of this chapter to lay a foundation on which interested readers can build. Those who pursue this field will find both a challenge and satisfaction in helping people who truly deserve our best effort. Finally, they will never be bored.

References

1. American Psychiatric Association. Diagnostic and Statistical Manual of Mental Disorders. 3rd ed., revised. Washington, D.C., 1987.

2. Barrera RD, Lobato-Barrera D, Sulzer-Azaroff B. A simultaneous treatment comparison of three expressive language training programs with a mute autistic child. J Autism Dev Disord. 10:21–37, 1980.

3. Carr E. Sign language. In: Koegel RL, Rincover A, Egel AL. eds. Educating and Understanding Autistic Children. San Diego, College-Hill Press, 1982a, pp 142–157.

4. Carr E. The motivation of self-injurious behavior. In: Koegel RL, Rincover A, Egel AL. eds. Educating and Understanding Autistic Children. San Diego, College-Hill Press, 1982b, pp 158–175.

5. Clarke S, Remington B, Light P. The role of referential speech in sign learning by mentally retarded children: A comparison of total communication and sign-alone training. J Appl Behav Anal. 21:419–426, 1988.

6. Collins DT. Head banging: Its meaning and management in the severely retarded population. Bull Menniger Clin 4:205–211, 1965.

7. de Lissovoy V. Head banging in early childhood: A suggested cause. J Genet Psychol. 102:109–114, 1963.

8. Eaves RC. The factor structure of autistic behavior. Presented at the Alabama Conference on Autism; May 15, 1990. Birmingham, AL.

9. Eaves RC, Hooper J. A factor analysis of psychotic behavior. Journal of Special Education. 21:122–132, 1987–88.

10. Harlow HF, Harlow MK. Social deprivation in monkeys. Sci Am. 207:136–146, 1962.

11. Kanner L. Autistic disturbances of affective contact. Nervous Child. 3:217–250, 1943.

12. Koegel RL, Rincover A, Egel AL. Educating and Understanding Autistic Children. San Diego, College-Hill Press, 1982.

13. Koegel RL, Traphagen J. Selection of initial words for speech training with nonverbal children. In: Koegel RL, Rincover A, Egel AL. eds. Educating and Understanding Autistic Children. San Diego, College-Hill Press, 1982, pp 65–77.

14. Konstantareas MM. Autistic children exposed to simultaneous communication training: A follow-up. J Autism Dev Disord. 17:115–131, 1987.

15. Levy DM. On the problem of movement restraint: Tics, stereotyped movements, and hyperactivity. American Journal of Orthopsychiatry. 14:644–671, 1944.

16. Lovaas OL. The Autistic Child: Language Development through Behavior Modification. New York, Irvington, 1977.

17. Lovaas OL. (Producer) Behavior Modification: Teaching Language to Psychotic Children [film]. New York, Appleton-Century-Crofts, 1969.

18. Lovaas OL, Berberich JP, Perloff BF, Schaeffer B. Acquisition of initiative speech in schizophrenic children. Science. 151:705–707, 1966.

19. Mahler M. On child psychoses and schizophrenia: Autistic and symbiotic infantile psychosis. Psychoanal Study Child. 7:286–305, 1952.

20. Nyhan WL. Behavior in the Lesch-Nyhan syndrome. Journal of Autism and Childhood Schizophrenia. 6:235–252, 1976.

21. Paul, R. Communication. In: Cohen DJ, Donnellan AM. eds. Handbook of Autism and Pervasive Developmental Disorders. Silver Springs, MD, V.H. Winston, 1987, pp 61–84.

22. Rank B. Adaptation of the psychoanalytic technique for the treatment of young children with atypical development. Am J Orthopsychiatry. 19:130–139, 1949.

23. Restak RM. The Brain. New York, Doubleday, 1979.

24. Rimland B. Infantile Autism. New York, Appleton-Century-Crofts, 1964.

25. Tarpley HD, Schroeder SR. Comparison of DRO and DRI on rate of suppression of self-injurious behavior. American Journal of Mental Deficiency. 84:188–194, 1979.

26. Wing L, Attwood A. Syndromes of autism and atypical development. In: Cohen DJ, Donnellan AM. eds. Handbook of Autism and Pervasive Developmental Disorders. Silver Springs, MD, V.H. Winston, 1987, pp 3–19.

Chapter 6
Learning Disabilities

William N. Bender

Functional Description

In the most general sense, a learning disability represents an unexplained inability to master learning-related tasks. By definition, a learning disability, or inability to learn, cannot be the result of low intelligence, socioeconomic factors, or poor sensory skills. Learning disabilities differ, and diagnosing two individuals as "learning disabled" does not mean that the learning problems of those individuals are the same. In fact, a consistent finding in research on learning disabilities is the amazing heterogeneity of learning problems included under the term.

Beyond this general definition, difficulty arises because of the number of different definitions used in the field. Definitions differ because of different theoretical perspectives on what a learning disability is. Theorists who focus on language delay have written definitions that focus on that aspect. Theorists who focus on visual motor performance have written definitions based on that aspect. Finally, the federal and state governments, as well as professional organizations, have proposed definitions designed to satisfy everyone.

A practitioner in the developmental disabilities is well advised to use the definition provided by the state in which he or she practices. Although some consistency has emerged based on federal legislation, definitions vary from one state to another. Generally, the state's Department of Education can provide a set of rules and regulations for special education services that includes the state definition of learning disability.

Operationalizing Definitions

Chalfant (1985) found at least five terms being used by different states to denote learning disabilities: learning disabilities, learning disabled, specific learning disabilities, perceptually impaired, and perceptual/communication disordered. Despite this diversity, there are several common aspects to most definitions. Examination of these components provides an organizational structure for understanding the current assessment procedures.

The Discrepancy Criteria

The most frequently used method of identifying learning disabilities is to measure the discrepancy between ability and achievement. The assumption that students with learning disabilities are not performing as well academically as they should has led to the development of mathematical formulas for identifying students with disabilities. These formulas are used to determine the degree of difference between intelligence, as measured on standardized intelligence quotient (IQ) assessments, and achievement in academic subject areas.

Four major types of ability/achievement discrepancy calculations (Chalfant 1985) have been used. First, practitioners calculated a discrepancy between grade placement and achievement level by subtracting the latter from the former. The result from this procedure suggested that a fifth grader who was reading at a second grade level must be disabled, a hypothesis that was clearly inadequate because intelligence level was not considered.

The "formula" calculations were the next to evolve. Because the foregoing procedure did not take into account the child's intelligence level, theorists developed formulas that did. These formulas usually involved calculation of an "expected achievement" level, based on intelligence score and grade placement, that was then compared to actual achievement. If the observed discrepancy was large enough, the child was considered learning disabled.

Standard score calculations were developed next because the formulas described above were based on mathematical manipulation of grade equivalent scores (for example, a 3.5 in reading), and such calculations were inappropriate mathematically because the standard deviations of the different grade equivalent scores are different. Consequently, the concept of a standardized score comparison was developed, whereby the practitioner would obtain an IQ score and an achievement score based on tests that have the same mean and standard deviation, thus yielding scores that are mathematically more comparable. Today, standard score calculation is the most common method of identifying children with learning disabilities.

The regression score table was developed from the standard score procedure. Repeated tests resulting in scores that are either very high or very low tend to yield scores that regress toward (or fall back toward) the mean, which can create error in simple subtraction of standardized scores. Thus, some states use "regression tables" that are basically standard score comparisons that take this regression into account.

In addition to the discrepancy between ability and achievement, other types of discrepancies have been used to identify a learning disability (Chalfant 1985). For example, many psychologists believe that different levels of scores on IQ tests, or different patterns of scores on the subtests of IQ tests, indicate a learning disability. It is not uncommon for practitioners to identify children as learning disabled based on this type of discrepancy.

As recently as 1976, the United States Department of Education indicated that a discrepancy that was unexplained by other factors was the only useful indicator of a learning disability. Also, Chalfant's (1985) report indicated that certain discrepancy procedures may be considered indicators of a learning disability. The Council for Learning Disabilities (1987) recommended that the use of discrepancy formulas be phased out, but the report did not recommend any type of alternative procedure. Despite this recommendation, the Council for Learning Disabilities did endorse the regression method for calculating discrepancy for states in which some measure of discrepancy was required. Finally, research has shown that practitioners regularly use discrepancies to identify learning disabilities (Chalfant 1985; Valus 1986).

The use of discrepancies has resulted in identification of children with learning disabilities only after they enter school. If a state's definition of learning disabilities stipulates a standard score discrepancy between IQ and reading achievement of 20 points as indicative of a learning disability, identifying children with learning disabilities at the age of four (prior to the use of school achievement tests) becomes problematic. Consequently, most children with learning disabilities are identified after the school years begin. Most students are identified as learning disabled when they are at the third and fourth grade levels.

The Psychological Process Criterion

The early assumption inherent in the definition of a learning disability was that some type of disability in perception, language, or cognition prevented an individual from learning. Numerous assessments of copying skills—referred to as visual motor performance—and motor movement skills have been used, as have language tests. Another common method for measuring "basic psychological processes" is to use standardized intelligence tests and to examine the discrepancies between various subscale scores on the tests based on visual perception and language skills. Thus, discussion of these mental or psychological processes includes terms such as perception, visual learning deficit, or auditory learning problems; receptive/expressive language (to be discussed in a later section); attention; and sensory integration, or the ability to combine information obtained from several senses, notably hearing and vision.

This component of the definition has always been problematic, because the theorists disagree on what the processes are and which should be measured (Ysseldyke 1983), and no exhaustive list of these processes has been proposed. Also, the measurement devices used as indicators of different types of perception are not adequate technically (Coles 1978). For these reasons the Council for Learning Disabilities (1987) recommended that measurement of such processes be terminated.

Nevertheless, Chalfant (1985) indicated that 18 states still require assessment of psychological processes in some fashion. Because there are no specifics as to what these processes entail, states vary greatly in required assessment practices. The best advice for the practitioner is to adhere to the rules and regulations published by the state Department of Education for assessment practices. These procedures can usually be obtained by interested professionals from the Department of Education in question.

The Exclusionary Criteria

The last part of the federal definition attempts to tell what a learning disability is not rather than what it is. Early definitions of learning disabilities included a phrase that suggested that learning disability was not a form of retardation and that mentally retarded children should not be considered learning disabled. This is always problematic because it is like trying to define the color red by pointing to things that are not red. Such attempts at definition inevitably suggest a real problem in the definition of the term.

During the 1960s, the exclusionary clause was expanded to include children who are culturally deprived or behaviorally disturbed. These exclusions also resulted in assessment problems because it is often difficult to tell different types of handicapping conditions apart. For example, a child with learning disabilities and a child with behavioral disorders often behave similarly, and no set criteria are provided to make the distinction.

Functional Characteristics

Given the heterogeneity among children referred to as learning disabled, it is difficult to identify functional characteristics that are universal to this population. Still, general characteristics that may be found in children with learning disabilities can be identified and used to illustrate the types of school problems that are characteristic of this group. (The practitioner is referred to the Summary at the end of the chapter for a complete list of characteristics that may be found in most children and youth with learning disabilities.)

The following list presents the types of characteristics frequently discussed as indicative of a learning disability. It is, however, merely a list of "potential" characteristics and should not be taken as a checklist for identification purposes. The research evidence clearly demonstrates the profound heterogeneity of learning disabled populations, and no characteristics list can be used as a single criterion for identification.

1. Neurologic impairment caused by impairment in cranial nerve function, demonstrated by a neurologic exam

2. Awkwardness of step or gait when walking

3. Awkwardness in use of one's hands for either gross motor or fine motor tasks

4. Difficulty in reading words on the blackboard, even with corrective lenses

5. Excessive hyperactivity, or inability to stay in his or her seat in the school room

6. Excessive distractibility, or inability to concentrate on a learning task for the same length of time as other children

Academic Skills

One of the best ways to understand this handicap is to review the types of academic, emotional, and social behavior problems that are associated with the condition. The following descriptions are taken from Bender (1991):

Bobby has failed several subjects in the fourth grade, and his mother believes that this is related to his low reading skill. Although he passes reading, he usually passes it with a D or a C. His parents are concerned and have spoken to the fourth grade teacher. The teacher has indicated that Bobby is in the lowest level reading group but that he still seems to be having problems. She also mentioned several other problem areas, including spelling and handwriting. Bobby has difficulty in writing a paragraph when one is assigned in class. Despite these difficulties, Bobby seems to have no difficulty with math, and he usually earns a B for that subject. His parents don't understand this, because they see that Bobby studies each night for at least 1½ hours.

Jessica earned below-average grades during her first year of school, but when she got to the second grade, she began to have problems with some of her work. She could not recognize words and did not understand the stories she read during reading time. She also had trouble when other students or the teacher read the story. Even though she could name the characters in a story, she could not remember the plot of the story very well, and if she had to tell the story to someone else, she tended to get the facts confused and could not recall the sequence of events. Despite this problem, Jessica was doing low-average work in math and could complete simple math operations as well as any other student.

Jason is in the tenth grade and has recently transferred into the local high school. The history teacher noted that he has a problem reading the text as well as reading questions on the unit tests. His homework, when he has it at all, is disorganized and indicates a problem understanding the material. His written work is barely readable, and his syntax is often confused. He writes in short sentences, and any understanding of paragraph structure seems to be totally lacking. Finally, Jason seems to realize that he is having significant problems with his work, and his self-concept has suffered. He is a proud teenager and doesn't like the other students to know that he has problems reading. Consequently, he doesn't like to share his work with the class, either verbally or in written form. After about a month, during which Jason received barely passing grades, the teacher asked for help.

Thomas never read well and had problems with handwriting since he was in first grade. When he got to the fourth grade, the teacher decided that he needed help in both of these areas, so she began to work with him during class. When she began, she was sure that the extra work would help, because Thomas seemed to be motivated to improve his reading. As she worked with him, she noted that he would often say one word when he meant another. Also, sometimes his thoughts were confused, and he was unable to communicate as clearly as the typical fourth grade child. It became apparent that the extra work did not help, so in desperation, the teacher approached the special education teacher to discuss having Thomas tested.

In each of the preceding descriptions, there was some indication of relative strengths and weaknesses. Students with learning disabilities tend to have some areas in which they do acceptable school work. Most of these students have difficulty with reading, language arts, written expression, or reading-based content subjects. However, there are students whose only disability seems to be in math. The types of memory problems that were evident when Jessica heard a story read are common, as are the organizational problems discussed as a characteristic of Jason. Finally, with older students such as Jason, there is often some degree of emotional and/or personality disturbance because the older students realize that they are different from their peers and they do not usually cope well with those differences. This can result in decreased self-concept and lower self-expectations.

Self-Care

Self-care is not a major problem for most learning disabled individuals. As indicated previously, most of these students are identified after the school years begin. Most parents report that children with learning disabilities seem to learn rudimentary self-care skills as quickly as their siblings. For example, tying shoes at the age of 3 or 4 years is not a problem (as it usually is for a moderately mentally retarded child) and nor is helping around the home difficult for learning disabled children.

Subtle differences probably exist, however, because of the lack of organizational abilities on the part of the child who is learning disabled. This deficit may result in an inability to follow directions for making the bed or bringing out all the white and light-colored clothes for washing.

Finally, dyslexic individuals, who represent a subgroup of the total learning disabled population (probably less than 2%), may need additional training in self-care skills throughout life. The true dyslexic will probably never read beyond the second- or third-grade level and will need special training for driving an automobile or using a city transportation system.

Receptive and Expressive Language

As it is in most children, receptive language is more developed in students with learning disabilities than is expressive language. There is typically some language delay, but not usually enough to determine that a handicap exists during the language-learning period characteristic of the second and third years of life. Consequently, the scanty research on early language development in children who are eventually diagnosed as having learning disabilities has not shown any potential for identifying this handicap at an early stage.

Children with learning disabilities tend to have the more sophisticated types of language problems. Typically, these children produce recognizable sentences and can participate, though minimally, in conversation. Whereas the problem in moderately and severely retarded populations may be eliciting rudimentary forms of language, the problems among children with learning disabilities concern use of language in academic and social situations.

Syntax and Semantics

Research on later language development has concentrated on syntax, semantics, and pragmatic language. Syntax refers to the formal relationships between words in phrases or sentences. Examples of such relationships include the subject–verb relationship or the relationship between the verb and the direct object. Semantics refers to knowledge and comprehension of words. Ability in this area is often measured by receptive vocabulary tests.

Most research on syntax and semantics has demonstrated deficits in children with learning disabilities (Wiig et al. 1977; Wiig et al. 1973). Children with learning disabilities demonstrate deficits in the ability to apply morphologic rules (for example, formation of plurals, verb tenses, and possessives) and difficulty in both comprehension of and expression of syntactic structures such as relationships between words in sentences and phrases. Understanding who a pronoun applies to and what function is served by a direct object or an indirect object are examples of this syntactic skill. These deficits are apparent both in the child's understanding of the language of others and in his or her own production of spoken language. Finally, at least one of these studies demonstrated that oral language production did not automatically improve with age as it does in most children (Wiig et al. 1977).

Pragmatic Use of Language

Pragmatics is the other level of language and the most recent to receive research attention. Pragmatics is the use of language in context. This aspect of language encompasses the social and cultural roles of the participants in the conversation (Boucher 1986). Theorists who study pragmatic language emphasize the ecologically based study of language in real communication situations rather than scores on a test that may not indicate true communicative skill.

Researchers in this area tend to measure the actual utterances a child makes when he or she communicates with other children and adults.

An important aspect of pragmatic language is the ability to adjust one's language to the speaker to enhance communication. For example, a person generally uses a more simplistic language with a young child than with an older person. This language adaptation is referred to as code switching. Such adaptations may be made in a number of ways, including using more simple sentences or using fewer modifiers in each complete thought.

Early research suggested that children with learning disabilities did not code switch as frequently as non-learning-disabled children (Boucher 1984; Bryan et al. 1981). Asking questions, responding to inadequate messages, and persuasion were noted as difficult skills to master for children with learning disabilities (Boucher 1986; Bryan et al.). These skills were cited as a possible reason for inadequate social skills among these children (Bryan et al. 1981).

Referential communication, another aspect of pragmatic language, requires that a child communicate specific information *to* another and evaluate the adequacy of communication *from* another. Giving or receiving instructions is one example of referential communication. Referential communication skills therefore, include awareness of accurate and inadequate messages as well as of choices based on such communication.

Several studies have suggested that children with learning disabilities are deficient in understanding and responding to inadequate communication (Donahue et al. 1980; Feagans 1983; Wiig et al. 1981). For example, Spekman (1981) created dyads, or paired groups, some of which included a child with a disability and some of which did not. Each child in each dyad was to communicate information and to act on information received from the partner in the dyad. This research design allowed for comparison of referential communication skills as well as of listening competence. The children were told they could ask questions regarding incomplete communications. Although no differences were found in their abilities to follow directions, to complete the task, or to ask appropriate questions, the children with learning disabilities gave less task-relevant information. These dyads demonstrated less success in completion of the task than did the dyads that included only normally functioning children.

The implications of this research for the practitioner are of concern. If a learning-disabled child demonstrates a pragmatic language disability in referential communication skills, that student will be less capable of giving instructions to his or her classmates and playmates. Consequently, this disability will affect the student's performance in group projects that require verbal participation of each group member. Also, the child will have problems responding to instructions given by the teacher or other members of the group. Clearly, a disability in referential communication presents real problems in the typical elementary school classroom.

A number of educational activities may be used to expand a child's success in pragmatic language skills. Any projects that require a child to communicate information to others utilizing referential communication skills can be a learning experience for these children. In giving directions to others, a child has to plan what the other needs to know, the order in which information should be presented, and the speed with which information should be given. By placing children with learning disabilities in that position and then discussing with them their efforts at communication, a more sophisticated level of pragmatic language may be obtained. Merely assigning these children to group projects without appropriate postcommunication follow-up will not result in improved communication skill. The com-munication must be examined and reconstructed so that the child understands the strengths and weaknesses of his or her communication efforts.

Impact of Language Deficits

Deficits in semantics, syntax, and pragmatic language skills in both the receptive and expressive areas often create additional problems in school performance. For example, such deficits often result in difficulty with written assignments, reading assignments, or group projects. The teacher and other practitioners must be sensitive to these language problems and to the effects of these problems on school tasks, and expectations for school work should be adjusted accordingly.

Adjustments that language deficits require may be simple or extensive. Many students with learning disabilities take tests orally rather than in written form. By allowing this form of testing, the teacher can get a true picture of the student's comprehension rather than a measure of comprehension that may be unduly influenced by the child's ability to read the test and write an answer. Other modifications that lessen the impact of language deficits include use of alternative texts, use of alternative reading materials that cover the same content but that are written at a lower reading level, use of graphic aids during lectures that students must listen to and determine the important information that should be included in the notes, and the frequent checking of notes taken by the student to ensure that the notes are complete.

Summary of Language Deficits

Although little evidence exists of major delays in expressive or receptive language in children with learning disabilities, more sophisticated language problems are well documented. Students with learning disabilities have deficits in both syntax and semantics that negatively affect their school performance in many spoken and written tasks. Perhaps a more debilitating handicap is the deficit in pragmatic language. Students with learning disabilities do not have the pragmatic language skills to adapt their language to the situation or to use referential communication skills—either receptive or expressive—in a fashion commensurate with their age group. Finally, some evidence suggests that, unlike nonhandicapped children, these language problems are not overcome with age. To alleviate these pragmatic language problems, specific instructional techniques such as frequent use of and feedback on referential communication skills are necessary.

Learning and Cognition

Several major areas of research involve cognition of students with learning disabilities, including intelligence, attention, and memory. The practitioner should be aware of the recent findings in each of these areas.

Intelligence

The definition of learning disabilities stipulates that children so diagnosed have average or above-average intelligence. Several research studies have indicated, however, that the anticipated IQ level for children with learning disabilities is approximately 90 to 93 (Gajar 1979; Webster and Schenck 1978). This range probably reflects several things. First, intelligence, as measured today in Western culture, is heavily dependent on verbal skill, and this dependence may deflate the average IQ levels reported above. In addition, these figures are based on samples of students with learning disabilities identified by the public schools, and identification procedures in public schools are not exact.

Some students with learning disabilities have a level of intelligence in the "gifted" range. These students are known as "gifted learning-disabled" students.

Some students with IQs above 130, or two standard deviations above the mean, also demonstrate an ability–achievement discrepancy, as discussed previously. Although these students may be at or above grade level academically, if there is a large discrepancy between their IQ and their achievement, they may be classified as learning disabled or as gifted learning disabled. Research studies that examine the characteristics of this group are recent and relatively rare. As a result, little is known about this group of students.

Attention

The construct of attention is more complex than it seems and involves at least three different types of skills. On-task behavior indicates the persistence or length of time a student can remain concentrated on a task. Focus of attention indicates the student's ability to inhibit distracting stimuli, and selective attention is a cognitively based process that involves choosing which aspects of a stimulus to attend to.

Research in each of these areas has indicated that students with learning disabilities suffer deficits compared with their agemates (Bender 1991; McKinney and Feagans 1983). For example, whereas the average on-task rates for nonhandicapped children range between 80% and 95%, the average rates of on-task behavior typically reported in the literature indicate that children with learning disabilities are on-task between 35% and 65% of the time (Bender 1991). This deficit in attention obviously has a negative affect on academic achievement.

Research has indicated that many children with learning disabilities can be trained to stay on-task for longer periods of time. This training, usually referred to as self-monitoring, was developed by Hallahan and his associates at the University of Virginia. The training involves a simple procedure that forces the child to ask himself or herself the question, "Am I paying attention?" on a periodic basis during a learning task. When such a procedure is utilized each day for a period of weeks, the child apparently forms the habit of monitoring his or her on-task skills. This training is relatively simple, and parents of children with disabilities have actually conducted this type of self-monitoring training with their own children during nightly homework sessions. Instructions are available in several sources (Bender 1991; Hallahan et al. 1982).

Research on the focus of attention is equivocal. In studies that used teacher perceptions of distractibility—the polar opposite of focused attention—as the measure of attention, the data typically indicate that students with learning disabilities are highly distractible, thus indicating a general inability to focus on a task (McKinney and Feagans 1983). However, in experimental studies in which the distracting stimulus is presented in a controlled fashion, such as distracting light shown on the page the child reads, students with learning disabilities seem to be no more highly distractible than nonhandicapped students (Zentall 1986; Zentall et al. 1978). More research, using both of these methods, is necessary before conclusions can be drawn regarding distractibility of students with learning disabilities.

Selective attention involves a conscious choice of particular aspects of the stimuli that deserve attention, and the results indicate that children with learning disabilities are not that involved with the task (Bender 1991). Typically, these students answer a question more impulsively than others and do not make the effort to attend selectively to the discriminative aspects of the stimuli that are used to answer the question. Research, at present, indicates that this deficit in selective attention is not due to a lack of desire to complete the problem correctly but rather to a lack of knowledge about the cognitive steps necessary to selective attention, that is what to attend to and what to ignore.

Selective attention skills may be developed for educational tasks by teachers who

assist the child in the thought process. When a child gives an answer that indicates incorrect thinking, the teacher should take a moment and reconstruct the child's selective attention process. Sometimes this can be accomplished by merely asking the child why that answer seems to be correct. The teacher may then be in a position to indicate to the child certain errors in attending to unimportant aspects of the problem of ignoring vital information in the formulation of the answer. This type of teaching requires small classes and a teacher who is highly responsive to the thought processes of the child.

Memory

The research on memory abilities of children with learning disabilities has also indicated problem areas. Memory may be divided into short-term memory, holding a stimulus in one's memory for a few seconds, or long-term memory, holding a stimulus anywhere from a few minutes to many years. Memory problems in children with learning disabilities tend to be associated with short-term memory. Once a child with learning disabilities learns something, that information is retained in a manner comparable to that of nonhandicapped children. Children with learning disabilities, however, have problems with short-term memory and with the cognitive strategies that are used to transfer stimuli into long-term memory (Ross 1976; Torgesen 1984).

To transfer a piece of information from short-term into long-term memory, most individuals develop some type of memory strategy. Many of us use verbal rehearsal to memorize names of persons we just met. Another common example: When nonhandicapped children are required to memorize pictures of various stimuli, they typically develop a classification system, place the pictures in the different classes or groups, and memorize the pictures in each group. Children with learning disabilities are much less likely to use these common strategies than are nonhandicapped children (Torgesen 1984).

Memory research is, however, optimistic because it indicates that, once a child with learning disabilities has been trained in an age-appropriate memory strategy, that child can usually use that strategy and improve his or her memory performance. A number of instructional strategies, generally referred to as "cognitive strategy training" or "learning strategies," are being used to enhance the performance of children with learning disabilities. These learning strategies generally include an acronym in which each letter represents a step for the student to perform. For example, the "RAP" strategy is a learning strategy that enables a child to memorize the major points from a paragraph of written text. The letters stand for: R—read the material, A—ask questions concerning the material, and P—paraphrase the material. When students with learning disabilities are trained to complete these steps, their ability to memorize important detail from written material increases.

Summary of Cognition

Research has shown that, in almost every aspect of cognition, children with learning disabilities demonstrate some deficits. The intelligence of these children is lower than the norm. Deficits are consistently demonstrated in both on-task attention measures and selective attention, and memory research has consistently indicated problems in memory transfer and memory strategies. With these deficits in cognitive skills that are intimately related to academic performance, it is not surprising that the cognitive deficits negatively affect the school work of these children.

These summary statements are, however, based on research on groups of children, and no automatic assumptions should be made regarding the cognition of a particular child with a learning disabil-

ity. For example, some children may have a disability based on memory deficit and still be able to perform educational tasks in a fashion similar to that of nonhandicapped children. Before making assumptions concerning the particular disability of a child, thorough assessment should be conducted to identify the type of disability that may be present in the individual case.

Capacity for Independent Living

Among students with learning disabilities, the capacity for independent living is not usually in question. These students typically live independently after completing school, and many have families, hold jobs, and lead relatively normal lives. Several factors result from the handicap, however, that may impair their capacity to function independently during their adult lives, including academic and social/emotional outcomes from the schooling process.

Academic and Cognitive Outcomes

Although long-term follow-up studies of students with learning disabilities are rare, there are some indicators that the types of academic and cognitive difficulties that students with learning disabilities experience during school persist after the school years (Gregory et al. 1986; Johnson 1984). For example, Gregory and colleagues (1986) conducted a retrospective study in which they compared outcome measures for learning disabled and nonlearning-disabled seniors in high school. Gregory and his coworkers used a data set designed to predict outcomes for all high school seniors in the secondary schools in America. Over 26,000 students completed a survey with information about themselves, and 439 of these students identified themselves as learning disabled. This group was compared to the nonhandicapped group on various academic variables, and the results demonstrated that the academic deficits of students with learning disabilities in reading, math, and language arts are apparent as late as the last year in school. Research on reading and academic skills has demonstrated that many students with learning disabilities finish school with academic performance around the fifth grade level. The reading level of adolescents with learning disabilities seems to peak at around the fifth or sixth grade level and improve little thereafter. Also, research indicates that the IQ–achievement discrepancy is still relatively large for most of these students. Johnson (1984) identified deficits in reading comprehension, written work, and verbal language problems that continue to plague adults who are learning disabled after the postschool transition period. These levels of achievement performance present problems either in further schooling or in entrance into the work force.

Because years of remedial schooling have failed to alleviate these academic problems, more schooling probably will not help. At this point, it is most beneficial for practitioners to assist the youth with learning disabilities to identify coping strategies that make normal independent living skills possible. Use of a functional skills curriculum during the later years of schooling seems to offer the best remedy for recurring academic problems. In a functional skills curriculum, daily-living skills such as completion of tax return forms, job applications, and medical insurance forms comprise the curriculum. With practice in those types of skills, the problems of living independently after school are alleviated somewhat.

Emotional and Social Outcomes

Another set of variables that may impair independent living skills includes social and emotional variables such as self-concept, peer relationships, and social interactions. Horn and coworkers (1983) reviewed a number of studies that suggested that the self-concept of adults with learning disabilities was lower than that of nonlearning-disabled comparison groups. Several more recent studies of self-satisfaction support this deficit in self-concept among adults with learning disabilities (Gregory et al. 1986; Pihl and McLarnon 1984).

The study by Gregory and coworkers (1986) also compared the locus of control of seniors with learning disabilities and nonlearning-disabled students. Locus of control involves the perception of control that one has over one's environment. A high level on "internal" control typically indicates that one feels fairly secure that one's actions can result in positive occurrences in one's environment, whereas a high level of "external" locus of control indicates that one feels rather helpless to affect change in one's own life circumstances. The data indicated that youth with learning disabilities demonstrate higher levels of "external" locus of control than would be desirable and that level of external control may have negative repercussions for independent living skills.

Finally, a number of emotional and social variables have been studied among the young adult learning disabled population that have not been studied in younger groups. The study by Gregory and colleagues (1986) included several other social and emotional variables including overall adjustment; self-ratings of personal attractiveness; satisfaction with peer group; trouble with the law; parental interests in the student's activities; adequacy of home-study facilities; and mother's absence from the home. On each variable, the seniors with learning disabilities demonstrated less positive outcomes than did the comparison group of nonhandicapped seniors.

This result does not demonstrate positive outcomes of special education treatment during the school years. These results indicate potential problems that young adults with learning disabilities may find in independent living. For example, trouble with the law, in the form of a simple parking ticket, requires reading, that is, the instructions on when and where to pay the fine, and some effort on the part of the person, should mistakes be made in that process.

Unfortunately, concern with emotional development and social skills among students and young adults with learning disabilities is relatively recent, and research on effective interventions for independent living skills is, at present, nonexistent. Although some research on social relationships during the school years has been conducted, little is known about how to increase social skills to facilitate independent living during the postschool period.

Economic Self-Sufficiency

Economic self-sufficiency in our society depends to a large extent on successful schooling in either a vocational program or a higher education program, and adults with learning disabilities frequently do attend college or vocational training programs after high school. In one study (Johnson and Blalock 1987), 23 of 93 adults with learning disabilities attended college, and 19 obtained degrees. To date, no study has been done on postcollege vocational experience for individuals with learning disabilities. Despite this lack of data, one may tentatively conclude that completing college indicates some degree of economic self-sufficiency for a sizable minority of adults with learning disabilities.

Additional data exist on the vocational outlook for adults with learning disabilities. Schalock and coworkers (1986) showed, in a postsecondary-school, 5-year follow-up study, that 72% of the students with learning disabilities were employed after school. These data are supported by several other studies of handicapped children (see Bender 1991 for review).

Based on these data, the prognosis for economic self-sufficiency for most adults with learning disabilities appears to be positive, and practitioners should let parents and the handicapped individuals themselves know this. There is, however, a sizable minority of persons with learning disabilities who are, apparently, not employed even 5 years after school ends.

Further, practitioners should endeavor to make vocational educational opportunities available for most students with learning disabilities during the secondary school years and thereafter. The content of such programs should focus on job-related skills as well as on work-related skills (for example, getting to work on time, punching the time clock) and interpersonal skills needed on the job (for example, getting along with other workers, supporting newer employees, requesting assistance as necessary). Only by providing a complete vocational training program such as this can the practitioner hope to improve the outlook for economic self-sufficiency for his or her clients.

Summary

One major factor in any discussion of characteristics of an intervention programs for children and youth with learning disabilities is the heterogeneity of the population. For example, whereas most students with learning disabilities may have problems in pragmatic language, not all students with this handicap do. Most of these students have problems in selective and sustained attention, but not all of them do. The following list of characteristics is not intended to be used as a diagnostic checkoff, but rather as a rough guide to the types of problems that may be noted in this population of students.

With this caveat in mind, some characteristics can be stipulated that may be found in many children with learning disabilities. The facts below are the types of characteristics that are presented in most introductory texts about learning disabilities. The types of interventions that alleviate each problem are also mentioned:

1. The ratio of males to females identified as learning disabled ranges from 2:1 to 5:1. There are many more males with this problem than females.

2. Self-care is not usually a problem with most students with learning disabilities, though higher-order, self-care skills that involve sequencing and organizational abilities may present problems.

3. Deficits exist among children and adolescents with learning disabilities in almost every area of language—semantics, syntax, and pragmatics—in both reception and expression. These deficits often result in difficulties in written language, speaking communication, and listening skills. Interventions are generally aimed at providing training in pragmatic language skills with frequent feedback about the adequacy of the spoken or written communication.

4. The average IQ of populations in public schools identified as learning disabled is approximately 90 to 93, or several points lower than the population norm for nonhandicapped children, even though the definition of learning disabilities stipulates that children identified as learning disabled have average or above-average IQs.

5. Cognitive deficits that are frequently demonstrated by this group include problems in both attention skills and memory. Research has shown that on-task time among students with learning disabilities is lower than that among nonhandicapped students, and the selective attention capabilities are less developed. Interventions for these attention skills include self-monitoring training of on-task behavior and direct cognitive strategy training in attention to various stimuli.

6. Students with learning disabilities have problems with short-term memory skills and with memorization ability. Educational interventions for these skills include memory strategies that include memorization of learning-strategy acronyms and use of verbal rehearsal and visual imagery to improve memory of textual material.

7. Neither mobility nor self-direction seems to be a major problem for this population.

8. Although most persons with learning disabilities do live independently after the school years, problems in both academic and emotional and social skills persist and may lead to complications during the postschool adjustment period. Functional skills curricula may alleviate some of the problems associated with low academic functioning; however, no research has been conducted on interventions to improve social and emotional functioning of young adults with learning disabilities.

9. Most students with learning disabilities are economically self-sufficient after the school years, and a sizable minority pursue higher education, either a 4-year college program or a vocational program. Increased attention to postsecondary vocational or college training should assist the young adult with learning disabilities to attain economic self-sufficiency.

References

1. Bender WN. Introduction to Learning Disabilities: Identification, Assessment, and Teaching Strategies. Needham Heights, MA, Allyn and Bacon, 1991.
2. Boucher CR. Pragmatics: The verbal language of learning disabled and nondisabled boys. Learning Disability Quarterly. 7:271–286, 1984.
3. Boucher CR. Pragmatics: The meaning of verbal language in learning disabled and nondisabled boys. Learning Disability Quarterly. 9:285–295, 1986.
4. Bryan T, Donahue M, Pearl R. Learning disabled children's peer interactions during a small-group problem solving task. Learning Disability Quarterly. 4:13–22, 1981.
5. Chalfant JC. Identifying learning disabled students: A summary of the national task force report. Learning Disabilities Focus. 1(1):9–20, 1985.
6. Coles GS. The learning disability test battery: Empirical and social issues. Harvard Educational Review. 48:313–340, 1978.
7. Council for Learning Disabilities. The CLD position statement. Journal of Learning Disabilities. 20:349–350, 1987.

8. Donahue M, Pearl R, Bryan T. Learning disabled children's conversational competence: Responses to inadequate messages. Journal of Applied Psycholinguistics. 1:387–403, 1980.

9. Feagans L. Discourse processes in learning disabled children. In: McKinney JD, Feagans L. eds. Current Topics in Learning Disabilities. Vol 1. Norwood, NJ, Ablex, 1983.

10. Gajar A. Educable mentally retarded, learning disabled, emotionally disturbed: Similarities and differences. Except Child. 45:470–472, 1979.

11. Gregory JF, Shanahan T, Walberg H. A profile of learning disabled twelfth-graders in regular classes. Learning Disability Quarterly. 9:33–42, 1986.

12. Hallahan DP, Lloyd JW, Stoller L. Improving Attention with Self-monitoring: A Manual for Teachers. Charlottesville, VA, University of Virginia, 1982.

13. Horn WF, O'Donnell JP, Vitulano LA. Long-term follow-up studies of learning disabled persons. Journal of Learning Disabilities. 9:542–554, 1983.

14. Johnson CL. The learning disabled adolescent and young adult: An overview and critique of current practices. Journal of Learning Disabilities. 7:386–391, 1984.

15. Johnson DJ, Blalock JW. Adults with Learning Disabilities: Clinical Studies. Orlando, FL, Grune and Stratton, 1987.

16. McKinney JD, Feagans L. Adaptive classroom behavior of learning disabled students. Journal of Learning Disabilities. 16:360–367, 1983.

17. Pihl RO, McLarnon LD. Learning disabled children as adolescents. Journal of Learning Disabilities. 17:96–100, 1984.

18. Ross AO. Psychological Aspects of Learning Disabilities and Reading Disorders. New York, McGraw Hill, 1976.

19. Shalock RL, Wolzen B, Ross I, Elliot B, Werbel G, Peterson K. Post-secondary community placement of handicapped students: A five-year follow-up. Learning Disability Quarterly. 9:295–303, 1986.

20. Spekman N. Dyadic verbal communication abilities of learning disabled and normally achieving fourth and fifth grade boys. Learning Disability Quarterly. 4:193–201, 1981.

21. Torgesen JK. Memory processes in reading disabled children. Journal of Learning Disabilities. 18:350–357, 1984.

22. Valus A. Achievement-potential discrepancy status of students in LD programs. Learning Disability Quarterly. 9:199–205, 1986.

23. Webster RE, Schenck SJ. Diagnostic test pattern differences among LD, ED, EMH, and multi-handicapped students. Journal of Educational Research. 72:75–80, 1978.

24. Wiig EH, Lapointe C, Semel EM. Relationships among language processing and production abilities of learning disabled adolescents. Journal of Learning Disabilities. 9:292–299, 1977.

25. Wiig EH, Semel EM, Abele E. Perception and interpretation of ambiguous sentences by learning disabled twelve year olds. Learning Disability Quarterly. 4:3–12, 1981.

26. Wiig EH, Semel EM, Crouse MAB. The use of English morphology by high-risk and learning disabled children. Journal of Learning Disabilities. 6:457–464, 1973.

27. Ysseldyke JE. Current practices in making psychoeducational decisions about learning disabled students. Journal of Learning Disabilities. 16:226–233, 1983.

28. Zentall SS. Effects of color stimulation on performance and activity of hyperactive and nonhyperactive children. Journal of Educational Psychology. 78:159–165, 1986.

29. Zentall SS, Zentall TR, Booth ME. Within task stimulation: Effects on activity and spelling performance in hyperactive and normal children. Journal of Educational Research. 71:223–230, 1978.

Chapter 7
Communication Disorders

Richard E. Talbott

Communication is the essence of what makes us human. (Author)

The most common theme running through all textual material on the developmentally disabled is the need to optimize the life potential of *each* individual. The perennial debate as to the distinctions, or lack thereof, among the disorders that may underlie developmental disabilities remains unresolved. Some authors, for example, suggest a clear and valid distinction between autism and mental retardation (Powers and Handleman 1984) whereas others emphasize the similarities between the two (Snell and Ronzaglia 1982). The specific cause underlying the behavioral manifestations of a given developmental disability may be important from an academic standpoint but is only important from a habilitative perspective to the extent that it impacts on that habilitative strategy.

The type and severity of communication disorders present in developmental disabilities range from mild expressive speech disorders to profound dysfunction of expressive or receptive language capabilities. Despite the severity of the communication deficit, the importance of maximizing the utilization of whatever communication potential exists for each individual cannot be overemphasized. The establishment of some communication channel is a sine qua non for all other habilitative intervention strategies, and the prognosis for such intervention is related directly to the level of communication achieved. Recent technologic developments in computer-assisted communication devices have unleashed a great heretofore untapped human resource. The ability to overcome the many barriers to communication imposed by several disabilities has made possible the actualization of life potentials that were beyond our reach in the not-too-distant past.

Society has finally begun to escape the Platonic construct of a general intelligence and the notion that "humans can be placed along a continuum of some highly abstract characteristic that is indifferent to the context in which it is actualized" (Kagan 1986). The adage that not everyone is gifted but everyone has gifts is especially relevant to the developmentally disabled population. The difficulty has often been the communication barriers that prevented the identification and nurturing of these individual strengths. One of the earliest and most critical components of any evaluation and subsequent remediational plan for the developmentally disabled (beyond medical intervention), therefore, should be the assessment of the communication status and potential of each individual. Modern research has provided and continues to enhance our capability to effectively evaluate and treat communication disorders.

The purpose of this chapter is threefold: to emphasize the need for the early identification and treatment of communication disorders, especially in the developmentally disabled population; to provide guidelines for professionals outside the communication disorders field for identifying and treating communication disorders; and to provide a definitional level acquaintance for other specialists working with developmentally disabled individuals with the diagnostic and therapeutic tools in communication disorders.

The Need for Early Identification and Intervention

The evaluation of communication disorders in the developmentally disabled is not as simple as it may seem. Communication disorders may or may not be present as a consequence of the underlying cause of the major developmental impairment. It may be a separate entity and, therefore, may require a different remedial approach than if it were the byproduct of another problem. The presence of one developmental difficulty or, indeed, the presence of one communication disorder, does not immunize the individual against other, perhaps more subtle, communication problems. It is not unusual that middle and outer ear pathologic conditions in the profoundly hard-of-hearing or deaf population go undetected much longer than they would in the normal hearing population simply because they are overlooked in the face of the more obvious problems. It is critical that, in dealing with the primary presenting problem, those responsible for planning and implementing remediation programs do not overlook the possibility of other more occult conditions.

The presence of a severe language disorder does not preclude the development of an unrelated speech problem. The primacy of the auditory channel in the development of language demands attention to transient middle and outer ear pathologic conditions. There are also other conditions that often are precipitated because of communication disorders and that may mislead the clinician in the evaluation of the developmentally disabled. Cantwell and Baker (1987) have examined the relationship between several psychiatric disorders and developmental disorders that are a consequence of speech or language disorders. It is the exception rather than the rule when a speech or language disorder does not carry with it the potential for an emotional overlay.

In evaluating the communication status of each individual, therefore, one must consider several possibilities: Is the communication disorder a consequence or an associated problem of the primary underlying condition? In either case, does this make a difference in the habilitative strategies that are appropriate? Is there an adequate plan for ongoing assessment of the communication status of each individual to ensure that no problem develops that goes undetected during the remediation process for the more obvious problems? Are there problems that are secondary to the communication disorder that may develop that perhaps can be ameliorated by early awareness and intervention?

Functional Description of Communication Disorders

Several taxonomies have been proposed to categorize communication disorders. In general, the types of communication disorders that are potentially deleterious to the developmentally disabled population are the same as those that affect the population as a whole. Certain conditions that result in developmental disabilities usually have an accompanying communication disorder; however, even when there are no obvious syndromal clues, one should not rule out the possibility of communication disorders concomitant with a developmental disability, especially in the infant and toddler age group.

Communication disorders can be broken down into those that are primarily expressive and those that are primarily receptive. The emphasis should be on the word primarily because it is unusual for either a receptive or expressive disorder not in some way to involve the other.

Receptive Disorders

Receptive disorders, or hearing losses, are divided into three categories based on the particular anatomic structures that are affected: conductive, sensori-neural, and central hearing losses.

Conductive Hearing Loss

Conductive losses are caused by pathologic conditions of the outer or the middle ear that interferes with the "conduction" of sound from the external environment to the more central auditory mechanisms for decoding. Any condition, therefore, that interferes with the transmission of sound to and through the middle ear is called a conductive hearing loss. Common causes of conductive hearing loss are excessive cerumen (wax) in the outer ear canal; infections of the outer or middle ear (otitis externa and otitis media, respectively); rupture of the tympanic membrane (ear drum); eustachian tube malfunction; and dislocation of the bones of the middle ear (incuostapedial disarticulation). Whenever there is an orofacial anomaly, one should rule out the possibility of an abnormal conductive hearing mechanism. A common orofacial anomaly that manifests in conductive hearing loss is Treacher Collins syndrome. The extent of the involvement of the middle and outer ear structures is dependent on the gestational age of onset; however, there is usually some involvement.

The good thing about conductive hearing loss is that it is responsive to medical treatment. The disturbing feature is that, left untreated, conditions causing conductive hearing loss, such as otitis media, can lead to life-threatening secondary conditions including mastoiditis, cholesteatomas, meningitis, and encephalitis. Again, regular evaluation to rule out these conditions is critical. One cannot depend on obvious signs of distress in the presenting client. For example, the classic ear flapping or pulling that is often seen in infants with middle ear infections is an unreliable indicator. The intensity of and the reaction to pain caused by middle ear pathologic conditions vary across individuals; therefore, it is important to schedule periodic examinations, especially with very young and generally unresponsive children.

Sensori-neural Hearing Loss

Sensori-neural hearing losses are caused by pathologic conditions affecting the inner ear structure or the eighth cranial nerve (auditory nerve). Sensori-neural losses can be caused by many factors. The typical "at-risk" indicators for sensori-neural hearing loss in infants are listed later in this chapter.

Hearing loss is also associated with many birth defects and syndromes (Northern and Downs 1978). Most of these birth defects cause one or more of the at-risk indicators for sensori-neural hearing loss. Common problems that have associated hearing loss include achondroplasia (chondrodystrophia fetalis calcificans); Alport's syndrome (hereditary nephritis and nerve deafness); Apert's syndrome (acrocephalosyndactyly); cleidocranial dysostosis (cleidocranial dysplasia, osteodental dysplasia); Crouzon's syndrome (cranio-facial dysostosis); Down's syndrome; Hunter's-Hurler's syndrome; Klippel-Feil syndrome;

osteogenesis imperfecta (Van-Der Hoeve's disease); congenital rubella; Treacher Collins syndrome–mandibulofacial dysostosis (first arch syndrome); Waardenburg's syndrome. This list by no means includes all defects with accompanying hearing loss but gives an indication of why the potential for hearing loss should be considered in almost any birth defect–syndrome situation.

Central Hearing Loss

A third category includes hearing loss caused by central pathologic conditions. Any neuropathologic condition that involves the central projections of the auditory mechanism may cause a central auditory problem. According to most texts on this subject, sensori-neural losses include those of the cochlea and the eighth nerve until it enters the brain stem. Pathologic disturbances of the auditory pathways from the brain stem to the cortex are usually referred to as central auditory problems. A major research goal facing audiologists is the development of tools for assessing auditory processing capabilities. It is difficult to identify the site of a central auditory lesion and to detect auditory processing disorders in part because of the redundancy in the auditory system. The auditory system is composed of multiple linkages and redundant neuronal populations that mask subtle problems. The great strides that are being made toward decoding this system have contributed and will continue to contribute substantially to our understanding of cognitive and language capabilities.

Expressive Disorders

Expressive communication disorders are usually divided into speech disorders and language disorders. As indicated in another section of this chapter, language disorders are of more concern than speech disorders in the developing child. This is not to discount the devastating effect that a strictly peripheral speech disorder might have on any given individual; however, the development of language and cognitive capability is so intrinsically interwoven that our primary concern is with language. A discussion of some of the most common speech disorders follows.

One of the most common speech disorders is an articulation disorder. Articulation refers to the movements of the articulators (tongue, lower jaw, cheeks, soft palate) that, when moved, help to produce distinct speech sounds. An articulation disorder is characterized by errors in the production of a phoneme. Articulation errors are typically categorized into omissions, substitutions, or distortions of the correct phoneme. Although many articulation problems are simple functional disorders that may resolve with maturation, articulation disorders should be carefully evaluated because they may be manifestations of subtle underlying neurologic problems.

Voice problems are also considered speech disorders. Speech production that is difficult to understand or unpleasant in its sound may be caused by a voice disorder. The term aphonia refers to the complete loss of the voice whereas dysphonia describes an unpleasant voice quality. Voice disorders can be functional or organic and range from breathiness or hoarseness to malfunctions of the vocal mechanism caused by tumors, polyps, or cysts. Voice disorders can also be related to resonance problems. Children with cleft palate or other orofacial anomalies often present either hyper- or hyponasality.

Disorders of fluency, known also as stuttering–cluttering disorders, often are obvious speech disorders; however, the line between a normal dysfluency and a fluency disorder is difficult to discern. In fact, the long-standing categorization of speech as being within normal limits to the extent that it does not call undue attention to itself, may remain the best diagnostic criterion for any of the speech disorders. The specific cause of fluency disorders is still unresolved. Theories about the causes of fluency disorders include conditioning, neurotic, diagnosogenic, or dysphemic. Therapeutic approaches to stuttering are as varied as the proposed causes, and no single unifying hypothesis as to cause or best treatment has yet evolved.

Speech production follows language development and therefore may be considered subservient to it. The association of language and cognitive development makes language important in the developing child. Language encompasses complex rules that need not be understood by the individual but that govern the basic comprehension and production of our communication system. This ability to use language is often called linguistic competence. Bloom and Lahey (1978) suggest that language can be divided into three components: form, content, and use.

The form of language includes the linguistic elements that facilitate the association of sounds and symbols with their meaning. Also included are the rules that govern sounds and their combinations (phonology), rules that govern the internal organization of words (morphology), and rules that specify how words are ordered (syntax). The content of language refers to its meaning or the rules governing semantics. The mental dictionary of the receiver, his or her lexicon, and the meaning associated with that dictionary are encompassed in semantics. Finally, the use component of language is dictated by rules of pragmatics that relate to the intent of the communication event. For a complete discussion of the inter-relation among the form, content, and use of language the reader is referred to Bloom and Lahey's (1978) work Language Development and Language Disorders.

A cause-and-effect relationship exists between disorders of hearing and disorders of speech and language. Although Lenneberg (1967) warned us long ago about the "critical period" during which language learning *could* take place, it has been typical for professionals to wait until children reach 3 or 4 years of age to begin language intervention. According to deVilliers and deVilliers (1978), the change from bilateral neural representation of language at an early age to a unilateral representation later is the neural basis for the critical period of cognitive readiness. Although the research literature contains different opinions regarding the specific neural mechanisms underlying this critical period, there is little doubt that congenital hearing loss causes immediate and irreversible changes in the morphologic structure of the neural system (Webster 1983).

Communication Disorders and Developmental Disabilities

Hearing Loss

As indicated previously, there is often a close relationship between conditions that manifest themselves in developmental disabilities and hearing loss. For example, approximately 10% to 30% of individuals with cerebral palsy present with an accompanying hearing loss (Apgar and Beck 1972). Children with Down's syndrome present with both sensori-neural and conductive hearing loss; as many as 25% of these children may have sensori-neural hearing loss (Strome 1981; Wilson et al. 1983; Keiser et al. 1981). Approximately 10% of all children and adults in residential institutions for the mentally retarded were hearing impaired in a study by Healey and Karp-Kortman (1975).

The important point for individuals working with developmentally disabled individuals is the fact that the prevalence of hearing loss is even greater in this population than it is in the normal population. The potential lifelong impact of an undetected hearing loss for these individuals emphasizes the importance of instituting programs to rule out or identify these losses when possible. Young (1985) suggested guidelines for hearing screening in programs serving developmental disabilities as follows:

Suggested Guidelines for Hearing Screening in Programs Serving Developmental Disabilities (Young et al. 1978)

I. Anyone having developmental disabilities (DD), regardless of age, without documented hearing testing shall be considered highest priority for receiving screening services.

II. Annual hearing level and middle ear immittance screening shall be provided for:

A. Children falling in the age range during which frequent upper respiratory infections are common.

Among children having DD the age range will extend to age 10.

B. Individuals older than 10 who may have DD and, as well,

1. Persistent congestion,
2. Frequent episodes of upper respiratory infections,
3. Draining ears or
4. Allergic reactions involving the ears, nose and/or throat.

Annual screening shall continue until such conditions are no longer chronic and/or are being managed medically.

C. Persons considered high risk for hearing loss, specifically those with:

1. Cleft palate,
2. Down's syndrome
3. Orofacial deformity or
4. Familial history of hearing loss.

III. After the age of 10 and 2 consecutive years of having hearing status documented as within normal limits without evidence of middle ear pathology, an individual with DD shall have . . .

A. Middle ear immittance screening annually, and
B. hearing status screening every 3 years.

IV. Individuals being considered for a change in placement (educational or vocational) shall be scheduled for a hearing screening, preferably prior to the change in placement or within 3 months of being in the new placement.

V. Individuals exhibiting regression in development and/or behavioral problems not previously characteristic for the person shall be referred for hearing screening as soon as possible.

VI. Otolaryngologic exam shall be an integral part of "hearing screening" for individuals having DD

A. Who are untestable in their community placement setting for either:

1. Hearing levels or
2. Middle ear immittance measurements; or

B. Who yield screening data (from on-site screening in the community) indicating the need for medical examination.

Several states have instituted mandatory hearing screening programs for infants in neonatal intensive care units or in the normal neonatal nurseries in all hospitals. States typically use an "at-risk" register to screen children initially and, upon failure, refer them for more definitive testing. Although there are some variations from state to state, most of the at-risk checklists contain the following items (McCormick 1988):

1. Family history of childhood hearing impairment

2. Congenital perinatal infection (rubella, cytomegalovirus, herpes)

3. Orofacial anomalies

4. Birth weight less than 1500 g

5. Hyperbilirubinemia at levels exceeding indications for exchange transfusion

6. Bacterial meningitis

7. Severe asphyxia—failure to institute spontaneous respiration by 10 min

8. Hypotonia to 2 hours of age

There are several advantages to screening all infants in the neonatal nursery. When there are obvious symptoms that put a newborn "at risk" for hearing loss, hearing screening will be done before the child is discharged from the hospital. However, when hearing loss is the only problem it may go undetected for months or even years. The effects of even mild to moderate hearing losses on normal language development can be significant. In addition, hearing loss may be only one manifestation of other problems, and its identification may alert the pediatric team to other problems. Recent advances in the technology available to the diagnostician have greatly improved our ability to confirm or rule out the presence of a hearing loss at an early age. This is especially advantageous when testing a child who is difficult to assess using standard measures. The following is a brief overview of the behavioral and electrophysiologic measures available for evaluating the auditory mechanism.

Behavioral Assessment

In addition to the high-risk factors that can alert one to a possible hearing loss, simple observation of reflexive movement (startle, auropalpebral, or orientation) or the lack thereof, to sound produced by devices that emit a sound spectrum of known intensity and frequency may be used to screen a child's hearing sensitivity (Parving 1985). Observing a child's play behavior with his parents may augment the information from the case history. The child's orientation to toys that produce sound, for example, may be an indicator of the presence of hearing. Calibrated sound generators of known frequency and intensity may be used in the neonatal nursery to elicit the reflexive responses mentioned above.

Behavioral Observation Audiometry

More accurate information regarding the child's hearing sensitivity may be obtained through behavioral techniques. Many tests that have been used for the easier-to-test population of infants have been adapted for the more-difficult-to-test child. Behavioral observation audiometry (BOA) relies on the observation of overt behavioral responses to acoustic stimuli. This procedure is often used when developmental age or handicapping conditions preclude the use of conditioned responses.

An important consideration when using BOA with difficult-to-test children is that the presence of handicapping conditions may limit the responsiveness and range of behaviors that can be observed in the child. Northern and Downs (1978) have developed norms for BOA that correlate closely with developmental age (Men-

cher and Gerber 1983). One shortcoming of BOA has traditionally been the effect of observer bias on the interpretation of the results. Gans did a number of studies using BOA in which scoring was evaluated systematically using a videorecorder. This procedure improved significantly the efficacy and validity of the procedure, especially with low-functioning children (Gans 1987).

Visual Reinforcement Audiometry

Visual reinforcement audiology (VRA) uses operant conditioning in which a behavioral response (usually a head turn) to frequency-specific sounds is reinforced with a visual reward. VRA is a reliable and accurate procedure for assessing auditory sensitivity in children as young as 6 months (Talbott 1987). In addition to ear-specific frequency thresholds, speech sounds can also be discriminated using VRA techniques (Thompson and Thompson 1972).

Another operant procedure allows children to respond to sounds by selecting between two responses, one resulting in the presentation of an audible reinforcer (pure tones and speech at various frequencies) and the other option offering no reinforcer. The procedure is valuable with children who do not respond well to visual reinforcers or who have limited motor movements (Silvia et al. 1978). An adaptation of VRA has been developed by Lancioni and colleagues (1989) whereby a classical conditioning procedure for the multiply handicapped was devised using an air puff as the unconditioned stimulus. Results indicated greater success in obtaining threshold data comparable to those obtained with VRA.

Tangible Reinforcement Operant Conditioning

Tangible reinforcement operant conditioning audiology (TROCA) is another approach to behavioral assessment of the difficult-to-test child. TROCA procedures, however, usually rely on button- or lever-pushing responses and therefore are only practical where a highly structured test condition is possible (Mencher and Gerber 1983). Play audiometry also may be used to obtain pure tone thresholds or speech reception information in the sound field or under earphones. Studies using this technique with brain-injured and retarded children have proved successful once a clear understanding of the task was established (Jerger 1984). The point of this study was that, given sufficient time and effort, behavioral information regarding the sensitivity and acuity of the child's hearing could be obtained.

Another approach to conditioning in behavioral assessment has been to combine sound with visual and vibrotactile stimuli. The added stimulus is faded out prior to conducting a threshold search; this approach is effective with visually impaired children and those suspected of having a profound hearing impairment.

Learning effect is an important contributor to any of the behavioral tests, and the need for testing on multiple days is often needed. Despite the sophistication of modern technology, the behavioral confirmation of the presence of usable hearing is a critical phase in the habilitation strategy for any individual child. The state of the art in physiology is not such that we can apply "Spocklike" (of space, not baby, fame) assessment of the child's system and obtain a definitive diagnosis. These new technologies, however, have greatly increased our diagnostic capabilities, especially in the very young or otherwise difficult-to-test individuals.

Physiologic and Electrophysiologic Assessment

Physiologic techniques offer an objective means of assessing the integrity of the auditory system from the periphery to the central auditory processing areas of the brain. Immittance and auditory evoked potential measurements have become standard clinical tools. The clinical applications of brain-mapping techniques, positron emission tomography (PET) scanning, nuclear magnetic resonance (NMR) imaging, and otoacoustic emission (OAM) show promise of becoming the "standard" procedures of the future. Not only are these fascinating new clinical tools enticing because of their diagnostic potential but they offer new insights into the basic mechanisms underlying communication and the basic cognitive processes. The following is a brief discussion of the principle underlying each of these measures and its clinical application.

Immittance Audiometry

One of the most beneficial applications of new technology to auditory diagnosis in the past 20 years has been the initial discovery and subsequent improvement in immittance audiometry. The physics of the measurement techniques and the engineering of the equipment involved are complicated; however, the basic principle is easy to understand. Simply stated, if one introduces a sound into the ear through the external auditory canal, the ear reflects a certain amount of the energy of that sound back out. Any time one attempts to cause the flow of energy from one medium to another there is some resistance to this transfer. In acoustic terms, the opposition to the movement of sound from one medium to another is called impedance. If one were to look at the amount of sound that was transferred rather than that which was rejected it would be called admittance. The combination of impedance and admittance is referred to as immittance—thus, the name for the testing equipment and the procedure—immittance audiometry.

This test is especially useful because the amount of sound energy that is reflected back from the tympanic membrane (ear drum) changes depending on the pathologic condition of the middle ear. A tympanogram is a plot of the energy being reflected as a function of variations in air pressure exerted in the ear by the measurement system. The "picture" generated by the energy reflected differs as a consequence of the state of the tympanic membrane, the condition of the ossicular chair (bones of the middle ear), the presence of fluid in the ear, the eustachian tube functioning, and others (Keith 1975).

This signature allows the audiologist to recognize the presence of hearing problems at the most peripheral level and, within certain limits, to have a good idea of what is causing the problem. These measurements can be made easily and quickly with modern equipment. A tympanogram may be obtained from the ear of even a restless, uncooperative child in as little as 5 seconds. In addition to giving a picture of the status of the middle ear, the ability to measure the effects of the middle ear muscle reflex permits assessment of the integrity of certain neural connections at a low brain-stem level.

The acoustic reflex is elicited by presenting a relatively intense sound to the ear. Under normal circumstances this stimulates the auditory nerve, which in turn stimulates the nerves going to the small muscles in the middle ear and causes them to contract. The contraction of these muscles alters the immittance of the middle ear and, therefore, can be detected by devices that measure immittance. This aspect of the test takes only a few more seconds of testing and provides additional information about the functioning of the auditory mechanism (McCandless and Allred 1978; Mencher and Gerber 1983). A study by Schwartz and Schwartz (1978) of infants 1 to 7 months of age showed that acoustic reflexes were absent in all 20 ears confirmed to have middle ear effusions. They suggested that a normal acoustic reflex response indicates normal middle ear function.

Acoustic reflex thresholds also may be used in predicting hearing sensitivity. Sensitivity prediction from the acoustic reflex (SPAR) correlates well with hearing sensitivity but not so well with audiometric slope (Hall and Bleakney 1981). In addition, most studies examining SPAR techniques have found predictions for normal hearing to be good whereas predictions of hearing loss are less accurate, especially for moderate hearing losses (Jerger and Hayes 1978). Results from specific applications to mentally retarded populations have been consistent with those obtained in the normal population (Niswander and Ruth 1977; Poole et al. 1982).

Auditory Brain-Stem Response

Computer technology combined with electroencephalographic (EEG) measurements has facilitated the development of auditory brain-stem response (ABR) measurements. This technique has proved useful with difficult-to-test children, including premature and multiply handicapped infants. The fact that ABR can be administered while the subject is asleep and that it is not affected by most sedatives (Jacobson 1985) gives it an advantage over most other techniques.

The technique involved is similar to that used in regular EEG measurement, in that electrodes are placed on the head, and the electronic equipment is configured to pick up the electrical voltage from the scalp. ABR measurement is called evoked potential measurement because the intent is to "evoke" the electrical activity of the brain that is caused by a specific sensory system (in this case the auditory system; however, visual and somatosensory responses also can be measured). The difficulty is that the activity of the brain that is caused by the presence of an auditory stimulus is extremely small compared with the ongoing electrical activity of the brain. This then requires the use of computer analysis and enhancement to cull out that electrical activity that is due to the auditory system from the background activity.

The use of computer technology and refinements in these electrophysiologic techniques permit the averaging to zero (or close to it) of the overall electrical activity of the brain, while at the same time evoking the activity that is attributable to the auditory system. Except for the minor discomfort of having electrodes (usually only three) placed on the head and ear phones on the ears, this is a noninvasive procedure for both screening and more in depth assessment of the auditory mechanism. ABR, currently one of the most popular screening methods of high-risk newborns, has a high degree of sensitivity, specificity, and cost effectiveness. It is important to remember, however, that ABR gives only a picture of the neural system's response, or lack thereof, to auditory stimuli. The speed of transmission (latency), the wave form structure, and the amplitude of the electrical response are all indicators of the way the neural system is responding to auditory input; however, ABR tests neural synchrony, not hearing threshold (Kileny and Magathan 1987; Cornacchia et al. 1982). ABR responses do not, unfortunately, reveal anything about the ability of the individual to use the information that is being conducted along the auditory pathways to the cortex.

Another variation of the brain-stem measurement technique is the measurement of the 40-Hz response. This method shows promise for determining the thresholds of the individual being tested; however, it is difficult to use because it is dependent on the state of the child. If the child can be kept quiet without sedation, the test may reveal significant information. With young infants, because of the lack of neural maturation, one can only estimate hearing sensitivity if the wave form is present; however, no conclusions can be reached if the wave form is absent (Fifer and Sierra-Irizarry 1988).

The use of neurophysiologic measures to evaluate special populations dates back to the 1960s when Rapin and colleagues were among the first to use the late evoked potentials to study auditory behavior in infants and young children with severe neurologic impairment (Rapin and Graziani 1967; Rapin et al. 1969). Specific disorders such as Down's syndrome have been extensively studied. As indicated before there seems to be an increased incidence of hearing loss in this population as well as of other neurologic differences (Brooks et al. 1972; Igarashi et al. 1971; Crome et al. 1966; Banik et al. 1975). In one study of 16 men with Down's syndrome, 15 men with retardation of unknown etiology, and 15 nonretarded men as control subjects, Squires et al. (1980) found support for the higher incidence of hearing loss among retarded populations. ABR studies to date show significantly shorter latencies, smaller amplitudes, and reduced interwave intervals in individuals with Down's syndrome (Stein and Kraus 1985).

Brain-stem electrophysiologic data contribute to our basic understanding of the role of the brainstem and higher cortical centers in other disorders as well. The suspected cause for infantile autism, for example, has shifted from an environmental to a neurophysiologic approach, even though the specific neurophysiologic basis of the disorder is yet to be fully understood. Schomer and Student (1978) were among the first to investigate the ABR response in infants and children with different psychopathologic abnormalities. They concluded that the abnormal behavior seen in their study group was caused by organic brain anomalies. Significantly longer ABR latencies, central conduction time, response variance, and other deviations from the normal responses have all been observed in studies of autistic children.

The development of ABR and associated electrophysiologic techniques has not only vastly increased our clinical assessment capabilities, especially for the very young and otherwise difficult to test; it is also providing another window to the neural mechanisms underlying many different conditions. Detection of auditory problems in children with autism and Down's syndrome is just one of the many problems associated with developmental disabilities that are being studied using ABR.

New Techniques

Immittance and ABR measurements have been used long enough to be considered everyday clinical tools for detecting auditory problems. Several other techniques described below have not been applied as extensively and yet show promise, from both a diagnostic and a research perspective. It is beyond the scope of this chapter to review completely all the new available techniques; however, the unique perspective that several of these measures provide deserves mention.

Positron Emission Tomography. Many neurophysiologic techniques do not provide a real-time analysis of the brain's activity. PET scanning permits a real-time look at the activity of the neural system while the subject engages in a specific task. A radioisotopically tagged substance containing glucose is injected into the subject's vascular system. During increased neural activity there is a large increase in glucose metabolism that can be observed using radiographic techniques designed to pick up the isotope. Subjects are instructed to engage in a number of cognitive tasks, and the specific part of the brain that is responsible can be observed because of the increased activity in that area. The obvious drawback is that, because this is *not* a noninvasive technique, there are limitations to its use.

Magnetic Resonance Imaging. Nuclear magnetic resonance (NMR) imaging techniques provide vastly improved images of the structures not only of the brain but of other soft tissue as well. The technique is actually a refinement of the spectrum prism studies first described by Newton.

The measurement takes advantage of electromagnetic radiation as first explained by James Clarke Maxwell. He noted that atomic nuclei possess a property known as spin and that associated with this spin is a magnetic property along the axis of rotation. If a magnetic field is applied to a sample having such nuclei, then the magnetic fields may align along the field like a compass. The atomic nuclei possessing spin obey the laws of quantum mechanics and have one of two orientations with respect to an applied field. Transitions between these states can be induced by applying an oscillating magnetic field.

This means that different chemical elements exhibiting this spin characteristic (not all elements do) give rise to signals of different frequencies. Tomogram techniques give us "slice" pictures of the body by combining Fourier transformations with computer matrix three-dimensional storage capacity, thereby producing NMR tomograms. These "pictures" are very lifelike, and structures can be recognized by even the untrained eye, which is not often the case with standard x-ray shadowgrams. The convolutions of the brain can be unfolded in vivo to permit a quantitative observation of asymmetries and areas of involvement for a given lesion (Jouandet et al. 1989). The NMR tomogram is an excellent tool for examining developmental disabilities that may manifest morphologic neural alterations.

One drawback with this measurement is that the patient or subject must be very still during the measurement. Almost any movement compromises the resultant "picture," therefore, such measurements are difficult to get with children.

Brain Mapping. Another recent breakthrough in neurophysiologic measurement is the so-called brain-mapping techniques. Again the major contributor to this new technology has been the computer. Brain mapping allows the cartooning of the electrical activity of the brain over time by transforming the electrical voltages generated at various positions on the head into colors representing either the frequency, time, or intensity domain of the electrical activity. Either evoked potential or ongoing EEG activity can be "mapped" by this technique.

A unique feature of this procedure is that the computer can store normative electrical data from many different individuals and then analyze and generate a statistical probability map emphasizing the differences in the activity of any individual brain's activity compared with the "normal" group. In the early 1980s, Duffy was the first researcher to make the techniques clinically available for general distribution. Since then, the diagnostic potential of applying this technology to special populations has been promising. Although mapping is still an experimental tool, interesting data have been generated in patients with such varied conditions as spasmodic dysphonia (Finitzo et al. 1987), dyslexia (Duffy et al. 1980), dementia (Duffy et al. 1984) and other defined brain lesions.

Intervention Strategies

As indicated previously, the major rationale for early identification is the importance of early intervention. The improved clinical tools and increased knowledge base for intervention has resulted in new emphasis on early identification programs. Technology has contributed to habilitation efforts for the developmentally disabled in the areas of auditory amplification and other augmentative communication devices. The importance of the auditory channel and the need to maximize the use of residual hearing in the deaf and hard of hearing have been accepted by most researchers. Rose (1983) suggested that hearing is basic to emotional, intellectual, and social development during infancy and that providing even a limited amount of sound to the hearing-impaired infant may minimize the possible deleterious effects of the hearing loss. For developmentally disabled children with hearing loss, early hearing-aid fitting is critical.

Early Fitting of Hearing Aids

There are five steps to consider when fitting the young child with hearing aids (Matkin 1986): otologic management; audiologic evaluation; selection of hearing aids; assessment of aided performance; and hearing aid monitoring. The essential first step in the process is medical management. Conductive hearing losses or other losses that can be treated medically should be treated before the individual is assessed for prosthetic intervention. Children who do not present with medically significant ear problems at an early age should be monitored for the development of problems later. Once no further medical treatment is needed, an assessment of the need for auditory amplification should follow.

Audiologic evaluation of the hearing mechanism should be done in conjunction with the otologic evaluation and treatment. Coordination between the medical and audiologic management of the individual is essential. The child should be evaluated and fit for appropriate hearing aids during medical intervention unless there is some well-documented medical reason not to do so.

It is beyond the scope of this chapter to discuss the evaluation techniques available for fitting the very young child with a hearing aid. It is important, however, for those working with the developmentally disabled to be aware that assessment for possible amplification should be started as soon as the hearing loss is identified. The audiologist can use probe tube microphone technology to measure the sound pressure levels generated in the external ear canal of very young children. This technique facilitates confirmation of the target amplification values and serves as a check that not too much amplification is delivered to the child's ear.

In addition, brain-stem and acoustic reflex measurements can be used to evaluate the potential benefits of amplification in children (Hall and Ruth 1985). These measurement techniques are not without some drawbacks when applied to hearing aid fitting; however, they do provide an objective tool for assessing the difficult-to-test child. It is also possible to surgically implant hearing aids in those children whose hearing loss is of such an extent that standard amplification procedures are not feasible.

Cochlear Implants

Cochlear implants involve the surgical implantation of an electrode array into the cochlea. These devices are designed to stimulate the cochlea electrically through either a single or a multiple electrode configuration. The early pioneering work by House and colleagues in California led to its approval by the FDA for use in deaf children across the country (House and Berliner 1984). It is based on the principle that the ear cannot be stimulated directly with sound, so the sound is converted into an electrical signal by an external transducer and then linked transcutaneously or percutaneously to an internal receiver that generates an electric impulse that stimulates the auditory nerve. The transcutaneous approach uses an electromagnet placed on the outside of the skin to generate electromagnet signals that travel through the skin and are picked up by the implanted receiver. Percutaneous linking on the other hand involves the direct coupling between the transmitter and the receiver, usually by an implanted hard-wire plug and socket system.

The cochlear implant system is the method of choice only when an individual shows no potential for success with conventional amplification. Electrical stimulation does not generate the same perception as acoustic stimulation. In addition, a major predictor for successful outcome with the cochlear implant is the quality of the auditory rehabilitation program that accompanies the physical implant. A tremendous amount of learning and auditory training must accompany use of the implant.

Augmentative Communication Devices

In addition to the typical hearing aid, the use of other augmentative communication devices has increased tremendously in the recent past. Advances in computer technology have contributed significantly to their development, however, augmentative communication is actually anything that is used as a supplement to verbal communication. The appropriateness of an augmentative communication device for a given individual depends on several factors: the extent of the disability and the effect of the disability on communication; the cognitive age of the individual; the initial cost of the device and its useful longevity; and the environment in which the device is to be used. The study of augmentative communication involves the following (Blackstone 1986):

1. Examination of various disabling conditions (cerebral palsy, mental retardation, amyotrophic lateral sclerosis, etc.) and their impact on an individual's ability to use primary communication techniques, such as speech and writing;
2. Development of specific strategies to facilitate the use of speech (that is, speech approximation, electrolarynx);
3. Development of specific techniques and strategies to facilitate the use of standard augmentative modes (gesture, pointing, etc.);
4. Study and development of special augmentative communication components, such as signing, communication boards, etc.;
5. Study of the impact of using special augmentative communication components;
6. Development of strategies for reducing the negative impact of using augmentative components;

7. Development of evaluation procedures to determine unmet needs and the most effective augmentative strategies for individuals having a wide range of physical, perceptual, and cognitive disabilities (varying in both type and degree);

8. Development of strategies for more effective use of augmentative communication components; and

9. Development of appropriate teaching materials and training procedures for mastery of these techniques.

Augmentative communication ranges from the simple use of gestures in the "normal" population to the use of computer-based communication boards for those with severe communication impairments. To help individuals with severe communication problems, the American Speech-Language-Hearing Association formed an ad hoc Committee on the Communication Processes of Nonspeaking Persons in 1978. This committee's work marked the beginnings of a newly developing field. In 1980 and 1981, conferences were held in Ontario, Canada that addressed augmentative and alternative communication topics.

Following this conference, the International Society for Augmentative and Alternative Communication (ISAAC) was formed in 1983. Through the efforts of these organizations several books and an ISAAC-sponsored journal *(Augmentative and Alternative Communication)* have been published. An international exchange organization called the International Project for Communication Aids for the Speech Impaired (IPCAS) includes Sweden, the United Kingdom, Canada, and the United States. A clear conclusion from all the work done thus far in this area is the need for a team approach to the management of augmentative communication programs. The expertise needed to develop the most appropriate augmentative communication strategy for any individual includes at a minimum input from the following fields: communication disorders; medicine; phys-

ical therapy; occupational therapy; engineering; computer technology; education; psychology; social services; vocational counseling. In addition, consultative services may be required of audiology, ophthalmology, orthopedics, neurology, rehabilitation nursing, and prosthetics to mention a few. For a complete overview of the history, evaluation techniques, and therapeutic strategies, the reader is referred to Augmentative Communication: An Introduction (Blackstone 1986).

Speech and Language Intervention

A critical controlling variable in developing communication skills in the very young child is the amount and kind of interpersonal interaction with parents and/or care givers, especially for those children with developmental disabilities. Several studies have shown that general developmental skill learning, including communication, is based on appropriate social interaction between the child and adult (Snow 1984; Marfo 1988). The intent to communicate is marked by the child's deliberate attention to an adult partner (Bates et al. 1979).

Because of the importance of this interaction in the development of communication skills, the professional working with the developmentally disabled must enhance this social and environmental interaction. The behavior of an interactive adult is critical to the facilitation of the child's initial communication abilities. The crucial feature is that the child's communicative attempts are recognized and that appropriate responses are made. As Snow (1981) points out, it is essential that the child understand the notion of signal. This understanding is the first step in developing the ability to communicate. Recent studies have shown that there is a tendency for some adults to be poor judges of communication attempts on the part of the child. In addition, adults who do identify such behavior are minimally facilitative if they do not also provide appropriate responses to the child's behavior (Wilcox et al. 1990). On the basis of these observations, Wilcox recommends a "partner information/education session(s) with a focus on facilitating a common definition of communication across a child's primary communication partners." This type of education seems especially critical when considering the gamut of developmental disabilities. The outward manifestation of the communication attempts of children with various presenting problems may vary substantially. It is important, therefore, that individuals charged with the overall coordination of programs for the developmentally disabled ensure appropriate professional assessment and guidance in the communication disorders area. For a detailed discussion of available intervention strategies, the reader is referred to Bloom and Lahey (1978), McLean & McLean (1974), and McLean (1983). In addition, an excellent discussion of language acquisition in general can be found in First Language Acquisition (Ingram 1989).

Summary

At the beginning of this chapter, we suggested that the acquisition of a communication base was a sine qua non for any other habilitative strategy for the developmentally disabled. Fortunately, our knowledge base and the complementary technology have increased tremendously over the past two decades. Computer technology has provided a window to the world for many individuals for whom interpersonal exchange was virtually impossible in the not-too-distant past.

From a holistic viewpoint, the importance of early assessment and intervention in the communication status of all developmentally disabled individuals cannot be overstated. The professional background of the "team leader" will vary as a function of the particular administrative model that

is brought to bear on behalf of these individuals. Regardless of the model, it is imperative that those charged with the overall management of the habilitative team be acutely aware of the need to obtain a communication assessment and intervention plan as soon as medical stability is established. A coordinated effort across all individuals who may be involved is essential to ensure homogeneity of effort. In addition, staff training with the various approaches that may be indicated in any given case often is as important as the direct therapy. As with almost every recommendation that has been made concerning the appropriate intervention on behalf of the developmentally disabled individual, the need for a coordinated, cooperative, and communicative interdisciplinary approach is an obvious conclusion.

References

1. Apgar V, Beck J. Is My Baby All Right? A Guide to Birth Defects. New York, Trident Press, 1972, pp 144–189.
2. Banik NL, Davidson AN, Palo J, Savolainen H. Biochemical studies of myelin isolated from the brains of patients with Down's syndrome. Brain. 98:213–218, 1975.
3. Bates E, Camaroni L, Volterra V. The acquisition of preformatives prior to speech. In: Ochs E, Scheffelin B. eds. Developmental Pragmatics. New York, Academic Press, 1979, pp 111–128.
4. Blackstone SW. ed. Augmentative Communication: An Introduction. Rockville, MD, ASHA, 1986.
5. Bloom L, Lahey M. eds. Language Development and Language Disorders. New York, Macmillan, 1978.
6. Brooks DN, Wooley H, Kanjilal GC. Hearing loss and middle ear disorders in patients with Down's syndrome (Mongolism). Journal of Mental Deficiency Research. 16:21–29, 1972.
7. Cantwell D, Baker L. Factors associated with the development of psychiatric illness in children with early speech/language problems. J Autism Dev Disord. 17:499–510, 1987.
8. Cornacchia L, Viglianii E, Arpini A. Comparison between brainstem evoked response and audiometry and behavioral audiometry in 270 infants and children. Audiology. 21:359–363, 1982.
9. Crome L, Cowie W, Slater E. A statistical note on cerebellar and brainstem weight in Mongolism.

Journal of Mental Deficiency Research. 10:69–72, 1966.

10. Duffy F, Albert M, McAnulty G. Brain electrical activity in patients with presenile & senile dementia of the Alzheimer's type. Ann Neurol. 16:439–448, 1984.

11. Duffy F, Denckla M, Bartels P, Sandni G. Dyslexia: Regional differences in brain electrical activity by topographic mapping. Ann Neurol. 7:412–420, 1980.

12. deVilliers JG, deVilliers PA. Language Acquisition. Cambridge, MA, Harvard University Press, 1978.

13. Fifer R, Sierra-Irizarry B. Clinical applications of the auditory middle latency response. Am J Otol. 9(suppl):47–56, 1988.

14. Finitzo T, Freeman F, Chapman S, Watson, B. Windows on the CNS in vocal controlled disorders. ASHA. 19:21–25, 1987.

15. Gans DP. Improving behavior observation audiometry testing and scoring procedures. Ear Hear. 9:92–99, 1987.

16. Hall J, Bleakney M. Hearing loss prediction by the acoustic reflex: Comparison of seven methods. Ear Hear. 2:156, 1981.

17. Hall J, Ruth R. Acoustic reflexes and auditory evoked responses in hearing aid evaluations. Seminars in Hearing. 6:251–277, 1985.

18. Healey WC, Karp-Nortman DC. The hearing-impaired mentally retarded: Recommendations for action. Rockville, MD, American Speech-Language-Hearing Association, 1975.

19. House WF, Berliner KI. Indications for and results of cochlear implants for total binomal deafness. Am J Otol. 5:520–523, 1984.

20. Igarashi M, Tokahashi M, Alford BR, Johnson PE. Inner ear morphology in Down's syndrome. Acta Otolaryngologia. 83:175–181, 1971.

21. Ingram D. First Language Acquisition: Method, Description and Explanation. New York, Cambridge Press, 1989.

22. Jacobson JT. ed. The Auditory Brainstem Response. San Diego, College Hill Press, 1985.

23. Jerger JF. ed. Pediatric Audiology. San Diego, College Hill Press, 1984.

24. Jerger JF, Hayes D. The cross-check principle in pediatric audiometry. Archives of Otolaryngology. 104:456–461, 1978.

25. Jouandet M, Tramo M, Herron D, Hermann A, Loftus W, Brazell J. Brainprints: Computer generated two dimensional maps of the human cerebral cortex in vivo. Journal of Cognitive Neuroscience. 1:88–117, 1989.

26. Kagan J. Cognitive development and strategies of assessment in young children. In: Kavanagh J. ed. Otitis Medicine and Child Development. Parkton, MD, York Press, 1986.

27. Keith RW. Middle ear function in neonates. Arch Otolaryngol. 101:376–379, 1975.

28. Keiser H, Montague D, Wold D, Maune S, Pattison D. Hearing loss of Down syndrome adults. Am J Ment Defic. 85:467–472, 1981.

29. Kileny PR, Magathan MG. Predictive value of ABR in infants and children with moderate to profound hearing impairment. Ear Hear. 8:217–220, 1987.

30. Lancioni GE, Coninx F, Smeets PM. A classical conditioning procedure for the hearing assessment of multiply handicapped persons. J Speech Hear Disord. 54:88–93, 1989.

31. Lenneberg EH. Biologic Foundations of Language. New York, Wiley Press, 1967.

32. Marfo K. ed. Parent-Child Interaction and Developmental Disabilities: Theory, Research, and Interaction. New York, Praeger, 1988.

33. Matkin N. Hearing Aids for Children in Hearing Aid Assessment and Use in Audiologic Habilitation. 3rd ed. Hodgson W, ed. Baltimore, Williams & Wilkins, 1986, p 172.

34. McCandless GA, Allred PL. Tympanometry and emergence of the acoustic reflex in infants. In: Harford ER, Bess FH, Bluestone CD, et al. eds. Impedance Screening for Middle Ear Disease in Children. New York, Grune and Stratton, 1978, pp 56–67.

35. McCormick B. ed. Pediatric Audiology. Philadelphia, Taylor and Francis, 1988.

36. McLean JE. Historical perspectives on the content of child language programs. In: Miller J, Yoder D, Schiefelbusch R. eds. Contemporary Issues in Language Intervention. Rockville, MD, American Speech-Language-Hearing Association, 1983.

37. McLean LP, McLean JE. A language training program for non-verbal autistic children. J Speech Hear Disord. 39:186–193, 1974.

38. Mencher GT, Gerber, SE. eds. The Multiply Handicapped Hearing Impaired Child. New York, Grune and Stratton, 1983.

39. Niswander PS, Ruth RA. Prediction of hearing sensitivity from acoustic reflexes in mentally retarded persons. American Journal of Mental Deficiency. 81:474–481, 1977.

40. Northern J, Downs M, eds. Hearing in Children. 2nd ed. Baltimore, Williams & Wilkins, 1978.

41. Parving A. Hearing disorders in children: Some procedures for detection, identification, and diagnostic evaluation. Int J Pediatr Otorhinolaryngol. 9:31–59, 1985.

42. Poole PB, Sheeley EC, Hannah JE. Predicting hearing sensitivity and audiometric slope for mentally retarded persons. Ear Hear. 3:77–82, 1982.

43. Powers MD, Handleman JS. Behavioral Assessment of Severe Developmental Disabilities. Rockville, MD, Aspen, 1984.

44. Rapin I, Graziani LJ. Auditory evoked responses in normal, brain damaged, cued deaf infants. Neurology. 17:881–894, 1967.

45. Rapin I, Graziani LJ, Lyttle M. Summated auditory evoked responses for audiometry: Experience in SI children with congenital rubella. International Audiology. 8:371–376, 1969.

46. Rose D. The fundamental role of hearing in psychological development. Hearing Instruments. 34:22, 24–26, 1983.

47. Schwartz DM, Schwartz RH. A comparison of tympanometry and acoustic reflex measurements for detecting middle ear effusion in infants below seven months of age. In: Harford ER, Bess FH, Bluestone CD, et al. eds. Impedance Screening for Middle Ear Disease in Children. New York, Grune and Stratton, 1978, pp 91–96.

48. Schwartz DM, Schwartz RH. Validity of acoustic reflectometry in detecting middle ear effusion. Journal of Pediatrics. 79:739–742, 1987.

49. Silvia DA, Friedlander BZ, Knight MS. Multi-handicapped children's preferences for pure tones and speech stimuli as a method of assessing auditory capabilities. American Journal of Mental Deficiency. 83:29–36, 1978.

50. Snell MD, Renzaglia AM. Moderate, severe, and profound handicaps. In: Haring NG. ed. Exceptional Children and Youth. 3rd ed. Columbus, Oh. Charles Merrill, 1982, pp 143–172.

51. Snow C. Social interaction and language acquisition. In: Pale P, Ingram D. eds. Child Language: An International Perspective. Baltimore, University Park Press, 1981, pp 195–214.

52. Snow C. Parent-child interaction and the development of communicative ability. In: Schiefelbusch R, Pickar J. eds. The Acquisition of Communicative Competence. Baltimore, University Park Press, 1984, pp 69–107.

53. Sohmer H, Student M. Auditory nerve and brainstem evoked responses in normal, autistic, minimal brain dysfunction and psychomotor retarded children. Electroencephalogr Clin Neurophysiol. 44:380–388, 1978.

54. Squires N, Aine C, Buchwald J, Norman R, Galbraith G. Auditory brain-stem response abnormality in severely and profoundly retarded adults. Electroencephalogr Clin Neurophysiol. 50:172–185, 1980.

55. Stein L, Kraus N. Auditory brainstem response measures with multiply handicapped children and adults. In: Jacobson J. ed. The Auditory Brainstem Response. San Diego, College Hill Press, 1985, pp 337–348.

56. Strome M. Down's syndrome: A modern otorhinolaryngological perspective. Laryngoscope. 91:1581–1594, 1981.

57. Talbott CB. A longitudinal study comparing responses of hearing-impaired infants to pure tones using VRA and play audiometry. Ear Hear. 8:175–181, 1987.

58. Thompson M, Thompson G. Responses of infants and young children as a function of auditory stimuli and test methods. J Speech Hear Res. 15:699–707, 1972.

59. Webster DB. A critical period during postnatal auditory development of mice. Int J Pediatr Otorhinolaryngology. 6:107–118, 1983.

60. Wilcox MJ, Kouri T, Caswell S. Partner sensitivity to communication behavior of young children with developmental disabilities. J Speech Hear Disord. 554:679–693, 1990.

61. Wilson WR, Folson RC, Widen JE. Hearing impairment in Down's syndrome children. In: Mencher GT, Gerber SE. eds. The Multiply Handicapped Hearing Impaired Child. New York, Grune and Stratton, 1983, pp 259–299.

62. Young C. Developmental disabilities. In: Katz J. ed. Handbook of Clinical Audiology. 3rd ed. Baltimore, Williams and Wilkins, 1985, pp 189–206.

Chapter 8
Deaf–Blind Handicapping Conditions

JoAnn M. Marchant

Federal legislation and regulations continue to refer to "deaf–blind" individuals, but current best practice in the field of special education dictates that such individuals be viewed as having "dual sensory impairments" or "multiple sensory impairments." These terms are more accurate because the label "deaf–blind" has usually included not only students who are deaf and blind, but also those who are visually and auditorially impaired.

It has always been difficult to determine the actual number of students in the United States with both vision and hearing impairments. Reporting systems vary from state to state and such students may be labelled as "deaf–blind," "multihandicapped," "severely/profoundly handicapped," or "blind" or "deaf." A national registry of students with multiple sensory handicaps has been established, but concern exists at the state and national levels that the available data are not accurate. It is significant to note that federal legislation in 1968 established 16 deaf–blind centers around the nation to serve children. In 1968, the estimates were that 250 children were served. In 1980, the 16 centers reported serving close to 6000 children through 300 regional service centers. In 1982, federal funding was expanded to individual states that have desired to manage their own programs for these students. In 1985 and 1986, other federal monies (Title VI-C) were targeted toward nonserved populations such as preschool students and students over 18 years of age. These Title VI-C funds have also been utilized to provide technical assistance centers to assist professionals and families.

The legislation in 1968 was the result of lobbying efforts by the directors of residential schools for the deaf and blind who realized that the rubella epidemic in the United States during 1963 to 1965 was going to affect the schools in 1969. Since that time, both residential and public school programs have faced serving larger numbers of students with severe multiple sensory handicaps (Benson and Turnbull 1986).

Unfortunately, many students are still found in institutional settings. The question regarding the definition of a deaf–blind student remains, as do problems related to appropriate curriculum, staff development, and instructional strategies. This chapter focuses on these issues and presents case studies of several students with dual sensory impairments.

Functional Description

Students who have dual sensory impairments may be blind, deaf, or have visual and auditory impairments. The Helen Keller National Center estimates that about 94% of such individuals have residual hearing or residual sight that can facilitate their educational programs. Because of the severity of their handicapping conditions, it is nearly impossible to assess these persons using formalized testing procedures to measure visual and auditory acuity and intellectual functioning. Many of these students are *functionally* vision and hearing impaired and demonstrate mental deficits. Model programs have demonstrated that instructional strategies utilized with visually impaired, hearing impaired, and severely/profoundly handicapped students are often effective with students with dual sensory impairments.

Program Components

As noted previously, the curriculum for students with dual sensory handicaps should include components that have been shown to assist students with a single handicapping condition. Such components are found in curricula for programs for blind, deaf, multihandicapped, and severely/profoundly handicapped individuals.

Ecologic Assessment

Skills that are taught to students with dual sensory handicaps should be those that the student needs to function in all the different environments in his or her daily life. An assessment for such skills must involve teachers, therapists, parents, and other significant individuals who work with each student. This team of persons must prioritize and agree to goals and objectives that will be implemented for each student. The educational program needs to be individualized so that each student learns skills that will be utilized in daily activities with his or her family. [See Appendix 8-1 at the end of this chapter for an assessment instrument for use with families in developing individualized education program.] Table 8-1 lists steps to be utilized in the ecologic curriculum development process.

This process represents a "top down" approach that focuses on the skills an individual needs to function independently in a variety of environments such as home, school, and community (Brown et al. 1979). This is a very different approach from the developmental approach, which attempts to move students along normal developmental sequences in areas such as language development and fine and gross motor and cognitive skills. Students with multiple handicaps often acquire new skills at a slow rate, so they may never acquire needed skills for adult life if the developmental model is utilized.

Orientation and Mobility Training

Welsh and Blasch (1980) defined orientation and mobility as the task of teaching

Table 8-1. Steps in Curriculum Design

Step 1. Delineate curriculum domains (vocational; domestic; community; recreation/leisure).

Step 2. Delineate the variety of current and subsequent natural environments in each domain in which students function/might function.

Step 3. Inventory and delineate the subenvironments within each environment.

Step 4. Inventory and delineate the activities performed by nonhandicapped persons in those subenvironments.

Step 5. Prioritize activities to delineate goals of the individualized education program.

Step 6. Delineate the skills needed to perform the activities.

Step 7. Conduct a discrepancy analysis to determine required skills not currently in the student's repertoire.

Step 8. Determine necessary adaptations.

Step 9. Develop an instructional program.

persons with visual impairments to move independently, safely, and purposefully through the environment. Orientation skills refer to the processes of utilizing remaining senses to establish one's position and relationships to all other significant objects in the environment. Mobility skills refer to one's ability to navigate from one's fixed position to another position in the environment.

Table 8-2 shows a basic outline of the orientation and mobility skills taught to a person who is totally blind. The outline goes from simple skills to advanced techniques for complex independent travel in many environments. Students with severe sensory handicaps may follow this traditional developmental sequence but at a slower rate.

This development approach may not be appropriate for all students with dual sensory handicaps. If progress is not noted, a functional orientation and mobility program should be developed using the six-step model in Figure 8-1; this is an ecologic approach with four main principles.

The first involves having orientation and mobility skills take place within and across the daily activities in which a student engages. Specific training takes place when travel is necessary, and instructional trials for an objective are done in several locations. An example is having a child practice using a cane on the way from the bus and on the path to the cafeteria.

The second principle involves the use of interspersed training trials. A student may be expected to complete independently only two skills involved in getting from one place to another. He or she will be physically prompted through the other skills. Instruction is provided when the skills designated for training are required. As the student masters the initial objectives, more of each route is added to his or her performance criteria.

The third principle involves setting up a functional motivation for travel. This principle builds in a "context instruction" phase whereby the teacher sets up an expectation that, at the end of the route, is an activity like riding the bus or eating lunch. In doing this, the teacher provides a context in which the student can perceive travel as necessary.

The fourth principle involves the use of systematic, data-based procedures. Fading or systematic use of "most to least" assistance prompting is used for initial instruction whereas "least to most" prompts and time delay are utilized in later stages of acquisition.

These instructional strategies allow traditional orientation and mobility skills to be taught as part of the functional education program. The student with dual sensory handicaps benefits when all members of the transdisciplinary individualized education program committee work together to teach orientation and mobility skills during the regular daily travel routes. This

Table 8-2. Scope and Sequence of Orientation and Mobility

Concept development
Basic techniques
    Sighted guide
    Protective and information gathering
    Forearm technique
    Trailing
    Lower body protective technique
    Independent room orientation
Introduction to cane techniques
    Touch technique
    Training with the touch technique
    Diagonal cane technique
    Touch and slide technique
    Stair travel
    Congested area cane technique
    Entering and exiting doorways, cars, and
        so forth
    Touch-and-drag technique
    Three-point touch technique
Residential travel
Light business travel
Major metropolitan travel
Rural travel
Snow travel and other adverse conditions

Figure 8-1. Functional Orientation and Mobility Model

I. Planned observations	II. Selection of routes for instruction

III. Baseline route analysis
Task analysis of routes
Instructional components
Baseline route analysis

IV. Context instruction and second baseline

V. Written instructional program
Select objectives
Performance criteria
Instructional techniques

VI. Implementation and data monitoring

model demands that there be continual communication among orientation and mobility instructors, vision specialists, and classroom teachers. Such collaboration results in more effective orientation and mobility training for these students in different school and community settings.

Functional Vision Programming

Four methods have traditionally been used to enhance residual vision: optical aids; contrast effects; vision stimulation; and vision training (Lundervol 1987). Students with dual sensory impairments benefit most from structured vision training. Such training is based on the sequential application of operant principles and data-based instruction (Snell 1978). In this approach visual behaviors are learned in naturally occurring situations, so that the use of residual vision results in specific, desirable, and functional consequences.

Visual skills are not taught as isolated skills, but rather in the context of learning other age-appropriate tasks and activities. This approach is very different from the traditional visual stimulation approach of using bright blinking lights in massed trials to stimulate visual skills.

This functional context vision training involves five steps:

1. Determine the targeted visual skill.
2. Select a training context.
3. Develop an instructional strategy for the visual skill.
4. Develop an instructional strategy for the other skills to be used as the training context for the visual skill.
5. Implement the programs and monitor progress using data.

Residual vision in students with multiple handicaps can be evaluated in a number of ways. Two assessments found to be useful with this population are the Parsons Visual Acuity Test and Langley and Dubose's Functional Vision Inventory. Classroom teachers should enlist the assistance of visual specialists in program development (Gee and Goetz 1985).

Such assessment data allow the team to identify what vision skills the student has and to understand what visual behaviors he or she lacks. Table 8-3 presents a list of different visual functions and possible measures of responses that a teacher may want to consider in setting objectives (Lundervold 1987).

When a specific vision objective has been pinpointed, the next step involves choosing a functional context in which to teach the desired skill. The skill should be taught in a functional setting using age-appropriate materials. It is also important to set up training activities that will motivate the student.

The instructional activities should be developed using current strategies for severely/profoundly handicapped programming. Reinforcers should be naturally occurring

Table 8-3. Visual Functions and Responses

Visual Function	Possible Responses Forms
Orient to presence of stimulus	Head turn, gaze shift, brief fixation (less than 1 second)
Fixation (bifoveal or monofoveal)	Sustained eye contact, presence of corneal light reflection
Accommodative convergence	Continuous fixation on object as it approaches nose; typically, fixation is broken as object moves within 4 inches of nose
Gaze shift	Fixation on one object, then on second object, without smooth tracking
Tracking	Smooth eye movement to follow object, both eyes aligned, head typically follows eyes
Scanning	Systematic search of visual display
Peripheral vision	Gaze shift to find object located on peripheral visual field

events whenever possible, and teaching activities should be carried out in as nonobtrusive a manner as possible in community-based settings. An example would be to teach scanning skills at the candy bar counter in the local grocery store during hours when the store is not crowded.

Functional Hearing Programming

Audiometric assessment is utilized to determine the presence and intensity of a hearing loss and to ascertain whether the loss is conductive or sensorineural in nature. Students with multiple sensory impairments are often difficult to test.

The single most useful test for audiologists is the auditory brain-stem response (ABR). This test is utilized when a student does not respond to a behavioral test. Behavioral tests use voluntary responses, whereas the ABR measures physiologic responses of the auditory mechanism. The ABR tests the general functional status of the auditory system, but does not provide an audiogram since it is not really a hearing test. It is of value with individuals who are severely delayed because it assesses the auditory system without any need to involve behavioral responses (Martin 1978).

Behavioral testing should be done in conjunction with physiologic assessment whenever possible. Visual reinforcer audiometry (VRA) procedures are useful because they require only primitive head-turn responses. Bright lights and mechanical toys are paired with sounds to elicit responses. Teachers can work closely with audiologists to test students with multiple sensory handicaps, because the teachers know what tangible objects or activities are reinforcing for individual children.

Once a hearing loss has been identified, the transdisciplinary team must decide whether to attempt use of a hearing aid and when to do so. Some children must be programmed to reduce tactile defensiveness or self-abusive behaviors before hearing aid amplification can be used.

If hearing aids are ruled out, or if additional input is needed, vibrotactile units can be utilized. These devices provide sensory input through vibrations on the skin. They use a microphone to pick up sounds and an amplifier to amplify and filter them. The signal is sent to a small vibrator that is attached to the arm or finger of the student. These units have proved most beneficial when used to supplement visual information (Martin 1978).

Establishing Communication

Teachers working with students who have dual sensory handicaps must develop systematic methods of communication with them. The communication strategies should capitalize on the individual strengths identified in the assessment of each child. The focus of establishing communication skills should be to enable each student to exert some control over his or her environment and to assist him or her in interacting with other people. These skills permit the student to bond with others and to feel comfortable in the classroom.

Cooley (1987) suggests that teachers utilize a variety of techniques to communicate with students who have dual sensory handicaps. One technique is to give the student opportunities to make choices during all activities. Two or more options should be presented whenever food, toys, or activities are selected. The student can be guided through touching each item and then prompted to make a choice.

A second strategy is to force each student to be as independent as possible. Guide students through part of a task and then wait for them to independently complete the activity. For example, have the student stand in front of a chair and feel the edge of the seat. Then wait for him or her to seat him- or herself independently.

Another suggestion involves having the teacher use physical prompts or signs to let a student know when he or she is approaching or leaving the student. A gentle touch on the arm or hand can signal arrival and a different handshake or pat on the shoulder can indicate that the teacher is leaving the student.

Special prompts should also be utilized to tell the student who is approaching. This can involve his feeling the person's hair or eyeglasses. Another suggestion is to have the teacher always wear the same perfume.

Object prompts can be utilized to let the student know what is about to happen. At lunch time, the student can feel the plate and utensils. Other specific prompts should be used to indicate when an activity is completed and it is time to do something else. Many teachers find it helpful to use the sign for "finished" to help students move from one activity to another. It is important that these strategies be carried out consistently across all environments and by all persons who interact with a student if they are to become functional for the child.

☐ Case 8-1: John

John is an 19-year-old man with dual sensory handicaps. He is profoundly deaf and has significant visual deficits. A transdisciplinary team has worked with him for many years. Team members include a special education teacher, job coach, orientation and mobility instructor, teacher for the hearing-impaired, audiologist, and vision teacher.

A transition plan was begun when he was 15 years of age. The focus has been to prepare him to work independently in the community while residing in the home of foster parents with whom he has lived for many years. He has been taught to get around the community using a public bus. He is employed at the Post Office as a mail sorter. His hearing loss presents no problem on this job, and magnification devices are used to alleviate his vision difficulties. A job coach helped him learn the job, and the special education teacher assists in money management and social skill development. An interagency agreement is in place to ensure that the local community service board will provide follow-up services when he completes his public school program. In addition to this support, a number of nonhandicapped employees at the Post Office have learned sign language to communicate with John on the job site. Although John has moderate mental retardation, his social skills are excellent, and he is nicely accepted by other workers.

☐ Case 8-2: Mary

Mary is a 10-year-old with profound mental retardation and multiple sensory physical handicaps. She is cortically blind, but she does respond to sounds with gazes and turns her head toward sounds on occasion. She smiles and coos when stimulated by touch and she seems to enjoy music. A team of professionals, utilizing modern technology, has rigged switch devices that allow Mary to activate toys and musical devices by eyebrow and tongue movements. She is also physically prompted to use switches to control devices in her environment such as the toaster. This technology allows her to participate partially in daily activities.

Staff members also communicate with her by telling her what is happening and by using tactile prompts during all activities. Different staff members wear different colognes to facilitate her identify of them.

Opportunities for choice are constantly presented to Mary. For example, two flavors of toothpaste are offered as well as two scents of soap during daily activities. Many instructional activities take place in community settings such as the mall or fast-food restaurants. The family and professionals plan together to be sure that everyone exposes Mary to multiple sensory experiences.

Constant communication among staff members, respite workers, and parents is required to assist Mary in interacting with her environment in all settings.

Summary

Educational programming for students with dual sensory handicaps has changed drastically in recent decades. Many of the strategies included in current best practices for this population parallel the programming suggested for students with severe or profound handicaps.

Such programming demands a commitment to systematic, data-based instruction. It requires teachers to be attuned to a student's attempts to communicate or interact with things around him or her. Programming for these students provides a real challenge to professionals from a variety of disciplines who must form working partnerships to design a truly individualized program to assist each student.

Appendix 8-1. Ecological Survey

_____   _____
               Student   Date

_____   _____
        Date of Birth/Current Age   Interviewer

I. FAMILY INFORMATION

                    Mother   Father

Name _____   _____

Occupation _____   _____

Persons Living in Household:

Name	Age	Relationship	How do they get along with son/daughter? (circle one)
_____	_____	_____	Good Fair Poor
_____	_____	_____	Good Fair Poor
_____	_____	_____	Good Fair Poor
_____	_____	_____	Good Fair Poor
_____	_____	_____	Good Fair Poor
_____	_____	_____	Good Fair Poor

Relatives outside the household with whom your son/daughter has regular contact:

Name	Age	Relationship	How do they get along? (circle one)
_____	_____	_____	Good Fair Poor
_____	_____	_____	Good Fair Poor
_____	_____	_____	Good Fair Poor

Medical problems of son/daughter or immediate family members:

_____

_____

Is son/daughter currently taking medication(s)? _____

If so, what is (are) the name(s) of the medication(s) and dosage(s)? _____

_____

Child care provider(s)   (circle one)

Day care center/ In-home care/ Other _____

Name, address, phone number _____

Does your child have a case manager from Dept. of MH/MR? _____

Name and phone number _____

Do you use respite services? _____

Where? _____

Does your son/daughter have a pet(s)? _____

Name(s) _____

What would you like for your son/daughter to be able to do by the end of the year that he/she does not do now? _____

_____

_____

II. Daily Routines/Domestic/Leisure

What does your son/daughter do to help at home? _____

Does your son/daughter go to the bathroom independently? _____

_____

Does your son/daughter dress him/herself? _____

_____

How does your child feed him/herself (spoon only, finger feed, and so forth)?

_____

_____

How does your child drink (cup, straw, bottle)? _____

What does your son/daughter do to occupy his/her leisure time? _____

_____

III. Community

Do you take your son/daughter with you when you go out? _____

Where do you go? _____

_____

Does your son/daughter participate in family activities? _____

What types (picnics, birthday parties)? _____

_____

IV. Vocational

What are your plans for your son/daughter after graduation? _____

_____

_____

Are you aware of what the school's vocational program has to offer? _____

_____

What living arrangements would you like for your son/daughter after graduation?

_____

_____

Where would you like to see your son/daughter work? _____

_____

How do you think your child will get to work? _____

_____

Do you know if your child is eligible to receive Supplemental Security Income and/or Social Security Disability Insurance? _____

_____

V. Communication

How do you communicate with your son/daughter? (circle one or more)

Verbal   Sign/Gesture   Augmentative Device   Other _____

Would you be willing to try any of these methods? _____

If so, which ones? _____

How do you want your child to communicate? _____

_____

Does your son/daughter have any patterns of behavior we should know about (that is, Does she/he jump up and down before needing to use the bathroom? Does she/he moan before displaying an inappropriate behavior?

_____

VI. Behavior Management

What does your son/daughter do that you are proud of? _____

_____

What does your son/daughter do that you wish she/he would stop? _____

_____

How do you usually discipline your child? _____

_____

In general, does your son/daughter usually listen to you–or do you have to punish him/her first to get him/her to listen? _____

_____

What does your son/daughter do after being praised? _____

_____

After being punished? _____

_____

VII. Additional Comments:

VIII. Additional Questions (to be used when appropriate)

Does your son/daughter partially participate in self-care? _____

_____

If yes, which tasks and to what extent? _____

_____

_____

_____

Does your son/daughter display a sucking action? _____

_____

Does your child use a wheelchair? _____   walker? _____

What mobility assistance do you feel your child will need as an adult? _____

_____

Does your son/daughter understand the meaning of

yes? _____   no? _____

Does your son/daughter turn his/her head when spoken to? _____

Toward a sound other than voice? _____

Does your son/daughter smile in response to a voice or presence of others? _____

Does your son/daughter react to everyday cues? _____

_____

If so, how? _____

Does your son/daughter initiate/terminate activities with the use of

body language? _____   switch? _____

verbalization? _____   other? _____

_____

References

1. Benson HA, Turnbull AP. Education of Learners with Severe Handicaps. Baltimore, Paul H. Brooks, 1986.
2. Brown L, Branston M, Hamre-Nietupski S, Pumpien I, Certo N. A strategy for developing chronologically age-appropriate and functional curricular content for the severely handicapped. Journal of Special Education. 13:81–90, 1979.
3. Cooley E. Getting in touch: Communicating with a child who is deaf–blind. (Videotape). Champaign, IL, Research Press, 1987.
4. Gee K, Goetz L. Outcomes of instructing orientation and mobility across purposeful travel routes in natural environments. Journal of the Association for Persons with Severe Handicaps. 11:1–11, 1983.
5. Lundervold D. Rehabilitation of visual impairments. Clinical Psychology Review. 7:169–185, 1987.
6. Martin F. Pediatric Audiology. Englewood Cliffs, NJ, Prentice-Hall, 1978.
7. Snell M. Systematic Instruction for the Moderately and Severely Handicapped. Columbus, OH, Charles Merrill, 1978.
8. Welsh R, Blasch B. eds. Foundation of Orientation and Mobility. New York, American Foundation for the Blind, 1980.

Chapter 9
Challenges for Service Providers

Pamela S. Wolfe

Since the call for "normalized conditions" for individuals with disabilities was first brought to the United States by Wolfensberger in the early 1970s, the field of special education and rehabilitation services has experienced rapid ideologic and implementational changes (Wolfensberger 1972). The simple, yet eloquent ideology behind the normalization principle has impacted on the perceptions of, and the services for, individuals with developmental disabilities. The principle provided a strong basis for deinstitutionalization, which placed increasing numbers of individuals with disabilities into the community and emphasized a professional responsibility to provide active treatment. Active treatment, contrasted with "custodial care," stresses the need (and the right) of individuals with disabilities to a treatment program that maximizes self-determination and independent functioning through consistent professional programming (Goldberg 1990).

Even individuals with the most severe and profound disabilities are now believed to be able to function successfully in integrated community settings, as evidenced in employment (Hill et al. 1987; Kiernan and Stark 1986; Mank et al. 1986; Moon et al. 1990), in residential settings (Amado et al. 1990; Larson and Lakin 1989), and in recreational activities (Banks and Aveno

1986). The concept of the least restrictive placement and environment is increasingly being replaced by a support service model. The support service model contrasts with a readiness model in which individuals with developmental disabilities "wait" to participate until needed prerequisite skills are in place. The support service model suggests that all individuals, regardless of the severity of their handicap, be placed with necessary supports instituted to allow full participation (Gardner 1990). It has become the challenge of professionals to provide the training and support necessary to sustain success in the environment.

The ideologic changes occurring in the field of special education and rehabilitation services have been mirrored by legislative mandates. Change is evident in research and demonstration, in formalized definitions, and in created venues for funding. Table 9-1 provides an overview of major legislation affecting service provision for individuals with developmental disabilities. Legislative changes have occurred in virtually every area of service provision ranging from education to residential and vocational services. Further, major legislation just recently passed by Congress (The Americans with Disabilities Act of 1990) has provided basic and far-

Table 9-1. Major Legislation Affecting Individuals with Developmental Disabilities

Date	Legislation	Provision
1970	The Developmental Disabilities Services and Facilities Construction Act (P.L. 91-517)	First introduced the concept of "developmental disabilities"
1971	Title XIX of the Social Security Act (P.L. 92-223)	Required ICFs/MR to provide "active treatment"
1975	Education for All Handicapped Children's Act (P.L. 94-142)	Guaranteed a free and appropriate education to all children
1978	Rehabilitation, Comprehensive Services, and Developmental Disabilities Amendment (P.L. 95-602)	Revised the definition of developmental disabilities to emphasize "functionality"
1984	Developmental Disabilities Act Amendment (P.L. 98-527)	Included employment-related activities as a priority
1990	Developmental Disabilities Assistance and Bill of Rights Act	Reauthorized the DD Act for three years and emphasized the empowerment of individuals with disabilities Placed particular emphasis on protection and advocacy
1990	Education of the Handicapped Act Amendments (P.L. 101-476)	Reauthorized parts of the EHA Changed the name of the law to Individuals with Disabilities Education Act (IDEA) to reflect people before disability Expanded the definition of disability to include children with autism and traumatic brain injury Increased emphasis on transition planning Provided support for projects for students with serious emotional disturbances
1990	Americans with Disabilities Act	Offered important civil rights for individuals with disabilities Extended rights to access in employment settings, public transportation, and public establishments

reaching legislative protection and advocacy for increased civil rights for individuals with disabilities (Amado et al. 1990).

Who Is Labeled Developmentally Disabled?

Those professionals working with individuals with developmental disabilities know all too well that definitions and labels rarely provide a comprehensive picture of the needs and strengths of the individuals with whom they work. The fields of education and of the helping professions have long struggled with issues of labeling, the stigma that may accompany them, and the inevitable ability of such labels to generate necessary funds. The Developmental Disabilities Assistance and Bill of Rights Act of 1990 addresses functional rather than categorical issues in the definition of developmental disabilities. The major components of the definition of developmental disabilities are listed in Appendix 9-1 at the end of this chapter. An individual categorized as developmentally disabled can be both mentally and physically impaired, with disabilities originating before the age of 22. Typical categories include epilepsy, cerebral palsy, mental retardation, and autism. According to the definition included in the Developmental Disabilities Act, individuals who are developmentally disabled show deficits in three of seven life activities: self care, language, learning, mobility, self-direction, capacity for independent living, and economic self-sufficiency. The Act defines disability in terms of what an individual is and is not able to do rather than in terms of a clinical diagnosis (Summers 1986). The move away from cause and effect to an emphasis on adaptive life activities highlights areas where human service professionals may be asked to provide assistance. Consider the contrast in utility in pinpointing service provision needs evidenced by the following two descriptions.

> Lisa is an 8-year-old girl who is mentally handicapped because of trisomy 21 and has a recorded IQ of 45 on the Weschler Intelligence Scale.

> Lisa is an 8-year-old girl who is developmentally disabled and who experiences significant difficulties in self-care, learning, and capacity for independent living.

Although service providers must always individualize, the second definition brings professionals much closer to knowing how they can assist Lisa.

Examining the definition of developmental disabilities further, an individual must show deficits in three life areas and must manifest the disability prior to age 22. An individual who has suffered a severe head injury at age 19 would probably be considered developmentally disabled because the injury sustained would probably limit life areas such as language, learning, capacity for independent living, and economic self-sufficiency. Conversely, an individual who was born with a congenital

hearing loss might not be considered developmentally disabled if he or she only experienced a deficit in language (Summers 1986). Although the definition itself may not provide an easy answer as to who is developmentally disabled, the definition places an important emphasis on functionality and draws attention to the need for diverse and extended services.

Meeting the Needs of the Developmentally Disabled

As they are personified by the Developmental Disabilities Act of 1990, the needs of individuals with disabilities may be unique, varied, and extensive. Over the course of a lifetime, an individual may have educational, independent living, economic self-sufficiency, and psychosocial needs.

Education

Perhaps nowhere has service provision for individuals with developmental disabilities been more comprehensive than in the educational setting. The Education for All Handicapped Children's Act (P.L. 94-142) set forth the right not only to a free and appropriate education, but also to any services deemed necessary to meet the needs of students with disabilities. The number of children receiving special education services has grown every year since 1976 with an overall increase of 21.2% since 1976–1977 (Amado et al. 1990). The newly amended Education of the Handicapped Act of 1990 (P. L. 101-476) has expanded the definition of disability specifically to include children with autism and traumatic brain injury. The amended Act also changed the name of the law to Individuals with Disabilities Education Act to emphasize the concept of person before that of disability.

The education of students with developmental disabilities has taken on a new and comprehensive meaning. Issues of "educability" of students, particularly those with severe disabilities, have been raging for some time (Bailey 1981; Kauffman and Krouse 1981) and continue to be evident in court cases (for example, *Timothy v. Rochester*, N. H. School District 84-733). Under the Education of the Handicapped Act Amendments (P.L. 101-476), the term "education" encompasses training in areas such as self-help, vocational training, and community living in addition to more traditional academic content. For example, a student with severe disabilities may spend a large part of his or her educational day in the community. A community-based outing such as a trip to a fast-food restaurant can provide the student with opportunities to increase his or her competency in skills such as money and word recognition and social situations. Similarly, a student who is blind may spend an equal amount of time in the community acquiring mobility skills and increasing opportunities for independence. The definition of developmental disabilities itself and current best practices together stress the need for functional, age-appropriate skills that will generalize to environments beyond the school doors.

Independent Living

The deinstitutionalization movement dramatically decreased the number of individuals residing in institutions and placed many individuals with disabilities into community residential settings. Although the total population of individuals with mental retardation in residential facilities has been stable (primarily because of a decrease in the number of children and youth living in out-of-home residential placements), there has been a change in the type of housing in which individuals with disabilities reside. Amado and colleagues (1990) report that in 1967, 85% of the developmentally disabled population lived in institutions but that this number decreased to approximately 34% by 1988. For many individuals, institutional living

has given way to residence in smaller, more normalized settings in the community. Amado and coworkers estimate that 23.9% of individuals with severe mental retardation and 17.8% of individuals with profound retardation are living in facilities of six or fewer residents. Residential options now include foster family care, semi-independent and supported living, state and nonstate group residences, state and nonstate institutions, and nursing homes. Table 9-2 provides the percentage of individuals with developmental disabilities in each residential option. Whereas institutional living continues to be a way of life for some, research is providing evidence that even those with the most severe disabilities can successfully live in the community if they are given adequate support (Amado et al. 1990).

Table 9-2. Residential Placements for Individuals with Developmental Disabilities during 1988

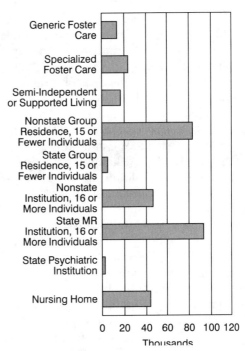

From Amado et al. 1990.

Economic Self-Sufficiency

The right to work is an important concept in our society; individuals who work are afforded greater opportunities for increased revenue and the greater respect of others. Two hundred and fifty thousand to 300,000 students exit school programs each year (Szymanski et al. 1990a). Once they are beyond the school doors, however, many individuals with disabilities find a startling lack of services. Individuals with disabilities are notoriously under-represented in the work force, with unemployment rates ranging from 58% (Wehman et al. 1985a) to 88% (Wehman et al. 1985b). Vocational options for individuals with developmental disabilities have traditionally consisted of day or activity centers. Available vocational options are expanding, however, and now include competitive or supported competitive employment. Supported employment is characterized by permanent, ongoing, or intermittent support, at least minimum wage, and opportunities for community integration (Wehman et al. 1988). The growth of supported employment has been marked. Wehman (1990), in a national analysis of supported employment, found an increase in supported employment participation of 226% from 1986 to 1988. Categories of disability represented in supported employment included mental retardation (70.5%), mental illness (16.7%), cerebral palsy (1.8%), sensory impairment (2.5%), and other (8.5%) (Wehman 1990). Although individuals with severe and profound mental retardation have been successful in supported employment, they comprise a relatively small portion of the population with disabilities who are placed (Kregel et al. 1989a, 1989b; Wehman 1990; Western Michigan 1990).

The primary impetus behind supported employment has been the placement of individuals with disabilities typically unable to be placed in community vocational settings. Such an emphasis on individuals with more severe disabilities has translated into service needs that may be extensive and long term. Cost-benefit analyses illustrate that even with extensive support and long-term assistance, supported employment is more cost-effective than other alternative day or activity programs (Brickey et al. 1985; Hill et al. 1987; Noble and Conley 1987). More importantly, however, the benefits of increased opportunities for economic self-sufficiency and integration cannot be overlooked. Exemplary supported employment programs emphasize work for at least minimum wages, thereby enhancing opportunities for community integration and self-respect. Although the often intangible rewards attained from competitive placements cannot always be factored into an equation, they certainly impact upon the sum.

Psychosocial Needs

All individuals have unique and varied needs. These needs typically do not fall neatly into service provision realms but are complex, inter-related, and subject to change over time. To fully serve individuals with developmental disabilities, professionals must be aware of the psychosocial needs of their clients. The illusive construct of "quality of life" must be considered. Although it is difficult to quantify, quality of life can be based on personal observations of an individual's needs, preferences, and aspirations (Inge et al. 1987). Quality of life includes tangible and intangible rewards and benefits such as self-esteem, wages, and friendships (Steere et al. 1990). For example, although securing and maintaining employment is a desired outcome for many individuals with developmental disabilities, it is not the only desired outcome. Professionals must view their clients in a "holistic" manner and examine aspects such as opportunities for integration, formation of friendships, and enhanced feelings of self-worth.

Integral to the issue of quality of life are opportunities for choice and client empowerment. In the past, the focus of much educational and service intervention has been on compliance. Now, professionals understand the need to foster independence and self-reliance (Wehman and McLaughlin 1981; Shevin and Klein 1984). Choice increases an individual's perceived independence, dignity, and self-worth. The ability to express choice has been evidenced and communicated by even those with the most severe disabilities (Dattilo and Rusch 1985; Guess et al. 1986; Houghton et al. 1987; Peck 1985). Choice must figure heavily into service planning and delivery for individuals with developmental disabilities; its inclusion represents advocacy for individuals with disabilities and the best chance of successful programming.

Issues for Services Providers

What follows are some major issues facing professionals working with individuals with developmental disabilities. Central issues emerging in the service profession field are outlined, and challenges to professionals are suggested.

Transdisciplinary Planning and Implementation

The terminology used to denote group planning and implementation of services has included "interdisciplinary," "multidisciplinary," and "transdisciplinary" models or approaches. Although their meanings vary slightly, all stress the need for input from many disciplines in service delivery. The need for an interdisciplinary approach to service provision is apparent in the legislation of P.L. 101-476 and is supported by The Developmental Disabilities Assistance and Bill of Rights Act of 1990. With the diverse needs of individuals with disabilities, many different disciplines must convene to provide optimal services. Though professionals are cogni-

zant of the need for coordination among their disciplines, actual service provision is often fragmented and uncoordinated. According to Giangreco (1990), related service professionals (occupational therapists, physical therapists, and communication specialists) believe that, whereas recommendations should be shared, the final authority of their discipline should be retained. With such territorial attitudes, programming efforts can all too easily fall to the wayside.

The need for an interdisciplinary approach is most marked in service provision for individuals with more severe disabilities. As the severity of the disability increases, so does the number of disciplines involved in providing services (Peterson 1980). Obviously individuals in need of the most extensive services cannot be faced with rhetoric such as "It's not my area." Szymanski and colleagues (1990b) have suggested the need for a "transdisciplinary model" for coordinating the efforts of service providers. Central to the model is the sharing of information and skills by professionals, with service delivery carried out by one or two facilitators (Orelove and Sobsey 1987). The transdisciplinary approach suggests use of an indirect model of services and utilization of role release. The

---

Challenges for Service Providers

- Understand that professional roles must be flexible and will change over time.
- Work to foster communication among professional disciplines through active listening, brainstorming, and the open sharing of ideas.
- Keep egos in check; remember that you work for the client first.
- Learn from others—do not feel that adhering to others' ideas in any way diminishes your professional status—it only enhances it.
- Recognize that different disciplines may have different beliefs and professional jargon (Orelove and Sobsey 1987).
- Value all ideas, even if they are different from your own.

---

indirect model of services centers on professionals working as consultants with other disciplines and requires role release or flexible role performance and facilitative communication (Orelove and Sobsey 1987). Whatever the terminology, the imperative is the same: cooperation and communication between service professionals.

Ecologic Approach to Planning and Service

Individuals interact with their environment in a complex way. Service planning and provision must incorporate a "systems approach" in meeting the needs of individuals with developmental disabilities (Powers 1988). A systems approach notes the characteristics and constraints of each level of a system (for example, individuals, groups, societies), and the inter-relationships between each system (Powers 1988). The approach notes that a change in one aspect of the system may impact in some manner on other parts of the system to create an imbalance that may cause stress. If a change in the system is to be implemented successfully, many aspects must be examined. For example, an educational program instituted in the school setting may have profound effects on the family of the student for whom the program was designed. Similarly, an individual participating in supported employment may effect change in the family and the community. Professionals must understand how service provision may impact on all the individuals who are participating in environments with the individual with a disability.

The ecologic approach to service provision, like the systems approach, stresses the need to examine the many elements that comprise an individual's life. Steps in an ecologic assessment typically include identification of domain areas (such as self-help, leisure or community living), identification of current and future environments, division of relevant environ-

Challenges for Service Providers

- Assess current levels of functioning and skills exhibited by the client.
- Assess levels of functioning needed in possible future environments.
- Utilize discrepancy analyses to assess strengths and weaknesses and gain a socially valid perspective of skills and behaviors of the general population.
- Be aware of the many environments in which your client/student may participate. Understand that needs and behaviors will change in different environments.
- Be aware that needs and skills will change throughout time and so will service needs.
- Understand that many individuals are involved in a person's life and each will affect service provision in a unique way.
- Examine both the strengths and weaknesses of your client. Utilize strengths to offset possible weaknesses.
- Understand how change can affect an individual and his or her environment and be sensitive to his or her needs.
- Be prepared to meet with resistance when instituting some changes.

ments into subenvironments, inventory of the subenvironments for needed skills, and examination of the activities to isolate required skills (Brown et al. 1979). For example, an ecologic approach for a teacher of a secondary student with severe disabilities would require that the teacher find out about possible future environments for his or her student. Possible future environments for a secondary student might include vocational programs such as supported employment placement, residential options such as group homes or supervised apartments, and possible recreational pursuits. The teacher could gather information by using a published ecologic inventory that aids in the identification of domain areas and prioritization of goals, or the teacher could informally interview professionals in potential future environments to pinpoint potential areas of need. Imagine the consternation of a parent whose child is denied acceptance in a group home due to inadequate self-care skills after 12 years of schooling in the special education system. By looking ahead and utilizing an ecologic approach, the teacher, families, and future service providers can project needs and begin working on necessary skills. Absence of an ecologic approach may result in lack of training necessary for success in future environments and perhaps overlap in training efforts.

Family Involvement in Service Provision

P.L. 94-142 brought family involvement in the educational process to light with the legislative mandate for parental participation. Recent legislation has also emphasized the importance of family support and input in service provision (for example, The Amended Developmental Disabilities Act of 1990 and The Amended Education for Handicapped Children Act of 1990). Parents have been given the right to informed consent, due process, and the educational planning of their child's curriculum. In

---

Challenges for Service Providers

- Understand the maxim "no man is an island" and be cognizant of how the family may affect service provision.
- Work toward understanding the "family systems approach" (Turnbull and Turnbull 1990).
- Understand the value of family input into service provision.
- Understand that needs change over time and that professionals must meet these changing needs.
- Be aware that family values may differ from service providers but must be respected and valued.
- Understand that families have different coping styles and may react to professional input and ideas differently.
- Work toward empowering parents with the means to institute change beyond professional intervention (Zigler and Berman 1983).
- Be aware of the impact your service suggestions (or demands) may place on the family.
- Be an advocate for the rights of the parents and family to institute change in their child's life.

---

fact, some have charged that many parents are undergoing a form of "professionalization" whereby they may be asked to undertake roles such as educator, decision maker, advocate, teacher, case manager, and program evaluator (Allen and Stefanowski-Hudd, 1987).

The amount and type of participation undertaken by parents and families obviously will vary. Professionals must encourage participation at whatever level parents feel most comfortable. The complex nature of interactions and of their effect on the family has been explored in both the family systems approach (Turnbull and Turnbull 1990) and the social support approach (Dunst et al. 1988). Both approaches examine the complex nature of the family and emphasize that family input must be valued and respected.

Transition from School to Work and Independent Living

The term "transition" conjures up many different meanings. Because transition typically denotes change or movement, individuals with developmental disabilities undoubtedly experience many different transitions during their lifetime. Transition can include movement from one educational setting to another or from one stage in life to another.

During times of transition, assistance from service providers is critical. Voids of service at times of change can translate into unsuccessful or poor transition or simply into no transition at all. The Amended Education of the Handicapped Act (1990) has emphasized the need for transition planning through increased grant revenue and the specification of vocational or educational goals as part of a student's individual education plan. A transition plan must be developed, if determined appropriate, by the age of 16, or in some cases, by the age of 14.

Transition planning should focus on vocational, residential, and social–interpersonal

Table 9-3. Services Anticipated in 1986–1987 for Students 16 Years of Age or Older Exiting the Educational System During the School Year 1985–1986.

Areas	%
Counseling/guidance	14.1
Transportation	4.3
Technologic aids	1.9
Interpreter services	0.6
Reader services	1.6
Physical/mental restoration	2.8
Family services	5.7
Independent living	5.2
Maintenance	4.0
Residential living	2.2
Vocational training	15.8
Postemployment services	6.0
Transitional services	7.4
Vocational placement	14.1
Evaluation of vocational rehabilitation services	12.6
Other services	1.7

From U. S. Department of Education (USDE), Office of Special Education and Rehabilitative Services, 1989.

domains (Halpern 1985). Table 9-3 outlines the types of services needed by students with disabilities leaving the school system. As Table 9-3 illustrates, there are many potential needs to be met. Wehman (1990) has suggested that transition is based heavily on the community and its characteristics and cannot be successfully implemented by schools or vocational rehabilitation agencies alone.

Successful transition includes plans for the sending and receiving programs to share information on eligibility requirements, entrance and exit criteria, program goals and objectives, follow-up and feedback procedures, and personnel responsible for promoting transition (Sileo et al. 1988). Further, all transition planning and execution must be concerned with many different quality outcomes. Quality-of-life issues should figure prominently in any transition planning. Steere and coworkers (1990) have outlined a process that may aid in the attainment of quality-of-life outcomes. The process helps guide the selection of employment placements. Table 9-4 outlines the major steps in the process.

Table 9-4. Outcome-Based Transition Planning for Individuals with Developmental Disabilities

1. *Orientation.* Establishment of transition planning team and appointment of a team leader: The team should include individuals who represent all the environments of the student or consumer. Members should be oriented to the intent and purpose of the meeting.

2. *Development of a Personal Profile.* Development of a "biographical sketch" outlining the student or client's characteristics (likes and dislikes) and achievements: The profile's purpose is to help team members identify appropriate employment matches with the individual's desired outcomes.

3. *Identification of Employment Outcomes.* Brainstorming session generating a list of potential quality-of-life outcomes: The list should contain hoped-for and dreamed-for outcomes in order of priority.

4. *Measurement System.* Outline of "standards of acceptance": Each outcome is further defined, and ideal and minimum standards are delineated. An outcome of increased community participation might include an ideal standard of one outing per day to a minimum standard of one outing per week.

5. *Compatibility Process.* Integration of outcomes and objectives with employment possibilities: Team members look for a match or degree of compatibility between available jobs and the consumer's abilities. Challenges to placement are outlined and potential solutions are generated through brainstorming. Potential solutions are ranked according to their feasibility, and "action plans" are drawn up. Action plans specify activities, personnel, timelines, and follow-up activities necessary to ensure that activities are successfully completed.

6. *Evaluation.* Team members continue to meet to monitor completion of team activities.

Adapted from Steere et al. 1990.

Although it is specific to employment outcomes, the model could be applied to other transition areas such as independent living.

The reality of transition for individuals with developmental disabilities is often long waiting lists for vocational and residential services and gaps in eligibility for services in movement from one service provision to another. For example, eligibility for special education does not necessarily ensure eligibility for vocational rehabilitation services (Szymanski et al. 1989); hence, many individuals may "graduate" into inadequate or wholly absent service provision.

Challenges for Service Providers

- Understand that transition will be on-going and will occur many times in an individual's life.
- Be aware that successful transition requires the cooperation of many different service agencies.
- Be aware that "multidisciplinary," "transdisciplinary," or team approach provides the most optimal transition services.
- Be aware that transition requires preplanning and projection of needed services from one service system to another.
- Understand the value of, and need for, quality communication between and among service delivery disciplines.
- Understand the roles and responsibilities of other professionals and how to work with other agencies.
- Have empathy for clients and consumers undergoing transition. Change is often difficult and may require time to adjust.
- Understand that transition may result in new and unique service needs for clients. Service providers must remain flexible and attuned to new needs.
- Focus on outcomes in transition that include aspects of quality of life.

Training in Socialization Skills and Increased Opportunities for Social Integration

Much of the ideology behind current best practice in the human service field is grounded in the belief that increased community integration can lead to greater opportunities for socialization between individuals with disabilities and their nondisabled peers. Social skill deficits are, however, evident in all categories of exceptional children (Strain and Odom 1986) and tend to become more debilitating without active intervention (Strain 1983). Acquisition and effective use of social skills are important to all individuals. Social skills enable individuals to foster friendships, increase opportunities to enjoy life, and are central to community survival; without appropriate social skills, simple pleasures and rights such as eating in a restaurant or holding down a job may be denied (Snell and Eichner 1989). Absence of appropriate social skills have often been cited as a factor in the job separation of individuals with disabilities (Greenspan and Shoultz 1981; Hanley-Maxwell et al. 1986; Lagomarcino 1990). Social skills allow individuals access to environments and relationships (Voeltz 1984) and must be taught and enhanced by professionals.

Challenges for Service Providers

- Understand the profound impact social skills can have on opportunities for social integration.
- Understand that interaction between individuals with disabilities and their nondisabled peers is a "two-way street" where all parties must want to participate.
- Understand that individuals differ as to the amount and kind of social interaction they desire.
- Social interactions should not be forced and must remain pleasurable for all parties involved.
- Be cognizant of promoting age-appropriate activities and actions in social interactions.
- Allow for the "dignity of risk" in social interactions. Often letting go and allowing an interaction to occur is difficult for service providers.
- Facilitate opportunities for social interactions through increased community integration.

Training of Professional Staff

Rapid changes in the field of developmental disabilities have resulted in many new roles for service providers. Changing roles

---

Challenges for Service Providers

- Understand the need for flexibility of professional roles and responsibilities.
- Understand that as needs arise, roles and responsibilities of service providers change and are redefined.
- Learn to communicate to facilitate professional and personal growth.
- Create a balance between advocacy for individuals with developmental disabilities and the inherent role of employee of a service system (Karan and Berger-Knight 1986).
- Work toward continued professionalism in the field by action and advocacy.
- Translate new changes in the field into current best practice for clients.

---

mean that service providers need to stay abreast of current changes and translate these new changes into satisfactory services for the consumers they serve. Throughout their professional career, professionals working with individuals with developmental disabilities may be called upon to play the role of communicator, facilitator, teacher, evaluator, negotiator, business person, advocate, or counselor. Some roles may be formally defined; others are only informally defined. The service delivery system for individuals with developmental disabilities is currently experiencing a shortage of qualified staff (Fifield and Smith 1985). Several professions related to vocational rehabilitation can expect rapid expansion because of increased need in community programs (Karan and Berger-Knight 1986). Further, preservice training is often discipline specific and may not adequately prepare professionals working with individuals with developmental disabilities (Richardson et al. 1985). Special education may not prepare professionals to work with adults with developmental disabilities or to work effectively with the rehabilitation system. Equally true is the fact that vocational rehabilitation counselors may not be trained in systematic instructional techniques (Kregel and Sale 1988). Table 9-5 outlines

competency areas important in supported employment training, but which apply equally to many service areas for professionals involved in work with individuals with developmental disabilities.

Utilization of the Community as a Training Site

Trends toward greater community integration of individuals with developmental disabilities mean that service providers need to learn to utilize the community as a training site. Use of the community can lead to greater generalization of skills to other environments (Sailor et al. 1988; Snell and Browder 1986; Stokes and Baer 1977; Thorpe et al. 1981) and provide

---

Table 9-5. Competency Areas for Professionals Working with Individuals with Developmental Disabilities

1. *Philosophical, legal, and policy issues.* Critical issues surrounding services for individuals with developmental disabilities, such as legislation and litigation, eligibility requirements, definitions, and related services provided by state and local agencies.
2. *Program Development.* Options and programs for individuals with developmental disabilities, assessment of client needs, and coordination of efforts among professional disciplines.
3. *Program Implementation.* Implementation of a service program.
4. *Program Management.* Understanding of legal issues, regulations, processes, and the allocation of personnel, equipment, and resources.
5. *Program Evaluation.* Evaluation of client progress and overall program effectiveness.
6. *Systematic Instruction.* Understanding of use of instructional techniques and use of prompts and reinforcers.
7. *Transition Planning.* Identification and analysis of skills needed in current and future environments of clients.

Adapted from Kregel and Sale 1988.

opportunities for integration with nondisabled peers (Mank et al. 1986; Moon et al. 1990; Wehman et al. 1985).

Although great gains can be made while training in the community, more than skill acquisition must be considered when in the public eye. Wolfensberger's definition of normalization places equal emphasis on the cultural normativeness of the outcomes of service delivery and the means used to achieve those outcomes (Wolfensberger 1972). Training occurring in the community must be concerned with how training is undertaken. Activities that are age-inappropriate or in any way demeaning may negatively impact on how individuals with disabilities are perceived (Bates et al. 1984). Professionals must work to foster community integration and remain sensitive to activities and behaviors occurring in the community.

Challenges for Service Providers

• Know your community and its needs and values.
• Understand other disciplines such as marketing, business, and personnel management and how these areas can impact on your profession.
• Understand the impact of actions and training occurring in the community. How individuals with developmental disabilities are treated wili influence attitudes toward, and expectations for, such individuals.
• Advocate and educate others to the benefits of increased integration.

Funding

A central issue in service provision for individuals with developmental disabilities is funding. During the 1980s, the amount of public funding for individuals with mental retardation and related conditions increased considerably, reaching approximately $12 billion in 1988 (excluding education and certain entitlement). Well over 100 federal programs provided funds for individuals with developmental disabilities as did state, local, and private sources (Amado et al. 1990). Whereas coordination between special education and vocational programs was stimulated by the 1984 Office of Special Education and Rehabilitation Services (OSERS) Transitional Initiative, use of different definitions for individuals with handicaps has often translated into inconsistent service delivery. The rehabilitation system is not an entitlement service like the educational system and may have an order of selection for clientele served (Szymanski et al. 1989). Differences in definition can result in ineligibility for individuals previously classified as disabled. Szymanski et al. note that eligibility for vocational rehabilitation services can be difficult for individuals with mild disabilities because their disability may not impact directly on employment and may render them ineligible for services. It is equally true that, because vocational rehabilitation programs require that individuals be expected to receive reasonable benefits from services, individuals with severe handicaps who have an unfavorable prognosis may be denied services. Funding for disability categories may also be discrepant. Kregel and colleagues (1989b) found that individuals with mental retardation could secure necessary funding for supported employment but that funding was not equally available for other disability categories such as cerebral palsy, brain injury, physical disabilities, and sensory impairments.

One of the most critical issues in funding provisions for individuals with developmental disabilities is lack of long-term funding. Long-term funding for rehabilitative services is often unstable, thereby creating funding lapses and inconsistencies. Lack of long-term funding may translate into inadequate services for individuals with developmental disabilities. Lack of long-term funding may mean that, although a client is initially provided a needed service, the service may be discontinued when funding expires. The needs of the client do not usually end when funding does. The issue of funding is further complicated by the inclusion of individuals with the most severe disabilities. Kregel and Wehman (1989) believe that differentiated funding levels should be established that reimburse programs based on the intensity and complexity of training and support needs. As more and more individuals with more severe disabilities take part in service delivery systems, the intensity of services may need to be factored into funding strategies and funding incentives provided to agencies taking on more severe cases (Moon et al. 1990).

Challenges for Service Providers

- Be knowledgeable about federal laws and how they may affect your clients.
- Be aware of model programs and utilize information and ideas to implement state-of-the-art practices.
- Utilize grant award opportunities for innovation.
- Lobby Congress for legislative change.

Changing Attitudes and Advocacy

Attitudes impact integrally upon service provision, funding, how individuals with disabilities are treated, and belief in what can be accomplished. Service providers need to continue to champion for the rights of individuals with disabilities to exercise choice, to work, and to access the services necessary to attain their full potential. Individuals with disabilities in the community and in integrated work settings must be the norm rather than the exception. Viewing individuals with disabilities in appropriate settings and demonstrating competence will further the development of more positive attitudes (Bates et al. 1984; Matson and Rusch 1986). Although contact alone cannot be assumed to induce more positive attitudes (Roper 1990), situations promoting the similarities between individuals with disabilities and their nondisabled peers may serve to enhance attitudes (Bak and Siperstein 1987). Finally,

service providers must place increased emphasis on accountability and quality of programming. As always, service providers must be accountable to those they seek to serve and must be able to validate socially the services they provide by continually asking if the services they provide are necessary and sufficient for the maximum functioning of their clients.

Challenges for Service Providers

- Work toward increased services for individuals with developmental disabilities.
- Strive for services that truly meet the needs of your clients rather than simply supply readily available services.
- Demonstrate accountability in programming and service provision.
- Assess techniques for training, methods, and skills for measures of social validity.

Implications for Future Service Delivery Planning and Research

Rob is a 2-year-old boy who has been totally blind since birth. Rob is entering the educational system for the first time.

Susan is a 12-year-old girl who experienced severe traumatic brain injury during an auto accident. Prior to the accident, Susan was in a regular sixth grade class. Now she has trouble walking independently, can no longer care for many self-care needs, and has trouble with memory loss. Susan's family is having a difficult time adjusting to the changes in their lives since the accident.

Melody is an 18-year-old girl who is severely mentally disabled. Melody has deficits in many life areas although she fiercely desires a "real job."

Glenn is a 46-year-old man with chronic mental illness. Glenn is living independently but still needs supervision in areas such as money management, time management, cooking, cleaning, and hygiene. Glenn loves living in the community and has recently expressed a desire to learn golf and tennis in order to "get in shape."

Service provision for individuals with developmental disabilities has substantially changed in the breadth and intensity of services provided. Advances in the educational field have meant that all students with disabilities, regardless of the severity of the handicap, can be educated in the least restrictive environment. Residential placements have moved from large institutional settings to a range of options including small, community-based settings. Vocational placements have similarly expanded to include a range of placements, many of which occur in the community. All of these changes have, and will continue to have, an impact on the services available to individuals like Rob, Susan, Melody, and Glenn. Where once Glenn may have resided in an institution, he may now successfully live in a group home or a supervised apartment. Likewise, Melody may leave the school system and be placed in a supported job in the community where she can earn competitive wages. The changes are, without a doubt, exciting. They offer chances for independence, increased self-esteem, and friendships for individuals with developmental disabilities. The changes also offer service providers in every service provision realm new challenges. Future challenges facing professionals include:

1. *The need to coordinate efforts among many different disciplines.* The educational and rehabilitation systems need to come together to provide a more successful transition for students like Melody in their move into the adult world. This coordination of effort will create new roles and redefine existing ones. The coordination of efforts represents the best chances of successful programming for individuals requiring diverse service needs.

2. *Provision of services that examine client outcomes.* Service providers will be challenged to focus on multiple student and client outcomes. No longer will simple placement in the community be enough. Individuals like Glenn will need to express their values and dreams to service providers who can help translate them into a realistic, yet satisfying, match in vocational and residential placements. Glenn may want to work in the community and receive benefits and wages that allow him to participate in his favored leisure pursuits. Professionals working with individuals like Glenn will need to work toward a satisfactory match between services and client needs.

3. *Inclusion of individuals with the most severe disabilities in services.* Professionals will need to work toward the continued inclusion of individuals with the most severe disabilities into the delivery system. A burgeoning in the assistive technology field will mean that many more adaptations can be made to accommodate individuals with disabilities. With assistance and support, individuals like Melody can be successfully employed in competitive worksites.

4. *Comprehensive training for professional staff.* The new and changing roles of professionals will require better training of professional staff. Training will need to focus on coordination of efforts between professionals and on strategies that foster communication and cooperation. Professionals working with new students like Rob just entering the school system will need to know characteristics of disabilities, systematic instructional techniques, and how to access community facilities outside the school.

5. *Development of comprehensive and coordinated funding sources.* Although all the individuals described above would probably be eligible for special education services, individuals like Melody and Glenn, who are outside of or who are leaving the school system, might not be able to receive needed services. Melody, who is severely disabled, may be judged a poor candidate for employment and may be

denied vocational rehabilitation services. Because of inconsistencies of long-term funding sources, Glenn may initially receive some services but then be denied further service when funding expires. Long-term and coordinated funding for services must be established to ensure that all individuals receive necessary services.

6. *The need for continued research in the field of developmental disabilities.* Research in the area of developmental disabilities must continue and should include a focus on more advanced technology to foster independence, examination of attitudes and how to enhance favorable attitude change, methods of fostering choice-making skills, and longitudinal data on outcomes in all facets of life of individuals who are developmentally disabled. Research represents forward movement in the field.

The challenges outlined throughout the chapter should not serve to daunt professionals working with individuals with disabilities but rather, suggest a means to generate an introspective look at services offered and areas where improvement can be made. Challenge does not denote insurmountable odds but offers a means with which to reach a goal. Individuals like Rob, Susan, Melody, and Glenn count on services providers undertaking the professional challenges facing them.

Appendix 9-1.   Federal Definition of Developmental Disabilities

"The term 'developmental disability' means a severe, chronic disability of a person 5 years of age or older which–
—is attributable to a mental or physical impairment or combination of mental and physical impairments;
—is manifested before the person attains age twenty-two;
—is likely to continue indefinitely;
—results in substantial functional limitations in three or more of the following areas of major life activity:
self-care
receptive and expressive language
learning
mobility
self-direction
capacity for independent living
economic self-sufficiency

—reflects the person's need for a combination and sequence of special interdisciplinary, or generic care, treatment, or other services which are of lifelong or extended duration and are individually planned and coordinated except that such term, when applied to infants and young children means individuals from birth to age 5, inclusive, who have substantial developmental delay or specific congenital or acquired conditions with a high probability of resulting in a developmental disability if services are not provided."
–The Developmental Disabilities Assistance and Bill of Rights Act Amendments of 1990

References

1. Allen DA, Stefanowski-Hudd S. Are we professionalizing parents? Weighing the benefits and pitfalls. Ment Retard. 25: 133–139, 1987.
2. Amado AN, Lakin KC, Menke JM. Chartbook on Services for People with Developmental Disabilities. Minneapolis, University of Minnesota, Center for Residential and Community Services, 1990.
3. Bailey JS. Wanted: A rational search for the limiting conditions of habilitation in the retarded. Analysis and Intervention in Developmental Disabilities. 1: 45–52, 1981.
4. Bak JJ, Siperstein GN. Similarity as a factor effecting change in children's attitudes toward mentally retarded peers. American Journal of Mental Deficiency. 91: 524–531, 1987.
5. Banks R, Aveno A. Adapted miniature golf: A community leisure program for students with severe physical disabilities. Journal of The Association for Persons with Severe Disabilities. 11: 209–215, 1986.
6. Bates P, Morrow SA, Panscofar E, Sedlak R. The effect of functional vs. non-functional activities on attitudes/expectations of non-handicapped college students: What they see is what they get. Journal of the Association for Persons with Severe Handicaps. 9: 73–78, 1984.

7. Brickey MP, Campbell KM, Browning LJ. A five year follow-up of sheltered workshop employees placed in competitive jobs. Ment Retard 23: 67–73, 1985.

8. Brown L, Branston MB, Hamre-Nietupski S, Pumpian I, Certo N, Gruenewald LA. A strategy for developing chronological age appropriate and functional curricular content for severely handicapped adolescents and young adults. Journal of Specific Education. 13: 81–90, 1979.

9. Dattilo J, Rusch FR. Effects of choice on leisure participation for persons with severe handicaps. Journal of The Association for Persons with Severe Handicaps. 10: 194–199, 1985.

10. Dunst CJ, Trivette CM, Deal A. Enabling and Empowering Families. Cambridge, MA, Brookline Books, 1988.

11. Fifield MG, Smith BC. eds. Personnel Training for Serving Adults with Developmental Disabilities. Logan, Utah State University Developmental Center for Handicapped Persons, 1985.

12. Gardner JF. Introduction: A decade of change. In: Gardner JF, Chapman MS. eds. Program Issues in Developmental Disabilities. A Guide to Effective Habilitation and Active Treatment. Baltimore, Paul H. Brookes, 1990, pp 3–18.

13. Giangreco MF. Making related service decisions for students with severe disabilities: Roles, criteria, and authority. Journal of The Association for Persons with Severe Handicaps. 15: 22–31, 1990.

14. Goldberg LJ. Legal rights of persons with developmental disabilities. In: Gardner JF, Chapman MS. eds. Program Issues in Developmental Disabilities. A Guide to Effective Habilitation and Active Treatment. Baltimore, Paul H. Brookes, 1990, pp 19–38.

15. Greenspan S, Shoultz B. Why mentally retarded adults lose their jobs: Social competence as a factor in work adjustment. Applied Research in Mental Retardation. 2: 23–38, 1981.

16. Guess D, Benson A, Siegel-Causey E. Concepts and issues related to choice-making and autonomy among persons with severe disabilities. Journal of The Association for Persons with Severe Handicaps. 10: 79–86, 1985.

17. Halpern AS. Transition: A look at the foundations. Except Child 51: 479–486, 1985.

18. Hanley-Maxwell C, Rusch FR, Chadsey-Rusch J, Renzaglia A. Reported factors contributing to job terminations of individuals with severe disabilities. Journal of the Association for Persons with Severe Handicaps. 11: 45–52, 1986.

19. Hill ML, Wehman P, Kregel J, Banks PD, Metzler HMD. Employment outcomes for people with moderate and severe disabilities: An eight-year longitudinal analysis of supported competitive employment. Journal of The Association for Persons with Severe Handicaps. 12: 182–189, 1987.

20. Houghton J, Bronicki GJB, Guess D. Opportunities to express preferences and make choices among students with severe disabilities in classroom settings. Journal of The Association for Persons with Severe Handicaps. 12: 18–27, 1987.

21. Inge KJ, Banks PD, Wehman P, Hill JW, Shafer MS. Quality of life for individuals who are labeled mentally retarded: Evaluation competitive employment versus sheltered workshop employment. Competitive Employment for Persons with Mental Retardation: From Research to Practice. Vol II. (monograph). Richmond, VA, Rehabilitation Research and Training Center, 1987, pp 211–232.

22. Karan OC, Berger-Knight C. Training and staff development issues in developmental disabilities. Remedial and Special Education. 7(6): 40–45, 1986.

23. Kauffman JM, Krouse J. The cult of educability: Searching for the substance of things hoped for; the evidence of things not seen. Analysis and Intervention in Developmental Disabilities. 1: 53–60, 1981.

24. Kiernan WE, Stark JA. Pathways to Employment for Developmental Disabilities. Baltimore, Paul H. Brookes, 1986.

25. Kregel J, Sale P. Preservice preparation of supported employment professionals. In: Wehman P, Moon MS. eds. Vocational Rehabilitation and Supported Employment. Baltimore, Paul H. Brookes, 1988, pp 129–143.

26. Kregel J, Shafer MS, Wehman P, West M. Policy development and public expenditures in supported employment: Current strategies to promote statewide systems change. Journal of The Association for Persons with Severe Disabilities. 14: 283–292, 1989b.

27. Kregel J, Wehman P. Supported employment: Promises deferred for persons with severe disabilities. Journal of The Association for Persons with Severe Handicaps. 14: 293–303, 1989.

28. Kregel J, Wehman P, Banks PD. The effects of consumer characteristics and type of employment model on individual outcomes in supported employment. J Appl Behav Anal. 22: 407–415, 1989a.

29. Lagomarcino TR. Job separation issues in supported employment. In: Rusch FR. ed. Supported Employment. Models, Methods, and Issues. Sycamore, Ill, Sycamore, 1990.

30. Larson SA, Lakin KC. Deinstitutionalization of persons with mental retardation: Behavioral outcomes. Journal of The Association for Persons with Severe Handicaps. 14: 324–332, 1989.

31. Mank D, Rhodes L, Bellamy GT. Four supported employment alternatives. In: Kiernan W, Stark J. eds. Pathways to Employment for Developmentally Disabled Adults. Baltimore, Paul H. Brookes, 1986, pp 139–153.

32. Matson JL, Rusch FR. Quality of life: Does competitive employment make a difference? In: Rusch FR. ed. Competitive Employment Issues and

Strategies. Baltimore, Paul H. Brookes, 1986, pp 331–337.

33. Moon MS, Inge KJ, Wehman P, Brooke V, Barcus JM. Helping Persons with Severe Mental Retardation Get and Keep Employment. Baltimore, Paul H. Brookes, 1990.

34. Noble JH, Conley RW. Accumulating evidence on the benefits and costs of supported and transitional employment for persons with severe disabilities. Journal of The Association for Persons with Severe Handicaps. 12: 163–174, 1987.

35. Orelove F, Sobsey D. Educating Children with Multiple Disabilities. A Transdisciplinary Approach. Baltimore, Paul H. Brookes, 1987.

36. Peck CA. Increasing opportunities for social control by children with autism and severe handicaps: Effects on student behavior and perceived classroom climate. Journal of The Association for Persons with Severe Handicaps. 10: 183–193, 1985.

37. Peterson CP. Support services. In: Wilcox BL, York R. eds. Quality Education for Severely Handicapped: The Federal Investment. Washington, DC, Bureau of Education for the Handicapped, 1980, pp 136–163.

38. Powers MD. A systems approach to serving persons with severe developmental disabilities. In: Powers MD. ed. Expanding Systems of Service Delivery for Persons with Developmental Disabilities. Baltimore, Paul H. Brookes, 1988, pp 1–16.

39. Richardson M, West P, Fifield MG. Preservice and professional training. In: Fifield MG, Smith BC. eds. Personnel Training for Serving Adults with Developmental Disabilities. Logan, Utah State University, Developmental Center for Handicapped Persons, 1985, pp 67–83.

40. Roper PA. Special olympics volunteers' perceptions of people with mental retardation. Education and Training in Mental Retardation. 25: 164–175, 1990.

41. Sailor W, Goetz L, Anderson J, Hunt P, Gee K. Research on community intensive instruction as a model for building functional, generalized skills. In: Horner RH, Dunlap G, Koegel RL. eds. Generalization and Maintenance. Lifestyle Changes in Applied Settings. Baltimore, Paul H. Brookes, 1988, pp 67–98.

42. Shevin M, Klein NK. The importance of choice-making skills for students with severe handicaps. Journal of The Association for Persons with Severe Handicaps. 9: 159–166, 1984.

43. Sileo TW, Rude HA, Luchner JL. Collaborative consultation: A model for transition planning for handicapped youth. Education and Training in Mental Retardation. 23: 333–339, 1988.

44. Snell M, Browder D. Community-referenced instruction: Research and issues. Journal of The Association for Persons with Severe Handicaps. 11: 1–11, 1986.

45. Snell ME, Eichner SJ. Integration for students with profound disabilities. In: Brown F, Lehr DH. eds. Persons with Profound Disabilities. Issues and Practices. Baltimore, Paul H. Brookes, 1989, pp 109–138.

46. Steere DE, Wood R, Panscofar EL, Butterworth J. Outcome-based school-to-work transition planning for students with severe disabilities. Career Development for Exceptional Individuals. 13: 57–70, 1990.

47. Stokes TF, Baer DM. An implicit technology of generalization. J Appl Behav Anal. 10: 349–367, 1977.

48. Strain PS. Identification of social skills curriculum targets for severely handicapped children in mainstream preschools. Applied Research in Mental Retardation. 4: 369–382, 1983.

49. Strain PS, Odom SL. Peer social initiations: Effective intervention for social skills development of exceptional children. Except Child. 52: 543–551, 1986.

50. Summers JA. Who are developmentally disabled adults? A closer look at the definition of developmental disabilities. In: Summers JA. ed. The Right to Grow Up. An Introduction to Adults with Developmental Disabilities. Baltimore, Paul H. Brookes, 1986, pp 3–16.

51. Szymanski ED, Hanely-Maxwell C, Asselin S. Rehabilitation counseling, special education, and vocational special needs education: Three transition disciplines. Career Development for Exceptional Individuals. 13: 29–38, 1990a.

52. Szymanski ED, Hanley-Maxwell C, Parker RM. Transdisciplinary planning for supported employment. In: Rusch FR. ed. Handbook of Supported Employment: Models, Methods, and Issues. Chicago, Sycamore, 1990b, pp 199–214.

53. Szymanski ED, King J, Parker RM, Jenkins WM. The state-federal rehabilitation program: Interface with special education. Except Child. 56: 70–76, 1989.

54. Thorpe HW, Chiang B, Darch CB. Programming generalization when mainstreaming exceptional children. Journal of Special Education Technology. 4: 15–23, 1981.

55. *Timothy W. v. Rochester, N.H.* School District 84-733 (1985).

56. Turnbull AP, Turnbull HR. Families, Professionals, and Exceptionality: A Special Partnership. 2nd ed. Columbus, OH, Charles E. Merrill, 1990.

57. U. S. Department of Education (USDE), Office of Special Education and Rehabilitative Services. Eleventh Annual Report to Congress on the implementation of Education for All Handicapped Children. Washington, DC, 1989.

58. Voeltz LM. Program and curriculum innovations to prepare children for integration. In: Certo N, Haring N, York R. eds. Public School Integration

of Severely Handicapped Students: Rational Issues and Program Alternatives. Baltimore, Paul H. Brookes, 1984, pp 155–183.

59. Wehman P. School to work: Elements of successful programs. Teaching Exceptional Children. 23:40–43, 1990.

60. Wehman P. A National Analysis of Supported Employment Growth and Implementation. Richmond, VA, Virginia Commonwealth University, Rehabilitation Research and Training Center on Supported Employment, 1990.

61. Wehman P, McLaughlin P. Program Development in Special Education. New York, McGraw-Hill, 1981.

62. Wehman P, Kregel J, Barcus JM. From school to work: A vocational transition model for handicapped students. Except Child. 52: 25–37, 1985.

63. Wehman P, Kregel J, Seyfarth J. Transition from school to work for youth with severe handicaps: A follow-up study. Journal of the Association for Persons with Severe Handicaps. 10: 132–136, 1985a.

64. Wehman P, Kregel J, Seyfarth J. Employment outlook for young adults with mental retardation. Rehabilitation Counseling Bulletin. Dec: 90–98, 1985b.

65. Wehman P, Moon MS, Everson JM, Wood W, Barcus JM. Transition from School to Work. New Challenges for Youth with Severe Disabilities. Baltimore, Paul H. Brookes, 1988.

66. Western Michigan University Supported Employment Evaluation Project. Supported Employment in Michigan. Fourteenth Quarterly Statistical Report: Summary Version. Kalamazoo, Michigan, College of Arts and Sciences, 1990, May.

67. Wolfensberger W. The Principle of Normalization in Human Services. Toronto, National Institute on Mental Retardation, 1972.

68. Zigler E, Berman W. Discerning the future of early childhood intervention. Am Psychol. 38: 894–906, 1983.

Chapter 10
Early Intervention

Rebecca J. Anderson
David C. Littman

*Legislation does not determine the
quality of service delivery: people do*
(Healy et al. 1989)

If all exceptional young children and
their families had the same resources, priorities, and concerns, then providing state-
of-the-art early intervention services would
be easy. In such a scenario, a few simple
research studies would answer the relatively few questions about how best to
serve the uniform population, and turning
the research results into practical information would be a straightforward, one-time-
only exercise. Curriculum materials for
teaching early interventionists would be
developed, and preparation programs using the materials could be established
wherever and whenever needed.

The reality is, of course, that the resources, priorities, and concerns of the
early-intervention population are incredi-
bly diverse. Early interventionists cannot
rely on a few simple research studies that
can be easily translated into practical
guidelines. Rather, numerous complex
studies of families, children, preparation
methods for early interventionists, and
specific intervention strategies are needed
to determine how to serve effectively the
diverse population of young children and
their families. Because of the quantity and
complexity of the information required to
provide early intervention, building the
bridge between research and practice is an
immense task that cannot be accomplished
by either researchers or practitioners alone.

Our intent in writing this chapter, as a
combination team of a practitioner and a
researcher, is to consolidate key information about early intervention in a concise,
practical, ready-to-use reference. Our goal
is to inform practitioners about what information is needed to provide early intervention services; where to get this information;
and how to use it.

The chapter begins with a review of
four of the primary reasons why we are
committed to providing early intervention
services and describes five "guiding philosophies" that appear over and over in
models of early intervention services. Then
comes the focus of the chapter: Content
information organized around a four-phase
model of service delivery in which assessment, program design, delivery, and program evaluation form a cycle that starts
over when the results of the evaluation are
used as part of the assessment for the subsequent trip through the cycle.

Why Provide Early Intervention Services?

1. *It's the law.* Individuals with Disabilities Education Act Amendments of 1991 or IDEA (formerly Public Law 99-457, the Education of the Handicapped Act Amendments of 1986), requires in all states a free and appropriate education for children age 3 through 5 years with disabilities. In addition, it requires states that accept IDEA funds to provide services to infants and toddlers, from birth through 2 years of age, with disabilities.

2. *It's the best time to begin.* Early intervention focuses on prevention and intervention. Both research results and demonstrated practice show that the earlier a problem is detected and the earlier treatment is begun, the more effective it is. Early intervention can alter, in a positive direction, overall development and learning (Lilly and Shotel 1987).

3. *It's cost effective.* Because we are a society with limited resources, we must be concerned with getting the most benefit for our expenditures in early intervention. It is clear from large-scale research efforts that the longer help is delayed, the more it costs. Shearer and Mori (1987) put it well:

> Early education models funded by the Handicapped Children's Early Education Program (HCEEP) and research findings have amply demonstrated the cost effectiveness of early intervention in terms of ameliorating the effects of handicapping conditions *and in preventing secondary problems* (emphasis added) that compound the original deficit.

4. *It works.* There is no longer any question that early intervention can be effective. There is, of course, controversy about just how effective particular types of early intervention may be for particular types of disabilities (Dunst 1986), but it is clear that well-considered, professionally delivered early intervention services can help virtually any child with a disabling condition and that early intervention saves time, money, and pain.

Guiding Philosophies

What follows is a brief description of five primary guiding philosophies that are integral to successful early intervention. Of course, these philosophies portray ideals: Most programs manifest each of these philosophies to a greater or lesser degree depending on the number of employees, their preservice and in-service training, and program budget limitations. For example, many teams use consultants who are available for only a small number of hours. This factor may make functioning as a team difficult. Nonetheless, the primary guiding philosophies are important components of early intervention service delivery and deserve special consideration. They are described briefly below and in more detail in the delivery section of this chapter.

1. Family involvement. Early intervention must (intent of IDEA) include the family. Key areas for family involvement include assisting the parents in adapting to the special needs of their young child; assisting the parents to utilize needed community resources; and facilitating mutually satisfying parent-child interactions (Niños Especiales Program 1986). Supporting the parental care-giving role should be a primary focus for services.

2. Case management. No single professional discipline or agency has all the necessary resources to address all of the needs of a young child with a disability and his or her family. Therefore, case management (often referred to as service coordination) is meant to provide a coordinated network of service delivery within and across community agencies specific to the needs of each young child and family. A single case manager, preferably someone who works directly with the young child and family,

should be identified for coordinating service delivery (Niños Especiales Program 1986).

3. Transdisciplinary approach. A transdisciplinary approach requires team members from multiple disciplines and includes the parents as equal team members, all working together as an interdisciplinary team. In addition, active teaching and learning across disciplines should occur as a result of early intervention services (Niños Especiales Program 1986), not only to enhance service delivery but to reduce the number of personnel directly working with infants and young children. If services are home based, this strategy reduces the number of personnel visiting the home (which can become overwhelming for family members).

4. Transition planning. Transition planning requires that intervention goals and instructional strategies reflect the development of skills that will be needed for success in each child's next environment (Niños Especiales Program 1986). Transitions frequently encountered in early intervention may include: (a) hospital to home, (b) home based services to center based services, (c) center based services to elementary school.

5. Cultural sensitivity. Cultural sensitivity is an important issue when a provider of early intervention services is of a cultural heritage different than that of the family and young child receiving services. Care-taking and child-rearing practices can differ enormously. Family members will be most responsive to suggestions and strategies that are consistent with their cultural values. Language barriers, cultural roles and norms, and socioeconomic factors are all important considerations when providing early intervention services (Niños Especiales Program 1986).

We will now incorporate these five guiding philosophies into the service delivery cycle. The critical focus for the remainder of this chapter is not why we need to provide early intervention services but how.

Assessment

Monitoring, screening, and assessment, the starting points in early intervention, represent the beginning of the service delivery cycle, which may begin at birth. If an infant is at risk for a developmental disability, he or she should be monitored by hospital staff or local follow-up clinics. Infants are typically monitored at regular intervals, such as every 3 or 4 months, for any signs of delayed development. Children with identified risk factors require more frequent observation. For example, a premature infant born with a very low birth weight of 2 pounds and respiratory distress syndrome needs intense developmental monitoring even if the outcome, medically, is positive. Infants with medical complications or questionable birth histories who require a stay in the neonatal intensive care unit or who are born to a substance-abusing mother need to be monitored.

The goal of screening in early intervention is to determine quickly whether administering a complete assessment battery (comprehensive testing in all developmental domains) is necessary, and if so, produce some clues regarding which assessment tools would be most useful. It is important to note that interventionists testing very young children need significant training (Meissels and Provence 1990).

After screening, infants and young children with poor or questionable results are typically referred to early intervention programs. It is important that early intervention programs have well-established eligibility criteria and referral procedures in place. Early intervention programs should not duplicate screening or assessment activities already performed but should expand testing that has been completed and establish services promptly when they are indicated. Sources of referrals may include professionals from medical, educational, and social agencies as well as family members.

The goal of assessment in early intervention is to collect enough information about the child's developmental status, medical status, and related family resources, priorities, and concerns to deliver needed services. Results from an initial assessment battery indicate whether intervention services are necessary and will provide a foundation of information on which the individualized family service plan (IFSP) or individualized education program (IEP) will be built.

This next step of the service delivery cycle is largely dependent upon the results of the assessment and the additional information collected. When designing a service plan it is necessary to have extensive knowledge not only of the child's status but also of the family's need for information and support and of the goals they have for their infant or young child. The initial assessment battery provides a baseline against which to compare future health status, developmental growth, and achievement of both child- and family-related goals.

Tools Needed in Early Intervention

There are different types of assessment tools, several developmental domains to test in, and a variety of standardized and criterion-referenced tools on the market. It is important that tools selected demonstrate high levels of validity and reliability. Interpretation of standardized assessments must also take into account cultural norms. For example, our experience suggests that, for young children of Puerto Rican heritage, social skills are often slightly above the norm and independent feeding skills are often slightly below the norm (tests normed on the Anglo culture). We believe that cultural differences (not biologic ones) in teaching social and feeding skills are responsible. Whenever possible, one should use tools that are already normed on the target population with which one intends to use them. When not possible, note this in the report.

To eliminate some confusion and expedite the assessment process, we have rec-

ommended types of tools to use in an assessment battery and, in some cases, a sample tool that, given our experience, may be most helpful to begin with. Table 10-1 contains a sample assessment battery with specific recommendations. The intent of this table is to assist practitioners and teams of practitioners to develop an early intervention assessment battery. It is only a beginning and should in no way be considered complete for all children and families. Table 10-1 includes tools for use with young children ages birth through 5 years. It also includes tools for practitioners to use collaboratively with families. The table begins with the category of general information. Before any testing takes place, the assessment battery and its purpose should be fully explained to the family, and written permission should be obtained. When possible, one should test the child in a familiar environment, with familiar objects, and ask a family member to help elicit desired behaviors. When this is not possible, one should rely more heavily on parent report than on behavior (or lack of it) elicited for unfamiliar people in an unfamiliar environment.

Demographic information (for example, names of family members, their ages, their relationship to the child) may now be collected. One should also collect current medical information (for example, diagnosis, medications) and a birth history (for example, length of gestation, weight at birth, APGAR scores, complications).

The next step is to administer a normative assessment tool. Normative assessment tools compare a child's developmental status with that of other children at the same chronologic age. A standard or percentile score of 100 is considered average (mean). A normative tool helps determine eligibility by indicating how far away from the mean a given child is. Over time, a normative tool establishes a pattern indicating whether a child is progressing closer to the mean or moving farther away from it. When combined with other sources, these

Table 10-1. Sample Assessment Battery in Early Intervention

Type of Tool	Purpose	Specific Recommendations
1. Tools for infants/young children		
General information	Permission slips signed by legal guardian (consent and release of information) Collect demographic data (child and family) Collect current medical information and birth history	Self-made forms specific to population and program needs are best
Normative	Provides a standard score Determines eligibility Overall program evaluation	Battelle Developmental Inventory (screening tool included) (Newborg et al. 1984)
Criterion referenced	Provides current levels of skill acquisition in all domains Assists with designing intervention plan	Carolina Curriculum for Handicapped Infants and Infants At Risk (0–2) (Johnson-Martin et al. 1986) Carolina Curriculum for Preschoolers with Special Needs (2–5) (Johnson-Martin et al. 1990)
Language specific	Specifically measures skill acquisition of receptive and expressive language (few language items on other tests at this age) Assists with designing intervention plan	Receptive and Expressive Emergent Language Scale (Bzoch and League 1970)
Behavior specific	Measures general behavioral characteristics (items not on other tests) Assists with designing intervention plan	Carolina Record of Individual Behavior (Simeonsson 1979)
Clinical evaluations	Conducted by specialists as needed Answers remaining questions Assists with designing intervention plan; for example, motor items tested within normal limits but quality of movement is poor	Team decision after reviewing previous tests results; for example, team decides clinical physical therapy evaluation is necessary
2. Family tools		
Community resources	Identifies services received from other local agencies and frequency of contact Identifies gaps in services Facilitates case management and interagency coordination Assists with designing intervention plan	Self-made checklist consisting of all local medical, educational, and social agencies, name of contact person, phone number, and frequency of use
Information	Allows caretakers to request and utilize information of current importance to them Assists with designing intervention plan	Self-made checklist specific to population served Need corresponding written pamphlets to distribute
Support	Primary caretaker identifies resources, priorities, and concerns regarding routine child-care tasks Assists with designing intervention plan	Family-Focused Intervention Rating Scale (Dunst 1983)

data can be a valuable measure of a program's effectiveness (for example, at preventing secondary causes of developmental delays). It is important to mention that young children with severe handicaps or progressive diseases (such as acquired immunodeficiency syndrome [AIDS]) will most likely move farther away from the mean as they age. For these populations, one should expect this pattern and use the information as a description of one's population (for example, when seeking additional resources). Normative tools are (typically) not the best tools to use for program planning. They often contain test items (for example, standing on one foot) that are not functional skills to teach. For this reason it is necessary to use a criterion-referenced tool.

Criterion-referenced tools provide information on which skills a given child can and cannot do. Many criterion-referenced tests include all developmental domains and some include a correlating curriculum. These tools are usually the most helpful for program planning as well as for documenting the achievement of new skills.

A language-specific tool is an important inclusion in an early childhood assessment battery. Language delays are common, as evidenced by the numerous language-based preschool programs in existence. Also, children with expressive language delays often receive poor scores for cognition (test items in this area may require a verbal response). It is important to determine whether assistive technology will be needed to facilitate interactive communication. A language-specific tool may help provide a more accurate picture.

Behavior-specific items are not typically included on the other types of tools previously mentioned. Measuring behavioral characteristics (for example, ability to console self) provides helpful information when developing intervention strategies.

Clinical observations, usually conducted by a specialist, should be utilized when any remaining questions are unanswered. For example, a given child might have test results within normal limits for motor development (for example, walks independently but gait is abnormal). When the quality of motor movement is poor, the child should be referred for a physical therapy evaluation.

Practitioners serving young children, age 3 through 5 years, are required to develop an IEP (not an IFSP). However, it is strongly recommended that practitioners serving this age group also address family resources, priorities, and concerns even though formal goals that address family desired outcomes are not required. In our experience, as global family needs are addressed and met (for example, getting food stamps, respite care), family members then actively seek specific information and skills to facilitate the development of their child. It is our hypothesis that as global needs are met, family members have more time, energy, and desire to devote to more specific activities that directly relate to their child's development. Practitioners need to help families identify their priorities and concerns, make the appropriate referrals, and follow up on them. The following tools are helpful in achieving these goals.

A community resource checklist facilitates case management and interagency coordination. It also assists with designing an intervention plan. It is recommended that each program develop a self-made checklist specific to the community it serves. This checklist should include all medical agencies that serve young children (for example, hospitals, clinics, private physicians), educational and intervention programs (for example, infant programs, day-care centers, preschool programs, head-start programs), social agencies (for example, food stamps, housing, counseling, job training). For each agency listed there should be space on the form to identify the name of the contact person and his or her phone number. An additional section should list the frequency of use.

In addition, an information checklist is recommended that is specific to the population served. This allows parents to identify what written information they are most interested in receiving at that time. Obviously, correlating written information (for example, pamphlets) needs to be available. Topic areas should include specific disabilities (for example, cerebral palsy, Down's syndrome); typical early childhood topics (for example, feeding, bedtime, toileting); developmental information (for example, how to facilitate key developmental milestones); and brochures on community resources.

Another support tool that is recommended is one that allows a primary care taker to identify resources as well as priorities and concerns with regard to routine child-care tasks. This tool should focus on the family's daily routine (for example, bathing, feeding, playing). We recommend the Family Focused Interview Rating Scale (Dunst 1983). This tool asks care takers to identify which family member performs given tasks and to rate how enjoyable or difficult it is. This tool is helpful for initiating dialogue with the family about the stresses in their life caused by caring for a young child with a disability.

Other possible tools include those that measure other areas of parental stress or of the home environment. A word of caution is necessary, however. It is not the practitioner's role to judge or "assess" family functioning. It is the practitioner's role to assist family members identify their own resources (for example, knowledgeable about child development) and priorities and concerns (for example, respite care) from *their* perspective. Taking prompt, direct action to assist families to build on their resources and address their identified priorities and concerns is a great method for establishing trust between family and practitioners.

Once an assessment battery is completed, the next step is a team meeting. We recommend completion of all tools within 1 month. Each team member should summarize his or her results. It is most helpful if a single summary page is completed at the meeting. A summary page should include overall test scores for the young child, identify areas needing intervention, list family identified resources, priorities, and concerns, as well as dates for future testing. The development of the intervention plan (be it IEP or IFSP) with the family and team members is now under way!

Figure 10-1 contains a simple checklist of items that we believe are essential. If most items are not complete for your team at this time, begin with a series of team meetings, prioritize goals and time lines, and share responsibility for completing these tasks. We have found that the checklist is a valuable roadmap to completing this process.

Designing Early Intervention Services

With the advent of IDEA, an IFSP is mandatory for any family receiving services under part H (ages birth to 3 years); IEPs are mandatory for children needing special services (ages 3 through 5 years). Because many practitioners are familiar with IEPs, the focus of this section is on designing individualized family service plans (IFSP).

An IFSP is required to document family status (resources, priorities and concerns) and to develop family-oriented goals and objectives. It is important to use strategies in service delivery that build upon family strengths. It is also important to assist families in their problem-solving efforts. Addressing family resources, priorities and concerns requires an additional set of strategies and services not required in an IEP. An IFSP is a comprehensive written plan of action developed collaboratively with the family, case manager, and other team members.

Table 10-2 includes a list of the legal requirements of an IFSP; descriptions of these requirements; where applicable, tools from the sample assessment battery that provide this information; and related examples as they might appear on an IFSP.

Figure 10-2 also contains a checklist for developing an IFSP. We recommend using this checklist during team meetings.

Figure 10-1. Assessment Checklist for Early Intervention Programs

Item	Completed (yes/no)	If Not, When	By Whom
1. Written eligibility criteria (correlates with program mission, state and federal regulations)			

2. Written referral procedures:
  A) receiving
  B) sending			

3. Written screening/assessment procedures
  a. Begins with a screening tool (unless completed before referral)
  b. Outlines typical sequence of tools
  c. Tools are valid and reliable
  d. Tools are culturally sensitive
  e. Includes: infant/young child tools:
    Normative referenced test
    Criterion-referenced test
    Test of language acquisition
    Test specific to behavior
    Additional clinical evaluation
 	
  Family tools:
    Community resources
    Need for information
    Need for support			

4. Assessment summary:
  a. Is conducted at a team meeting
  b. Identifies a case manager
  c. Is informative to outside agencies
  d. Summary report includes:
    Schedule of future testing
    Present levels of functioning
    Family resources, priorities, and concerns			

Delivering Early Intervention Services

Three issues arise in the service delivery phase of the early intervention cycle: where services are delivered; who delivers the services; and how the five guiding philosophies appear as real concerns when delivering services.

1. Where should services be delivered? A primary concern when delivering services is location. Ideally a continuum of options exists. Three typical options include home-based service (service providers visit families at home), center-based service (preschool, day-care center), or a combination of the two.

Delivering services in the home might be the option of choice when the focus of the intervention is facilitating parent-child interactions, providing significant support services to the family, or serving an extremely medically fragile child (in some cases services may need to begin in the hospital). Center-based services are usually the option of choice when intervention emphasizes peer interaction or a primary care taker is unavailable for home visits. Children typically make the transition from home-based to center-based services between the ages of 2 and 3 years; however, age alone should not determine the location of services; individual child and family needs should play the major role.

Table 10-2. Individualized Family Service Plan Contents, Requirements, and Examples

IFSP Requirements*	Descriptions	Related Tools	Sample Item
Present levels of child development in all domains	Domains include cognition; receptive/expressive language; gross and fine motor skills; self-help; and social-emotional development	Battelle Developmental Inventory, Carolina Curriculum for Handicapped Infants and Preschoolers	Gross-motor skills: Jerry is able to sit independently although muscle tone is slightly low. Pull to stand is emerging.
Statement of resources, priorities, and concerns	Statement of family desired outcomes relating to the enhancement of the child's development	Potentially all family tools used	Parents report a strong network of family and friends. Ms. Smith (mother) is interested in written information on Down's syndrome. Mr. Smith (father) is interested in visiting preschool programs in the local community.
Identify a case manager	Person responsible for facilitating clear communication between self, family, other team members, and community agencies		Jennifer Reilly, infant specialist.
Long-term goals and short-term objectives	Expected outcomes to be achieved by child and family, written in measurable terms including: criteria, procedures, and timelines used to determine degree of progress	Potentially all child and family tools used	Long-term goal: Jerry will walk independently. Short-term objective: Jerry will pull to stand and maintain a standing position, with support provided at hip level from Ms. Smith, for 5 consecutive minutes during three consecutive therapy sessions.
Specific early intervention services	A list of all services that address the unique needs of child and family including: method, frequency, and dates of initiated and anticipated duration of services	Community resources checklist	Nutrition services from county Child and Family Services One visit per month from 1/89 to 1/92.
Steps for transition	A list of activities that support the move of the child from one service delivery setting to another; includes documenting activities such as parent information, visitations and selection of new site, communication with staff at new site, follow-up phone calls.	Potentially all child and family tools used (although indirectly)	Appointments will be scheduled for parents and infant specialist to visit each of the three local preschool programs. This will be completed by 3/30/91.
Parental consent			

*IFSP = individualized family service plan

Figure 10-2. Individualized Family Service Plan Checklist

Item	Comments
1. Legal requirements	
a. Present levels of performance	
b. Schedule of future evaluations	
c. Statement of resources, priorities, and concerns	
d. Case manager	
e. Goals and objectives	
f. Specific services	
g. Transition plan	
h. Signature of legal guardian	
2. Goals and objectives	
a. Assessment results	
b. Desired outcomes and needs of the family	
c. Increased independence for child and family	
d. Terminology used is understandable to all	
3. Intervention strategies	
a. Are comprehensive and collaborative	
b. Build on identified strengths	
c. Address unique priorities and concerns	
d. Result from team decisions	
e. Are culturally competent issues	

2. Who should deliver services? This is a complex issue. Medical personnel (for example, nurse, occupational therapist), educational personnel (for example, infant specialist, special educator), social services personnel (for example, social worker, psychologist) comprise an interdisciplinary team. Team members ideally provide a variety of direct services, meet regularly, and provide ongoing consultation and training to each other.

The services to be provided should be a team decision and should be documented in the intervention plan. Decisions should be based on family input, assessment results, and team discussion. The decisions should also address these questions: Who on the team is best equipped to provide a comprehensive set of services, including case management, to a specific child and family? Which team members need to be available to provide training and consultation to the primary service providers of the

intervention plan? Is someone outside the team needed for a specific service?

3. What is the role of the guiding philosophies? The guiding philosophies, first mentioned in the introduction of this chapter, play a significant role in the implementation of an intervention plan. A goal statement for each guiding philosophy is therefore followed by a brief "real life" scenario.

1. The primary goal of **family involvement** is to assist each family maintain or develop a sense of confidence and competence with respect to their care-taking role.

☐ Case 10-1: Carmen

Part of the care-taking role includes medical appointments. A young mother, Rosa, of a premature infant, Carmen, requested the support of her home visitor (an early child special educator) when attending medical visits for her daughter. Now that she was at home following a lengthy stay in the neonatal intensive care unit, Carmen needed to visit a nurse practitioner monthly (to evaluate and monitor health care issues, including asthma). Carmen was also scheduled to visit a neurologist (to evaluate and monitor neuromotor development) and an ophthalmologist (because of retinopathy) routinely.

After further discussion Rosa revealed that she felt intimidated and overwhelmed with so many medical appointments for her daughter. She speaks English well but it is her second language. Rosa sometimes felt uncomfortable asking questions during these medical appointments. Rosa felt most comfortable with the nurse practitioner because they spoke on the phone frequently and a rapport had already developed.

The home visitor agreed to accompany Rosa on several visits each to the neurologist and the ophthalmologist. The purpose of this level of support was to assist Rosa in feeling confident and competent in her new care-taking role. The home visitor provided initial support with her presence; reassured Rosa that her questions were appropriate and that she had a right to ask them; and faded support (for example, phone call after visit) as Rosa's comfort level with this activity increased. It is important to point out that the home visitor did not take over the care-taking function by asking questions "for" Rosa.

2. The primary goal of **case management** in early intervention is the coordination of overall service delivery with a community focus.

☐ *Case 10-2: Christopher*

A 3-year-old boy, Christopher, attends a local integrated preschool program. Christopher has spina bifida, and his service providers include a nursery school teacher, a physical therapist, an occupational therapist, and a nurse. The team, including his parents, felt most comfortable with the physical therapist being case manager.

Case management services provided by the physical therapist include meeting regularly with other team members to discuss Christopher's needs (for example, helping him learn to maneuver his new wheelchair; notes to his parents about his school activities; inviting the family and their social worker to important meetings; maintaining all records on Christopher; attending medical visits as necessary (for example, when his wheelchair needed altering).

3. The primary goal of utilizing a **transdisciplinary approach** within an interdisciplinary team is to provide ongoing, active consultation and needed training across disciplines.

☐ *Case 10-3: John*

A 6-month-old infant, John, and his father have been receiving home visits from both an infant specialist and a physical therapist. The father's primary concern is John's high muscle tone. Although John responds positively to social interactions he is not yet initiating them. The infant specialist and the physical therapist decided to train each other in specific activities and strategies necessary to facilitate increased initiations of social play and increased motor development, respectively. This transdisciplinary approach included joint home visits initially while training each other; exchange of related written information; alternating home visits after training was complete; each taking responsibility for addressing both goal areas simultaneously with John and his father; continued consultation (meetings and by phone); and additional joint visits as needed to update activities for John.

4. The primary goal of **transition planning** is to help assure success for each child when moving from one location of service delivery to another.

□ *Case 10-4: Janet*

Janet is 4 years old and has been attending a local head-start program as well as receiving speech and language services. She has made significant improvement in her use of spontaneous language. Some sounds, however, are still difficult to understand, and it is expected that she will continue to need speech therapy next year when she enters kindergarten.

A transition plan for this child began 1 year prior to discharge. Transition activities included providing information to the family and the public elementary school about Janet and her expected needs; scheduling a team meeting that included the family and a representative from the elementary school such as the principal; assisting parents visit recommended programs; selecting a kindergarten placement (an IEP was developed by a team that comprised parents and current and new staff); inviting the kindergarten teacher and the speech therapist to a team meeting to review Janet's current progress and ask questions; forwarding records to the new placement site; scheduling a time for Janet to visit her new classroom; and follow-up phone calls made by the case manager to family and new staff working with Janet (2 weeks after class started).

5. The primary goal of **cultural sensitivity** is to maintain family involvement and provide services consistent with the needs of a minority population.

□ *Case 10-5: Roberto*

Roberto is an 18-month-old boy with Down's syndrome. He and his family have recently migrated from Puerto Rico. Culturally sensitive services to this family included a Spanish-speaking home visitor; extensive support services (instead of referrals, direct assistance dealing with other community agencies was provided such as helping the father enroll in English classes); including the aunt (a frequent care taker) as well as the mother in decisions about intervention goals and strategies; learning about their culture; and respecting the family's right to maintain their language, values, and customs.

In summary, service delivery needs to be comprehensive. Providing early intervention services that are genuinely family oriented and culturally sensitive, utilizing case management and a transdisciplinary approach, and preparing for transitions will indeed be providing comprehensive services.

Program Evaluation

Evaluation: Everybody hates it but everybody's got to do it.

Fortunately, there is another way to look at evaluation, and it is the way that we suggest in this chapter: "Evaluation: That's figuring out what we (team) did well and what we can do better."

The primary viewpoint of this chapter is that early intervention is an ongoing cycle of activities that does not culminate in, but begins anew, with evaluation. Thus, rather than feeling pressured by evaluation—feeling that evaluation is the point at which one is tested to see whether one has performed well enough—evaluation should be used as the device that answers the most important question that faces us all in early intervention: What should we do next? Our view of evaluation, then, is that its primary role should be formative rather than summative.

Summative evaluation addresses questions of an early intervention program's effectiveness at the end of the program's life. This means that summative evaluation occurs only once: when the child no longer needs intervention services. Formative evaluation, on the other hand, happens during the entire intervention process. Formative evaluation helps early interventionists determine how to improve services for individual children and is, therefore, much more important within the four-phase cycle of early intervention.

We describe below four evaluation problems that early interventionists have frequently asked us to help them with, and we give what we hope will be useful, usable answers. Table 10-3 identifies each of the four evaluation problems and offers brief suggestions for addressing each from the formative viewpoint.

1. Evaluating developmental progress. The evaluation of a child's progress is crucial for the effective improvement of early intervention services. Because the goal of early intervention is progress of the child through controlled, directed change, it is necessary constantly to monitor the child's status so that it is possible to control change effectively (Bricker and Littman 1982). Hence, formative evaluation of the child's progress must be a major emphasis. Formative evaluation information should

be collected from all team members, and all team members should be aware of all the information. If all members of the team know the results of the frequent evaluations of the child's status, then the results can be used formatively when it is useful to modify, or re-design, the child's intervention plan. Table 10-3 suggests what aspects of a child's performance are useful in this kind of formative evaluation, which seems best addressed by criterion-referenced measures.

Children who are being evaluated summatively (for example, before transition to a new service delivery setting) can be assessed with both norm-referenced and criterion-referenced assessments. The norm-referenced assessments give the new service professionals an objective picture of the child compared with other children, and the criterion-referenced measures provide information that can be extremely useful in devising new intervention goals.

2. Evaluating family desired outcomes. As it is for the child, the focus of evaluation for the family is formative. Interventionists should always have the goal of helping the

Table 10-3. Evaluation Problems and Suggestions

Evaluation Problem	Suggestions for Frequency
1. Child progress	
a. Individual	Frequent: Use for IFSP or IEP modification* (for example, tools in Table 10-1)
b. All enrolled	Occasional: Use to improve procedures for IFSP or IEP modifications (for example, tools in Table 10-1)
2. Family desired outcomes	
a. Individual	As above (for example, tools in Table 10-1)
b. All enrolled	As above (for example, tools in Table 10-1)
3. Consumer satisfaction	
a. Families	Frequent: Use to improve trust and involvement (for example, survey)
b. Other agencies	Occasional: Use to insure effective interagency coordination (for example, survey)
4. Program effectiveness	Occasional: To improve one or more phases of service delivery cycle (collective/all measures)

*IEP = individualized education program
 IFSP = individualized family service plan

family adapt to changes in the family and in the social environment. Because the goals specified in a family intervention plan typically focus on directed adaptive change, it is vital to keep track of whether the intervention strategies are producing the desired change (for example, Are family desired outcomes attained?). This approach requires formative evaluation that identifies areas in which the direction of change under the current intervention strategies is appropriate and areas of change that may benefit from shifts in intervention strategies or, just as frequently, in the outcomes.

3. Evaluating consumer satisfaction. If people are not happy with either the help they receive or the people who help them, they are likely either to drop out of the service system entirely or to go "shopping" for a "better" situation. One of the most important roles of formative evaluation is, therefore, to maintain an awareness of how families feel. Perhaps more than any of the other three evaluation problems, consumer satisfaction requires frequent monitoring (for example, survey).

4. Evaluating overall program outcome. Even when the overall program outcome is evaluated and summative evaluation intuitively seems most appropriate, the evaluation should be performed with a view to program improvement. Although many evaluation techniques commonly associated with summative evaluation are used for this purpose (for example, pre- and post-intervention measurements), the *interpretation* of the measures can, and should, be used formatively with the main goal of improving the program.

Realistic, useful evaluation is done for one simple reason: to determine what to do next to improve whatever one is evaluating. Evaluation feeds into all four phases of the service delivery cycle described in this chapter. Indeed, formative evaluation of the evaluation procedures themselves can be an extremely valuable activity and should be undertaken whenever one has the feeling that "something is wrong (or right!) but I just cannot put my finger on it." Evaluation is the process of putting one's finger on the problem. Thus, addressing any of the four evaluation problems described previously can have a significant impact on the assessment, design, delivery, or program evaluation phase of the early intervention cycle.

Summary

In summary, we have suggested that early intervention should be viewed as a four-phase cycle in which each phase influences all the others and is, in turn, influenced by them. Beginning with assessment, the early intervention cycle proceeds to program design, delivery, and program evaluation that serve the purpose of collecting valuable information that can be used to improve service delivery on the next pass through the cycle. Of course, this is an abstract view of the process that is useful for presenting the material we wanted to communicate, and, if readers now believe that the phases are not really laid out in a line but rather feed back and forth into one another, they are correct.

To assist readers who would like more detailed information, a brief resource list (books and journals) is provided in Appendix 10-1. The categories include assessment, families (working with them), general (early intervention), medical, parents (especially for them), and technology. Numerous resources are available at university libraries. We have selected a few that, in our opinion, may be most helpful.

Our goal has been to help service delivery personnel see their activities as an integral part of a community wide service delivery system. Knowledge is the key to power and if we have given you any knowledge in this chapter that has empowered you (as we hope you will empower the children and families you serve), then we are satisfied.

Appendix 10-1.   Key Resources in Early Intervention

Assessment

Bailey D, Woolery M. Assessing Infants and Pre-schoolers with Handicaps. Columbus, Ohio, Merrill Publishing Company, 1989.

Linder TW. Transdisciplinary Play-Based Assessment. Baltimore, Paul Brookes, 1990.

Meisels S, Provence S. Screening and Assessment: Guidelines for Identifying Young Disabled and Developmentally Vulnerable Children and Their Families. Washington, DC, National Center for Clinical Infant Programs, 1989.

Families (Working with Them)

Bennett T, Lingerfelt BV, Nelson DE. Developing Individualized Family Support Plans: A Training Manual. Cambridge, MA, Brookline Books, 1990.

Dunst C, Trivette C, Deal A. Enabling and Empowering Families: Principles and Guidelines for Practice. Cambridge, MA, Brookline Books, 1988.

Healy A, Kessee P, Smith B. Early Services for Children with Special Needs: Transaction for Family Support. Baltimore, Paul Brookes, 1989.

Johnson BH, McGongigel MJ, Kaufman RK. Guidelines and Recommended Practices for the Individualized Family Service Plan. Chapel Hill, NEC TAS CB #8040, 1989.

McWilliam RA. Family-Centered Intervention Plans. Tucson, AZ (in press).

General

Odom SL. Journal of Early Intervention [Division Manager, CEC, 1920 Association Drive, Reston, VA 22091].

Topics in Early Childhood Special Education (Journal). [Pro-Ed, 8700 Shoal Creek Boulevard, Austin, TX, 78758].

Bricker D. Early Intervention for At-Risk and Handicapped Infants, Toddlers and Preschool Children. [VORT Corporation, PO Box 60132, Palo Alto, CA 94306.] 1989.

Linder TW. Early Childhood Special Education Program Development and Administration. Baltimore, Paul Brookes, 1983.

Meisels SJ, Shonkoff JP. Handbook of Early Childhood Intervention: Theory, Practice and Analysis. Baltimore, Paul Brookes, 1988.

Odom SL, Karnes MB. Early Intervention for Infants and Children with Handicaps. Baltimore, Paul Brookes, 1988.

Parents

Dinkmeyer D, McKay GD, Dinkmeyer JS. Early Childhood Step: Systematic Training for Effective Parenting of Children Under Six (includes video). Circle Pines, MN, American Guidance Services, 1989.

Featherstone H. A Difference in the Family, Living with a Disabled Child. New York, Basic Books, 1980.

Finne N. Handling the Young Cerebral Palsied Child at Home. New York, E.P. Dalton, 1974.

Greenspan S, Greenspan NT. First Feelings: Milestones in the Emotional Development of Your Baby and Child. New York, Viking, Penguin, 1985.

Harrison H. The Premature Baby Book, A Parent's Guide to Coping and Caring in the First Years. New York, St. Martins Press, 1983.

Parks S. Make Every Step Count: Birth to One Year. Palo Alto, CA, VORT Corporation, 1986.

Special Care: For Families of Preterm and High Risk Infants (magazine). San Diego, CA, Special Care Productions.

Medical

Blackman JA. ed. Infants and Young Children: An Interdisciplinary Journal of Special Care Practices. Frederick, MD, Aspen.

Blackman JA. Medical Aspects of Developmental Disabilities in Children Birth to Three. Rockville, MD, Aspen, 1984.

Ensher GL, Clark DA. Newborns at Risk: Medical Care and Psychoeducational Intervention. Rockville, MD, Aspen, 1986.

Technology

Behrmann MM. ed. Integrating Computers into the Curriculum. A Handbook for Special Education. Boston, MA, College Hill Press (Division of Little, Brown), 1988.

Wright C, Namura M. From Toys to Computers: Access for the Physically Disabled Child. San Jose, CA, Christine Wright, 1985.

References

1. Bricker D, Littman D. Intervention and evaluation: The inseparable mix. Topics in Early Childhood Special Education. 1: 23–33, 1982.
2. Bzoch K, League R. The Receptive-Expressive Emergent Language Scale for the Measurement of Language Skills in Infancy. Gainsville, FL, Tree of Life Press, 1970.
3. Dunst CJ. Family-Focused Intervention Rating Scales. Morganton, NC, Family, Infant and Preschool Program, Western Carolina Center, 1983.
4. Dunst CJ. Overview of the efficacy of early intervention programs. In: Bickman L, Weathersford DL. eds. Evaluating Early Intervention Programs for Severely Handicapped Children and Their Families. Austin, TX, PRO-ED, 1986.
5. Healy A, Keesee PD, Smith BS. Early Services for Children with Special Needs: Transactions for Family Support. Baltimore, MD, Paul H. Brooks, 1989.
6. Johnson-Martin NM, Attermeier SM, Hackner B. The Carolina Curriculum for Preschoolers with Special Needs. Baltimore, MD, Paul H. Brooks, 1990.
7. Johnson-Martin NM, Jens K, Attermeir S. The Carolina Curriculum for Handicapped Infants and Infants At-Risk. Baltimore, MD, Paul H. Brooks, 1986.
8. Lilly TJ, Shotel JR. Legal issues and the handicapped infant: From policy to reality. Journal of the Division for Early Childhood. 12: 4–12, 1987.
9. Meissels S, Provence S. Screening and Assessment. Washington, DC, National Center for Clinical Infant Programs, 1990.
10. Newborg J, Stock J, Wnek L. Battelle Developmental Inventory. Allen, TX, DLM-Teaching Resources, 1984.
11. Niños Especiales Program. A Comprehensive Guide to Serving Puerto Rican Families in Early Intervention. Unpublished manual. Farmington, CT, Pediatric Research & Training Center, 1986.
12. Niños Especiales Program. An Introduction to Individual Family Service Plans in Early Childhood Special Education. Unpublished workbook. Farmington, CT, Pediatric Research & Training Center, 1987.
13. Shearer MS, Mori AA. Administration of preschool special education programs: Strategies for effectiveness. Journal for the Division for Early Childhood. 11: 161–170, 1987.
14. Simeonsson R. Carolina Record of Individual Behavior. Chapel Hill, NC, School of Education and Frank Porter Graham Child Development, 1979.

Chapter 11
Special Education

Kathryn A. Blake

The focus of this chapter is ways to solve problems subsumed under the following general problem: how to select and deliver the most appropriate special education services for developmentally disabled pupils.

At the same time, we consider a frequently occurring concurrent problem—the many times severely handicapped, multiply handicapped youngsters are labeled retarded or less intelligent than they really are because their handicaps, and the resulting deprivation of experience, prevent them from developing and expressing intellectual abilities they have. Given this label, they are treated as less intelligent. In turn, given this treatment, they function at a less intelligent level. This labeling, expectancy, and self-fulfilling prophecy sequence can lead to some terrible mistakes. On the other hand, if the sequence is broken, there can be some incredible victories. For example, see Brown (1955) and Lee and Jackson (1991).

One should consider Helen Keller as a keystone to understanding the general problem of how to select and deliver the most appropriate special education services for developmentally disabled pupils and the concurrent problem of labeling, expectancy, and the self-fulfilling prophecy.

Helen was the child of well-to-do parents. She was born in rural Alabama in the late 1800s. Her case was a classic one. She developed normally until she was about 18 months old. Then, following a childhood illness, she developed encephalitis. In turn, the brain destruction caused by the encephalitis left her blind and deaf. In addition, she did not have speech and language because the illness occurred while she was still prelingual or while she was just beginning to learn language. The Kellers tried hard to get services for Helen but few were available in that time and place. Therefore, Helen grew to middle childhood without intervention. Anyone looking at Helen might, in the parlance of the day, have called her feebleminded. She did not have speech and language, her social and emotional behavior was on an early childhood level, and she showed little grasp of her environment. At this point, the Kellers found Annie Sullivan. Annie recognized Helen's intellectual brilliance and potential for learning. She communicated to Helen the concept of language—that symbols stand for concrete and abstract entities. Given Helen's grasp of this concept of language and the technique of finger spelling in the hand, Annie went on to help Helen develop the strengths that helped to circumvent her limitations. Finally, Helen graduated from Radcliffe College and became a world-renowned author and lecturer. For more details, see such works as Joseph Lash's Helen and Teacher and Helen's writings, for example, The Story of My Life; Three Days To See; and The World I Live In.

More specifically then, the problem in providing special education services to developmentally disabled pupils is to describe the limitations caused by their handicaps, to go beyond these limitations to find their strengths, and to build a program of services that will capitalize on their strengths and circumvent their limitations. Above all, the task is not to miss the Helen Kellers among us, that is, not to slip too quickly into the label "severely mentally retarded" and with that label make the error of false expectancies and of the self-fulfilling prophecy.

This chapter is devoted to special education services that one can use to help solve problems in dealing with developmentally disabled pupils. That is, we consider special education services that are available for developmentally disabled pupils and how pupils are placed for the delivery of these services. As we do so, we consider how special education services articulate with other services and best practices for particular problems described elsewhere in this book. Then, we look at how special education services are organized within federal law.

We illustrate our points with the case of Geoffrey, a 14-year-old boy, classified as developmentally disabled. He is in school at present. His diagnosis is cerebral palsy—severe, spastic, quadriplegia. His speech and hearing are normal. His receptive language is adequate within the context of his physical limitations and the ensuing restricted experiences. He is limited in expressive language. He does not articulate words—not surprisingly, because the muscles in his speech-production apparatus are spastic. At this time, he has not learned alternative modes of communication to put together messages he wishes to convey. He has some use of his right arm and hand but no use of his left. He is limited in self-care and mobility.

Definitions

Definitions for two sets of services are pertinent: special education services and related services, as defined in the Education of the Handicapped Act.

Special Education Services

Special education services generally are the set of activities used to deliver instruction to handicapped pupils. More specifically, the following definition is used in The Education of the Handicapped Act [P.L. 94-142 as amended. 34 *CFR*, Sec. 300.4— Sec. 344-14 (excerpts)].

- *Special education* means specially designed instruction at no cost to the parents to meet the unique needs of a handicapped child, including classroom instruction, instruction in physical education, home instruction, and instruction in hospitals and institutions.
- This term includes speech pathology, or any other related service, if the service consists of specially designed instruction, at no cost to the parents, to meet the unique needs of a handicapped child, and is considered *special education* rather than *related service* under state standards.
- The term also includes vocational education if it consists of specially designed instruction, at no cost to the parents, to meet the unique needs of a handicapped child.
- The terms in this definition are defined as follows:
  - *At no cost* means that all specially designed instruction is provided without charge, but does not preclude incidental fees which are normally charged to non-handicapped students or their parents as a part of the regular education program.
  - *Physical education* is defined as follows: The term means the development of: physical and motor

fitness, fundamental motor skills and patterns; and skills in aquatics, dance, and individual and group games and sports (including intramural and lifetime sports). The term includes special physical education, adapted physical education, movement education, and motor development.

- *Vocational education* means organized educational programs which are directly related to the preparation of individuals for paid or unpaid employment, or for additional preparation for a career requiring other than a baccalaureate or advanced degree.

Related Services

The Education of the Handicapped Act requires that professionals provide related services in coordination with special education services. Related services are defined as follows:

> *Related services* include transportation and such developmental corrective, and other supportive services as are required to assist a handicapped child to benefit from special education, and includes speech pathology and audiology, and psychological services, physical and occupational therapy, recreation, early identification and assessment of disabilities in children, counseling services, and medical services for diagnostic and evaluation purposes. The term also includes school health services, social work services in schools, and parent counseling and training.

Coordination among Services

Coordination among services is the articulation of work focused on common objectives. There are many common elements in the activities professionals use in delivering several special education and related services to pupils. Using these elements in a mutually reinforcing way facilitates work with developmentally disabled pupils. Or-

ganizing this work within a case management team operation is a good technique. See Chapter 12, Case Management Services, for a description of case management.

Geoffrey's situation provides an illustration. His expressive language is limited because of the spasticity of the muscles in the speech apparatus and because of extremely limited experience related to the severe spastic quadriplegia and legal blindness.

A prime goal is to improve Geoffrey's expressive language so that he can communicate in academic, personal, social, and business situations. In turn, this prime aim requires that Geoffrey learn something to communicate and that he learn to use various speech- and language-production devices, computers, and other writing devices.

The teachers and the therapists can, and should, coordinate their services as they work with Geoffrey on these activities. For example:

1. The special education teachers, the regular education teachers, and in time the vocational education teachers should focus on the content of his expressive language. As he works on this content, the teachers should have him incorporate the techniques that the therapists are working on with him.

2. The speech and language therapists should focus on such activities as relaxation, breath control, correct placement of his tongue and other parts of his speech apparatus, and use of the various speech- and language-production devices. The speech and language therapists should have him practice these techniques on the content he is learning with the teachers and on the techniques he is learning with the physical and occupational therapists.

3. The occupational therapists and the physical therapists focus on such matters as increasing his hand and arm use through work on muscle relaxation and specific movements as well through learning to operate computers and other communication devices. As they do so, the physical and

occupational therapists should have him practice these techniques with the content he is learning with the teachers and the techniques he is learning with the speech and language therapists.

The case manager's role is to facilitate communication and cooperation among these specialists as well as among these specialists and Geoffrey's family to be sure that they all reinforce each others' work. In addition, the case manager has a responsibility to see that all of this activity stays focused on Geoffrey's movement toward more independent personal, vocational, and community living activities.

Instructional Planning and Placement

Instructional planning involves selecting from among components and systems for teaching a pupil. Placement involves locating a pupil for delivering instruction.

Figure 11-1 is a model of the sequence of activities we use in instruction. We employ seven components in two phases. Phase 1 is identifying present performance levels. Phase 2 is developing instructional programs. Here we use six activities:

1. Selecting instructional objectives
2. Selecting instructional sequences
3. Selecting instructional rates
4. Selecting instructional procedures
5. Deciding about instructional settings
6. Evaluating results of instruction.

Present Performance Levels

Present performance levels are the pupil's status on the new behavior specified in an objective to be taught and on the knowledge and skills required to learn that new behavior. That is, the information about present performance levels indicates whether the pupil is ready for working on the objective.

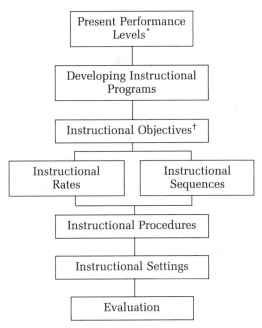

Figure 11-1. Instructional Model Sequence

*Also labeled Entering Behavior or Prerequisite Skills
†Also labeled Curriculum, when collected in a set

One faces several problems in dealing with present performance levels of a developmentally disabled pupil. A primary problem is to get valid and reliable estimates of the pupil's present performance levels. Evaluating severely handicapped, multihandicapped pupils is extraordinarily complex. One must meet two conditions before one can use norm-referenced instruments with anyone, that is, before one can compare a pupil to the norm group. These requirements apply also to the developmentally disabled pupil.

The first condition pertains to standard procedures of testing. The pupil being tested and the pupils in the norm group must have the same directions, use the same way of responding, and generally receive the test under the same circumstances. The norms do not apply if one violates this condition and does not give the test under the standard procedures. The test may be easier or harder for the pupil being tested than it was for pupils in the norm group. In turn, this could make the scores wrong in indicating what the pupil is really able to do.

The second condition in using norms in norm-referenced testing pertains to the pupil's background of experience with the language and materials in the test. The pupil being tested must have had the same chances as pupils in the norm group to learn the language used in the test and to learn how to use materials like those in the test items. If the pupil being tested has had either restricted experience or different experiences, for him or her the test items are not accurate ways to sample the behavior they are supposed to sample. He or she may be more capable than he or she shows on the test.

In most cases, one cannot meet these conditions with severely handicapped pupils. For example, their handicaps lead to restricted experiences—not experiences common with the norm group. In addition, their handicaps preclude their responding to the tests in the standard way that members of the norm group did when the norms were being established. As a result of these and similar problems, too often the evaluation techniques yield further measures of the handicap, not measures of the characteristics of interest.

For example, consider Geoffrey's situation. A psychologist evaluated Geoffrey within the framework of the Vineland Social Maturity Scale and other developmental scales. Given the results, he classified Geoffrey as severely mentally retarded. Of course, he had no basis for this classification. He did not get a measure of Geoffrey's intellectual potential. Instead, he got further measures of Geoffrey's cerebral palsy, his speech and language impairments, and their combined effect on Geoffrey's experience and his ability to perform items in the developmental scales.

A tragic error was nearly made here. Once a pupil is given a label one tends to treat the pupil according to that label, and he or she becomes the condition named in the label. The error was, however, prevented when a teacher put notes in Geoffrey's records indicating that he had a great sense of humor. What happened was that Geoffrey kept up with the activities in his surroundings. When funny things happened—often subtle things—he laughed. That is, he showed humor appropriate to the situation.

In time, monitors from the Special Education Department made the 3-year evaluation of the special education program in which Geoffrey was enrolled. Monitors saw the comments about Geoffrey in his records and went on to interview Geoffrey's teacher further.

Geoffrey's show of appropriate humor raised a flag on the situation. Severely mentally retarded pupils seldom show such characteristics. Therefore, the state monitors questioned Geoffrey's evaluation and classification. Finally, he was referred to a long-established center organized to evaluate severely handicapped pupils. The evaluators used diagnostic-prescriptive teaching. As a result of their work, they rejected the diagnosis of severe mental retardation and eliminated it from Geoffrey's records. Subsequently, teachers and therapists acted accordingly.

In the original diagnosis, we did not get an estimate of Geoffrey's intellectual ability. Instead, we got a further description of his cerebral palsy, his limited speech and language, and their effects on his experiences. Further evaluation eliminated this error.

The problem of reliably and validly assessing severely multihandicapped pupils has been widely considered. For example, see Kaufman (1990) and Luftig (1989). As one deals with the present performance levels of multihandicapped, severely handicapped pupils, one seeks to solve the problems with procedures like the following. One should leave alone characteristics that one has to infer, such as intellectual potential. Instead, one should follow a diagnostic-prescriptive teaching model.

The diagnostic-prescriptive model involves the sequence of selecting an instructional objective, teaching it intensively, and seeing how, and how much, the pupil learns. By successive approximations, one achieves the appropriate levels and procedures for teaching the pupil. Then, one sees how far and how fast he or she can go.

In assessing present performance levels, one should approach the youngster as if he or she were Helen Keller. As Annie Sullivan said, "I treat her like a seeing child because I expect her to act like a seeing child."

Developing Instructional Programs

Instructional programs include multiple components: instructional objectives, instructional sequences, instructional rates, instructional procedures, instructional settings, and instructional systems.

1. Instructional objectives are statements about what the pupil should be able to do if he or she learns through instruction. They are based on the goals for the pupil. They guide the selection of the instructional procedures and the evaluation procedures.

2. Instructional sequences are arrangements of instructional objectives in the order they are to be taught. Most sets of objectives for a given topic are arranged from simple to complex. That is, the objectives with no prerequisites are learned first. In turn, they become prerequisites for learning more complex skills.

3. Instructional rates are based on the timing for presenting the objectives, that is, how fast they are presented or how much time is spent on each objective. Instructional schedules are based on instructional rates.

4. A curriculum is a set of instructional objectives. A scope and sequence chart for a curriculum shows which objectives are included and the order in which they are organized.

5. Instructional procedures are the methods, media, and equipment used to help pupils reach their objectives.

6. Instructional methods are recurrent patterns of teacher behavior. They include teacher presentation (lectures, demonstrations), student problem solving (inquiry training, experimenting), group work (discussion, debate), individual work, direct experience (consultants, field trips), and behavioral techniques.

7. Instructional media are materials and machines. They include print media (textbooks, workbooks), audio, visual, and audiovisual media (photographs, audio tapes, video tapes, three-dimensional models), prototypes (games and simulations), and programs (programmed text, computer-assisted instruction).

8. Special equipment comprises devices to compensate for particular handicaps. Such devices include computers, braille writers, and so on.

9. Instructional settings are the ways personnel and space are arranged for delivering instruction to particular pupils or groups.

10. Personnel allocation refers to how pupils, teachers, and teacher aids are organized. Common patterns are tutoring, independent study, solitary activity, small groups, and large groups.

11. Space allocation is how facilities are arranged for instruction. Frequently used patterns are common areas, carrels, special centers, and depositories.

12. Instructional systems are sets of activities put together to teach a particular topic. Each package includes the several instructional components described in Figure 11-1 and in the text.

A problem in developing instructional programs for developmentally disabled pupils is how to select program elements based on a pupil's present performance levels. In the interests of normalization, one should select as much as possible from the programs for nonhandicapped pupils. At the same time, as necessitated by the pupil's present performance levels, one makes different selections than one would make for nonhandicapped pupils.

Selections differ for each developmentally disabled pupil depending on his or her present performance level. Sometimes, one selects only different objectives, sometimes only different schedules, sometimes only different procedures, or sometimes only different settings. Further, one sometimes makes different selections for more than one instructional component. Again, one should fit the program to the pupil's characteristics—his or her present performance levels.

Geoffrey's instructional activities are focused on life-management activities such as consumer economics and academics (for example, language-related tasks including listening to and reading literature and written composition; mathematics; social studies; and the sciences). In addition, Geoffrey's instructional program has a heavy emphasis on expressive communication through oral means and electronic assistive devices. In these latter activities, Geoffrey's teacher works closely with the speech and language, physical, and occupational therapists. Geoffrey's teachers use some of the same instructional procedures they use with other pupils. The difference is they devote more time to individual work. In addition, they adjust Geoffrey's instructional schedule to allow him more time for all of his work. See Stepping Out (1991), Bos and Vaughn (1991), Langone (1990), McDonnell et al. (1991), and Widerstorm et al. (1991), for more information about instructional activities for developmentally disabled youngsters.

Placement for Instruction

Educational placement is a tool for locating a pupil for convenient delivery of educational services to him or her. These placements are accompanied by barrier-free facilities and barrier-free transportation. There are a number of options for placing developmentally disabled pupils for their special educational services. Selecting among these options is governed by the principle of the least restrictive environment, based, in turn, on the goal of normalization.

The following is a list of frequently used options for special education placement of developmentally disabled pupils. The options are arranged from least restrictive to most restrictive.

- Regular class
- Regular class with consultation assistance to the teacher
- Regular class with assistance by itinerant specialist
- Regular class plus resource-room help
- Regular class with part-time special classes
- Full-time special class
- Full-time residential school
- Instruction in a hospital
- Instruction at home

When one is selecting placement options for a developmentally disabled pupil, the goal is to find the least restrictive environment. That is, given the instructional objectives in his or her individualized education program (IEP), the pupil is placed in the least restricted—most normal—environment in which instruction based on these objectives is being delivered to other pupils. For example, if the instructional objectives in the IEP of a 14-year-old developmentally disabled pupil were to achieve the social studies objectives outlined in the eighth grade curriculum, he or she could study social studies with the regular eighth grade class. The teacher may or may not need consultant help. If, on the other hand, another 14-year-old pupil's IEP specified the social studies objectives of the third grade curriculum, he or she would not work with the chronologically younger (9-year-old)—nonhandicapped third graders. Such a placement would not meet the normalization requirement. Instead, a more appropriate placement for instruction would be a resource room or a special class.

Placing developmentally disabled pupils in the least restrictive environment often causes management problems. For example, a developmentally disabled pupil who has hand and arm involvement that precludes handwriting and handling books and papers requires special accommodation such as audiotaping or videotaping of class notes, using devices to hold and turn the pages of books, and using computers or oral presentation for preparing papers, projects, and tests.

Geoffrey's IEP has life-management objectives as well as academic objectives that are on grade levels of pupils who are younger than he is chronologically. Therefore, he is enrolled in a special class for instruction to meet these objectives. Given his attention span and his propensity to keep up with his environment, he has objectives for music and literature on an eighth grade level commensurate with his chronologic age. He participates with the regular eighth-grade class to pursue these objectives.

Organization within the Law

Governing Law

Education-related legal and human rights of developmentally disabled pupils are heavily protected at the federal and state levels. These legal protections are based on a solid foundation of constitutional law, common law, and statutory and regulatory law. In addition, developmentally disabled citizens are governed by the same laws as all other United States citizens. Table 11-1 portrays the body of law affecting handicapped citizens.

Constitutional Source

Part 1 of Amendment 14 is the primary constitutional source for special education law. The four key clauses are the citizenship clause, the supremacy clause, the due process clause, and the equal protection clause.

Table 11-1. The Body of Law Affecting Handicapped Citizens

A. All citizens including handicapped citizens—the founding documents
1. The Declaration of Independence of the Thirteen American Colonies
2. The Constitution of the United States of America

B. Handicapped citizens only—statutes and administrative regulations
1. The Education of the Handicapped Act, The Handicapped Children Protection Act, and Other Amendments
2. The Rehabilitation Act and Amendments (Services)
3. The Rehabilitation Act and Amendments (Sections 501, 503, and 504)
4. The Developmental Disabilities Assistance Act
5. The Civil Rights Act of 1964 and The Civil Rights Restoration Act of 1987
6. The Architectural Barriers Act
7. The Fair Housing Amendments of 1988
8. The Air Carriers Access Act
9. The Social Security Act
10. The Perkins Act (Vocational Education)
11. The Americans with Disabilities Act of 1990
12. The states' statutes and regulations

C. Handicapped citizens only—policy statements, rulings, and decisions from
1. The United States Supreme Court
2. The United States Circuit Courts of Appeal
3. The United States District Courts
4. The states' courts
5. The United States Office of Education—Office of Special Education and Rehabilitation Services (OSERS)
6. The United States Office of Education—Office of Civil Rights (OCR)
7. The states' education agencies
8. Other federal and state executive departments

D. All pupils including handicapped pupils—the school law
1. All statutes and regulations and all rulings and decisions, for example, child abuse and neglect, freedom of expression

E. All citizens including handicapped citizens—the general law
All statutes and regulations and all rulings and decisions, for example, business law, criminal law

[Citizenship clause]: All persons born or naturalized in the United States and subject to the jurisdiction thereof, are citizens of the United States and of the State wherein they reside. [Supremacy clause]: No State shall make or enforce any law which shall abridge the privileges or immunities of citizens of the United States; [due process clause]: nor shall any State deprive any person of life, liberty, or property, without due process of law; [equal protection clause]: nor [shall any State] deny to any person within its jurisdiction the equal protection of the laws.

Common Law

The case law supporting the present-day status of handicapped pupils' rights and protection is strong. The ground-breaking ruling is in *Brown v. Board of Education of Topeka, KS* (1954). In *Brown*, the United States Supreme Court affirmed that the equal protection and due process clauses of the *Fourteenth Amentment* are in force in educational decisions. Starting with the precedents in *Brown* and capitalizing on the cultural and legal zeitgeist, a number of cases were brought and decided in favor of handicapped students. For example, some early landmark decisions are in *Diana v. State Board Of Education; Larry P. v. Riles; Mills v. D.C. Board of Education; Pennsylvania Association for Retarded Children v. Commonwealth of Pennsylvania*; and *Wyatt v. Stickney*. Several important principles were established in such cases (for example, the right to free public education; the right to nondiscriminatory evaluation; the right to be educated with nonhandicapped peers; the right to adequate consultation with parents; and the right to adequate instruction with proper goals).

The complaints and remedies in these cases pertained to specific federal jurisdictions like the Northern District of California and the Eastern District of Pennsylvania. The remedies, or principles, were nation-alized, made general to all pupils in the United States, in the federal statutory and regulatory law.

Subsequently, the second round of litigation began. These cases focused on clarifying existing legislation. Examples of such cases include *Lora v. Board of Education; Debra P. v. Turlington; Marshall et al. v. Georgia; Board of Education v. Rowley*; and *Lachman v. Illinois State Board of Education*.

Statutory-Regulatory Law

Since the mid 1800s, federal statutes provided education, treatment, and care for people who have handicaps. Emphasis on all handicapped school children, however, began in the late 1950s and early 1960s. The statutory enactments paralleled, incorporated, or negated the judicial enactments. Some landmark statutes are named in Table 9-1. Most of these laws have been amended extensively over the years.

These statutes, and their accompanying regulations, prescribe and guarantee a large number of specific rights and protections for handicapped people that can be generalized as the right to a free appropriate public education from infancy through adulthood; the right to vocational rehabilitation services and appropriate vocational education; the right to nondiscriminatory evaluation; the right to confidentiality and control over records; and the right to procedural due process.

Requirements

The Education of the Handicapped Act mandates that handicapped youngsters from infancy through age 21 receive a free appropriate public education. Implementing this mandate involves a wide range of detailed regulations for required best practices to be followed at the state and local levels. These regulations pertain to such matters as identifying eligible participants, funding services, personnel training, procedural safeguards (for guaranteeing due process, protection in evaluation, placement in the least restrictive environment, and confidentiality of information), programming for transition from school to adult roles, and legal representation in administrative and judicial disputes. Several sources have information about these regulations and their interpretation in administrative and judicial rulings. Five examples are Rothstein's (1990) Special Education Law; the American Bar Association's Mental and Physical Disabilities Law Reporter; LRP Publications' National Disability Law Reporter and their Education of the Handicapped Law Report; and Tucker and Goldstein's (1991) Legal Rights of Persons with Disabilities: An Analysis of Federal Law.

The IEP exemplifies these requirements. (For more details, see Larsen and Poplin [1980] and Strickland and Turnbull [1990]). The IEP is the keystone to a free appropriate public education. Simply, in a pupil's IEP, one should start with his or her present level of performance and set goals; then, marshall whatever services are needed to help the pupil move from his or her present performance level to the goals established. In more detail, the term individual education program means the following.

- A written statement for each handicapped pupil
- Developed in a meeting by
  - a representative of the local education agency or of an intermediate education unit who is qualified to provide, or supervise the production of, specifically designed instruction to meet the pupil's unique needs
  - the teacher
  - the pupil's parents or guardians
  - whenever appropriate, the pupil.
- The statement includes
  - the pupil's present levels of educational performance

- annual goals, including short-term instructional objectives
- the specific educational services to be provided to the pupil (that is, instructional services, nonacademic services, related services, and services to insure procedural safeguards
- the extent to which the pupil will be able to participate in regular education programs
- the projected date for initiation of and anticipated duration of the services
- appropriate objective criteria and evaluation procedures
- a schedule for determining, at least annually, whether the pupil is achieving the instructional objectives

An IEP must be developed for all pupils regardless of where they are located during instruction—public school, private school, hospital, residential school, or home. The conference to plan the IEP must be conducted within 30 days after the beginning of the school year or 30 days after the pupil becomes eligible for special education services.

We use 17 steps to design an IEP according to the preceding guidelines and to specify the pupil's placement for receiving the IEP (Figure 11-2). IEPs done in depth with frequent evaluations and revisions are extremely important to developmentally disabled pupils. For example, the core of Geoffrey's IEP is the selection of elements considered in the sections on Coordination of Services and on Instructional Planning and Placement. That is, the developers (the parents-advocates, the special educators, and the related service providers) work together to plan specific activities for Geoffrey, ways these activities can be coordinated, and how they can be evaluated.

Accountability

Given that judicial decisions and statutes-regulations are general rules, honorable

Figure 11-2. Relationships Among Components and Steps in the Individualized Education Program

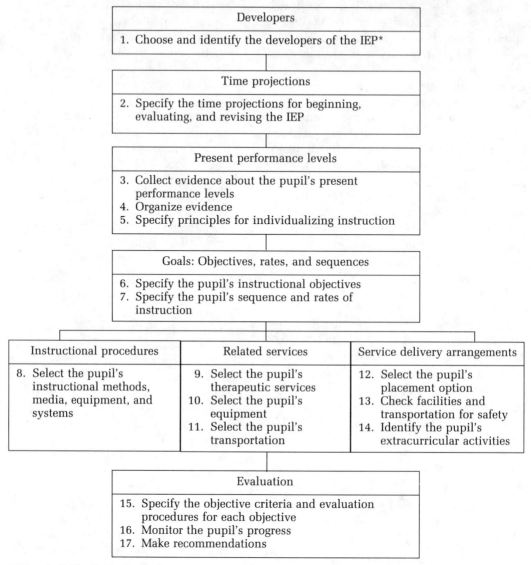

*IEP = individualized education program

people often disagree about how these rules should be applied in specific cases. In addition, given the pressures of day-to-day situations and variations in the levels of personnel training, sometimes there are actions that may constitute negligence or malpractice. Consequently, one must be concerned about accountability. Three major areas of accountability are monitoring programs, dealing with individual disputes, and deciding about personnel liability.

Program Monitoring

The Education of the Handicapped Act requires and has procedures for insuring that special education programs be monitored at least every 3 years. The federal Office of Special Education and Rehabilitation Services monitors programs in state departments of education. In turn, the state departments of education monitor programs in local school districts.

The monitoring essentially involves investigating whether the requirements of the laws are being observed. Procedural due process is observed. Deficient programs are given ample time to remedy problems. Failure to remedy problems can result in loss of funding.

Program monitoring is especially important for special education programs in which developmentally disabled pupils are enrolled because some developmentally disabled pupils have complex problems. As a result, their special education services can be complicated and long term. Lapses from legally required standard practices can occur. For example, inappropriate instruments were used to evaluate Geoffrey's present performance levels, and Geoffrey was inappropriately classified as severely intellectually retarded.

State department of education monitors found the problem. The Education of the Handicapped Act and the state requirement for nondiscriminatory evaluation had clearly been violated. That is, Geoffrey had been subjected to a discriminatory evaluation. As a result of the monitors' work, the legal violation in Geoffrey's situation was recognized and rectified. Again, program monitoring is crucial.

Individual Disputes

Section 504 of the Education of the Handicapped Act and The Handicapped Children's Protection Act include requirements and procedures for dealing with disputes about actions with respect to an individual pupil. In addition, there are important precedents in the judicial law. *Smith v. Robinson; Quackenbush v. Johnson City School District; Burlington School Committee v. Department of Education*; and *Taylor v. Board of Education* are examples of the many cases here.

A parent–advocate who disagrees with a decision may request an administrative hearing at the local school district level. Either party may appeal the decision of the local hearing officer to the state education agency level. In turn, appeals may be made to the federal level either to the Office of Special Education and Rehabilitation Services or the Office of Civil Rights.

A case may be moved to the federal courts once administrative remedies are exhausted, or, in some specified cases, before administrative remedies are exhausted. Within the federal court system, the route is the district courts, the circuit courts of appeal, and the Supreme Court. Using attorneys' services is allowed in all of these actions. Prevailing plaintiffs in court disputes may claim reimbursement for attorneys' fees and other litigation expenses.

The courts also may award prevailing plaintiffs reimbursement for expenses such as cost of private placement while disputes about placement are being resolved. This is so if it is reasonable to expect that so much time will be required to resolve the dispute that the pupil will be harmed by observing the Education of the Handicapped Act requirements that the pupil remain in his or her current placement until a final decision is forthcoming.

The courts also may award funds for compensatory education. That is, school districts may have to pay the costs of programs to rectify losses resulting from programs not supplied when they should have been or losses resulting from incorrect practices.

The complexity of developmentally disabled pupils' limitations may lead to ambiguity about the nature of the best decisions or to decisions that are costly to implement. Consequently, disputes arise frequently. The procedures for resolving disputes through administrative hearings and the federal courts are extremely important for developmentally disabled pupils. The provision in The Handicapped Children's Protection Act for awarding costs to the prevailing plaintiffs makes these avenues more widely available to parties who have legitimate complaints.

Consider again Geoffrey's initially being subjected illegally to discriminatory testing. The state department of education monitors found the problem and it was rectified without dispute. However, Geoffrey's parents-advocates also would have had another avenue for resolving the problem. They could have disputed the initial evaluation procedures. In turn, they could have sought redress through administrative hearings ranging from the local school level, through the state level, to the federal level in the United States Department of Education. Lacking a satisfactory resolution, they could have gone into the Federal Court system.

The plaintiffs (Geoffrey's parents-advocates) could have asked that the discriminatory evaluation cease and that nondiscriminatory evaluation be used. They also could have asked that funds be supplied for compensatory programs to make up for time lost and errors made as a result of the original incorrect evaluation.

Personnel Liability

The question here is, Can a pupil, or his or her parent-guardian, recover monetary damages from personnel whose failure to act (dereliction of duty) or whose wrongful action (malpractice) caused harm to the pupil? At present, the answer to this question is unclear.

The relevant federal statute is in The Civil Rights Act, Section 1983, Civil Action for the Deprivation of Rights. This section holds that:

> Every person who subjects, or causes to be subjected, any citizen of the United States or other person within the jurisdiction thereof to the deprivation of any rights, privileges, or immunities secured by the Constitution and laws, shall be liable to the party injured in an action at law, suit in equity, or other proper proceeding for redress.

The body of tort law also may pertain.

Persons claiming to be harmed have brought a number of suits for damages. In some cases, the courts have awarded money damages, for example, *Rodriguez v. Board of Education*. In some cases, they have not, for example, *Braun v. Board of Education*.

The doctrine of sovereign immunity is one major reason for this ambiguity or inconsistency even in cases where fault was obvious. The doctrine of sovereign immunity ("the king can do no wrong") has its roots in English common law. Extended to present-day United States law, sovereign immunity means that one cannot sue the government. However, there are two exceptions. The first exception is when a Constitutional right is violated. Cases brought under Section 1983 are in this category.

The second exception pertains to claims based on statutes. Governmental immunity generally is based on common-law precedent and on Amendment 13 of the United States Constitution. This immunity can be abrogated in two ways: a state can specifically waive immunity in a case, and Congress can write a waiver into a particular statute as it did in 1986 with an amendment to Section 504 of the Rehabilitation Act.

It is fairly clear, as we considered earlier, that a person can successfully claim reimbursement for expenses incurred in rectifying errors. On the other hand, the extent to which one can claim damages for harm caused by personnel dereliction of duty or malpractice is unclear. This matter probably will be clarified in the near future, given the increasing numbers of cases occurring, the laws providing for awarding expenses to prevailing plaintiffs, and the highly specific standards for best right practices being enacted in the laws and their amendments.

The option of recovering monetary damages for harm is important to developmentally disabled pupils and their parents or guardians for three reasons. One, some developmentally disabled pupils have such severe and complex problems that they can come to harm quickly if they are not carefully supervised and treated with correct procedures. Two, the Education of the Handicapped Act has long required and provided for comprehensive personnel training; so, personnel working with developmentally disabled pupils can learn right practices and precautions. Three, the Education of the Handicapped Act, and several other laws, specifically prescribe certain standard best practices; as do researchers and widely disseminated practitioners' handbooks.

Let us consider once again the example of Geoffrey's situation. The Education of the Handicapped Act's system for insuring accountability led to the problem being found and rectified. However, Geoffrey did lose opportunity for development while he was being incorrectly educated as a severely intellectually retarded pupil. In addition, the problems of evaluating severely handicapped pupils and the dangers of misclassification and of the self-fulfilling prophecy have long been known. Training programs and publications have widely disseminated this knowledge. As a result, Geoffrey's parents-advocates could explore the possibility of a liability action for damages.

References

1. Bos C, Vaughn S. Strategies for Teaching Students with Learning and Behavior Disorders. Boston, Allyn and Bacon, 1991.
2. Brown C. My Left Foot. New York, Simon & Schuster, 1955.
3. Burgdorf RL. ed. The Legal Rights of Handicapped Persons: Cases, Materials, and Text. Baltimore, Paul H. Brookes, 1980.
4. Education of the Handicapped Law Report. Horsham, PA, LRP Publications, Serial.
5. Kaufman AS. Assessing Adolescent and Adult Intelligence. Boston, Allyn and Bacon, 1990.
6. Keller H. The Story of My Life. New York, Doubleday, 1903.
7. Keller H. Three Days To See. Atlantic Monthly. 151: 34–42, 1933.
8. Keller H. The World I Live In. New York, Appleton-Century, 1938.
9. Langone J. Teaching Students with Mild and Moderate Learning Problems: Boston, Allyn and Bacon, 1990.
10. Larsen SC, Poplin MS. Methods for Educating the Handicapped: An Individual Education Program Approach. Boston, Allyn and Bacon, 1980.
11. Lash J. Helen and Teacher. New York, Dell, 1990.
12. Lee CM, Jackson R. Faking It: A Look into the Mind of a Creative Learner. Portsmouth, NH, Heinemann, Boynton and Cook, 1991.
13. Luftig RL. Assessment of Learners with Special Needs. Boston, Allyn and Bacon, 1989.
14. McDonnell J, Wilcox B, Hardman M. Secondary Programs for Students with Developmental Disabilities. Boston, Allyn and Bacon, 1991.
15. National Disability Law Reporter. Horsham, PA, LRP Publications, Serial.
16. Rothstein LF. Special Education Law. New York, Longman, 1990.
17. Stepping Out: A Dynamic Community Based Life Skills Program. Verona, WI, Attainment Company, 1991.
18. Strickland B, Turnbull AP. Developing and Implementing Special Education Programs. 3rd ed. Columbus, OH, Merrill, 1990.
19. Tucker BP, Goldstein BA. Legal Rights of Persons with Disabilities: An Analysis of Federal Law. Horsham, PA, LRP Publications, 1991.
20. Widerstorm AH, Mowder B, Sandall SR. At Risk and Handicapped Newborns and Infants: Development, Assessment, and Intervention. Boston, Allyn and Bacon, 1991.

Chapter 12
Case Management

Susan H. Neal
Beth A. Bader

Many different opinions exist as to what case management for people with developmental disabilities should be. These opinions have been operationalized into an array of service models, many claiming to be "state-of-the-art" or "best practice." In this chapter, we have chosen not to discuss the models that exist but rather to focus on the tools that case managers need to facilitate the integration of people who are developmentally disabled with their personal environments. Looking at people as individuals is repeatedly emphasized throughout the chapter. The focus in the following pages is on the values needed to provide the most effective and least obtrusive support for consumers as they go about meeting the challenges in their day-to-day lives.

When case managers are clear as to the values held regarding the people with whom they are working, it is possible to face the job with enthusiasm, energy, and creativity. If not, the potential for continuing frustration and eventual professional burnout exists. Case managers develop and test their values through experience rather than through any specific educational training. People usually do not go to college with the goal of becoming a case manager, but case management skills are increasingly being taught within the curriculums of many different professions. Any profes-

sional can hold and practice the values inherent in case management. Therefore, the information in this chapter is intended for any person acting in the capacity of a case manager regardless of his or her formal academic training.

Case Management: What It Has Been; What It Is; What It Can Be

The label "case management," given to what can be considered the most important support service for consumers with developmental disabilities, too often connotes depersonalization and control. For years, professionals in all of the social services have designated the people who are on the receiving end of services as nameless, faceless cases, cases that are in need of being "managed." Professionals tend to forget that human beings sooner or later resist control and show their resistance, either appropriately or inappropriately, through their behavior. In the past the people whose behavior was perceived as being inappropriate, usually those people who were argumentative, injurious, or not considered socially appropriate in their actions, were prioritized as needing case management. These were the people who did not easily fit into the system, who were not easily amenable to existing rules and control. Yet, these same people were the ones who were given more control, more case management. Thus, the cycle tended to perpetuate itself, managing the people who needed to be managed.

People with developmental disabilities have traditionally been targeted as needing case management. Usually it is their behavior excesses or deficits, or just the fact that they are considered less than capable, that gets them and their families into the service system. People with developmental disabilities are considered to belong to a group of people with similar characteristics and needs who are incapable of negotiating service systems to get their needs met. Thus, each "case" belonging to this disability group has often been considered as needing case management provided by a case manager (that is, someone who is faster than a speeding discharge plan and able to leap tall bureaucratic mazes in a single bound).

The myths of disability "groups" and "super" case managers are slowly being dispelled within the field of developmental disabilities. Each person with a disability label is considered an individual who is challenged by specific barriers because of the characteristics of his or her disability. Instead of being labeled as clients, people are being referred to as persons or, sometimes, as consumers of the supports and services that will assist in eliminating the barriers created by their disabilities. As professionals gain more experience in the delivery of services, they see the efficacy and cost effectiveness of providing the level of support the individual needs rather than fitting the individual into existing programs.

Although it is slowly being recognized that not everyone who has a developmental disability needs case management, case managers are seen as the key that links the consumer with the needed supports. Professionals who are providing case management are seen less and less as managers

and more as facilitators. Case managers cannot provide and do everything as a "superperson," but they can coordinate a team consisting of the consumer, professionals, family, and friends who can identify and put in place the supports that are needed. Therefore, the responsibility of service provision is spread among the team members, with the case manager providing the quality assurance that what team members say is needed is actually delivered and that it has the intended effect in the day-to-day life of the consumer.

Case management is not a paper shuffling, administrative function. Neither is it a daily skill training, direct care, or pure advocacy service. Rather, it is the nucleus of the system of support that is provided to, and received by, a person who wants such a service. Case management does not have to be provided to, or on behalf of, every consumer of the developmental disability service system. It can be done by the consumer or his or her family or care giver or both as long as the support that may be needed at any time as the consumer lives, learns, works, and socializes within the community is available.

When it works well, case management is the hub of services and the focus of support. It can facilitate the efficiency and effectiveness of a system while it meets the individualized needs of consumers. Case management can improve the responsiveness of service providers and the satisfaction of consumers, their families, and service providers. Beyond its own activities, case management has the potential to enhance the quality of programming throughout the service delivery system. In most systems, case management activities take place from the time of entry to successful completion of programming. Through these activities, case management can effect program planning and development, implementation and coordination of services, and evaluation of programming and support.

The success of case management in promoting quality services often depends greatly, sometimes solely, on who is fulfilling the role of case manager. For example, because it is the case manager who identifies resources to meet the needs of a consumer, the options are usually limited to his or her scope of awareness of resources and to what he or she sees as appropriate given the abilities of the consumer. If a case manager is working with an 18-year-old woman who is severely mentally retarded and feels that work experience is unrealistic and currently not important, then transition services with supported employment will not be seen as an option. Another case manager working with this same woman might see work experience as important and refer to transitional services. In this example, what the consumer receives depends on the person providing the case management. Agency policies and procedures, team process, and supervision can all impact on the quality of case management, but the values and abilities of the case manager are the major factors for success. How a case manager perceives the people who are served, the job responsibilities, and the role within the agency determines the quality of interactions and interventions. These perceptions are directly tied to values.

Values

A case manager needs a set of values that respects and supports the lives of consumers and their families. Before continuing to address the idea of what case management can be, it is helpful to identify some of the values that make case management successful. These values help establish a framework from which responsive case management can be developed. This is not a prioritized, inclusive list of values that guarantee good case management, but instead is a foundation for best practice.

All People Are Individuals

The value that all people are individuals is essential for quality case management. We work in a world of categories and too often determine needs based on diagnosis and disability. Checklists, standardized tests, and other resources that can help case managers be more efficient in their work are becoming more popular. As case loads become larger, case managers do not have the time to really get to know the people they are serving. Formalized assessments give ranges, but spending time with a person, and his family, in natural settings, exposes the person's uniqueness. A standardized test can indicate that a woman is mildly mentally retarded. It does not, however, indicate that she likes to embroider, has a brother she is very close to, that she can cook but cannot tell time, and that she usually sleeps 10 hours a night. All of this information is useful as programs are planned and activities are suggested. Her level of mental retardation will be less significant in her day-to-day life. This day-to-day life is where case management takes place. When a case manager does not know the uniqueness of the people he or she is working with, services are not supportive.

The majority of outcomes through case management services are dependent on the relationship between the case manager and the consumer and his or her family. A case manager who enjoys a rapport with a consumer and his or her family will be more successful than the case manager who has a poor relationship. A positive relationship with a consumer and his or her family can facilitate obtaining better information about the person's uniqueness and therefore enable a better job of matching needs to services. It can also provide the mutual respect and understanding that is necessary for a working partnership, which is important to quality case management.

□ Case 12-1: Katie

An example of what can happen when a case manager does not take the time to know the consumer and family is reflected in the case of Katie, a 12-year-old girl who is developmentally disabled. A case manager had been working with Katie and her family for about a year. On several occasions the case manager spoke with the mother, whose main concern is friendship for her daughter. Katie has also stated to the case manager that weekends were boring away from her friends at school. The case manager began looking for a recreation program that would provide socialization for Katie on weekends. It took many months for the case manager to find an appropriate program. The case manager was determined to find an integrated program that would provide opportunities for friendships with children who were disabled and children without disabilities. Finally, after having many telephone conversations with staff and administrators, placing Katie on a waiting list, and securing transportation, the case manager arranged for the girl to attend a Saturday afternoon recreation program at a local community center. The case manager, pleased with success, called to give the family the good news. The case manager's excitement ended when she learned from the girl's mother that the family was Jewish and that Saturday is their day of worship. The family preferred that their children not participate in outside activities on Saturdays. The case manager felt frustrated that so many months of work had gone to waste and embarrassed that she had not known this basic fact about the family. The family was shocked at how little the case manager knew about their daughter's life and were distressed at not being informed of the case manager's plans earlier in the process. This case clearly demonstrates that the best intentions and plans can be inappropriate if family life-styles and preferences are not considered.

Families Make Decisions

Getting to know consumers and their families well takes time. All successful relationships in our lives develop over time through many face-to-face interactions.

Relationships between case managers and the people they serve are no exception. It is impossible to know the likes and dislikes of people or how they spend their days through letters, staff meetings, and telephone conversations. A relationship with the consumer develops through visits to the home, eating together, shopping together, or participating in daily activities. One creative case manager uses Christmas shopping as an excellent way to get to know the people in her case load. Through this one activity, she obtains information on family transportation, decision making, fiscal management, traditions, and individual interests and likes as gifts are selected. She arranges this shopping trip to be informal and as close to what the family would do as possible. The case manager then uses the information gathered from this trip to support activities in the future. For example, if the consumer feels unable to find transportation for an activity, the case manager will remind the family of how they were able to find transportation for Christmas shopping. She reinforces their resourcefulness and supports their decision making and problem solving as a family. This case manager is able to do her job well because she takes the time to know the people she serves.

All consumers come to case management services with some type of support system. It can be the natural family or foster parents, siblings, other relatives, neighbors, a landlady, or roommates. These support persons cannot be ignored; in fact, they can be the most useful resource to the case manager. These people usually remain constant in the consumer's life whereas case managers come and go. Members of this support system offer advice and suggestions to the consumer throughout involvement with the case manager. Through experience, case managers realize that final decisions are made in families or in other support groups, and not in meetings. Consumers and families who may not verbalize their feelings in meetings do let case managers know in some way what they will, and will not, do. Involving members of the support system in program planning helps case managers offer appropriate assistance. This is not to say that the final decision should be left to family and friends in all cases. For some consumers, the final decision must be their own. The value expressed here is that the role of family and friends must be clearly seen, respected, and supported by case managers. This can be accomplished by keeping the support individuals informed, providing opportunities for input, and using them as resources. It cannot be accomplished by inviting family or friends to participate only in periodic, formal staff meetings. Involvement of the support persons should be a partnership with the case manager as all activities are planned, implemented, and monitored.

In providing case management, a significant value is that all services are accountable, first and foremost, to consumers and their families. Services exist for consumers and not vice versa. The consumer's welfare and dignity must be considered when making program decisions. Issues such as maintaining confidentiality, setting criteria for admission and discharge, charging fees, referring to other services, and keeping records can all greatly impact the lives of consumers. These issues must be addressed by upholding the personal worth of consumers and respecting their differences. Policies and procedures for operating programs cannot be based on the premise that the population being served is a homogeneous group. Case management services must be responsive to people by adhering to approaches that support the individual, not approaches that simply make the office run better.

All People Have Basic Wants

The final value to be discussed is that people with disabilities want the same basic things that people without disabilities want out of life. They want to live in a home with family or housemates, have friends and neighbors, go to school, work, and socialize within their community. A lot has been written about community integration and the importance of family and friends. Along with promoting integration, case management can also provide consumers with challenges that help them grow as individuals. In any setting, case managers can challenge consumers with activities such as making decisions, encouraging self-direction, developing personal preferences, and using their natural support system effectively. Case management has not evolved at the same pace as other programs such as vocational and residential services, which have improved by accepting the abilities of consumers and challenging them to enhance their abilities. In some case management services, consumers work in supported employment and participate in supported living arrangements yet continue to have case managers who make all doctors' appointments, provide transportation, and remain the direct contact with the physician instead of the consumer. Case management services that do not support the consumer's existing skills and that do not promote learning new skills can put the entire service delivery off balance. Case managers need consistently to encourage consumers to use their own skills.

Values Framework and Challenge

Using the values as a framework, it is easy to see the tremendous potential for case management. Case management is the key to coordinated, responsive services, across programs and agencies. A level of quality assurance is provided by case managers through their partnership with consumers and families and their sharing of information on resources throughout the service delivery system and community. As case managers promote the importance of family, friends, and community participation for all people, they support integration through all of the activities. Finally, case managers can facilitate learning of new skills and maintenance of existing skills for consumers in areas imperative for successful community integration. Skills such as making choices, communicating, solving problems, and advocating for oneself can be naturally taught and encouraged by case managers in their day-to-day interactions with consumers and families.

The challenge for case managers and their supervisors is to take these values and operationalize them within their systems. This attempt is often complicated by agency policies and procedures, standards and regulations, and unfortunately sometimes by other staff in the system. It helps to remember that everything will not change overnight. Change may be a slow process that initially occurs with a few consumers. To meet its full potential, however, it is necessary to assess all activities, or components, of case management to ensure that these values are reflected in the work.

Components

The components of a case management service delivery system must allow for flexibility in meeting individual needs and take into consideration consumer preference in choosing how the service components will be used. In other words, what a case manager offers to a consumer should be unique to that person, and the consumer should have a say in the type, frequency, location, and extent of involvement by the case manager in his or her life. What is undesirable is a rigid system in which a consumer must meet an exact criterion to be eligible for and remain a client of the service. Too often, eligibility and service criteria become exclusionary rather than inclusionary, and consumers become the square pegs trying to fit into case management round holes.

There must also be flexibility in identifying who the consumer of the case management service really is. When an individual is served outside of the context of family, friends, neighbors, and care givers, there is often conflict between what the case manager wants for the consumer and what others see as needed. The following description of Sarah's situation is an example of what can happen when the case manager is required to question whose interests need to be represented.

In this example, conflict between Sarah's family and the team will, in all certainty, be the entire focus of the upcoming meeting unless the case manager can get across that Sarah is not the only consumer whose interests need to be represented. It would do no good for the case manager to decide that Sarah is the consumer and to alienate her family by saying that since Sarah is her own guardian, what she wants should occur. On the other hand, neither does it help Sarah if the case manager represents her parents' interests, thus preventing her from taking advantage of a less restrictive service option. The role of the case manager must be that of facilitating compromise so that the consumer receives what he or she desires and agrees is needed, while not alienating any potential support provider who is needed for maximizing achievement of success.

The function or role of the case manager is not only that of facilitator, but also of coordinator, advocate, team leader, and provider of service linkage and quality assurance. But what does a case manager do to accomplish all of these roles? Most activities of a case manager fall into four primary categories: assessment, planning, implementation, and review.

☐ *Case 12-2: Sarah*

Sarah is a 36-year-old woman who has lived all her life with her parents, Mr. and Mrs. Smith, who are now approaching retirement age. Although they have never filed a petition to become Sarah's court-appointed guardians, Mr. and Mrs. Smith have always acted in this capacity, insisting that they sign every document on Sarah's behalf. Sarah has cerebral palsy, which has severely limited her physical and expressive communication abilities. For the past year, the staff at the sheltered workshop that Sarah has attended since graduating from school have targeted her for supported employment services. The staff have shown Sarah various job sites and feel extremely confident that her nonverbal communication indicates that she wants to work at the local YMCA. Sarah's parents refuse to give permission or to sign release forms for the supported employment program because they fear that if the job does not work out, Sarah will have lost her space at the workshop and will have to wait at home until a new job site is available. Mr. and Mrs. Smith are both still working and will not consider leaving Sarah home alone. The workshop and supported employment program want to accept Sarah's signature mark on a release form so that they can go ahead with the transfer. They are absolutely sure that they have Sarah's informed consent and that she knows the risks involved. The case manager has decided to call a team meeting before Sarah is transferred from the workshop.

Assessment

A case manager must have adequate information about the consumer and his or her personal environment before any other service delivery can effectively occur. Case managers have traditionally not had available an assessment protocol designed specifically for their use. Instead, they have had to rely on formal assessments done by other professionals and on the verbal information provided by the consumer and current care givers. Often all that is available is medical information, intelligence testing, and educational-vocational evaluations. This information usually is not current, nor have the results and recommendations been compared with each other.

What is most revealing about a consumer is a situational assessment that combines verbal and observational information about what the person is actually able to do at home and in the community. A case manager does not have to be the one who actually conducts such an assessment, but it is extremely helpful to be a part of the process and have firsthand knowledge of the consumer's capabilities.

An assessment barrier that is frequently identified is that there are not enough professionals in a given community with experience in evaluating people with developmental disabilities. It is often difficult to obtain a psychologic evaluation that includes an assessment of adaptive behavior in addition to an intelligence score. Rather than go without this information, case managers can themselves use an adaptive behavior assessment tool and use the information in conjunction with a narrative summary that describes the consumer's current status. If nothing else, a good narrative description of what a person does at home, in school or the workplace, in social situations, and with family and friends can suffice.

After all of the assessment information is collected, it must be compared and, from it, the consumer's strengths and limitations identified. It is best if the consumer and the care providers who know the consumer best are the ones who identify the strengths and limitations with the case manager. These are the people who form the basis of a program-planning team that directs the focus of all services and supports that a consumer receives.

Planning

The strengths and limitations of a consumer serve as the framework upon which services and supports are planned. Supports are needed both to maintain and to strengthen what a person does well and also to assist the person in developing the skills and competencies needed in his or her life. The case manager is essential to ensuring that the supports identified as needed are what the consumer has agreed are needed and wanted, and that they are neither too restrictive nor too broad to be effective. To accomplish this, the case manager serves as the team leader or at least as a team member with major monitoring responsibilities.

Services and supports are identified in conjunction with goals and objectives. In addition to the consumer himself, the case manager should have the best overall understanding of what the consumer wants and needs to accomplish. The case manager must ensure that the team establishes a long-range goal on which all other service providers base their goals and objectives. Sometimes it makes the most sense to have a team meeting at least once a year during which a mutually agreed on overall goal for the consumer is set, and potential objectives and program strategies are discussed. Then each provider of the supports or services that have been set as priorities works at a later time with the consumer to establish specific, short-range (that is, less than 1 year) program goals and objectives. The case manager must make sure that all of the program goals and objectives fit into the framework of the overall goal set by the team.

There are times when a case manager does not have a team within which to work. In these instances, the "team" becomes the consumer, others chosen by, or who are acting on behalf of, the consumer (that is, family, legal guardian, advocate), and the case manager. Service planning occurs whether or not an interdisciplinary team is present, but, when the team is small, the case manager has a greater responsibility for knowing the availability of potential services and supports and subsequent linkage activities.

Implementation

Not only does the case manager provide coordination and direction for the consum-

er's planning team; he or she also must frequently develop goals and objectives for the case management activities. The case manager is usually responsible for what are called service coordination objectives, which specify what the case manager will do on behalf of the consumer. Service coordination objectives are different from behavioral objectives, which focus on what the consumer will achieve. Both types of objectives should be written so that progress can be measured (that is, who will do what, by when, using what kinds of supports).

It is important for the case manager to have written documentation of what activities are being done. Documentation is kept either in an activity log, which is summarized periodically, or as narrative notes that are put in the record each time the case manager does something on behalf of the consumer. It is important that the activities be tied back to the goals and objectives. If they are not, there must be reassessment of, and any necessary revisions made to, the objectives.

Review

Case managers have the responsibility of providing the quality assurance that all services and supports being received by the consumer are having the intended effect. There are many ways that this can be accomplished, from regular, on-site observation of the consumer to a paper review of data submitted by other service providers. No single way of review can be recommended, but what is done must be consistent and least invasive in the lives of the consumer and the care givers. The maximum time frame in which a review process occurs should be semi-annually. A quarterly review is preferred. If a case manager's review of services and interventions is not seen as needed at least once every few months, then the question must be raised as to whether the consumer actually needs case management services.

The periodic review of a consumer's service plan provides part of the assessment information upon which future goals and objectives are set. It is important that information gathered from the reviews regarding progress, or lack of progress, be shared with the consumer as well as with all other team members.

The necessary components of case management (that is, assessment, planning, implementation, and review) remain the same, regardless of whether the consumer is a child, an adult, or a senior citizen. Nor do they change in relation to where the person lives: within a family, in a supervised setting, or independently in his or her own home. What does change is how each of the components is delivered by the case manager and how the consumer interacts and grows within the process. The next section provides guidance to case managers in evaluating the effectiveness of what they do.

Program Evaluation

Services delivered to individuals with developmental disabilities traditionally have been evaluated using standards set by national accreditation bodies, by state and local licensing authorities, or by a combination of both. Case management is usually not a licensed service, and only recently have standards evolved specific to the activities of a case manager. Evaluation strategies other than standards to measure service delivery outcomes can provide more qualitative information for use in evaluating how case management is being received by consumers and their families. This is important because it is no longer enough to justify the effectiveness of case management activities to funding sources, agency administrators, and utilization reviewers by presenting data that specify numbers served, frequency of contacts, documentation deficiencies corrected, and goals accomplished.

Evaluation of case management service delivery should always be approached from the perspective of the consumer. The question, "What kind of success is being evaluated?" must be asked and answered in terms of the success of the consumer, not just in terms of what the case managers have accomplished. Evaluation strategies should measure the successes of the individual consumer, as well as the successes of all who are served within a given service delivery system. Below are suggestions for evaluation strategies that can be built into the assessment of case management at the individual consumer, the agency, and the service system levels.

The Individual

Most of the time, an individual's achievement, or lack of achievement, of the goals and objectives listed on his or her individual service plan is what constitutes evaluation of progress. Case managers are responsible for monitoring the implementation of program strategies and often share in the blame when the consumer does not respond as expected. To avoid this, the case manager can influence the development of program goals and objectives so that they are written narrowly enough to ensure success yet at the same time broadly enough to challenge the consumer. One must always remember that success is what motivates individuals to continue to achieve. People with developmental disabilities are not exceptions to this rule.

In addition to assuming responsibility for monitoring consumers' responses to specific skill training, it is equally important to look at how well consumers are integrated into their homes and family activities, whether they are involved in the same activities as their peers who are not disabled, and whether, as shown by their behavior, they like what they are doing. Perhaps most important is the need to look at whether the individuals are making choices on a day-to-day basis. If the case management is effective, then not only will the individuals have the opportunity for making choices, they will also demonstrate their ability to make decisions no matter how basic their choices or how challenging their disabilities.

The Agency

Administrators of service agencies focus not only on the effectiveness of the service provided, but also on whether the outcomes justify the cost of delivering the service. One of the best ways of looking at this is to examine how case managers spend their work time. It is suggested that the administrator look beyond the ratio of direct and indirect service hours to a more qualitative assessment of what case management activities are actually required to achieve a particular outcome (for example, the transition of a student from school into employment or of an adult from living with his or her family to another setting). The time a case manager spends handling the behavior crisis of a person living with elderly parents is probably significantly different from that spent if the person lived in a staff-supervised setting. Examining the actual case management activities done with specific consumers reveals trends in case loads. These trends can provide objective indicators for planning and resource allocation purposes.

The System

The effectiveness of case management within a service delivery system can be evaluated by looking at how well people with developmental disabilities are integrated into the community. It is helpful to determine the number of segregated preschools, schools, day support programs, apartment buildings, recreational programs, church groups, Boy or Girl Scout troops, and senior citizen programs. This type of evaluation is important, not as a value judgment against segregated settings, but rather as an indication of the level of integration and participation of people with developmental disabilities in day-to-day community activities. One way of determining this is to ascertain who are the friends of people who are disabled. If the friends of consumers are limited only to care givers or other consumers that they live with or are with during the school or work day, then case management is not being effective in facilitating community integration.

It is important to remember that evaluation is not just an activity that occurs every so often. Assessment of case management service delivery should begin at the planning stage, before service is initiated with any consumers. The same approach used with individual program planning can be applied to overall case management service delivery: The need for case management is assessed by identifying strengths and limitations; goals and objectives are developed, and services are implemented; outcomes are reviewed and used for further modifications in the delivery of the service. Approaching evaluation as an evolving process ensures that case management is "doing what it should be doing."

Preparation and Supervision

The role of case managers is increasing in importance as the service delivery system improves. Best practice such as community integration and family-centered services relies heavily on successful case management. These new challenges and responsibilities will be met by case managers who have the values, knowledge, and skills necessary to do the job well. Ensuring that case managers are competent and comfortable in their roles demands that attention be given to preservice and inservice training, technical assistance, and ongoing supervision. All areas of personnel preparation and work evaluation need to reflect and support creative, responsive case management. A match must occur between what is known about case management and its potential, and the activities that teach, monitor, and evaluate the components of case management.

Case management is no longer perceived as a single activity within all staff roles, but rather as a role that involves many activities. It is becoming a position with a career track for professionals, and not an entry level position that serves as a stepping stone to other jobs within an agency. For example, in Virginia it is not difficult to find case managers who have been in this role for 10 to 15 years. The knowledge and skills needed to do case management are increasing as the service evolves. Training in topics such as communication, negotiation, assessment, group interaction, team leadership, and family dynamics has become important to prepare case managers for their work. In addition, case managers can benefit from training that defines their role, discusses current best practice, and describes the potential of case management services. Case management is emerging as a curriculum in preservice training, but presently these courses are few in number, with no specific degree program.

The time is right for colleges and universities to begin offering course work and specialized degrees in case management. This training should be interdisciplinary because it is known from experience that no one discipline is best prepared for the role and that the work of the case manager is interdisciplinary in nature. Preservice training for case managers also needs to provide many hours of contact with consumers and families in their homes and communities. A practicum, for example, could be for all students to provide 6 hours per week of free respite to families with children who are disabled. This simple change from agency-based to a family-based field experience would be invaluable to students who are preparing for the case manager role. Students would experience firsthand family dynamics, interactions

with parents, siblings, and consumers, and at the same time, provide an invaluable support to these families through respite services. This could be an ongoing, free service to families as students enter the curriculum year after year.

On the job, case managers face many challenges and demands that make ongoing training and supervision necessary. Case managers need training and technical assistance that help them understand their community, agency, and role within the organization. They need to be encouraged to be inquisitive and creative but to also know their limits of authority and of responsibilities. Technical assistance is needed to help case managers use their time wisely, stay on track with their activities, and expand their knowledge of resources to meet individualized needs of consumers. As case management continues to develop, it is important regularly to expose case managers to current trends through training opportunities.

The case manager's supervisor will, in most agencies, be the key source of information and skill development. It is the supervisor who will be asked for assistance in prioritizing activities, identifying resources, clarifying policies, procedures and regulations, and solving problems. The supervisor's role is a balance between administration and the case manager, always keeping consumer satisfaction as a priority. For example, a case manager currently working in early intervention services uses a family-centered approach whereby families are making many of the decisions that professionals have made in the past. If this case manager works in an agency whose administration believes all final decisions need to be made by staff, the family-centered approach will be in conflict with agency policy. The supervisor of case management services will need to educate the administration about this approach and its importance and at the same time support the work of the case manager.

To promote quality case management, the supervisor needs to commend case managers when integration occurs and dependence on the case manager decreases. Supervisors are the key to stopping the "superperson" syndrome of case management. Case managers need to ensure that as much autonomy and decision making as possible is left to the consumer and family. A supervisor can help the case manager assume the role of facilitator and maintain the values important to successful case management, as described in this chapter. It is easy to become overly helpful in providing case management services. Supervisors and coworkers can provide objective insights and useful suggestions as case managers adapt services to meet the changing needs of consumers and their families. It is sometimes difficult to draw the line between encouraging independence and "dumping" on the family and consumer. Supervisors need to guide case managers as they address these difficult issues on an individual consumer basis.

The importance and demands of the supervisors of case management services have also increased. There are in-service training needs for supervisors, because many of these supervisors were case managers who were promoted because of a job well done. Training that addresses team leadership, policy analysis, current trends in services, management, and staff development will help supervisors in their roles.

Summary

The success of case management is not determined by the discipline of the case manager, the model of the service, or the type of agency administering the service. The success is dependent on the values of the people providing the service, the provision of services that facilitate community life, and agency administration that supports its case managers. It is time to be creative and innovative in case management services and break with tradition. Questions about size of case load, preferred model, and which discipline makes the best case manager will, unfortunately, keep the system in its traditional, outdated approach. Instead, it is now time to question whether there is sufficient time for interactions, whether services are flexible enough to meet changing needs, and whether collaboration is occurring among many disciplines to provide the best services possible.

Chapter 13
Supported Employment

Trudie Hughes
Paul Wehman

Within the past decade many states have developed a major interest in supported employment as a vocational outcome for adults with developmental disabilities who have never worked before or who have never been considered candidates for employment (Wehman and Moon 1988). Many individuals who were labeled developmentally disabled spent their time at home, at segregated workshops, or in day-activity centers (Buckley and Bellamy 1986).

Supported employment models ranging from individual placement models, enclaves, mobile work crews, and entrepreneurial models have been developed to provide a wider range of vocational options for persons with severe disabilities. Individuals with developmental disabilities have been major beneficiaries of supported employment because historically they have not been employed in competitive settings.

The purpose of this chapter is threefold: First, the characteristics of several supported employment models are presented. Second, how people with different disabilities are participating in supported employment is reviewed. Finally, the effects of recent legislation on employment opportunities for individuals with developmental disabilities are summarized. Several case studies are presented following the main discussion.

Vocational Options prior to Supported Employment

Since the 1960s, community-based day and vocational programs for persons with disabilities have been developed on a hierarchical system in which individuals are expected to progress toward competitive employment. At the highest level are the individuals with the least severe disabilities. They are included in regular program workshops in which the focus is on preparation for competitive employment. These workshops generally offer work evaluation and work adjustment and are typically funded by state vocational rehabilitation agencies and other agencies responsible for time-limited services. Studies of workshop requirements by Johnson and Mithaug (1977) and Mithaug et al. (1977) showed that most workshops had similar requirements such as the ability to communicate basic needs, to exhibit safety skill awareness, to maneuver around the workshop, to work uninterrupted for sustained periods without leaving the work station, and to respond appropriately to interruptions.

Those individuals that cannot meet these requirements generally are sent to work-activity and day-activity programs. Work-activity programs are designed to build work-related skills so the individual can climb the hierarchical workshop ladder. Day-activity programs generally focus on daily living skills and recreation. These services are usually funded by state and federal funds such as Medicaid and Social Service Block Grants (Bellamy et al. 1988).

Although these services are still in existence today, other vocational options have emerged through supported employment initiatives from the U. S. Office of Special Education and Rehabilitative Services in 1984, Developmental Disabilities Act of 1984 and 1987, added amendments to the Rehabilitation Act (PL 99-506) 1986, and the Americans with Disabilities Act of 1990 (PL 101-336) to name just a few.

The Rehabilitation Act of 1986 (PL 99-506) was a major initiative for service providers of supported employment services. It authorizes supported employment as a viable rehabilitation goal for vocational rehabilitation agencies and provides new emphasis on rehabilitation engineering as a needed service. In addition, it provides funds to states to develop supported employment programs.

A recent piece of legislation that will influence vocational opportunities is the Americans with Disabilities Act of 1990 (PL 101-336). The purpose of this act is:

1. To provide a clear and comprehensive national mandate for the elimination of discrimination against individuals with disabilities;
2. to provide clear, strong, consistent, enforceable standards addressing discrimination against individuals with disabilities;
3. to ensure that the Federal Government plays a central role in enforcing the standards established in the Act on behalf of individuals with disabilities; and
4. to invoke the sweep of congressional authority, including the power to enforce the fourteenth amendment and to regulate commerce, in order to address the major areas of discrimination faced day-to-day by people with disabilities. (Americans with Disability Act, 1990).

To date the Americans with Disabilities Act is the most powerful public law preventing and hopefully stopping discrimination in all aspects of a person's life, ranging from employment to housing and transportation. The employment section of this law covers many issues dealing with discrimination in obtaining and maintaining employment for persons with disabilities. For example, an employer cannot limit, segregate, or classify a job applicant such that the opportunities or status of such applicant or employee is adversely affected because of his or her disability. An employer cannot deny equal jobs or benefits to a qualified individual because of his or her disability. The employer must make reasonable accommodation to the known physical or mental limitations of an otherwise qualified individual with a disability (Americans with Disabilities Act, 1990). If this law is recognized and obeyed, it can have a major effect in breaking down the barriers that prevent individuals with disabilities from experiencing equal opportunity in all aspects of life.

What Is Supported Employment?

According to the Federal Register (1987), supported employment is "Paid work in a variety of settings, particularly regular work sites, especially designed for handicapped individuals: (i) for whom competitive employment has not traditionally occurred; and (ii) who, because of their disability, need intensive ongoing support to perform in a work setting." Several key components of supported employment exist within this definition. These components will be further defined to clarify the concept of supported employment.

1. Paid employment. For a position to be considered supported employment, the employer must comply with wage and hour regulations for that position. Some individuals are paid at minimum wage or above,

although provisions can be made for disabled individuals to be paid at a rate commensurate with their productivity levels.

2. Integration. Integration is essential to achieving the goal of ensuring that handicapped workers have opportunities for physical and social contact with nondisabled coworkers and the general public. According to Shafer and Nisbet (1988), it is important to consider the capacity of the setting and the level realized by nondisabled workers when considering integration.

3. Ongoing support. A key characteristic that distinguishes supported employment from other vocational services is the ongoing support offered. This support can include but is not limited to direct training, indirect intervention at the worksite, or advocacy issues away from the worksite. The level of ongoing support depends on the needs of the individual worker; however, federal guidelines mandate that an employment specialist must personally visit the work site at least two times per month.

4. Workers with severe disabilities. Supported employment is specifically designed to serve those individuals who, because of the severity of their disability, cannot obtain or maintain employment without ongoing support. Persons who are able to sustain employment independently are not candidates for supported employment. According to Bellamy and coworkers (1988), the term severe disabilities is used to describe individuals who need intensive, ongoing support to live and work in community settings. These individuals are not typically served by vocational rehabilitation and other job-training programs.

As stated previously, supported employment reflects a variety of models such as enclaves, mobile work crews, individual placement, and entrepreneurial models. Supported employment is characterized by the inclusion of individuals with the most severe disabilities in a place-and-train model where both integration and wages are highly valued (Kiernan and Stark 1986;

Rusch 1986; Wehman and Moon 1988). Implementing supported employment programs requires coordinated efforts from several groups, each of which has different responsibilities and outlooks toward the success of the individual's employment opportunities. Employers provide the job opportunities; vocational rehabilitative agencies fund, regulate, and evaluate employment programs; employment specialists or job coaches provide the intensive job training and ongoing support; significant others advocate for the services needed; and the individual with a disability has the power to choose the type of supported employment model and the type of work to perform (Bellamy et al. 1988).

The employment specialist or job coach has a diverse and challenging position. He or she is responsible for providing initial community screening, client screening, job placement, intensive job site training, task analysis, data collection, assessment, orientation and training of coworkers, coordination of transportation, and ongoing follow-along and advocacy (Rusch 1986; Wehman 1981; Bellamy et al. 1988). The employment specialist must have the flexibility to wear many hats at one time. He or she must possess not only the ability to present the supported employment program to the business community, and train individuals with disabilities in a variety of work settings, but also the stamina to be effective in advocacy and tenacious in follow-along services.

Descriptions of Supported Employment Models

Individual Placement Model

The individual placement model enables individuals with moderate and severe disabilities to be placed, trained, and provided support in integrated community competitive jobs with the assistance of an employment specialist or job coach. According to this model, an individual with a disability is hired at minimum wage or above by a community business or industry. The employment specialist provides intensive job training, advocacy, and support from the first day of employment (Moon et al. 1986). As the employee gains the necessary skills to work independently and his or her performance reaches the employer's standards, the employment specialist gradually reduces the time and intensity of training provided to the employee. At any time during employment, the employment specialist can provide additional training, advocacy, and support whenever necessary to maintain employment. Additional training usually occurs if there has been a change of job duties, added job duties, change of equipment used, or change of supervisor and coworkers. All of these factors can indirectly or directly affect the employee's work performance, which may require training or support or both from the employment specialist. A major factor to consider is the job match. When the employment specialist considers a job for an individual, he or she must consider the individual's job preference. If that individual does not like the type of work, he or she will not put forth the effort necessary to succeed. In addition, the employment specialist must also look at the individual's physical ability, social skills, behavioral problems, safety skills, shift hours, and transportation needs.

Some of the benefits of the individual placement model are:

1. It allows the disabled employee maximum choice for job selection that meets his or her individual preference and abilities.

2. It offers the greatest opportunity for integration among nondisabled workers and the general public because the workplace is centered in the community. In addition, the individual with the disability is not grouped with other individuals with disabilities, which reduces the likelihood of coworker involvement.

3. It allows the individual to earn competitive wages (Kregel et al. 1990).

4. It offers flexibility in identifying jobs, the limitation being what the community has to offer. Jobs may range from computer work to secretarial to landscaping to dishwashing.

Mobile Work Crew Model

The mobile work crew model comprises workers with severe disabilities (generally 4 to 8) and one supervisor, usually a human service worker with a supported employment agency. The crew typically travels from one business to another performing custodial work, grounds maintenance, housecleaning or janitorial and other needed services. Work contracts are drawn up between the agency and the business, and the human service worker provides the training, supervision, and transportation from site to site and is always present on the job site. Potential for contact with the public is an important consideration in work site selection to insure optimal integration opportunities. Integration usually takes place when the crew interacts with the public during breaks and mealtime. This model is flexible in relation to the local job market and meets the needs of urban, suburban, or rural areas (Bellamy et al. 1988; Bourbeau 1985; Mank et al. 1986).

Benefits of the mobile work crew include:

1. It offers flexibility in program design. In rural areas the program may be operated using a single crew comprising 4 to 6 individuals. In more populous areas, the program may use multiple crews serving 24 to 28 individuals.

2. It provides flexibility as to work performed. Workers may stay on one crew or rotate crews to experience a variety of working conditions.

3. Crew members usually earn higher wages, higher than those earned by individuals doing piecework, depending on the contract developed between the business and the supported employment agency (Bourbeau 1985).

Enclave Model

The enclave is one of the most commonly accepted supported employment models. It is characterized by a group (generally up to eight) of workers with severe disabilities who are trained and supervised by a human service worker within a local business. The individuals are employed in an integrated host business or industry, and access to employment opportunities is provided to all employees of the host business or industry. The individual is paid wages commensurate with his or her productivity and may be paid directly by the host business or industry or by the human services support organization (Rhodes and Valenta 1985). The human service worker does not fade from the job site. The ability to provide continuous supervision and flexible and shared decision making between the host business or industry and the human service support organization is an advantage of the enclave model (Bellamy et al. 1988).

Benefits of the enclave model are:

1. It provides real job opportunities within a company; consequently, program employees experience the full range of employment outcomes, including reasonable income for work performed, integration with nondisabled coworkers, and good working conditions.

2. It provides ongoing support that allows persons with severe disabilities to perform their work (Rhodes and Valenta 1985).

Entrepreneurial Model

The entrepreneurial model is a manufacturing or subcontracting not-for-profit operation employing approximately 15 individuals with severe disabilities, as well as workers without disabilities, and providing one type of product or service. Individuals with severe disabilities typically have spent most of their lives in institutions and often display inappropriate social behaviors, making it difficult for them to be ac-

cepted in competitive employment environments. This supported employment option was developed by the Specialized Training Program (STP) at the University of Oregon.

The individuals with severe disabilities are trained and supervised by 2 to 3 human service workers who do not fade from the job site. Because the model relies on contractual assembly work (O'Bryan 1985), the success of the program depends on securing ongoing contract work from industry. Workers are generally paid subminimum wages commensurate with their productivity (Bellamy et al. 1988). Companies using this model typically share the profits among all employees through salary increases, bonuses, improved benefits, and profit sharing. Management salaries are usually funded through local agencies in conjunction with the board of directors.

Benefits of the entrepreneurial model include:

1. Worker wages average twice the national average for individuals in work activity centers.

2. It offers a higher quality work environment than does an activity center.

3. It offers the individual a permanent job rather than a time-limited training program (O'Bryan 1985).

Current Status of Supported Employment

Between 1978 and 1990, the supported employment program of Virginia expanded from a single university-based demonstration program at Virginia Commonwealth University to a statewide system serving 2702 individuals. As of September 30, 1990, 70% of the 2702 served were individuals with mental retardation and over 40% of all individuals served were reported to have a secondary disability such as cerebral palsy, convulsive disorder, or hearing, language, or visual impairments (Kregel et al. 1990).

The three most popular supported employment models used for those 2702 individuals were as follows:

Individual placement model	76%
Enclaves	12%
Work crews	6%

According to Wehman and Moon (1988), the main issue that faces vocational rehabilitation services is how credibly to manage supported employment programs. Specific problems include:

1. The limited funding and training resources available.
2. Increased pressure to serve the most difficult individuals.
3. Some vocational rehabilitation personnel, ranging from direct counselors to supervisors and state administrators, do not support the benefits of supported employment.

Unless attitudes and funding priorities change, current supported employment programs may greatly diminish or disappear completely. A major challenge that faces providers of supported employment in the 1990s is to include individuals with *all* severe disabilities, not just those who have mental retardation. Thus far, supported employment research has been primarily descriptive in nature and has not focused on *cross-disability* comparisons. As noted previously, differential analyses of individuals who are mentally retarded have dominated the literature. There is, however, a need to evaluate the efficacy of the supported employment model for other difficult-to-place individuals such as those with brain injuries or mental illness, and to assess for differences across disabilities. What follows is an overview of data that address these two issues.

Overview of Supported Employment Outcomes among People with Multiple Disabilities

The Employment Data Management System

The Virginia Commonwealth University Rehabilitation Research and Training Center on Supported Employment (VCU-RRTC) operates a comprehensive management information system designed to monitor the employment outcomes of targeted severely disabled workers from Virginia and a number of other states and localities. The Supported Employment Information System (SEIS) consists of client employment outcome data generated from 96 local programs from Virginia, North Dakota, and Nevada, as well as from federally funded demonstration programs operated by the United Cerebral Palsy Association, VCU-RRTC, and six school programs in California and Florida. As of March 31, 1989, the database contained information on 1760 persons with disabilities placed in employment.

Nature of All Clients in the Database

The 1760 clients placed into supported employment who make up the database have a variety of primary disabilities. The overwhelming majority (77%) are diagnosed as having mental retardation; 11% have chronic mental illness or other emotional disorders; and the remaining 12% have other primary disabilities. Of the persons with mental retardation as either a primary or secondary disability, 9% are in the severe and profound category; 33%, in the moderate category; 44%, in the mild category; and 13% are in the borderline category. Fifty-seven percent of the individuals are men, and 27% are individuals from identified minority groups. The mean age of individuals in the database working as of 31 March 1989 was 31.4 years.

As noted previously, supported employment is intended for persons who have previously had difficulty in obtaining and maintaining competitive employment. The previous employment histories of 1411 individuals in the database are presented in Table 13-1. For example, 43% of the individuals reported no earnings in the year prior to referral for supported employment. *The average wage earned in the previous year was $1,655 for the 57% who did earn wages.* Those not earning wages include individuals who entered supported employment directly from secondary special education programs, persons on waiting lists, previously unserved persons in adult activity centers with no paid work opportunities, or persons institutionalized or hospitalized immediately before entering supported employment.

Analysis of Clients with Multiple Disabilities

The study that follows examines a subset of 278 persons placed in supported employment. These individuals have chronic mental illness (CMI), cerebral palsy (CP), traumatic brain injury (TBI), or a dual diagnosis of chronic mental illness and men-

tal retardation (CMI/MR). Over 60% of all persons lived in supported or dependent residential arrangements such as with their parents or in group homes. It should be noted that these individuals have had little or no competitive employment history and have shown themselves to be extremely resistant to job placement using traditional types of vocational rehabilitation. The mean length of coma for persons with traumatic brain injuries in the referral pool for placement is 55 days. At referral, the disability groups received federal disability income benefits that ranged from 41% for the CMI population to 93% for the cerebral palsy population.

As Table 13-2 indicates, 168 persons across the four disability groups were working in supported employment as of 31 March 1989. There were 349 placements made to date of the 278 individuals, with some persons receiving replacement assistance. A total of $1,048,881 in wages have been earned cumulatively by persons in these 349 placements, ranging from $143,870 for persons dually diagnosed as mentally retarded and chronically mentally ill to $517,808 for persons with chronic mental illness. These

Table 13-1. Previous Employment History of All Clients

Salary in Year Prior to Supported Employment

Individuals reporting no earned wages in year prior to supported employment, %	43.0
Average wages earned by consumers who reported earning in year prior to supported employment, $	1655

Adult Activity Center Attendance

Individuals who had previously attended an adult day center program, %	24.1
Average length of adult day program attendance, *mo*	35

Sheltered Workshop Attendance

Individuals who had previously attended a sheltered workshop, %	52.1
Average length of sheltered workshop attendance, *mo*	44

Community-Based Work Experience

Individuals with previous community-based work experience, %	36.1
Average length of competitive employment experience, *mo*	31

wages were earned in competitive employment by persons who for the most part had a limited to nonexistent recent work history.

A primary indicator of effort and time spent on the placement and retention of the persons working is the cumulative recording of intervention hours spent by staff. The hours and percent of time of staff intervention are shown in Table 13-3. The level of intervention by category varies across the four disability groups. The highest percent of time, ranging from approximately one third to one half of the intervention time of the employment specialist, involved *actively training* at the job site the individual with a disability. The "Inactive Time on Job Site" category represents time spent at the job site by the employment specialist between periods of active involvement or observation with the client. Comparatively large amounts of time are also spent by the employment specialist in direct employment advocacy with job site personnel including employers, coworkers, and supervisors. Persons with traumatic brain injury or cerebral palsy have a noticeably higher mean intervention time than do persons with CMI or MR/CMI.

The types of work are reflected in Table 13-4. The food service and janitorial-custodial areas are the largest sources of employment for the LMI (57%) and MR/CMI (79%) populations. Clerical-office work provides the largest source of employment

for both the TBI (37%) and CP (49%) populations. Sick leave benefits were secured for 31% to 42% of the individuals categorized as disabled; similar levels were obtained for paid vacation and medical insurance.

Table 13-5 shows the specific reasons why separations from employment took place. It is important to note that job separations because of employer-initiated terminations occurred with noticeably more frequency (52.4%) than did resignations or layoffs for persons with traumatic brain injuries compared with persons in the other three disability groups. Table 13-5 shows the larger number of reasons given for separations, with the leading reasons being medical health problems, taking a better job, and not wanting to work.

Table 13-6 shows the percent of persons by disability who were employed in an initial or subsequent job for the indicated number of months after placement. The percent of persons employed twelve months after initial placement in supported employment ranged from 60% for the CMI population to 93% for the MR/CMI dually diagnosed population.

Implications of Analysis

The implications of this analysis give reason to be cautiously optimistic that some persons with multiple disabilities who have traditionally been unemployable

Table 13-2. Placement Outcomes for Clients with Multiple Disabilities*

Client Characteristics	CMI	CP	MR/CMI	TBI
Employed as of 31 March 1989, n	85	37	23	23
Placements (cumulative), n	205	51	46	47
Working in jobs (cumulative), n	157	47	31	43
Mean hourly wage, $	4.10	4.66	3.75	4.45
Mean time worked per week, h	22	35	37	32
Cumulative gross wages, $	517,808	179,394	143,870	207,809

*CMI = chronic mental illness; CP = cerebral palsy; MR = mental retardation; TBI = traumatic brain injury.

Table 13-3. Staff Intervention Hours Provided by Category*

Category of Intervention Time	CMI		CP		MR/CMI		TBI	
	h (90)							
Active time on job site	3493	(33.4)	3015	(30.3)	2831	(53.8)	4662	(44.4)
Inactive time on job site	935	(8.9)	439	(4.4)	610	(11.6)	1446	(13.8)
Travel and transport time	1474	(14.1)	1317	(13.2)	555	(10.5)	1428	(13.6)
Consumer training time	1180	(11.3)	303	(3.1)	330	(6.3)	381	(3.6)
Consumer program development	324	(3.1)	701	(7.1)	92	(1.7)	567	(5.4)
Direct employment advocacy	1587	(15.2)	2384	(24.0)	401	(7.6)	892	(8.5)
Indirect employment advocacy	1038	(9.9)	856	(8.6)	172	(3.3)	607	(5.8)
Consumer screening and evaluation	426	(4.1)	930	(9.4)	275	(5.2)	509	(4.9)
TOTAL	10,457	(100%)	9948	(100%)	5267	(100%)	10,495	(100%)

*CMI = chronic mental illness; CP = cerebral palsy; MR = mental retardation; TBI = traumatic brain injury

Table 13-4. Types of Work*

Type of Work	CMI (*n* = 205)	CP (*n* = 51)	MR/CMI (*n* = 46)	TBI (*n* = 46)
	%			
Food services	29.8	21.6	28.3	13.0
Janitorial-custodial	26.8	7.8	50.0	21.7
Unskilled labor	1.5	0.0	0.0	4.3
Bench work-assembly	4.9	5.9	13.0	0.0
Laundry	1.5	2.0	0.0	0.0
Stock clerk-warehouse	12.2	9.8	2.2	15.2
Transportation	2.0	0.0	2.2	0.0
Clerical-office	13.7	49.0	2.2	37.0
Groundskeeping	3.4	2.0	2.2	2.2
Human services	4.4	2.0	0.0	6.5
TOTAL	100	100	100	100

*CMI = chronic mental illness; CP = cerebral palsy; MR = mental retardation; TBI = traumatic brain injury

may be able to work with supported employment. The results of this study were not experimentally controlled and are therefore subject to obvious methodologic problems, not the least of which is subject selection bias by participating programs. Participating clients were selected for placement by many programs not necessarily on the basis of ability but rather on the basis of family support, transportation availability, willingness to take a less desirable job, or willingness to risk loss of Social Security payments. Furthermore, local economic conditions in different regions

Table 13-5. Reason for Separation from Employment*

Separation Reason	CMI	CP	MR/CMI	TBI
			%	
Transportation problem	3.0	0.0	0.0	0.0
Does not want to work	11.9	15.4	6.3	9.5
Took better job	12.9	7.7	18.8	0.0
Economic situation	5.0	7.7	12.5	9.5
Medical-health problem	14.9	15.4	6.3	28.6
Slow work	5.0	7.7	6.3	0.0
Low quality work	5.9	7.7	0.0	4.8
Poor social skills	0.0	0.0	0.0	8.8
Poor attendance-tardy	7.9	0.0	0.0	9.5
Insubordinate behavior	2.0	0.0	6.3	14.3
Aberrant behavior	4.0	0.0	0.0	4.8
Parental interference	0.0	7.7	0.0	0.0
Poor work attitude	4.0	7.7	0.0	4.8
Employer uncomfortable	2.0	7.7	6.3	0.0
Poor job match	9.9	0.0	18.8	4.8
Seasonal layoff	4.0	7.7	0.0	0.0
Other	5.9	7.7	18.8	4.8

*CMI = chronic mental illness; CP = cerebral palsy; MR = mental retardation; TRI = traumatic brain injury

Table 13-6. Employment Retention Rates at Various Intervals after Placement

Disability Groups*	3 Months		6 Months		9 Months		12 Months	
				n (%)				
MR/CMI	28	(89.3)	27	(77.8)	23	(82.7)	15	(93.3)
TBI	34	(82.4)	27	(59.3)	20	(55.0)	16	(62.5)
CP	42	(83.3)	32	(81.3)	24	(87.5)	15	(80.0)
CMI	130	(69.2)	99	(66.7)	75	(64.0)	47	(59.0)

*CMI = chronic mental illness; CP = cerebral palsy; MR = mental retardation; TBI = traumatic brain injury

of the country vary markedly, which makes uniform evaluation of program success difficult.

Nevertheless, the persons who are presented as working have one major attribute in common: Historically, they have been considered by the rehabilitation system as unemployable. Their preplacement work history clearly supports this perception; the mean salary is less than $1700 per year per person. Hence, the first finding of this study is that supported employment appears to be an effective means of helping people with severe disability go to work. The lack of a randomized control group does make it impossible, however, to conclude that supported employment was *the* reason for these persons working competitively.

We believe that this report provides an important benchmark, or baseline, from which to evaluate future efforts at vocational rehabilitation and job placement of persons with multiple disabilities and who have no appreciable work history. It would appear that these individuals can work competitively with job coach help; that persons with cerebral palsy and brain injury are able to participate in somewhat higher paying jobs; and that job retention is better by individuals with cerebral palsy and mental retardation-mental illness. To reduce job terminations for individuals with brain injuries or mental illness, closer liaison with a physician is probably necessary.

Although the previous material presents an excellent overview and analyses of supported employment, a case study approach is optimal to present implementation issues and problems. Therefore, in the final section that follows, we present several actual cases.

Case Studies of Competency in Supported Employment

□ Case 13-1: Taylor

□ Employee Characteristics

Taylor is a 22-year-old man who has been assessed by school psychologists as having severe mental retardation (IQ score of 24 on standardized intelligence tests). Medical records report that he has trisomy 21 with ventricular septal defect, a serious cardiac defect. Taylor takes heart medication daily and is not allowed to lift more than 25 pounds or to work in excessive heat. He has no sensory or motor impairments and is overweight. His speech is unclear and difficult to understand. Psychologic evaluations indicate significant deficits in language development with verbal understanding assessed at the 5-year level. School records and observations reveal that Taylor initiates interactions frequently and is often immature, with excessive touching and flirting.

Taylor has lived with his family for 9 years, and prior to that, he lived in a residential institution for persons with severe and profound mental retardation. His educational program since leaving the institution has been a self-contained classroom in an integrated high school. Taylor's school curriculum provided community-based training in janitorial and food service jobs at a local manufacturing center, supply center, and the school cafeteria. His training included dusting, bussing tables, sweeping, operating a dish machine, emptying trash, mopping, and potscrubbing. His teachers report that he can perform the tasks correctly and that he works at a slow rate.

□ Employment Record

With the help of a special university project and local school personnel, Taylor was placed as a dishwasher at a restaurant 8 months before his graduation. He was hired to work 16 hours a week on Friday and Saturday nights. His schedule increased to approximately 20 hours a week after 5 months. Taylor was paid $3.50 an hour beginning the first day of employment. Additional benefits include medical insurance, a free meal, and a bonus incentive plan. Taylor has received one bonus check of $100.00 for working 500 hours. His family transports him to and from work.

Taylor's job is operating a dish machine, putting dishes away, sweeping, mopping, and emptying trash. A copy of a detailed task analysis of daily activities used for training necessary job skills is found in Table 13-7.

After 1 year of employment, the supervisor changed Taylor's job tasks to wrapping potatoes for baking, making french fries, operating a dish machine, and emptying trash. Two other dishwashers work during the same hours and Taylor assists them as needed. The supervisor and

Table 13-7. Individualized Task Analysis and Special Training Strategies

Trainee: Taylor	Job Site: Western Sizzlin Restaurant
Employment Specialist: Shelia M.	Job Title: Dishmachine Operator

Approximate Times	Task Performed	Task Analysis–Diagrams–Special Training Techniques
4:55–5:00	1. Put on uniform.	1a. Put on apron and tie. b. Put on hat.
	2. Punch time card.	2a. Locate card in rack. b. Locate "in" on card. c. Line "in" up with red nozzle on clock. d. Pull black lever to clock in.
5:00–7:00	3. Load dishes onto racks.	3a. Pick up plates, hold in left hand. b. Shake apart, put in rack. (Black behind silver in same row.) c. Repeat until all black plates are removed from table. d. Remove salad plates and bowls from bus pan. e. Put dishes in rack. f. Repeat *d* and *e* until rack is full.
	4. Place full rack over sink.	4a. Lift rack and carry to sink area. b. Use water hose to rinse dishes.
	4a. Rinse with hose.	
	5. Load dishes onto racks.	5. Repeat *Step 3*.
	6. Place full rack over sink.	6. Repeat *Step 4*. If busy, it is better to load rack, place over sink area and spray both racks at one time.
	7. Put two racks into dish machine.	7. Take racks over to sink and push or slide into dish machine.
	8. Close machine door.	8. Take handle with hand and pull door completely down.
	9. Turn on dish machine.	9a. Use index finger and push white button to the right. b. Hold for approximately 2 to 3 seconds. c. Release button.
	10. Load glasses, cups, and soup bowls.	10a. Remove glasses, cups, and soupbowls from buspan. b. Carry and load into racks located above sink area. c. Repeat *a* and *b* until the racks become full. (This is to be done throughout the loading process. It may be an hour before the rack is full.)
	11. Put glasses, cups into dish machine.	11a. When one of the racks is filled with glasses, cups, or soup bowls, put in dish machine. b. Repeat *Step 7*.
	12. Close machine door.	12. Repeat *Step 8*.
	13. Turn machine on.	13. Repeat *Step 9*.
7:00–8:00	14. Continue loading racks with dirty dishes.	14. Repeat *Steps 3 to 13*.

Table 13-7. Continued

Trainee: Taylor	Job Site: Western Sizzlin Restaurant
Employment Specialist: Shelia M.	Job Title: Dishmachine Operator

Approximate Times	Task Performed	Task Analysis–Diagrams–Special Training Techniques
	15. If caught up on work (loading), wash pans and plastic containers.	15a. Go to sink and remove dirty pans. b. Bring pans to work area near sink. c. Spray with water hose the inside of pans. d. Scour with green pad if needed. (This is to loosen food only.) e. Put pans on flat rack. f. Slide through dish machine. (Make sure two racks are in the machine before turning it on.) g. Turn machine on. Repeat *Step 9*.
	16. Wash silver 16a. Locate push cart.	16a. When silver rack bottom is covered with knives, forks, and spoons, carry rack to sink. b. Rinse with hose. c. Push rack of silver into dish machine. Make sure two racks of dirty dishes are in machine. d. Turn machine on. Repeats *Steps 8* and *9*.
8:00–9:00	17. Catch clean dishes.	17a. When machine cuts off, lift machine door. b. Pull out two racks of dishes. c. Stack dishes at end of counter (bowls, cups).
	18. Catch clean silver.	18a. Pull rack with silver out of machine. b. Pour silver on counter. c. Sort knives and put into round containers. d. Sort forks and put into round containers. e. Sort spoons and put into round containers. f. Sort soup spoons and put into container.
	19. Wash silver second time.	19. When silver containers become at least half full, push silver back into machine and wash again (two racks needed in machine).
	20. Load clean dishes onto push cart.	20a. When caught up, put black plates on top of cart. b. Put smaller dishes on second and bottom rows. c. Continue until all clean dishes are on cart.
	21. Carry clean dishes to front line and store.	21a. Push loaded cart to front (grill area). b. Unload black plates first. Place on top of counter behind grill. c. Repeat *b* for remaining dishes. Place red plates, potato plates, salad bowls, and small bowls along under table behind french fry area. Salad plates belong on counter beside desserts.
	22. Load glasses, bowls.	22. If down time, repeat *Step 10*.

Table 13-7. Continued

Trainee: Taylor	Job Site: Western Sizzlin Restaurant
Employment Specialist: Shelia M.	Job Title: Dishmachine Operator

Approximate Times	Task Performed	Task Analysis–Diagrams–Special Training Techniques
9:00–9:30	23. BREAK. a. Order meal, continue to work, then punch out.	23a. Order meal at cashier stand. b. Carry meal ticket to order desk. c. Go to time clock, locate time card. d. Locate "out" on card just under the punched "in" 5:00. e. Line "out" up with red nozzle on clock. f. Pull black lever to clock out. g. Go to very back of restaurant and eat meal.
9:30	24. Punch in.	24. Follow *Step 2*. Punch directly under time he punched out.
9:30–Closing	25. Load or catch dishes, pans, silver, plastic containers.	25. Follow *Steps 3 to 22*.
	26. Sweep visible trash from floor.*	26a. Use broom to collect debris. b. Use dust pan to collect debris. c. Discard in trash can.
	27. Put Tide and water in bucket.	27a. Put 2 cups of Tide in bucket. b. Use hose to fill bucket with water.
	28. Scrub floor with scrub brush and Tide solution.	28a. Start in prep area, dip brush in solution. b. Pull out and scrub floor. c. Repeat *a* and *b* when brush becomes dry. d. Continue until floor is completely scrubbed.
	29. Hose floor down.	29. Repeat *Step 27*.
	30. Remove excess water from floor with squeegee.	30. Use squeegee to push excess water into floor drain.
	31. Before leaving, all pans and dishes must be washed and put away.†	31. Repeat *Steps 3 to 22*.

*Step 26 is exchanged with second dishwasher. One cleans floor and the other continues to do dishes. Pans will be coming from salad and potato bar.
†Make sure dish room is clean before leaving.

coworkers, without assistance from the employment specialist, trained Taylor to perform the new job tasks.

□ Problems Presented and Nature of Intervention

Taylor was trained by the employment specialist to perform the job tasks, to use the time clock, to order his meal at break time, and to socialize appropriately with coworkers. As the task analytic data indicated that Taylor was completing the job to the company's standards, the employment specialist gradually reduced her time on the job site. Initial training during the first month required 89 hours of trainer intervention time. The employment specialist began fading the second month, and reduced her time to 1 hour per shift during the third month. The total intervention time after 18 months of employment is 161 hours. Taylor continues to receive ongoing follow-along services by the employment specialist. His work performance is monitored by job site visits, supervisor evaluations, and phone calls to the family.

Taylor's supervisor's evaluations during the first 2 months on the job indicated that Taylor needed improvement in speed and consistency. The employment specialist used behavioral training strategies to teach skill acquisition and production rate before fading from the job site. Two additional supervisor evaluations reported that Taylor was frequently tardy and absent. The employment specialist identified the problem as a change in scheduling that resulted in an increase in Taylor's hours that Taylor failed to comprehend because Taylor's employer notified him verbally of the change. To prevent future recurrences of tardiness and absenteeism, arrangements were made for the employer to send a note home to the family notifying them of schedule changes.

After Taylor had been employed for 11 months, the employment specialist made a follow-along visit to the job site and observed him lifting potato boxes weighing 50 pounds. Coworkers reported that they volunteered to provide assistance but that Taylor repeatedly initiated the task independently. After lifting the boxes, Taylor would grasp his chest and close his eyes. The coworkers and supervisors would respond by asking Taylor if he was all right and suggesting he take a break. The employment specialist intervened and modeled initiating asking for assistance as the opportunity to lift the boxes occurred. Reinforcement was provided by the coworkers and the employment specialist for requesting assistance. After several weeks of training, the behavior was eliminated.

□ Outcome Measures

Taylor has earned over $5,000 in wages and has paid $1,235 in taxes after 18 months of employment. Since Taylor has been employed, he has lost over 8 pounds, which is a significant improvement. His family, teachers, and employment specialist state that his immature social behaviors have decreased. Taylor's family reports that he is allowed to stay home alone now, which was not permitted before he began working. Assessment data indicate that Taylor's work rate has increased from a slow to an average pace. In addition, the performance evaluations show that Taylor adapts to task changes more easily since the beginning of his employment. The employer consistently rates Taylor's work performance positively on supervisor evaluations and states that "he reduces the tension in the kitchen."

□ Case 13-2: John

□ Employee Characteristics

John is a 23-year-old man whose primary diagnosis is autism. His psychologic test data suggest wide discrepancies in John's abilities. His mental age at 18 was reported at 8 years (Peabody Picture Vocabulary Test). Intelligence test records place him in the moderate range of mental retardation with an IQ of 45. His reading and math skills are at eighth and third grade levels, respectively, according to the Slosson Oral Reading Test and the Wide Range Achievement Test (WRAT), which were also administered at age 18.

He is described as "highly active" and deficient in social and language skills. His movements are quick and abrupt. His verbalizations are inappropriately loud, one- to three-word staccato phrases. He avoids eye contact and makes short repeated glances at people when forced to interact with them. He sometimes hums or uses language in a self-stimulatory manner.

Other inappropriate behaviors include walking too fast, pushing people out of his way, perseverating words and phrases, and flipping objects with his fingers. When he is upset or frustrated, John has been observed to walk at a fast pace, sometimes in circles, repeating a word or phrase over and over again.

John's school services included a period from age 12 to 18 in a residential program for individuals with autism. His vocational training consisted of assembling food packets, shelving books in the library, and filing papers. At age 18, he returned home and was provided school services outside the classroom that consisted of one-on-one instruction provided by a homebound instructor in the school central office building. His educational program focused on vocational training and applied academic skills. Vocational training involved sorting mail in the central office mail room and reshelving books in the professional library. John was described as being difficult to train and extremely dependent on teachers' verbal and physical prompting.

□ Employment Record

The year before John's last year in school, he was selected for participation in a supported competitive employment program. Through this program, a supported work employment specialist located a 28-hour-per week position for John at a local bank operations center as a Proof Operator in September of his last year in school. The job involved using a specialized computer terminal to enter bank transaction items into the bank's main computer system.

After two and one half months of training, it was decided that John would not be able to complete the job duties of the Proof Operator position without constant supervision because of the many variations and exceptions that occurred in the work that would require John to make judgments.

John's employer at the bank identified another position at the bank that he felt might be a more appropriate match to John's abilities. After the employment specialist completed a thorough analysis of the position, John was started in the second position.

This position, called a Lockbox Clerk, required sorting and processing installment loan payments; it included separating the payment coupons from the checks, determining whether the payment had arrived by the due date, and then balancing the amounts paid using an electronic calculator. He was also responsible for deciding when items needed to be rejected and routed to the loan department. Handwriting was required to mark items or batches of items to indicate the actions to be taken. Sample portions of the task analyses for both the proof operator and lockbox clerk positions can be seen in Table 13-8.

□ Problems Presented and Nature of Intervention

The position of Proof Operator was determined not to be an appropriate job match because of incomplete job analysis information. Because of the nature of the job, many details were identified after several weeks of doing the job. After he decided that the job was too difficult, the work supervisor, together with the employment specialist, identified the second position of Lockbox Clerk.

Standard job-site training procedures included use of an ecologic and task analytic approach with behavioral and systematic instructional procedures being applied (Moon et al. 1986). The employment specialist provided intensive one-on-one training for all job and social skills; all work-related communication with coworkers and supervisors necessary for the completion of job duties (for example, asking for more work, notifying a supervisor of equipment malfunction); and instruction in how to use the city buses, how to order

Table 13-8. Proof Operator and Lock Box Clerk Jobs in a Bank

Closing a Proof Machine

1. *Look* on the journal tape, *find* the last sequence number (on the left side).
2. *Write* this number on your Batch Log Sheet (END SEQUENCE NUMBER _____).
3. *Press ND* key, *DN* key, 5 and the _____ key.
4. *Press ADD* key and __*__ key.
5. *Add* up all of the batches from the Batch Log Sheet (hit debit key after each number).
6. *Press* _____ key.
7. The two subtotals should be the same. *Write* numbers on Log Sheet–TOTAL BATCHES.
8. *Press* __*__ key and *release ADD* key.
9. *Press ND* key, *DN* key and __*__ key.
10. *Press* 1, 9, *PROG* key and _____ key. *Write* two numbers on Log Sheet–ITEM COUNT.
11. *Tear* off top proof journal tape. *Circle* total and *put* your name and the date on it.
12. *Tear* off second proof journal tape. *Fold* it up. *Circle* the total and *put* your name and the date on it. *Put* a rubber band around the tape.
13. *Sign* Batch Log Sheet and *fill* in STOP TIME _____.
14. *Fill* in Time Sheet.
15. *Turn* Time Sheet, Batch Log Sheet, Proof Journal Tapes (both), first practice item, and adding machine tapes into *supervisor*.
16. *Turn* the machine off and *cover* the machine. Be sure your work area is clean.

Lock Box Clerk Task

1. Compare check with document.
2. Decide action to take with items.
   - If check matches, put in "accept" stack.
   - If check is slightly larger, put in "accept" stack.
   - If check is much larger, put in "reject" stack.
   - If check is less, put in "reject" stack.
3. Write correct department on other bank mail.
4. Send items to loan department.
5. Decide when check is a deposit or loan payment with no document.
6. Keep all correspondence.
7. Write AN on front of envelope (if not listed on Corr).
8. Check for date and final payment written on document.
9. Check for bank name and signature on check.
10. If either is missing, pass to coworker to stamp.
11. Write correct description on front of envelope (Corr, Ck Reject, Ck/No Doc, Final Payment/Ck Reject).
12. Stop to add up stacks of checks and documents.
13. If adding machine tapes match, rubber-band stacks.
14. If adding machine tapes do NOT match, search for error.
15. Correct error.

lunch in the employee cafeteria, and how to spend break time appropriately.

In this position, the particular problems presented during training were fading prompts, dealing with exceptions, communicating with supervisor and coworkers, and printing legibly and small enough to fit into spaces on forms.

To fade prompts, the employment specialist implemented a question prompt procedure, "John, what do you do?" followed by a period of withholding any verbal interaction until John finally began to initiate the behaviors independently. Positive reinforcement for independent initiating was given in the form of verbal praise. Care was taken to deliver reinforcement intermittently to avoid transferring the dependence to the reinforcer, which would inhibit John's initiation of the subsequent behavior required in the task sequence.

To help John record correctly the exceptions that occurred in processing the loan installments, the employment specialist developed a checklist of procedures with "if–then" routines for processing irregular items. John's reading skills were utilized to train him to read brief instructional cues placed on his desk blotter that told him what action to take for a given type of exception. Each time an exception occurred, the employment specialist prompted John to refer to the written instructional cues, match the type of exception, and carry out the action as instructed. After many repetitions of this training to recognize an exception, go to written cues, and complete the action as written, John is able to handle the exceptions independently. The prompt fading procedure was also used. The one behavior that John could not be trained to do was to make a judgment about how much over or under the loan document amount a check amount could be to be accepted or rejected. This part of the job was negotiated out of the job duties to be done by a co-worker.

Interactions with coworkers and supervisors were trained by the employment specialist utilizing systematic procedures. As the employment specialist began to fade intervention time, she began prompting John to ask the room supervisor for more work or assistance rather than to ask her. She also assisted the supervisor and coworkers in asking John for items or giving him instructions by modeling the behaviors and then having John ask for them. Prompt fading in this instance was achieved by the employment specialist gradually becoming less available for John and coworkers and supervisors. Handwriting problems were solved by modifying some forms to accommodate John's large printing and by teaching John to use abbreviations.

On the second position, John began to perform duties and other work-related behaviors according to pre-established criteria based upon the employer's standards. The employment specialist began gradually to reduce intervention time at the job site. The supervisory role of the employment specialist was transferred to the worksite supervisor during the gradual reduction of time from the job site. The employment specialist was able to fade to a level of intervention of less than 1 hour per week. She continued frequent phone contact with the parents and employer and visited the job site once a week.

Two reasons can be offered to explain the high number of intervention hours. First, job development and job analysis in the high technology business world are more complex than the typical employment settings that have been common for supported employment consumers. Supported employment professionals need more experience in employment settings other than service industries such as food and janitorial services. Far fewer hours might have been possible in a simpler job placement. However, to place John in a position that did not utilize his higher level skills would be to underemploy him for the sake of programmatic efficiency. Secondly, the wide discrepancies between John's abilities and inabilities made consumer assessment information difficult to translate for appropriate job match.

□ *Outcome Measures*

Beginning the first day of employment in the Lock Box Clerk position, John earned $4.80 per hour working 20 hours per week. His cumulative wages earned at the time of this report were over $8,700 with over $2,000 paid in taxes. His supervisor at the bank has said that John is one of his more accurate workers; "he never makes a mistake." In addition to the primary financial gains, marked improvements in John's adaptive behavior are evident.

By the time John graduated from school he was performing the job at above 95% accuracy, and his production rate was approaching the standards of the employer. Employer evaluations indicated a high level of satisfaction with John's performance.

□ Case 13-3: Jim

The following case history illustrates the practical implementation of compensatory and cognitive remediation techniques.

□ Employee Characteristics

Jim is a 34-year-old man who sustained a head injury in an automobile accident approximately 4 years ago. He was subsequently in a coma for 2 months and was hospitalized for 4 months. As a consequence of his brain injury, he moved slowly, walked with a leg brace and cane, and had severe ataxia of the right hand and a drooping left eyelid that partly obscured his vision. His speech was difficult to understand because of slowness and dysarthria. Primary cognitive impairments included memory dysfunction, reduced learning ability, poor planning and organizational skills, distractibility, limited self-awareness, and inconsistent error recognition.

□ Employment Record

This unmarried man had held a number of jobs before his injury. After leaving high school, he joined the Marines and served 3 years as a unit dietary clerk. His responsibilities included typing, collating, and filing daily reports on his company's activities. Additional preinjury employment included work as a house painter, automobile painter, route driver, and maintenance worker. He was referred to our supported employment program because he was unable to maintain employment despite the efforts of vocational rehabilitation professionals using traditional techniques. The client had been labeled as severely disabled.

On referral for supported employment, Jim expressed interest in obtaining a clerical job similar to his previous military position. After 3 months of job development, he was offered a position as a microfilm clerk with a national electronics retailer. Jim was encouraged to accept the position because he had expressed interest in performing similar job responsibilities, had previously worked in a similar setting, and according to his neuropsychologic evaluation, possessed sufficient skills to master the work responsibilities. The job was a fulltime position and involved organizing documents, processing checks, checking and correcting accounting errors, microfilming processed documents, and restocking boxes.

□ Problems Presented and Nature of Intervention

An employment specialist assigned to Jim determined that he required training in two primary areas, document processing and microfilming. Initially, half of Jim's work was completed by the employment specialist. To facilitate hiring, the employment specialist guaranteed the employer that a normal workload would be completed daily. (The work completion guarantee is characteristic of our supported employment program.) Jim learned all the steps necessary for the processing tasks within 30 days. A level of 98% to 100% accuracy was established. Microfilming accuracy levels exceeded 85% after 1 month. During the first 2 or 3 months, Jim was processing 20 to 30 units per day. By 3 months after placement, and with the aid of compensatory strategies, he was able to complete 250 to 300 units per day with 98% accuracy.

Jim experienced many problems, especially during the first 4 months of employment. Specifically, he forgot the steps required for task completion; had a relatively high error rate in arithmetic operations; had poor error recognition; was slow and unable to meet production standards; and had difficulty operating equipment safely and efficiently. The causes of Jim's problems were the many cognitive and physical impairments he had sustained as a consequence of his brain injury.

Jim had difficulty remembering the steps required to complete various tasks. For example, he would begin to photocopy documents before ensuring that he had the complete set of documents organized in the correct sequence. A task analytic approach was utilized to teach Jim. The task was initially broken down into a series of components. Jim was taught to master each of the components in sequence. Several weeks after acquisition, however, the employment specialist observed that Jim occasionally omitted several steps. The employment specialist developed a special notebook that described each step in the job completion process. The notebook served as a memory aid. Furthermore, coworkers were informed about the availability of the notebook and were instructed to encourage Jim to refer to it if he appeared confused or disoriented.

Our client also had difficulty learning how to load film cartridges. Absolutely correct performance of the task was critical. On occasion, Jim was required to repeat several hours of filming because the film had been loaded incorrectly. To facilitate learning, the employment specialist arranged for Jim to practice loading the camera using several dummy rolls of film. Practice loadings supervised and checked by the employment specialist resulted in successful skill acquisition with a 0% error rate within 1 week of initiation. The employment specialist continued to monitor and track all film cartridges for an additional 3 weeks.

Jim often forgot to reset the date on a machine used to stamp documents. The employment specialist wrote a note that asked, "Have you changed the date?" and placed it in a location where Jim could see it while operating the machine. Because the switches on the microfilming machine were often dislodged by normal movement of the machine and by people bumping into it, the employment specialist also attached notes indicating the correct settings near each important switch and dial. Although this intervention strategy was relatively simple, the visual cues provided an effective and permanent solution to problems that could have had serious consequences.

Jim occasionally demonstrated problems with error recognition and correction. For example, he would place processed documents in an incorrect sequence and merge them with documents awaiting processing. A clear Plexiglas divider was used to separate completed work from work to be completed.

In addition, the employment specialist obtained random work samples as part of a quality control process. A baseline was initially established by checking 50% of the completed work. At first, Jim's baseline was below the 99% accuracy rate required by his employer. To improve Jim's self-awareness, accuracy rates were graphed and placed in a visible area in Jim's work station. A bold line was drawn to indicate the acceptable level of accuracy. Over a 6-week period, Jim's work reached a consistent and acceptable range of quality. The employment specialist also instructed Jim in methods of checking his work. Apparently, he was motivated to self-monitor partly because he felt uncomfortable having his work closely monitored by the employment specialist. Jim was able to work more independently. Positive feedback from the employment specialist and supervisors was increased, and performance quality improved to acceptable levels within a 2-week period.

Later, environmental distraction became a problem for Jim, causing his overall production rate to decrease. The employment specialist determined that auditory rather than visual stimuli were the source of distraction. The first remedy tried was moving the work situation away from a busy doorway. Jim was also discouraged from listening to his radio while working. Finally, his work station was turned so that he would not face the doorway. The three initial modifications were successful. As an alternative, Jim purchased a headset for his radio. The headset proved effective in closing out unwanted noise and allowing him to focus on a single, pleasant auditory stimulus—music. Jim eventually purchased a cassette player, which gave him greater freedom of movement.

A series of interventions was also implemented to assist Jim in compensating for his physical limitations. His work table was elevated with two pieces of wood to minimize the necessity of extended movement and to improve his posture. Large paper clips were substituted for smaller ones, and butterfly clips were made available for organizing larger stacks of documents. A bowl was purchased to hold the paper clips, enabling easier and quicker access, which was initially restricted because of Jim's poor fine-motor control. An electric stapler was substituted for a manual one, allowing Jim to staple documents using his single steady hand. Rubber fingertip covers were introduced to speed handling and filing of documents. Finally, a back cushion was added to his chair to increase comfort and reduce fatigue.

□ *Outcome Measures*

One month after Jim was hired, the company upgraded his classification from trial to permanent employee. He was given a raise from $4.50 to $5.00 per hour with full fringe benefits. Jim has received 712 staff hours of assistance during his 88 consecutive weeks of employment. He is now earning $5.60 per hour. To date, he has earned $19,471 as a microfilm clerk. He continues to work 39 hours per week, with periodic opportunities for overtime. He recently moved from his brother's home to his own apartment. Because of his improved financial status, he has been able to purchase a stereo and a car and to spend more time in recreational activities with friends. He has maintained a high level of work performance and requires only periodic visits from an employment specialist to help reinforce appropriate work-related skills.

References

1. Americans with Disability Act of 1990, Public Law 101-336.
2. Bellamy GT, Rhodes L, Mank DM, Joyce A. Supported Employment: A Community Implementation Guide. Baltimore, Paul H. Brookes. 1988.
3. Bourbeau P. Mobile work crews: An approach to achieve long-term supported employment. In: McCarthy P, Everson JM, Moon MS, Barcus JM. eds. School to Work: Transition Youth with Severe Disabilities. Richmond, Virginia Commonwealth University, Rehabilitation, Research and Training Center, 1985.
4. Buckley J, Bellamy GT. National survey of day and vocational programs for adults with severe disabilities: A 1984 profile. In: Ferguson P. ed. Issues in Transition Research: Economics and Social Outcomes. Eugene, OR, Specialized Training Program, 1986.
5. Federal Register. Final Regulations. Voc. 52 (157, pp. 30546–30552). Washington, DC, Government Printing Office, 1987, August.
6. Johnson J, Mithaug D. A replication of sheltered workshop entry requirements. In: Bellamy GT, Rhodes L, Mank DM, Albin JM. eds. Supported Employment: A Community Implementation Guide. Baltimore, Paul H. Brookes, 1977.
7. Kiernan W, Stark J. Pathways to Employment for Adults with Severe Developmental Disabilities. Baltimore, Paul H. Brookes, 1986.
8. Kregel J, Wehman P, Revell WG, Hill M. Supported employment in Virginia 1980–1988. In Kregel J, Wehman P, Shafer M. eds. Supported Employment for Persons with Severe Disabilities: From Research to Practice. Monograph Vol 3. Richmond, Virginia Commonwealth University, Rehabilitation, Research and Training Center, 1990.
9. Mank DM, Rhodes LE, Bellamy GT. Four supported employment alternatives. In Kiernan WE, Stark JA. eds. Pathways to Employment for Adults with Developmental Disabilities. Baltimore, Paul H. Brookes, 1986.
10. Mithaug DE, Hagmeire LD, Haring NG. The relationship between training activities and job placement in vocational education of the severely and profoundly handicapped. In: Bellamy GT, Rhodes

L, Mank DM, Alvin JM. eds. Supported Employment: A Community Implementation Guide. Baltimore, Paul H. Brookes, 1977.

11. Moon S, Goodall P, Barcus M, Brooke V. eds. The Supported Work Model of Competitive Employment for Citizens with Severe Handicaps: A Guide for Job Trainers. rev. ed. Richmond, Virginia Commonwealth University, Rehabilitation Research and Training Center, 1989.

12. O'Bryan A. The STP benchwork model. In: McCarthy P, Everson J, Moon S, Barcus M. eds. School-to-Work Transition for Youth with Severe Disabilities. Monograph. Richmond, Virginia Commonwealth University, Rehabilitation Research and Training Center, 1985.

13. Rhodes LE, Valenta L. Enclaves in industry. In: McCarthy P, Everson J, Moon S, Barcus M. eds. School-to-Work Transition for Youth with Severe Disabilities. Monograph. Richmond, Virginia Commonwealth University, Rehabilitation Research and Training Center, 1985.

14. Rusch FR. Competitive employment issues and strategies. In: Bellamy GT, Rhodes L, Mank DM, Albin JM. eds. Supported Employment: A Community Implementation Guide. Baltimore, Paul H. Brookes, 1986.

15. Schloss P, Wolf R, Schloss C. Financial implications of half and fulltime employment for persons with disabilities. Except Child. November: 54:272–276, 1987.

16. Shafer M, Nisbet J. Integration and empowerment in the workplace. In: Barcus M, Griffin S, Mank D, Rhodes L, Moon S. eds. Supported Employment Implementation Issues. Monograph. Richmond, Virginia Commonwealth University, Rehabilitation Research and Training Center, 1988.

17. Wehman P. Competitive Employment: New Horizons for Severely Disabled Individuals. Baltimore, Paul H. Brookes, 1981.

18. Wehman P, Moon MS. eds. Vocational Rehabilitation and Supported Employment. Baltimore, Paul H. Brookes, 1988.

Chapter 14
Behavior Management: Focus on Self-Injury

David Pitonyak

The volume of literature concerning self-injurious behavior has increased significantly in the last 20 years (Johnson and Rea 1986). Although a significant portion of this literature deals with the possible causes of self-injury, the bulk of the literature is concerned with treatment. This emphasis on treatment is not surprising given the serious nature of these behaviors and the need to develop effective interventions (Johnson and Baumeister 1978). Indeed, the seriousness of self-injury often dictates that the intervention be direct, precluding extended analysis of causal variables.

As Favell and her colleagues (1982a) point out, little is known about the causes of self-injurious behavior. Self-injury is strongly associated with medical conditions such as the Lesch-Nyhan syndrome, but specific causal relationships have yet to be established (Cataldo and Harris 1982). Severity of self-injury is related to institutionalization, history of chronicity, and a number of organic disorders (Schroeder et al. 1978). There is evidence that impoverished environments may cause self-injury, but the principal evidence to support such claims is based on research with primates; any generalization of these findings to humans must be done with caution (Schroeder et al. 1986).

Carr (1977), in a careful review of the literature, arrived at five possible hypotheses concerning the origins of self-injurious behavior:

1. Self-injury is a learned behavior maintained by positive reinforcement.
2. Self-injury is a learned behavior maintained by negative reinforcement (avoidance of or termination of an unpleasant event).
3. Self-injury is a self-stimulatory behavior that provides tactile, vestibular, and kinesthetic input.
4. Self-injury is the result of an aberrant physiologic process.
5. Self-injury is used to reduce guilt and establish ego boundaries.

Each of Carr's five hypotheses is discussed below.

Hypotheses To Explain Self-Injurious Behavior

The Positive Reinforcement Hypothesis

The positive reinforcement hypothesis claims that self-injury "is a learned operant, maintained by positive social reinforcement, which is delivered contingent upon the performance of the behavior"

206

(Carr 1977). Lovaas and colleagues (1965) showed that self-injurious behavior could be affected by the laws of operant behavior. They demonstrated that the self-injurious behaviors of a 9-year-old girl increased when care givers responded to those behaviors with social attention. They also showed that the behaviors decreased when social attention was withheld.

In a later report (Lovaas and Simmons 1969), the social reinforcement hypothesis was tested by physically and socially isolating the subjects. Each subject's self-injury was gradually reduced to negligible levels when this procedure was used. At the beginning of the isolation period, there was an increase (over baseline levels) in the frequency and intensity of self-injury. This increase was similar to the extinction burst phenomenon reported in the animal literature (Skinner 1938). These studies demonstrate that the discontinuation of reinforcement for a previously reinforced response results in a temporary increase in the frequency or magnitude of the response. The presence of an extinction burst has been suggested as further support of the positive reinforcement hypothesis (Carr 1977). A number of subsequent investigations have also shown that social reinforcement can serve to maintain self-injurious behavior (Carr and McDowell 1980; Durand 1982; Durand and Crimmons 1988).

Social reinforcement is not the only form of reinforcement that may maintain self-injury. Other reinforcers, such as tangible reinforcers, have also been shown to affect the frequency and intensity of self-injury (Durand and Crimmins 1988; Edelson et al. 1983). The precise form of positive reinforcement can differ widely from individual to individual; that is, individuals may engage in self-injury for very different—even aberrant—forms of reinforcement (Favell et al. 1982a). For example, it has been shown that physical restraint is reinforcing for some individuals (Favell et al. 1978; Foxx and Dufresne 1984), and its

use as a contingency for self-injury may actually strengthen and maintain the behavior (Favell et al. 1981).

The Negative Reinforcement Hypothesis

The negative reinforcement hypothesis claims that self-injury "is maintained by the termination or avoidance of an aversive stimulus following the occurrence of a self-injurious act" (Carr 1977). This hypothesis suggests that "individuals may expose themselves to aversive stimulation—like self-injury—in order to avoid even more aversive consequences" (Schroeder et al. 1980).

Several authors have reported anecdotally that individuals may engage in self-injury to escape from unpleasant situations. For example, Freud and Burlingham (1949) described an institutionalized girl who engaged in head-banging to escape being put to bed. Jones et al. (1974) described a 9-year-old autistic girl who forcefully thrust the back of her hand into her upper front teeth whenever demands were placed on her. Her self-injury resulted in the immediate termination of demands and the application of mechanical restraints.

Evidence for the negative reinforcement hypothesis also comes from a number of studies that investigated the effects of task demands on self-injury. The purpose of this research was to show that self-injury may serve as an escape response. Carr and colleagues (1976), for example, observed that self-injury was far more likely when difficult versus easy tasks were presented to an 8-year-old boy with childhood schizophrenia. They reasoned that the boy's self-injury would decrease during high-demand situations if his teacher said, "OK, let's go," a signal that normally ended the situation. In contrast, they reasoned that a signal such as "The sky is blue" (a signal that never resulted in the termination of a demand situation) would have no effect on the rate of self-injury. Both of these hypotheses were substantiated. Gaylord-Ross and coworkers (1980) showed that the self-injury of a 16-year-old girl varied when she was asked to perform different tasks. When she was asked to assemble a puzzle (easy), little or no self-injury occurred, but presentations of a button-sorting task (difficult) produced high rates of self-injury. In more recent studies, researchers have confirmed these early findings (Durand 1982; Durand and Crimmins 1988; Iwata et al. 1982).

The Self-Stimulation Hypothesis

The self-stimulation hypothesis holds "that a certain level of stimulation, particularly in the tactile, vestibular, and kinesthetic modalities, is necessary for the organism, and that, when such stimulation occurs at an insufficient level, the organism may engage in stereotyped behaviors, including self-injurious behavior, as a means of providing sensory stimulation" (Carr 1977). In this view, some persons are thought to be insensitive to normal levels of environmental stimulation and engage in self-injury to fulfill that need (Cataldo and Harris 1982). Although few experimental studies have been conducted to confirm this hypothesis (Edelson et al. 1983), there are various anecdotal and experimental reports that lend credence to the hypothesis.

Levy (1944) noted that orphan children who were restricted to their cribs without toys engaged in self-injury. When these infants were given toys to play with, their self-injurious behavior disappeared, presumably because of the increased tactile and kinesthetic stimulation. Dennis and Najarian (1957) discussed similar behaviors among a group of orphan children who were left alone in their cribs because of understaffing, attributing the self-injury to "stimulation hunger." Experimental evidence for the self-stimulation hypothesis includes interesting evidence from animal studies (Berkson 1968; Harlow and Griffin 1965; Harlow and Harlow 1971). Berkson (1968), for example, observed groups of

monkeys who were separated from their mothers at birth to assess the influence of separation on the development of stereotyped behaviors. In addition to a variety of stereotyped behaviors observed in the monkeys (for example, self-sucking, crouching, and bodyrocking), Berkson observed a number of self-injurious behaviors, including eye poking, self-biting, and body rubbing. Monkeys raised with their mothers rarely showed any stereotyped or self-injurious behaviors. Berkson concluded that stereotyped behaviors are self-stimulatory in nature, occurring when there is an absence of adequate stimulation.

Research has also shown that certain forms of self-injury in humans (for example, eye poking) may be maintained by sensory reinforcers (for example, visual). Favell and colleagues (1982b) taught institutionalized children to manipulate toys that provided sensory input thought to be similar to input the children were achieving through self-injury. The reinforcement value of the toys was thought to compete with the reinforcement value of the childrens' self-injury, resulting in decreases in these behaviors. The authors wrote, "it may be argued that the pervasive deficiencies of these clients kept them in a chronic state of sensory deprivation."

Repp and coworkers (1988) suggested that self-injury may function as an individual's "adaptive" way of controlling the level of activity in his or her total environment. They found that the mere presence of tasks resulted in decreased levels of self-injury and self-stimulation among three students with profound mental retardation. "Interestingly," they write, "this is the opposite procedure suggested by the negative reinforcement hypothesis," which assumes that the individual engages in self-injury to escape task demands.

The Aberrant Physical Process Hypothesis

It is known that self-injury can result from aberrant physiologic processes such as the

Lesch-Nyhan syndrome (Nyhan 1976), Cornelia de Lange syndrome (Bryson et al. 1971), and otitis media (de Lissovoy 1963). For example, destructive biting of lips, tongue, and fingers is often associated with the Lesch-Nyhan syndrome, which results from a genetic flaw in purine metabolism (Jones 1982). Purine is a chemical compound produced by the body during normal activity, the metabolic end product of which is uric acid. Because the biting of lips, tongue, and fingers is prevalent in individuals afflicted by the syndrome, it has been hypothesized that self-injury results from a specific biochemical abnormality (Seegmiller 1972). To date a specific abnormality has not been identified, though biochemical studies do point to abnormalities involving the neurotransmitter serotonin and dopamine (Cataldo and Harris 1982).

Carr (1977) has argued that "several lines of evidence mitigate against a purely organic explanation" of self-injury. First, there are reports of individuals with Lesch-Nyhan syndrome who do not engage in self-injury (Nyhan 1968; Seegmiller 1972). Second, operant techniques such as extinction, time out, and differential reinforcement of other behaviors (DRO) have been shown to be effective in treating the self-injurious behaviors of individuals with Lesch-Nyhan syndrome (Duker 1975). One would not expect such individuals to respond to operant procedures if their self-injury was controlled by biochemical abnormalities. Finally, Duker (1975) noted that children with Lesch-Nyhan syndrome have been observed to engage in self-injury more frequently with adults who paid attention to the behavior(s). Given these observations, it seems likely that self-injury is controlled by both organic and environmental factors (Carr 1977).

Psychotropic medications have been used widely to treat self-injurious behavior in developmentally disabled persons (Singh and Millichamp 1985). Despite their widespread use, there exists little in the way of hard data to support the treatment of self-injury with psychotropic medications (Singh and Millichamp 1985). In one study of the long-term effects of treatment on the self-injurious behavior of persons living in a state facility for mental retardation, for example, Schroeder and coworkers (1978) reported sobering results; they found that only 26% of the persons treated exclusively with psychotropic medications showed improvement. This figure compares with figures obtained in studies of individuals who were treated with behavior modification alone (90% showed improvement) and individuals who received no treatment at all (21% showed improvement). As Singh and Millichamp (1985) point out:

> The most notable aspect of research in this area is that the data are so meager. While drugs are used extensively with the mentally retarded, there is little empirical evidence attesting to the efficacy of these drugs in the treatment of self-injury. What little data there is suggests that drugs may not be as effective as some clinicians may assume. For example, an observational study of physician's drug prescriptions for self-injury suggested that clinicians may prescribe a series of different drugs and/or the same drug in different doses in the belief that eventually a drug or dosage will be effective.

In conclusion, despite research that links self-injury with aberrant physiologic processes, it is generally believed that a purely organic basis for self-injury is untenable. Instead, an interaction of organic and environmental variables is suggested (Carr 1977). From this viewpoint, the successful treatment of self-injury will require the manipulation of organic and environmental events. The use of psychotropic medications to treat self-injury has little empirical support. Researchers have called for controlled studies that isolate the effects of psychotropic medications on self-injury (Cataldo and Harris 1982; Singh and Millichamp 1985).

The Psychodynamic Hypothesis

Prior to the 1960s, a major body of literature concerning self-injury was psychodynamic in nature (Johnson and Rea 1986). Proponents of psychodynamic approaches have proposed that individuals have a difficult time distinguishing the self from the external world and that self-injury is an attempt to create a "body reality" (Carr 1977). Beres (1952) suggested that self-injury was an individual's means of alleviating guilt, and Menninger (1938) suggested that children engaging in the behavior do so because they must displace anger toward their mothers. Hoffner (1950), describing self-biting as "oral aggressiveness," suggested that self-injury could result from a variety of events, including a mother's refusal to breast feed her child and the absence of a "pain barrier" that regulates such behavior in normal children. Others have suggested that self-injury serves an "autoerotic" and "auto-aggressive" function (Freud 1954; Freud and Burlingham 1949; Klein 1932). Klein (1932), for example, suggested that the night-time head banging of a young girl "meant having sadistic coitus with her mother, in which she played the part of her supposedly sadistic father."

A major problem with psychodynamic theory has been the difficulty of operationalizing concepts such as "body reality," "guilt," and "anger displacement" (Carr 1977). Few treatment strategies based on the approach have produced meaningful outcomes when studied empirically (Bachman 1972; Favell et al. 1982a). Indeed, in a widely cited study, Lovaas and colleagues (1965) demonstrated that strategies designed to alleviate guilt in an individual who engaged in self-injurious behavior actually resulted in a worsening of the problem. In contrast, the use of reinforcement and extinction strategies (described below) resulted in significant improvements in both the frequency and intensity of the individual's behaviors.

Treatment of Self-Injurious Behaviors by Operant Procedures

Since the 1960s, operant procedures have been used widely to treat the behavior problems of persons with developmental disabilities (Berkson and Landsman-Dwyer 1977). Despite the relatively low incidence of self-injury, a great deal of the operant literature has been concerned with its reduction (Johnson and Rea 1986). Comprehensive reviews of this literature are available (for example, Gorman-Smith and Matson 1985; Horner and Barton 1980; Romanczyk 1986; Schroeder et al. 1980).

What follows is a selective review of the operant literature related to the reduction of self-injury. Studies reported in this review have been chosen because they are representative of a specific type of operant procedure or procedures used within the last 20 years to reduce these and other problem behaviors. This review is divided into two sections: the reduction of self-injury using aversive procedures and the reduction of self-injury using nonaversive procedures.

The Reduction of Self-Injury Using Aversive Procedures

It should be noted the term "aversive" is not synonymous with the term "punishment." Schroeder and colleagues (1980) emphasize that "punishment consists of delivering an intense stimulus immediately contingent on the occurrence of self-injury, to reduce self-injury." The stimulus need not be aversive, but its use must result in the suppression of self-injury to be classified as a punisher (Azrin and Holz 1966). In the review that follows, not all of the procedures did, in fact, result in a suppression of self-injury. Thus, "aversive" hereafter reflects a general class of procedures designed to suppress self-injury, regardless of their actual effect.

Most of the behavior-reduction strategies reported in the operant literature have emphasized the use of aversive procedures (LaVigna and Donnellan 1986). Mesaros (1983), for example, in an extensive review of the major behavioral journals from 1968 to 1982, found that of the 96 articles dealing with autism, 85% of the behavior reduction strategies were punitive. More recently, Lennox and coworkers (1988) were "surprised at the number of aversive procedures . . . still being evaluated in the literature relative to the number of positive approaches." In their review of seven major behavioral journals from 1981 to 1985, 65% of the strategies used to treat self-injury were considered aversive.

The purpose of this section is to review selectively the use of aversive procedures to reduce self-injurious behaviors. These procedures can be grouped into five major categories: extinction; time out from positive reinforcement; overcorrection; electric shock; and other punishers.

Extinction

Extinction involves withholding the reinforcer maintaining the self-injury. The effectiveness of the extinction procedure depends on an ability to identify and control the reinforcer (Horner and Barton 1980). If that reinforcer is care-giver attention, the use of the extinction procedure requires ignoring episodes of the behavior. If that reinforcer is escaping from an unpleasant activity, the extinction procedure involves preventing escape from the activity (Favell et al. 1982a).

Lovaas and coworkers (1965) and Tate and Baroff (1966) found that simple extinction had no effect on the frequency of self-injury. These results are difficult to interpret, however, because no measure of adult attention was reported in either study. Carr (1977) has suggested that adults may have inadvertently paid attention to their self-injury on an intermittent basis: "This situation is likely because of the difficulty of ignoring an individual when that individual is engaging in dan-

gerous high-frequency head banging or face slapping."

Lovaas and Simmons (1969) attempted to remedy the problem of inadvertent adult attention by arranging for the noncontingent isolation of two boys with severe mental retardation. The boys were isolated separately in an observation room for 1.5 hours per day to test the effectiveness of the extinction procedure. One boy produced 2750 self-injurious responses, and the other, 900 responses in the first session. There were 25,000 and 9000 total responses, respectively, before the behaviors were extinguished. Notably, there was no change in the frequency of self-injury for either boy in other settings.

Watson (1967) cautioned that extinction could be inappropriate in treating severe forms of self-injury. Bucher and Lovaas (1968) abandoned an extinction procedure because a young girl "could have inflicted serious self-injury or even killed herself during an extinction run." Because of these problems, extinction was abandoned as a strategy in a number of studies (Corte et al. 1971; Myers 1975; Wolf et al. 1967); the investigators in each case replaced extinction with other techniques. In a relatively small number of cases, simple extinction has been used effectively (Jones et al. 1974; Ross et al. 1974; Wright et al. 1978). Wright and coworkers (1978), for example, instructed care givers to leave the room whenever a 9-month-old baby engaged in ruminative vomiting. The vomiting gradually disappeared over a 2-month period, and these results were maintained for an 18-month period.

Despite the success of the extinction procedure in a limited number of studies, it is generally thought that the risks to individual safety are too great to warrant its use in severe cases of self-injury (Horner and Barton 1980; Schroeder et al. 1980). Additionally, problems with generalization, durability, and substitution of other behaviors have been reported (Duker 1975; Jones et al. 1974; Miron 1971).

Time Out from Positive Reinforcement

Time out from positive reinforcement consists of "removing an individual from the opportunity to obtain reinforcement contingent upon each occurrence of self-injury" (Favell et al. 1982a). The forms of time out vary widely (for example, contingent observation, withdrawal time out, seclusion time out, response cost), but all involve the removal of the individual from reinforcement or visa versa (Schroeder et al. 1980). This removal period typically ranges from several seconds to 30 minutes.

One of the earliest reports of time out for self-injury was by Wolf and coworkers (1964). The study involved a 3.5-year-old boy who engaged in head banging, face slapping, hair pulling, and face scratching. His mother reported that the boy "was a mess, black and blue and bleeding" after these episodes. Previous attempts to treat the behaviors with drugs and restraint had failed. The boy was placed in his room contingent upon episodes of self-injury and left alone until he stopped. His behaviors were decreased to near-zero levels in 5 months. Wolf and colleagues (1967) treated the same boy again 3 years later for face slapping. The boy's behavior was particularly troublesome to the boy's preschool teachers. Efforts to use an extinction technique failed, and the authors implemented a time-out program (removal to a separate room) where the behavior reached near-zero levels after three time-out periods.

Nunes and colleagues (1977) withdrew vibratory stimulation contingent upon self-injury from a 16-year-old boy with mental retardation. Self-injurious behavior was reduced to zero in three home and school environments in 31 days. No generalization data were presented. The study is unique in that it introduced vibratory stimulation to the boy first and then used the vibrator as a reinforcer that could easily be withdrawn.

It is important to note that time out is effective only when the individual is functioning in an environment in which reinforcement is available (Birnbrauer 1976;

Solnick et al. 1977). Thus, most procedures should be accompanied by efforts to enrich the environment (Favell et al. 1982b). Similarly, the success of a time-out program depends upon the amount of reinforcement an individual is able to obtain while *in* time out. For individuals who find self-stimulatory behaviors to be reinforcing, the opportunity to go to a room and self-stimulate may be rewarding rather than punishing (Solnick et al. 1977). Likewise, an individual who is attempting to escape from an unpleasant or uncomfortable activity may find time out reinforcing. Both of these issues were addressed in a study by Rolider and Van Houten (1985). The self-biting behavior of a 9-year-old boy with autism was treated by a procedure termed "movement suppression time out." The authors describe the procedure:

> Movement suppression consisted of telling the child to go immediately to the corner while guiding or forcing him into the corner as quickly as possible. [Tom] was positioned with his chin against the corner, both hands behind his back, with one hand on top of the other and both feet close together touching the wall. Whenever the child moved or made a verbalization the parents said "Don't move" or "Don't talk" in a very firm, loud voice while pressing the child into the corner by placing one hand against the child's upper back between the shoulder blades . . . this procedure was applied even if the child only moved a small amount such as wiggling a finger or shifting weight from one leg to the other. The parent stood behind the child very closely so the procedure could be implemented following any movement or verbalization. This procedure lasted approximately three minutes, and the child was then told he could leave the corner.

The procedure was implemented after a less intrusive procedure—DRO—had failed to reduce the self-biting. After 14 administrations of the program, the self-injury was nearly eliminated. In five follow-up sessions 2 and 3 months after the program was initiated, the self-biting was at the zero-level. In their discussion section, the authors note that the procedure, which includes physical restraint, was relatively easy to administer. They caution against the use of the procedure with larger persons, however. "The procedure might be less effective or safe when applied to strong combative adults or adolescents. Under these conditions the corner should be padded."

In addition to the problems of removing an individual to time out and holding him or her there when he or she is struggling, care must be exercised to ensure that the individual will not hurt himself or herself if left alone. Favell et al. (1982a) recommend that if the individual cannot be protected from self-harm, time out should not be used.

Overcorrection

Overcorrection is a complex combination of procedures that "require the misbehaving individual (a) to overcorrect the environmental effects of the inappropriate act, and (b) to practice overly correct forms of relevant behavior in those situations where the misbehavior commonly occurs" (Foxx 1978). When an individual engages in self-scratching, for example, he or she might be required to keep the hands open while extending them over the head, at right angles to the body (for example, Azrin et al. 1975). The procedure requires the individual to practice such movements for extended periods of time. If necessary, the care giver uses manual guidance to ensure compliance. Another form of overcorrection has been applied to individuals who engage in rumination (chewing and reswallowing vomitus) (for example, Foxx et al. 1979). In these cases, the individual would be required to cleanse his or her mouth with mouth wash and clean his or her face for extended periods of time.

Epstein and colleagues (1974) have identified several components in overcorrection: negative feedback; time out from positive reinforcement; verbal re-educative instructions; compliance training, such as gradual guidance or shadowing; and negative reinforcement. Schroeder and coworkers (1980) state that these procedures should be related directly to the self-injury, be applied immediately following the self-injury, and be performed in a rapid manner so as to be inhibiting.

Azrin and Wesolowski (1975) manually guided a mentally retarded woman through a clean-up procedure after she vomited and taught her to vomit in the toilet. The procedure was successful in reducing the vomiting to near-zero levels. Prior to the use of the overcorrection program, a time-out and required relaxation program had failed. Borresson (1980) notes that adult attention and demands were both motivational variables in the self-biting of a 22-year-old man with mental retardation. After several attempts to control this behavior with alternative procedures (including extinction, mechanical restraint, and DRO) had failed, a forced running program was implemented. The procedure involved guiding the man up and down a four-step stairway upon each occurrence of self-biting. Physical guidance was provided to increase the rate of stair climbing beyond a normal rate. A minimum of two staff persons was necessary to implement the procedure, which took less than 1 minute. Additionally, edible reinforcers were delivered for compliance, toy play, and appropriate social behaviors. The procedure was effective in reducing the self-biting from baseline levels in excess of 1000 times per day to less than two times per day after 34 days. A reversal was conducted in which the behavior returned at frequencies in excess of baseline levels (more than 2000 times per day). When treatment was reinstated, the self-biting was reduced to 3.7 times per day after 10 days.

Foxx and coworkers (1979) used a combination of satiation and oral hygiene procedures to reduce the rumination behaviors of an adult man and woman, both of whom were mentally retarded. The satiation condition simply consisted of allowing both individuals to have double portions of lunch. During the satiation and oral hygiene condition, the authors required both individuals to cleanse their mouths with an oral antiseptic (Listerine) for 2 minutes contingent upon rumination. Both were required to swab or brush the insides of their mouths with the antiseptic and then wipe their lips with a cloth that had been dipped in the antiseptic. When necessary, the care giver used manual guidance to ensure compliance. When the individual was resistant, the care giver performed the oral hygiene procedure. The results of the study revealed that satiation alone reduced the ruminating behaviors of these two individuals by 45% and 84%. The addition of the oral hygiene procedure resulted in near-zero levels of the behavior. Maintenance of these results after 4 months was reported. This procedure, without the satiation condition, was used by Singh and colleagues (1982) with monozygous twins, both profoundly retarded, who engaged in ruminative behaviors. The authors reported success in treating rumination, but also noted collateral increases in self-stimulatory behaviors (for example, rocking, waving, or rubbing parts of the body). Several authors warn that overcorrection may be inappropriate for self-injury and other problem behaviors (Foxx and Bechtel 1982; Kelly and Drabman 1977; Rapoff et al. 1980; Zehr and Theobald 1978). Rapoff and colleagues (1980), for example, found that overcorrection resulted in an immediate increase in self-injury to levels that were unacceptable. They indicate that, even had the procedure proved effective, "it was quite time consuming and impractical." Kelly and Drabman (1977) report a similar finding:

> Discontinuance had little to do with the staff's judgments of the treatment's effectiveness. The teachers simply did not like to perform the procedure. Although we strongly reinforced their efforts, the response cost of overcorrection outweighed any reinforcers we could practically provide.

Foxx and Bechtel (1982) warn that overcorrection may not be appropriate with individuals who are physically strong enough to combat their care givers; this warning is echoed by others as well (Favell et al. 1982a; Kelly and Drabman 1977).

Electric Shock

There have been more published reports on the use of electric shock to control self-injury than on any other single technique (Favell et al. 1982a). It is considered one of the most effective procedures for reducing self-injury (Carr and Lovaas 1983) and also one of the most controversial (Mauer 1983).

Electric shock is typically delivered from a hand-held device sometimes referred to as a "shock rod." These devices are designed to deliver a peak shock of 1400 volts at 0.4 mA (Harris and Ersner-Hershfield 1978). The tip of the shock rod typically includes two protruding terminals through which the shock travels to the surface of the skin. Carr and Lovaas (1983) describe the pain delivered by the shock rod this way:

> Subjectively, the pain has been described as being similar to that experienced when one is hit with a leather strap or a willow switch. However, shock is not as dangerous as either of these events nor does it leave a durable, radiating pain. In fact, the pain is localized and stops as soon as the shock is terminated.

Contingent application of shock has been shown to result in an immediate and dramatic reduction of self-injurious behavior (Corte et al. 1971; Lovaas and Simmons 1969; Risley 1968; Tate and Baroff 1966). A study by Lovaas and Simmons (1969) is representative of the effects of shock on self-injury. An 8-year-old boy, diagnosed as severely retarded, was treated for head banging. His head banging, which began when he was 2 years old, involved the beating of his temples and forehead with closed fists. At the time of treatment, he was in full restraints in an institution. Various psychotropic medications had been tried, but had failed. During the baseline condition, the boy engaged in an average of 250 blows to the head in a 5-minute session. When the treatment condition was introduced, the behavior declined to a near-zero level after 12 administrations of shock over four sessions. In conditions in which shock was not introduced, however, self-injury remained high.

Generalization of treatment effects outside of the experimental situation is a significant problem with electric shock (Horner and Barton 1980). The reduction of self-injury tends to occur only in the presence of the shock rod; thus some researchers have suggested that the procedure be implemented in all situations (Corte et al. 1971; Foxx et al. 1986). Another problem with shock is that subjects have been known to "show marked aversion to the sight of the hand-held shock stick" (Lichstein and Schreibman 1976); one report speaks of a boy who cried and shivered whenever the experimenter approached him (Bucher and King 1971). The use of electric shock is also associated with the development of other undesirable behaviors. For example, Bucher and Lovaas (1968) reported that one child became aggressive toward other children during nonexperimental time periods.

It should be noted that there have been positive emotional side effects to shock. Lovaas and colleagues (1965), for example, observed that many of the children exposed to shock in their study seemed more alert, smiled, and appeared happy. Others have reported similar findings (Carr and Lovaas 1983; Merbaum 1973; Lovaas and Simmons 1969; Tate and Baroff 1966).

Finally, discussions of the effectiveness and ethics of using shock have a long history (Johnson and Rea 1986). Shock is an extremely restrictive procedure that is highly subject to abuse (Favell et al. 1982a). Therefore, a number of guidelines have been established for its use (for example, Foxx et al. 1986). Additionally, a number of regulations governing shock and other punishment techniques have emerged as a result of increased litigation in the mental health field (Griffith 1983). A number of advocacy groups, including The Association for Persons with Severe Handicaps and the Association for Retarded Citizens have called for the cessation of electric shock as a treatment option.

Other Types of Punishment

Several other procedures have been demonstrated to be effective punishers of self-injury. These procedures include forced inhalation of ammonia capsules (Baumeister and Baumeister 1978; Tanner and Zeiler 1975), lemon juice sprayed into the mouth (Becker et al. 1978; Simpson and Sasso 1978); water mist to the face (Murphey et al. 1979), and forced swallowing of vomitus (Simpson and Sasso 1978). As Favell and colleagues (1982a) point out, "Some of these events are associated with possible physical side effects, ranging from chapped skin (with water mist) to mucous membrane damage (with ammonia)."

Concluding Remarks on Punishment

The contribution of the operant literature to the understanding and treatment of self-injury is undeniable. Prior to the emergence of operant conditioning as a major approach to the behavior problems of persons with severe disabilities, behaviors such as self-injury were thought to be "untreatable" (Johnson and Rea 1986). As stated previously, however, the use of aversive procedures to reduce self-injury and other problem behaviors has come under increasing scrutiny (National Institute of Health 1989).

In a comprehensive review of the "aversive" literature, Guess and colleagues (1987) examined 38 studies published between 1964 and 1985 that employed aversive procedures (punishment and overcorrection).

The studies represented 115 experiments and 364 subjects who exhibited a variety of problem behaviors, including self-injury. (Note: the authors also examined studies employing negative reinforcement procedures, but none of these involved self-injury.) Each study was evaluated in terms of treatment effectiveness or efficiency; maintenance of effects; generalization of effects; side effects; and acceptability of experimental design.

Punishment procedures (for example, electric shock, ammonia tablets under the nose, or lemon juice sprayed into the mouth) were used to treat self-injury far more often (49%) than any other behavior type (for example, self-stimulation [26%], disruptive behaviors [8%], aggression toward other people [5%]). These procedures were said to be 90% to 100% effective in reducing problem behaviors overall (data were not provided for self-injury specifically), and most were said to bring about such effects quickly (the average for self-injury was 9 hours). Seventy-one percent of the self-injury studies reported maintenance of effects; however, data were rarely reported beyond a 12-month period. Fewer than half of the studies reported generalization; of those that did, less than one third (29%) reported generalization of effects to nontreatment settings. Both positive and negative side effects were reported in 71% of the studies. Positive side effects included increases in "learning, performance and other adaptive behaviors" and negative side effects included resistance to instruction and avoidance behaviors. Finally, the authors concluded that 64% of the studies were inadequately designed or contained no description of an experimental design. Examples of design flaws included the use of AB designs or confounding order effects (ABCAC, ACAD).

Guess and coworkers (1987) also examined the effects of overcorrection (for example, forced body movement, restitution) on self-injury. Although most of the studies in their review targeted stereotyped or self-stimulatory behaviors (45%), many targeted self-injurious behaviors (30%). Overcorrection, like punishment, was shown to be effective in reducing problem behaviors (90% to 100% reductions in over half the studies). These effects were said to occur with a mean time of 35 hours for self-injury. It should be noted, however, that there was considerable variability in the number of hours required (1 to 480 hours). Maintenance was reported in an average of 53% of the studies; however, 94% of these were for 12 months or less. Less than one third (32%) of the studies reported generalization of effects to nontreatment settings. Side effects were noted in 42% of the studies. Positive side effects included increased attention to tasks and persons, whereas negative side effects included increases in resistant behaviors and aggression toward others. Eight of the 12 studies regarding self-injury used adequate designs. The four remaining studies "had unacceptable designs (AB) or were confounded by order effects (ABC)."

In summary, punishment and overcorrection proved to be effective procedures for reducing self-injury *in the short term.* Few studies provided follow-up data beyond a 12-month period. Most researchers failed to report data on the generalization of effects, and of those that did, almost half found no degree of transfer across settings. Negative side effects were noted in a significant number of studies, including severe emotional reactions and resistance and avoidance behaviors. Positive effects included increases in learning and adaptive behaviors. Most punishment studies were faulted for poor experimental design.

According to LaVigna and Donnellan (1986), the literature is "biased" toward aversive procedures. They point out that "punishment is the way we have been shown and taught to solve behavior problems" since childhood; this applies to researchers and practitioners alike. They point out that "neophytes" entering the profession "are likely to emulate their peers and colleagues" and model the use of punishment. The widespread attention punishment has received as an "effective" procedure may have led some to a false impression that "punishment is superior" to nonaversive techniques.

Guess and colleagues (1987) raise questions concerning the effects of punishment on the perceived value of persons with developmental disabilities. A fundamental concern is: Do the interventions that are intended to enhance the well-being of the individual actually detract from the individual's worth and value in society? The authors assert that aversive procedures may lead to the depersonalization of the individual receiving treatment. Depersonalization "involves the separation in the therapist's view of the person from the technology to treat an aspect of that person." Finally, critics have questioned the short- and long-term effects of aversive procedures on the care giver (for example, Turnbull et al. 1987). They question the effects of aversive procedures on the therapeutic relationship. As Bucher and King (1971) reported, one boy cried and shivered whenever the experimenter approached him. In the National Institutes of Health's recent position paper on self-injurious behaviors (1989), the authors stated:

> Less visible side effects associated with behavior reduction approaches include the potential for abuse in the application of these procedures, the psychological effects on staff, and most important, the negative and demeaning social image that the use of some of these procedures conveys to the general public about persons with developmental disabilities.

The Reduction of Self-Injury Using Nonaversive Procedures

As stated previously, most of the behavior reduction strategies reported in the operant literature have been punitive in nature (LaVigna and Donnellan 1986). Although the literature related to nonaversive alternatives to punishment is expanding (for example, Evans and Meyer 1985; LaVigna and Donnellan 1986; McGee et al. 1987), it is generally agreed that empirical support for these methods is scarce (Axelrod 1987a; Snell 1987). The purpose of this section is to review the use of nonaversive procedures to reduce self-injury. The section is divided into four parts: treatment of self-injury by rearrangement of antecedent stimulus conditions; treatment by differential reinforcement strategies; treatment based on a functional analysis of self-injury; and treatment as a comprehensive, composite approach.

Rearrangement of Antecedent Stimulus Conditions

This class of nonaversive procedures is based on the principle of stimulus control. This principle refers to the fact that self-injury is much more likely to occur in some situations than in others. Determining which situations control self-injury allows the interventionist to manipulate relevant anecedents (such as high demands) rather than consequences. As Favell and colleagues (1982a) point out:

> Which specific situations control high or low rates of self-injury depends on the individual's reinforcement history in those situations. In many cases, self-injury tends to occur when reinforcement that has previously been given is not forthcoming or when demands are placed on the individual. In such situations, the self-injury is likely to have been reinforced by the resumption of reinforcement or the withdrawal of demands, respectively.

Procedures based on the stimulus control principle can be divided into two approaches. One approach involves identifying the stimulus conditions that are associated with low rates of self-injury and then providing the individual with access to these conditions. For example, Carr and coworkers (1976) determined that an 8-year-old boy's self-injurious behaviors increased when he was presented with commands to perform a task. In contrast, telling the boy a story did not result in an increase in self-injury. By mixing commands in with "story telling," the authors noted a reduction in the overall frequency of self-injury without reducing the level of commands. Similarly, Weeks and Gaylord-Ross (1981) noted that demand situations resulted in significantly higher rates of self-injury than did low-demand or no-demand situations. By providing the subjects with assistance for difficult tasks (errorless learning), the rates of self-injury were significantly reduced during difficult task periods. Other examples of this approach include the provision of vibratory stimulation (Bailey and Meyerson 1970; Dura et al. 1988) and opportunities for toy play (Favell et al. 1982b; Mulick et al. 1978).

A second approach to self-injury based on the stimulus control procedure involves identifying and then rearranging the conditions associated with high rates of the behavior(s). As Favell et al. (1982a) point out, the research in support of this approach is "scant":

> Although research in this area is scant, the clinical value of eliminating or changing situations which are reliably associated with self-injury is clear. Such situations will differ across clients, but may include barren environments with few activities, little reinforcement for appropriate behavior or lack of social contact of any kind.

Touchette et al. (1985) offer an interesting case study that involves this second approach. They identified, through the use of their scatter plot diagram, a strong association between a subject's self-injury and a particular staff person. By simply altering the schedule of this staff person, the rates of self-injury were significantly reduced. They also showed that the aggressive behaviors of a 14-year-old girl were strongly associated with demands; activities associated with low rates of the behaviors were alternated with demands, and significant reductions in her aggressive behaviors were achieved.

Differential Reinforcement Strategies

The principle of differential reinforcement is key to a number of nonaversive procedures. Baumeister and Rollings (1976) suggest that the principle of differential reinforcement should be the "backbone" of any behavioral treatment program; its use in the treatment of self-injury requires that reinforcement be provided for appropriate, noninjurious behaviors, whereas less (ideally no) reinforcement is provided for self-injury (Favell et al. 1982a).

Two specific forms of differential reinforcement will be discussed here: DRO and the differential reinforcement of alternative responses (ALT-R). It should be noted that DRO and ALT-R strategies have been applied in many studies, typically as components of treatment packages that contain aversive procedures (Woods 1980). Thus, it is difficult to assess the effectiveness of the DRO and ALT-R contingencies alone because of the confounding effects of other procedures (for example, Repp and Deitz 1974). Nevertheless, there are studies in which each procedure was applied by itself to self-injury.

Differential reinforcement of other behaviors is a popular technique with high public acceptability (Horner and Barton 1980). In DRO, reinforcement is provided following periods of time in which self-injury is absent. In other words, the individual receives reinforcement for refraining from self-injury.

Repp and coworkers (1976) used a DRO procedure to reduce hand-biting in a 14-year-old girl with severe mental retardation. They began by reinforcing the absence of self-injury for 1-second intervals and gradually increased these intervals over time. They do not report generalization. Luiselli and coworkers (1978) used DRO to treat, across three school environments, the self-biting of a 10-year-old boy with moderate mental retardation. Starting with 1-minute intervals, the authors were able to delay reinforcement for the nonoccurrence of self-injury to 20-minute intervals in fewer than

25 days. The authors did not report results beyond the 25-day period.

Frankel and colleagues (1976) reduced aggression and head banging in an 8-year-old girl by reinforcing a variety of task and play behaviors with candy and praise. Although the authors did not report results beyond a 40-day period (the girl was moved to another institution "where a different type of program was carried out"), the behaviors were reduced to near-zero levels. The authors also noted that the procedure was implemented after two time-out programs had failed to reduce the girl's self-injury and:

> A surprising by-product of this approach was the reinstatement and perhaps enhancement of the social reinforcement properties of the teachers. The disappearance of these properties might well have been responsible for the failure of the isolation booth program . . . as teachers were cast in the role of dispensers of aversives.

One of the most interesting studies using DRO to reduce self-injury was conducted by Favell and colleagues (1978). The authors determined that mechanical restraints were reinforcing to three individuals who engaged in self-injury. Restraints were subsequently used to reinforce differentially the nonoccurrence of self-injury. This procedure was implemented after aversive techniques, including the contingent use of lemon juice, had failed. The authors did not report results beyond 14 weeks.

Finally, Lockwood and Bourland (1982) used DRO and the availability of toys to reduce the self-injury of two non-ambulatory children who were profoundly mentally retarded. They found that the availability of toys was not sufficient to reduce self-injury, but that the availability of toys and reinforcement for the absence of self-injury was effective. The authors did not report results beyond 80 treatment sessions, each lasting approximately 1 hour.

Differential reinforcement of alternative responses is among the most widely recognized and used of the alternatives to punishment (LaVigna and Donnellan 1986). This procedure calls for the differential reinforcement of behaviors that are topographically incompatible with self-injury.

Saposnek and Watson (1974) taught a 10-year-old boy to slap the experimenter's hand rather than his own. Reinforcing the hand slapping reduced the levels of self-injury significantly and enabled the subject to participate in a variety of educational and recreational activities. More recently, Heidorn and Jensen (1984) reported the effects of an ALT-R procedure in which the head gouging of a 27-year-old man was successfully treated. This procedure included the prevention of escape from unpleasant activities. After initial success with the program, the subject's daily dosage of chloral hydrate was reduced, but the self-injury increased; however, the behavior was gradually reduced to previous levels after the procedure was reinstated. A similar increase in self-injury occurred when the subject moved to another living unit, but again the self-injury returned to a low frequency when the procedure was implemented in the new setting. The study utilized information gathered through a functional analysis, and it was hypothesized that the man engaged in his self-injurious behavior for social attention (positive reinforcement) and to escape demands (negative reinforcement). Similarly, Carr and Durand (1985) determined that adult attention and high-demand situations maintained a variety of disruptive behaviors in school-aged children, including self-injury. They taught the children how to solicit adult attention and assistance that significantly reduced their disruptive behaviors.

Functional Analysis of Self-Injury

The basic premise underlying differential reinforcement strategies is that the reinforcement of appropriate behaviors relative to problem behaviors should result in a decrease of the latter. An emerging concept, that of "functional equivalence," is based on the premise that treating problem behaviors may require more than the reinforcement of alternative or incompatible behaviors; instead, treatment may depend upon the reinforcement of behaviors that serve the same *function* as the problem behavior (Favell and Reid 1988). In this view, self-injury is seen as a form of nonverbal communication that helps the individual to achieve positive ends. For example, it is thought that self-injury may help some individuals escape from unpleasant activities. The self-injury of these individuals may be functionally equivalent to saying, "I need to take a break." Knowing this, it should be possible to teach the individual appropriate ways to communicate a need for breaks. In this way, the reinforcer maintaining self-injury (the termination of demands) is used to reinforce a communicative alternative (Dunlap et al. 1987).

Teaching functionally equivalent behaviors depends on the identification of the reinforcers maintaining the individual's self-injury. In recent years, a number of studies have attempted to isolate systematically the reinforcers that maintain self-injury; this process, which often includes an analysis of the antecedent conditions that precipitate problem behaviors, has been referred to as "functional analysis" (Axelrod 1987b). Horner and colleagues (1991) have stated that a functional analysis is designed to define operationally the problem behavior; to determine the "times and situations" when the problem behavior "will and will not be performed across the full range of typical daily routines"; and to delineate the maintaining reinforcers of the problem behavior.

Iwata and colleagues (1982) showed that the self-injurious behaviors of nine developmentally disabled children, ranging in ages from 1 to 17, were motivated by one or more of the following variables: escape from demands (negative reinforcement); social attention (positive reinforcement); and a sensory variable (self-stimulation). The authors argued that the treatment of self-injury should be based foremost on an understanding of the variables that maintain the behavior(s).

Several studies have used functional analysis techniques to develop interventions for self-injury. Carr and colleagues (1976) showed that the self-injurious behaviors of an 8-year-old boy were more frequent in the presence of demands and less frequent when simple declarative statements were made. When the authors reduced or modified the demands (by interspersing stories about familiar activities), the boy's self-injury was reduced. The authors suggested that interspersing low- and high-demand tasks, coupled with positive teacher interactions, would result in low levels of self-injury and task participation. Gaylord-Ross and coworkers (1980) showed that by substituting difficult tasks with easy tasks and by using errorless learning teaching strategies, the self-injurious behaviors of a 16-year-old girl with severe mental retardation could be reduced. Bird and colleagues (1989) taught a 27-year-old man with profound mental retardation to communicate his need for breaks by handing his teachers a token that signaled the termination of demands. As he became more proficient at communicating his need to take breaks, the authors gradually increased task demands while consistently honoring his requests for breaks.

Researchers have also used functional analysis techniques to develop treatment programs for self-injury motivated by positive reinforcement. Carr and Durand (1985) taught three children with severe disabilities to ask for assistance in completing their school work. The children were taught to ask, "Am I doing good work?" or to say, "I don't understand" to solicit adult attention. The authors showed that these communicative responses, which were followed by adult attention, led to reductions in self-injurious, aggressive, and destructive behaviors. Durand and Kishi (1987) reported similar results in a study using a technical assistance model that focused on the use of functional analysis techniques. In their study, students with profound disabilities were taught to let their teachers know that they needed help or attention. The functional assessment used in this study was the Motivation Assessment Scale (Durand 1988), a 16-item questionnaire.

Favell and coworkers (1982b) hypothesized that the self-injurious behaviors of six profoundly mentally retarded young adults were motivated by "visual, tactile, gustatory or other sensory consequences." The authors provided these individuals with toys that presumably provided similar consequences (for example, a chew toy) as their self-injury (for example, hand mouthing) and showed significant reductions in their behaviors. An interesting finding from this study and other studies was that a lack of stimulation in the environment may be a significant factor contributing to the development and maintenance of self-injurious behaviors (for example, Horner 1980; Iwata et al. 1982; Repp et al. 1988).

A number of authors have suggested that the use of functional analysis techniques may lead to a reduction in the use of aversive techniques (Axelrod 1987b; Durand 1987; Favell et al. 1982b; O'Neill et al. 1990). Durand (1987) has asserted that treatment approaches that ignore the function(s) of problem behaviors, whether aversive or nonaversive, may fail to produce lasting results. He writes:

> . . suppose an individual is hitting herself to escape tasks because they are difficult or unchallenging. Techniques that involve punishing her for her self-injury or reinforcing her for not hitting herself both fail to provide her with appropriate means of leaving work, and they do not address the issue of whether the tasks themselves are appropriate. Thus, conceptually, these types of interventions may not be able to produce lasting reductions in problem behavior. Using the case described above,

the individual will presumably continue to escape from tasks, and may attempt novel responses (e.g., aggression, destroying materials) toward this end.

At present, a relatively small number of researchers employ functional analysis techniques, despite the clear utility of understanding what a behavior means before intervening (Gardner and Cole 1983; Johnson and Rea 1986). Lennox and coworkers (1988) reported that in nearly two thirds (64%) of the studies they reviewed from 1981 through 1985 did not report a pretreatment functional analysis.

A Comprehensive, Composite Approach to Treatment

Treatment of self-injury often involves single interventions such as DRO, time out, or overcorrection. Favell and Reid (1988) pointed out that "such a focus on singular and relatively narrow interventions undoubtedly reflects the appropriate scientific mandate of attempting to isolate the effects of single interventions or elements of treatment." The effective treatment of self-injury, however, may demand changes to a variety of variables in the individual's "social and physical environments." In 1982, the Association for the Advancement of Behavior Therapy called on researchers and practitioners to move away from the "sequential application of single techniques" toward the development of multifaceted intervention packages that take into account biologic and environmental influences on behavior. This emphasis on comprehensive treatment packages reflects a growing understanding that self-injurious behaviors may serve multiple functions.

Berkman and Meyer (1988) successfully treated the self-injurious behaviors of a man named "Mr. Jordan" who had been institutionalized for 39 years because his behaviors were thought to be "untreatable" in the community. Treatment consisted of a comprehensive array of "program and placement changes," including movement from the institution to a community residence, participation in a community job placement, and access to a variety of community recreational activities. The intent of this treatment "package" was to "modify the circumstances associated with his self-injurious behaviors and replace them with functional alternatives." According to the authors, the key to the program's success was allowing Mr. Jordan to make decisions about the intervention package itself; that is, he was asked to make decisions about where he wanted to live, work, and recreate. They write:

> Although Mr. Jordan's self-injury was clearly related to the institutional setting, to have *imposed* [sic] community living upon him might have resulted in a similar negative pattern. Instead, the emphasis was upon both the different environments and activities as well as upon increasing his own decisions and choices in the context of meaningful and more normalized social relationships.

Despite the lack of experimental control in their study, Berkman and Meyer argue that their treatment package was probably responsible for the changes, given Mr. Jordan's long history of self-injurious behavior and his resistance to other treatment efforts. They encourage practitioners to consider major changes in the individual's "life-style" *before* intervening with individual behaviors. Recently, the Rehabilitation Research and Training Center on Community-Referenced Nonaversive Behavior Management in Oregon initiated a similar study in which several people with long histories of institutionalization and treatment-resistant behavior problems are involved. The purpose of their study is to delineate, if possible, the critical variables in such intervention packages.

It seems clear that researchers and practitioners are "moving away from a time when the expectation is that manipulation of a single variable will produce dramatic, durable, and generalizable changes in the behavior of persons with very severe behavior problems" (R. Horner, personal communication). The emphasis on comprehensive, composite approaches to self-injury may reflect the field's growing awareness that singular approaches to such problems may be "clinically misleading" and "contrary to good clinical practice" (Favell and Reid 1988).

Summary

The volume of literature concerning self-injurious behavior has grown considerably over the last 20 years. Because of the serious nature of the behavior, most of the published studies have dealt with treatment versus theoretical issues. Few studies have dealt with the causes of self-injurious behavior.

A number of hypotheses concerning the factors that cause and maintain self-injury have been described. These include the positive reinforcement hypothesis, in which self-injury is viewed as a learned behavior that is maintained by positive reinforcement; the negative reinforcement hypothesis, in which self-injury is viewed as a learned behavior maintained by the termination of unpleasant stimuli following the behavior; the self-stimulation hypothesis, in which self-injury is viewed as a means of achieving sensory stimulation; the aberrant physical process hypothesis, in which self-injurious behavior is said to result from an aberrant physiologic process such as the Lesch-Nyhan Syndrome; and the psychodynamic hypothesis, in which self-injury is said to result from a variety of intrapsychic phenomena such as the need to establish ego boundaries.

The use of operant techniques to treat self-injury has been widely documented since the 1960s, with most of these techniques involving aversive components. Increasingly, questions are being raised about the use of aversive procedures with persons who are severely disabled. Unfortunately, the number of studies supporting nonaversive approaches to self-injurious behavior are few, and those that do exist tend to involve persons who exhibit the least serious forms of the behavior. Professionals, advocates, and consumers alike are calling for research concerning non-aversive approaches to serious forms of self-injurious behavior.

An emerging concept, that of "functional equivalence," is based on the premise that treating problem behaviors may require more than the reinforcement of alternative or incompatible behaviors; instead, treatment may depend upon the reinforcement of behaviors that serve the same *function* as the problem behavior (Favell and Reid 1988). In this view, self-injury is seen as a form of nonverbal communication that helps the individual to achieve positive ends. A growing number of researchers are exploring the use of functional analysis techniques to determine how the social and physical environments affect self-injury. Researchers are also calling for "comprehensive, composite" approaches to self-injury that involve multiple treatment components.

References

1. Axelrod S. Book Review: Doing it without arrows. The Behavior Analyst. 10: 243–251, 1987a.
2. Axelrod S. Functional and structural analysis: Approaches leading to reduced use of punishment procedures? Res Dev Disabil. 8: 165–178, 1987b.
3. Azrin NH, Holz WC. Punishment. In: Honig WK. ed. Operant Behavior: Areas of Research and Application. New York, Appleton-Century-Crofts, 1966.
4. Azrin NH, Wesolowski MD. Eliminating habitual vomiting in a retarded boy by positive practice and self-correction. Journal of Behavior Therapy and Experimental Psychology. 6: 145–148, 1975.
5. Azrin NH, Gottlieb LH, Hughart L, Wesolowski MD, Rahn T. Eliminating self-injurious behavior by educative procedures. Behavior Research and Therapy. 13: 101–111, 1975.
6. Bachman JA. Self-injurious behavior: A behavioral analysis. J Abnorm Psychol. 80: 221–224, 1972.
7. Bailey J, Meyerson L. Effect of vibratory stimulation on a retardate's self-injurious behavior. Psychological Aspects of Disability. 17: 133–137, 1970.
8. Baumeister AA, Rollings JP. Self-injurious behavior. In: Ellis NR. ed. International Review of Research in Mental Retardation. 8: 1–34. New York, Academic Press, 1976.
9. Baumeister AA, Baumeister AA. Suppression of repetitive self-injurious behavior by contingent inhalation of aromatic ammonia. Journal of Autism and Childhood Schizophrenia. 8: 71–77, 1978.
10. Becker J, Turner SM, Sajwaj T. Multiple behavioral effects of the use of lemon juice with a ruminating toddler-age child. Behav Modif. 2: 267–279, 1978.
11. Beres D. Clinical notes on aggression in children. In: Eissler RS. ed. The Psychoanalytic Study of the Child. New York, International Universities Press, 1952.
12. Berkman KA, Meyer LH. Alternative strategies and multiple outcomes in the remediation of severe self-injury: Going "all out" nonaversively. Journal of the Association for Persons with Severe Handicaps. 13: 76–86, 1988.
13. Berkson G. Development of abnormal stereotyped behaviors. Developmental Psychology. 1: 118–132, 1968.
14. Berkson G, Landsman-Dwyer S. Behavioral research on severe and profound mental retardation (1955–1974). American Journal of Mental Deficiency. 81: 428–454, 1977.
15. Bird F, Dores PA, Moniz D, Robinson J. Reducing severe aggression and self-injurious behaviors with functional communication training. Am J Ment Retard. 94: 37–48, 1989.
16. Birnbrauer JS. Mental retardation. In: Leitenberg H. ed. Handbook of Behavior Modification. New York, Appleton-Century-Crofts, 1976.
17. Borresson PM. The elimination of a self-injurious avoidance response through a forced running exercise. Ment Retard. 18: 73–77, 1980.
18. Bryson Y, Sakati N, Nyhan WL, Fish CH. Self-mutilative behavior in the Cornelia de Lange syndrome. American Journal of Mental Deficiency. 76: 319–324, 1980.
19. Bucher B, Lovaas OI. Use of aversive stimulation in behavior modification. In: Jones MR. ed. Miami Symposium on the Prediction of Behavior, 1967; Adversive Stimulation. Coral Gables, Fla, University of Miami Press, 1968.

20. Bucher B, King L. Generalization of punishment effects in the deviant behavior of a psychotic child. Behavior Therapy. 2: 68–77, 1971.

21. Carr EG. The motivation of self-injurious behavior: A review of some hypotheses. Psychological Bulletin. 84: 800–816, 1977.

22. Carr EG, Newsome CD, Binkoff JA. Stimulus control of self-destructive behavior in a psychotic child. J Abnorm Child Psychol. 4: 139–153, 1976.

23. Carr EG, McDowell JJ. Social control of self-injurious behavior of organic etiology. Behavior Therapy. 11: 402–409, 1980.

24. Carr EG, Lovaas OI. Contingent electric shock as a treatment for severe behavior problems. In: Axelrod S. ed. The Effects of Punishment on Human Behavior. New York, Academic Press, 1983, pp 221–245.

25. Carr EG, Durand MV. Reducing behavior problems through functional communication training. J Appl Behav Anal. 18: 111–126, 1985.

26. Cataldo MF, Harris J. The biological basis for self-injury in the mentally retarded. Analysis and Intervention in Developmental Disabilities. 2: 21–39, 1982.

27. Corte HE, Wolf MM, Locke BJ. A comparison of procedures for eliminating self-injurious behavior of retarded adolescents. J Appl Behav Anal. 4: 201–213, 1971.

28. de Lissovoy V. Head banging in early childhood. J Genet Psychol. 102: 109–114, 1963.

29. Dennis W, Najarian P. Infant development under environmental handicap. Psychological Monographs. 71: 1–13, 1957.

30. Duker P. Behavior control of self-biting in a Lesch-Nyhan patient. J Ment Defic Res. 19: 11–19, 1975.

31. Dunlap G, Johnson J, Winterling V, Morelli MA. The management of disruptive behavior in unsupervised settings: Issues and directions for a behavioral technology. Education and Treatment of Children. 10: 367–382, 1987.

32. Dura JR, Mulick JA, Hammer D. Rapid clinical evaluation of sensory integrative therapy for self-injurious behavior. Ment Retard. 2: 83–87, 1988.

33. Durand VM. Analysis and intervention of self-injurious behavior. Journal of the Association for the Severely Handicapped. 7: 44–53, 1982.

34. Durand VM. In Response: "Look homeward angel" A call to return to our (functional) roots. The Behavior Analyst. 10: 299–302, 1987.

35. Durand VM. The Motivation Assessment Scale. In: Hersen M, Bellack AS. ed. Dictionary of Behavioral Assessment Techniques. New York, Pergamon Press, 1988.

36. Durand VM, Kishi G. Reducing severe behavior problems among persons with dual sensory impairments: An evaluation of a technical assistance model. Journal of the Association for Persons with Severe Handicaps. 12: 2–10, 1987.

37. Durand VM, Crimmins DB. Identifying the variables maintaining self-injurious behavior. J Autism Dev Disord. 18: 99–117, 1988.

38. Edelson SM, Taubman MT, Lovaas OI. Some social contexts of self-destructive behavior. J Abnorm Child Psychol. 11: 299–312, 1983.

39. Epstein LH, Doke LA, Sajwaj TE, Sorrell S, Rimmer B. Generality and side effects of overcorrection. J Appl Behav Anal. 7: 385–390, 1974.

40. Evans IM, Meyer LH. An Educative Approach to Behavior Problems: A Practical Decision Model for Interventions with Severely Handicapped Learners. Baltimore, Paul H. Brookes, 1985.

41. Favell JE, McGimsey JF, Jones MJ. The use of physical restraint in the treatment of self-injury as a positive reinforcer. J Appl Behav Anal. 11: 225–241, 1978.

42. Favell JE, McGimsey JF, Jones MJ, Cannon PR. Physical restraint as positive reinforcement. American Journal of Mental Deficiency. 85: 425–432, 1981.

43. Favell JE, Azrin NH, Baumeister AA, et al. The treatment of self-injurious behavior. Behavior Therapy. 13: 529–554, 1982a.

44. Favell JE, McGimesey JF, Schell RM. Treatment of self-injury by providing alternate sensory activities. Analysis and Intervention in Developmental Disabilities. 2: 83–104, 1987b.

45. Favell JE, Reid DH. Generalizing and maintaining improvement in problem behavior. In: Horner R, Dunlap G, Koegel R. eds. Generalization and Maintenance. Baltimore, Paul H. Brookes, 1988, pp 175–195.

46. Foxx R. An overview of overcorrection. J Pediatr Psychol. 3: 97–101, 1978.

47. Foxx RM, Snyder MS, Schroeder F. A food satiation and oral hygiene punishment program to suppress chronic rumination by retarded persons. J Autism Dev Disord. 9: 399–412, 1979.

48. Foxx RM, Bechtel DR. Overcorrection. Progress in Behavior Modification. 13: 227–228, 1982.

49. Foxx RM, Dufresne D. "Harry": The use of physical restraint as a reinforcer, timeout from restraint, and fading restraint in treating a self-injurious man. Analysis and Intervention in Developmental Disabilities. 4: 1–13, 1984.

50. Foxx RM, McMorrow MJ, Bittle RG, Bechtel DR. The successful treatment of a dually diagnosed deaf man's aggression with a program that included contingent electric shock. Behavior Therapy. 17: 170–186, 1986a.

51. Foxx RM, Plaska TG, Bittle RG. Guidelines for the use of electric shock to treat aberrant behavior. Progress in Behavior Modification. 20: 1–34, 1986b.

52. Frankel F, Moss D, Schofield S, Simmons JQ III. Case study: Use of differential reinforcement to suppress self-injurious and aggressive behavior. Psychological Reports. 39: 843–849, 1976.

53. Freud A. Problems of infantile neurosis: A discussion. The Psychoanalytic Study of the Child. 9: 40–43, 1954.

54. Freud A, Burlingham D. Infants without Families. New York, International University Press, 1949.

55. Gardner WI, Cole CL. Selecting intervention procedures: What happened to behavioral assessment? In: Karan OC, Gardner WI. eds. Habilitation Practices with the Developmentally Disabled Who Present Behavioral and Emotional Disorders. Madison, WI, Rehabilitation Research and Training Center in Mental Retardation, 1983.

56. Gaylord-Ross R, Weeks M, Lipner C. An analysis of antecedent response, and consequence events in the treatment of self-injurious behavior. Education and Training of the Mentally Retarded. 15: 35–42, 1980.

57. Gorman-Smith D, Matson JL. A review of treatment research for self-injurious and stereotyped responding. J Ment Defic Res. 29: 295–308, 1985.

58. Griffith RG. The administrative issues: An ethical and legal perspective. In: Axelrod S. ed. The Effects of Punishment on Human Behavior. New York, Academic Press, 1983, pp 317–338.

59. Guess D, Helmstetter E, Turnbull RH, Knowlton S. Use of aversive procedures with persons who are disabled: An historical review and critical analysis. Seattle, WA, Association for Persons with Severe Handicaps, 1987.

60. Harlow HF, Griffin G. Induced mental and social deficits in rhesus monkeys. In: Osler SF, Cooke RE. eds. The Biosocial Basis of Mental Retardation. Baltimore, Johns Hopkins Press, 1965.

61. Harlow HF, Harlow MK. Psychopathology in monkeys. In: Kimmel HD. ed. Experimental Psychopathology. New York, Academic Press, 1971.

62. Harris SL, Ersner-Hershfield R. Behavioral suppression of seriously disruptive behavior in psychotic and retarded patients: A review of punishment and its alternatives. Psychol Bull. 85: 1352–1375, 1978.

63. Heidorn SD, Jensen CC. Generalization and maintenance of the reduction of self-injurious behavior by two types of reinforcement. Behavior Research and Therapy. 22: 581–586, 1984.

64. Hoffner W. Oral aggressiveness and ego development. International Journal of Psychoanalysis. 31: 156–160, 1950.

65. Horner RD. The effects of environmental "enrichment" program on the behavior of institutionalized profoundly retarded children. J Appl Behav Anal. 13: 473–491, 1980.

66. Horner RD, Barton ES. Operant techniques in the analysis and modification of self-injurious behavior. Behavior Research of Severe Developmental Disabilities. 1: 61–91, 1980.

67. Iwata BA, Dorsey MF, Slifer KJ, Bauman KE, Richman GS. Toward a functional analysis of self-injury. Analysis and Intervention in Developmental Disabilities. 2: 3–20, 1982.

68. Johnson WL, Baumeister AA. Self-injurious behavior: A review and analysis of methodological details of published studies. Behav Modif. 2: 465–487, 1978.

69. Johnson WL, Rea JA. Self-injurious behavior treatment and research: A historical perspective. Advances in Learning and Behavioral Disabilities. 5: 1–23, 1986.

70. Jones FH, Simmons JQ, Frankel F. An extinction procedure for eliminating the self-destructive behavior in a 9-year-old autistic girl. Journal of Autism and Childhood Schizophrenia. 4: 241–250, 1974.

71. Jones IO. Self-injury: Toward a biological basis. Perspect Biol Med. 26: 137–143, 1982.

72. Kelly JA, Drabman RS. Overcorrection: An effective procedure that failed. Journal of Clinical Child Psychology. 6: 38–40, 1977.

73. Klein M. An obsessional neurosis in a six-year-old girl. In: Strachey A. ed. The Psycho-Analysis of Children. New York, Delacorte Press/Seymour Lawrence, 1932, pp 35–57.

74. LaVigna G, Donnellan A. Alternatives to Punishment: Solving Behavior Problems with Nonaversive Strategies. New York, Irvington, 1986.

75. Lennox DB, Miltenberger RG, Spengler P, Erfanian N. Decelerative treatment practices with persons who have mental retardation: A review of five years of the literature. American Journal of Mental Deficiency. 92: 492–501, 1988.

76. Levy DM. On the problems of movement restraint: Tics, stereotyped movements and hyperactivity. Am J Orthopsychiatry. 14: 644–671, 1944.

77. Lichstein KL, Schreibman L. Employing electric shock with autistic children. Journal of Autism and Childhood Schizophrenia. 6: 163–173, 1976.

78. Lockwood K, Bourland G. Reduction of self-injurious behaviors by reinforcement and toy use. Ment Retard. 20: 169–173, 1982.

79. Lovaas OI, Freitag G, Gold VJ, Kassorla IC. Experimental studies in childhood schizophrenia: I. Analysis of self-destructive behavior. Journal of Experimental Child Psychology. 2: 67–84, 1965a.

80. Lovaas OI, Schaeffer B, Simmons JQ. Building social behavior in autistic children by use of electric shock. Journal of Experimental Research in Personality. 1: 99–109, 1965b.

81. Lovaas OI, Simmons JQ. Manipulation of self-destruction in three retarded children. J Appl Behav Anal. 2: 143–157, 1969.

82. Luiselli JK, Helfen CS, Colozzi G, Donnellon S, Pemberton B. Controlling the self-inflicted biting of a retarded child by the differential reinforcement of other behavior. Psychological Reports. 42: 435–438, 1978.

83. Mauyer A. The shock rod controversy. Journal of Clinical Child Psychology. 12: 272–278, 1983.

84. McGee JJ, Menalascino FJ, Hobbs DC, Menousek PE. Gentle Teaching: A Nonaversive Approach to Helping Persons with Mental Retardation. New York, Human Services Press, 1987.

85. Menninger K. Man Against Himself. New York, Harcourt, Brace & World, 1938.

86. Merbaum M. The modification of self-destructive behavior by a mother-therapist using aversive stimulation. Behavior Therapy. 4: 442–447, 1973.

87. Mesaros RA. A review of the issues and literature regarding positive programming and contingency management procedures for use with autistic children. Unpublished manuscript. Madison, WI, University of Wisconsin, 1983.

88. Miron NB. Behavior modification techniques in the treatment of self-injurious behavior in institutionalized retardates. NIMH Bulletin of Suicidology. 8: 64–69, 1971.

89. Mulick J, Hoyt R, Rojahn J, Schroeder S. Reduction of a "nervous habit" in a profoundly retarded youth by increasing toy play: A case study. Journal of Behavior Therapy and Experimental Psychology. 9: 381–385, 1978.

90. Murphy R, Ruprecht M, Baggio P, Nunes D. The use of mild punishment in combination with reinforcement of alternate behavior to reduce the self-injurious behavior of a profoundly retarded individual. American Association for the Education of Severely/Profoundly Handicapped Persons. 4: 187–195, 1979.

91. Myers DV. Extinction, DRO, and response-cost procedures for eliminating self-injurious behavior: A case study. Behavior Research and Therapy. 13: 189–191, 1975.

92. National Institutes of Health. Consensus development conference statement: Treatment of destructive behaviors in persons with disabilities. Washington, DC, US Government Printing Office, 1989.

93. Nunes DL, Murphy RJ, Ruprecht ML. Reducing self-injurious behavior of severely retarded individuals through withdrawal of reinforcement procedures. Behav Modif. 1: 499–514, 1977.

94. Nyhan WL. Lesch-Nyham syndrome: Summary of clinical features. Fed Proc. 27: 1034–1041, 1968.

95. Nyhan WL. Behavior in the Lesch-Nyhan syndrome. Journal of Autism and Childhood Schizophrenia. 6: 235–252, 1976.

96. O'Neill RE, Horner RH, Albin RW, Storey K, Sprague JR. Functional analysis: A practical assessment guide. Sycamore, IL, Sycamore Publishing, 1990.

97. Rapoff MA, Altman K, Christophersen ER. Suppression of self-injurious behavior: Determining the least restrictive alternative. J Ment Defic Res. 24: 37–46, 1980.

98. Repp AC, Deitz S. Reducing aggressive and self-injurious behavior of institutionalized retarded children through reinforcement of other behaviors. J Appl Behav Anal. 7: 313–325, 1974.

99. Repp AC, Deitz SM, Deitz DED. Reducing inappropriate behaviors in classrooms and in individual sessions through DRO schedules of reinforcement. Ment Retard. 14: 11–15, 1976.

100. Repp AC, Felce D, Barton LE. Basing the treatment of stereotypic and self-injurious behaviors on hypotheses of their causes. J Appl Behav Anal. 21: 281–289, 1988.

101. Risley TR. The effects and side effects of punishing the autistic behaviors of an autistic child. J Appl Behav Anal. 1: 21–34, 1968.

102. Rolider A, Van Houten R. Movement suppression time-out for undesirable behavior in psychotic and severely developmentally delayed children. J Appl Behav Anal. 4: 275–288, 1985.

103. Romanczyk RG. Self-injurious behavior: Conceptualization, assessment, and treatment. In: Gadow KD. ed. Advances in Learning and Behavioral Disabilities. Greenwich, CT, JAI Press, 1986, pp 29–56.

104. Ross RR, Meichenbaum DH, Humphrey C. Treatment of nocturnal head-banging by behavior modification techniques: A case report. Behavior Research and Therapy. 9: 151–154, 1974.

105. Saposnek DT, Watson LS. The elimination of self-destructive behavior of a psychotic child: A case study. Behavior Therapy. 5: 79–89, 1974.

106. Schroeder SR, Schroeder C, Smith B, Dalldorf J. Prevalence of self-injurious behavior in a large state facility for the retarded. Journal of Autism and Childhood Schizophrenia. 8: 261–269, 1986.

107. Schroeder SR, Schroeder CS, Rojahn J, Mulick JA. Self-injurious behavior: An analysis of behavior management techniques. In: Matson JL, McCartney JR. eds. Handbook of Behavior Modification with the Mentally Retarded. New York, Plenum Press, 1981, pp 61–115.

108. Schroeder SR, Bickel WK, Richmond C. Primary and secondary prevention of self-injurious behaviors: A life-long problem. In: Gadow KD. ed. Advances in Learning and Behavioral Disabilities. Greenwich, CT, JAI Press, 1986, pp 63–85.

109. Seegmiller JE. Lesch-Nyhan syndrome and the X-linked uric acidurais. Hospital Practice. 7: 79–90, 1972.

110. Simpson RL, Sasso GM. The modification of rumination in a severely emotionally disturbed child through an overcorrection procedure. American Association for the Education of the

Severely/Profoundly Handicapped Review. 3: 145–150, 1978.

111. Singh N, Manning P, Argell M. Effects of an oral hygiene punishment procedure on chronic rumination and collateral behaviors in monozygous twins. J Appl Behav Anal. 15: 309–314, 1982.

112. Singh NN, Millichamp CJ. Pharmacological treatment of self-injurious behavior in mentally retarded persons. J Autism Dev Disord. 15: 256–267, 1985.

113. Skinner BF. The Behavior of Organisms. New York, Appleton-Century-Crofts, 1938.

114. Snell M. In Response: In response to Axelrod's review of Alternatives to Punishment. The Behavior Analyst. 10: 295–297, 1987.

115. Solnick JV, Rincover A, Peterson CR. Some determinants of the reinforcing and punishing effects of time out. J Appl Behav Anal. 10: 415–424, 1977.

116. Tanner BA, Zeiler M. Punishment of self-injurious behavior using aromatic ammonia as the aversive stimulus. J Appl Behav Anal. 8: 53–57, 1975.

117. Tate BG, Baroff G. Aversive control of self-injurious behavior in a psychotic boy. Behavior Research and Therapy. 4: 281–287, 1966.

118. Touchette PE, MacDonald RF, Langer SN. A scatter plot for identifying stimulus control of problem behavior. J Appl Behav Anal. 18: 343–351, 1985.

119. Turnbull RH, Guest D, Backus LH, Barber PA, Fielder CR, Helmstetter E, Summers JA. A model for analyzing the moral aspects of special education and behavioral intervention: The moral aspects of aversive procedures. In: Dokecki PR, Zaner RN. eds. Ethics of Dealing with Persons with Severe Handicaps: Towards a Research Agenda. Baltimore, Paul H. Brookes, 1987, pp 167–210.

120. Watson LS. Application of operant conditioning techniques to institutionalized severely and profoundly retarded children. Mental Retardation Abstracts. 4: 1–4, 1967.

121. Weeks M, Gaylord-Ross R. Task difficulty and aberrant behavior in severely handicapped students. J Appl Behav Anal. 14: 449–463, 1981.

122. Wolf M, Risley T, Mees P. Application of operant conditioning procedures to the behavior problems of an autistic child. Behavior Research and Therapy. 1: 305–312, 1964.

123. Wolf M, Risley T, Johnson M, Harris F, Allen KE. Application of operant conditioning procedures to the behavior problems of an autistic child: A follow-up and extension. Behavior Research and Therapy. 5: 103–111, 1967.

124. Woods TS. Bringing autistic self-stimulatory behavior under S-Delta stimulus control. Journal of Special Education. 4: 61–70, 1980.

125. Wright DR, Brown RA, Andrews ME. Remission of chronic ruminative vomiting through a reversal of social contingencies. Behavior Research and Therapy. 16: 134–136, 1978.

126. Zehr MD, Theobald DE. Manual guidance used in a punishment procedure: The active ingredient in overcorrection. Journal of Mental Deficiency Research. 22: 263–272, 1978.

Chapter 15
Community Living

Tom Clees

Children, youth, and adults with developmental disabilities encounter many transitions throughout their lives, as do those who do not possess a disability. Perhaps the ultimate transition is that to the postschool world. During this period, individuals typically embark on their careers, take up their own residences, develop new relationships with individuals in their communities, and continue their education and/or training to advance their skills. This period presents not only many new responsibilities, but also an increasing demand to exhibit independence in meeting them. For many individuals with disabilities, these challenges become barriers; these individuals enter the community with fewer skills and greater dependence on significant others than do the nondisabled citizens in their communities. The result is many poor postschool adjustments and, potentially, a loss of independent living status. People with developmental disabilities are not as likely to be assimilated into their communities as are individuals with no accompanying disability labels. Numerous databases have documented the cumulative failure of current publicly funded educational and vocational programs to consistently provide services that are predictive of postschool success for these individuals in the areas of

independent living (Edgar and Levine 1987), employment and wages (Hasazi et al. 1985), and postschool education and training (Fairweather and Shaver 1991; SRI International 1989). This general lack of assimilation, however, cannot be directly attributed to (that is, is not caused by) individuals' respective exceptionalities. Rather, inconsistencies in the quality, degree, and coordination of the services they receive during and after their school years are clearly the best predictors of poor adjustment to the community.

What skills, then, are needed to meet the challenges found in one's community? What are the barriers to successful transitions? What community living options do disabled individuals have, and how and what supports are needed to assist individuals in acquiring and maintaining their status as workers, players, and residents in their respective communities? These questions are the focus of the current chapter and are all related to the concept of independence.

Independence

Independence, or more functionally stated, "independent living," is typically viewed as an outcome, but it has also been described as both an outcome and a process

228

(Fisher, 1989). As an outcome, functioning independently within the community requires that an individual exhibit a wide range of skills across numerous settings and in the absence of supports not normally present, such as those provided by state or federal agencies (for example, vocational rehabilitation). For many individuals, particularly those with disabilities, independent living is best described as a terminal goal that they are in the process of reaching. The ongoing process of providing a person with residential, financial, educational, career, and other supports to assist him or her to acquire functional skills across all relevant skill domains has, as its terminal goal, the maintenance of those adaptive responses once the supports have been faded to the minimum required to maintain the individual's status within the community. From this perspective, individuals utilize available supports to acquire skills and services that move them along a continuum of greater independence while maintaining their status as citizens within their own communities.

Many individuals require some degree of supervision to function within and outside of their residences. This assistance varies depending on the needs of the individuals served. Some examples include assistance in meal preparation or transportation to work, the use of augmentative communication devices, social skills training, and physical care.

Community living skills, or those competencies that individuals must utilize to function independently, are typically grouped into broad skill areas, or domains. Whereas conceptualizations differ in the number of domains they utilize to represent skills and in the number of competencies and subcompetencies falling within each domain, the domains generally include skills related to daily living (for example, domestic and mobility skills), personal-social interactions (for example, communication and interpersonal skills), and employment (for example, job seeking and work performance skills).

Thus, one's independence is a matter of degree and is determined by

1. The extent of his or her community living skills

2. The resources and support services required by the individual to acquire and maintain those skills in relevant settings (that is, to function as a working, playing resident of his or her community)

3. The extent, availability, and quality of the resources and support services in the individual's community.

This last factor is crucial. A deficit in either the scope, quality, or availability of assistance or in one's success at accessing needed assistance, adversely affects one's acquisition of new skills and the likelihood that one will acquire or maintain community living status.

For example, Laurie, a young adult with a physical disability that precluded her from traveling independently, lived alone in an apartment located in a rural setting; she required minimal assistance to maintain her independent living status (for example, transportation to and from work; assistance in shopping). Her employer described her as a superior worker who interacted well with her fellow employees. Her transportation had been provided or otherwise coordinated by a nondisabled neighbor with whom Laurie worked and who served as an advocate for her. Because the coworker–advocate moved away, Laurie was faced with the loss of consistent transportation. Thus, her job, her income, and, potentially, her status in the community could no longer be maintained unless she moved to a group home in an area with more support services, which she unhappily did. As unfortunate and common as this scenario is, there are many individuals to whom community-based career, residential, or mobility supports have never been available; or these individuals have been denied access because of the limited number of existing services or other people's priorities, misconceptions, or prejudices.

For the current chapter, the terms "independent living" and "independence" always imply "independence from" any setting more restrictive than the community. Such restrictive settings are those that segregate people with disabilities from the general population.

Barriers to Independent Living

Rusch and colleagues (1986) identified six obstacles to competitive employment that, with minor addenda (/), apply equally well as barriers to independent living or to integration. These obstacles include specific employee/resident skill and behavior deficits; deficient assessment and training procedures; disregard for social validation of work/residential goals and (training) procedures; lack of a systematic approach to service delivery; inadequate personnel preparation; and economic and policy considerations that deter efforts to promote competitive employment/independent living. To this list of barriers may be added public opinion and the concept of readiness as a determinant of integration.

The first three items address what should be taught, how it should be taught, and the social validity, or functional significance, of each. These concerns are addressed in the Community Living Skills section of this chapter. The remaining items represent problems in the systems of service delivery and in the priorities and policies that determine levels and types of support. Fragmentation and duplication of services, a lack of communication and collaboration among schools, agencies, and community programs, and misconceptions regarding individuals' potentials exemplify these problems.

The types of supports and the degree to which they are provided to individuals are certainly affected by the availability of resources and are greatly determined by a set of guiding principles, or philosophy of operations (Pancsofar and Blackwell 1986).

The principles of normalization and least restrictive environment have greatly influenced the current range of school and postschool service delivery models. Pancsofar and Blackwell (1986) cited Wolfensberger, who described normalization as:

> The use of means which are culturally normative to offer a person life conditions at least as good as the average citizen's and to as much as possible enhance or support personal behaviors, appearances, status and reputation to the greatest degree possible at any given time for each individual according to his or her developmental needs.

The least restrictive environment (LRE) is engendered in The Education for All Handicapped Children Act, P.L. 94-142, which states that:

> . . . to the maximum extent appropriate, handicapped children, including children in public or private institutions or other care facilities, are educated with children who are not handicapped, and that special classes, separate schooling, or other removal of handicapped children from the regular educational environment occurs only when the nature or severity of the handicap is such that education in regular classes with the use of supplementary aids and services cannot be achieved satisfactorily . . . (section 612{5}B).

These principles have greatly affected the way in which persons with developmental disabilities are perceived and treated. Although individuals with disabilities have clearly benefitted from a growing philosophy of "community," there have been and remain difficulties not only with the implementation of practices related to the principles but also with their conceptualization as related to service models. The "deinstitutionalization" movement and the evolution of a "continuum of services" exemplify these problems.

In the earlier phases of deinstitutionalization, many individuals were taken from state institutions and ". . . dumped into the community without having the necessary skills to cope successfully in their new environment and without easy access to support and follow-up services that see that the transition was successful" (Heward and Orlansky 1988).

The difficulties faced by many deinstitutionalized individuals can be viewed either as a function of their lack of readiness to move into the community or as a function of an inadequate system of services with which to support them (regardless of their disabilities or skill levels).

The former view, that of readiness, is embodied in the concept of the least restrictive environment and implies a continuum of services approach to providing services. This is evidenced in the preceding citation regarding LRE, which has provisions for ". . . public or private institutions, . . . special classes, special schooling, or other removal . . ." The harsh reality is that the least restrictive environment is actually the least restrictive environment *given* the current distribution of services.

There is certainly a discrepancy between the number of people with disabilities who could hold jobs with support in an integrated setting and who could live with support in their own apartments, homes, or small transitional group homes, and the number who do. In analyzing their data on community placements and outcomes, Seyelman and colleagues (1978) concluded that clients of virtually any intellectual functioning level can succeed in the community, given the provision of adequate supports. Wehman's (1986) data refute any notion that people with disabilities cannot be productive members of the work force. This is true even for those whose disabilities may be severe (for example, persons with severe mental retardation). If supports are the key to maintaining one's status within the community, then this conclusion can easily be expanded to include virtually all levels and types of disabilities. Unfortunately, people with handicapping conditions are vastly under-

represented in integrated employment and residential settings. According to Lakin and Bruininks (1985), "When services are viewed across a continuum from highly integrated to highly segregated, it can be seen that there is clear discrimination against those clients who have the most severe handicapping conditions." This being the case, there needs to be a redistribution of fiscal supports and support services such that they are tied to residences, employment settings, and supports (for example, career education and training, transportation) that are integrated into disabled peoples' communities. The greater this redistribution, the more commonplace it will become to see disabled individuals working and residing in the community.

Living Arrangements and Employment Outcomes

Figure 15-1 depicts a continuum of services for each of three outcomes: educational, employment, and residential. The continuum runs from highly segregated services and settings that expect and perhaps foster extreme dependency to those that are integrated, or normalized, and that require either a high degree of independence or considerable support. Although this continuum is well entrenched across each of the outcomes, there has been some realization that the severity of disability should not determine one's place on the waiting list for services nor whether the setting in which he or she is served is integrated. Supported employment models have taken the lead in operationalizing this realization by providing citizens with severe disabilities the opportunity to work in integrated settings with whatever support they require. Much of this success may be owed to the school-to-work transition priority that was established by the Department of Education a few years ago (Will 1984). This priority fostered collaboration within and between educational programs and service agencies. Since then, the meaning of the term "transition" has been expanded to include transitions to all aspects of community life.

Living Arrangements

The categories of residential outcomes shown in Figure 15-1 represent the general continuum of placements or options associated with serving developmentally disabled individuals. Independent living arrangements include many types of residences. Individuals are considered to be living independently, however, only if they are receiving no supports other than those generally available to those who do not have disabilities. Supported living arrangements include assistance in maintaining community status in either a nonagency-owned,

-leased, or -managed residence or an agency-owned, -leased, or -managed residence.

The second of these two options includes, primarily, supervised living in an apartment or group home that has been built or leased by the same agency that provides the support. The degree of supervision provided in group homes varies depending on the type of residence it is. Today group homes range from smaller (a few individuals) to larger (10 or so, although group homes in which 20 or more people reside are still present) and from transitional in nature to long term. Transitional group homes are generally those in which people reside while they are either preparing to move to a more independent living arrangement (a readiness approach) or waiting for supports to be made available in

Educational Outcomes

Regular classroom	Regular classroom with consultation	Separate class (self-contained)	Separate school	Residential facility or school	Homebound or hospital environment

Employment Outcomes

Competitive employment	Supported, integrated competitive employment		Sheltered employment in integrated setting (enclave)		Sheltered employment: transitional extended work activities

Residential Outcomes

Independent living	Supported living in own apartment or home	Supported living in group home or apartment: small, transitional large, long-term	Nursing home: intermediate care facility convalescent or county home		State or private residential facility

Integrated (normalized) services that require a high degree of independence or of support ←——————→ Segregated services that foster extreme dependence

Figure 15-1. Continuum of educational, vocational, and residential outcomes associated with a "readiness" approach to service delivery

less restrictive settings. Some individuals who reside in group homes do so on a long-term basis, primarily because of a lack of the available supports they require to live in more normalized residences. This is because agency costs are tied to facilities. Although group homes have greatly contributed to the integration of disabled individuals into the community as well as kept people from living in more restrictive settings such as nursing homes or institutions, the fact that the buildings themselves and the support services share the same budgets means that there is less to spend on supporting individuals in the mainstream. (Note: Many group homes are actually classified as Intermediate Care Facilities for the Mentally Retarded, or ICF/MR, and fall under the heading of nursing facility).

Whereas a continuum-of-care model is intended to provide whatever level of assistance individuals need, perverse funding incentives, particularly at state and local levels (Copeland and Everson 1985), have unnecessarily made it less expensive to provide care in more restrictive settings.

Housing Support and Supported Living

Some individuals require assistance to function within their residences, whether they own, rent, or, in some cases, share them with their families. Just as the supported employment model has demonstrated that individuals can, if given proper support, hold real, paying jobs in integrated employment settings, there is a growing, although somewhat younger, movement to provide individuals with whatever supports they need to own, rent, or otherwise reside in nonagency managed homes, regardless of their disabilities. This is a consumer-centered model, which is generally referred to as an individualized, person-centered, or *housing-support* strategy to assist individuals to acquire normalized living options within their communities (Racino and Taylor 1989). This approach is part of the conceptualization of supported

living discussed previously. In a broader sense it addresses not only living arrangements, but also other aspects of community life, such as employment and recreation. The basis of the supported living model of community living is the contention that living in one's community is a matter of individual rights, not of placement decisions made by significant others. This supported living approach rejects the continuum-of-services model and the principle of LRE as they pertain to current community living options. Despite ample demonstration that individuals with severe disabilities are, if given adequate supports, able to function within their respective communities (Hill et al. 1983), there is ". . . still a pervasive tendency to believe that people have to acquire certain prerequisite skills before they're eligible or 'ready' to live where they choose." (Karan et al. 1990).

Racino and Taylor (1989) have summarized the problems associated with the continuum concept:

1. People with severe disabilities get relegated to the "most restrictive" end of the continuum.

2. The most restrictive placements, such as institutions, are not necessary.

3. The continuum implies that people need to leave their homes every time they acquire new skills.

4. The most restrictive placements do not prepare people for the least restrictive placements.

5. The continuum concept confuses restrictions of people's rights with intensity of their support and service needs.

6. The continuum directs attention to physical settings rather than to the services and supports people need to be integrated in the community.

The major barrier to housing-support strategies is the generally accepted, facility-based funding approach to residential services. The development of facility-based residences, predominantly group homes or apartments, intermediate care facilities and other nursing homes, and residential facilities (that is, institutions), is determined not by the community-living support needs of individuals, but by perceived group needs within a continuum-of-services model. This results in the construction, purchase, and rental by agencies of a variety of residences, thus precluding the utilization of funds for expanding community-living support options.

In a facility-based approach, which is typical in most communities, individuals must reside in licensed, agency-owned or -rented residences run by state, private, or private nonprofit agencies, in order to receive services. Leaving the agency-run facility means the loss of services, because the services are tied to the residence (that is, the services do not generally follow the person). A partial solution to this problem is The Home and Community Based Medicaid Waiver, which provides for services to be delivered in alternative settings such as the first option above (that is, supported living in a nonagency-owned, -leased, or -managed residence). Because it eliminates the cost associated with the agency facility, this option can provide a way to increase the level of supports to meet individuals' requirements for living in a preferred setting. Although many disabled individuals may be able to apply such benefits to community integration services, as is the case with Wisconsin's Medicaid Waiver Community Integration Program, few are even aware of such an option nor are their parents, guardians, or advocates. Even when they are, few communities have developed programs that are comprehensive enough to allow persons to exercise such options (that is, there are not ample support systems to allow individuals to contract out, or buy, the services they require to live independently of state-developed residences).

For persons to benefit from the supported living approach identified here, housing, support services, and funding options must all be available and coordinated. Racino and Taylor (1989) have identified some of these options in relation to one's place of residence. These and others are presented in Table 15-1. The provision or coordination of support services is the responsibility of the agencies with whom the disabled person contracts. Such agencies may be state- or county-funded or private and paid through reimbursement for services. Grass roots organizations, or those consisting of families, friends, and advocates of disabled individuals, including service providers, influential members of the community, and professionals, can affect policy through advocacy, as well as help to coordinate and supplement services (for example, provide transportation or drop in). One key element in this supported living model is that service providers do not also function as landlords. This allows the services provided by the agency and designated service personnel to follow a consumer to a new home or apartment, should the individual still wish to employ them. In a facility-based approach, agencies must fill slots as they open. The slots are filled based on the type and severity of a person's disability, not on his or her desire to move into it. In addition, individuals may become trapped in a facility-owned residence because the services they receive cannot be provided if they live elsewhere.

Restrictive settings are created by the belief that they are necessary. They are perceived to be necessary because there are not enough resources to provide, on a consistent and comprehensive basis, the level of services required to assist disabled individuals of all levels of severity to live within their communities in the places of their choosing (or that, on their behalves, are advocated as normalized). Because most disabled individuals do not receive the support that would allow them to live in typical community residences, they do not live in them. This reinforces both the misconception that they are unable to do

Table 15-1. Supported Living Options Available to Disabled Consumers in a Housing-Support (That Is, Nonfacility-Based) Supported Living Model

Living Arrangements	Support Strategies (examples of agency and other supports)	Funding Strategies
Own or rent own house, apartment, condominium	Live-in employee (physical-household care; meal; skill development)	Salary and wages
Own and lease out part of residence	Drop-in or on-call employee (maintenance; emergencies)	Trusts for housing Subsidies Medicaid waiver programs
Jointly own or rent with roommate(s)	Volunteers (errands; shopping)	Supplemental security income
Live alone, or with nonsupported roommate(s) in parent- or guardian-owned or -rented residence (without owner)	Advocates (coordination; finances; friendship) Paid companion (recreation; interaction) Adaptations or modifications (accessibility, augmentative communication devices)	Low-income tax credits Cooperatives Purchases through housing associations Private subsidies
Live in cooperative Foster home	Transportation (to work, medical, education-training, recreation) Family or friends Acquisition of housing (finding housing, furnishings)	

Adapted from Racino and Taylor 1989.

so and the erroneous conclusion that a continuum of restrictive settings is necessary.

Numerous residential options are available to or imposed on persons with disabilities. A full range of living arrangements has been identified in the literature (Baker et al. 1977; Heal et al. 1980; Lensink 1980; Thompson 1977), and has been summarized by Pancsofar and Blackwell (1986). This range is presented in Table 15-2. Although there are clear differences between the degrees of independence required to function (with no support) within some of these options (for example, institutions versus nursing homes versus group homes versus independent living), in total they should be viewed as a list of residential classifications, not as a strict continuum related to the residential services generally afforded persons with disabilities, as represented in Figure 15-1.

Employment Outcomes

The continuum of competitive and sheltered employment outcomes for disabled individuals is briefly described below.

Independently, Competitively Employed

Competitive employment is work that produces valued goods or services at minimum wage or above, offers opportunities for advancements, and is in an integrated setting (Rusch 1986). Integrated settings are those that contain, primarily, nonhandicapped persons. Competitive employment settings, when compared to others, are the most advantageous because they offer greater wages and benefits; integration with nonhandicapped persons; normalized settings; greater opportunity for advancement; and improved perceptions by family and friends (Wehman et al. 1985b).

Table 15-2. Living Arrangements: Available Options and Residential Placements*

Independent Living—A site where an individual lives with a roommate, a spouse, or alone; usually an apartment or duplex, but occasionally a house

Single-family homes—a free-standing, single-family home in an average residential neighborhood

Shared home—Two or more handicapped persons may prefer to share a single-family home and the cost of needed modification; often the sharing is between handicapped and congenial, able-bodied persons

Individual or shared apartment—In large or small building, apartments occupied by a single handicapped person, or shared by two or more, have been used successfully with or without services, depending on need

Group of individual apartments—Group of apartments, on one floor or scattered throughout the building or scattered among several buildings in an apartment complex

Dwelling in new apartment building—Some percentage of the living units in a large public or private apartment building can be designed for the handicapped

Elderly housing project—Project for the elderly that is designed with special facilities may have a percentage of the units set aside for the handicapped, with provision of the additional services needed

Congregate housing—A residential environment, assisted independent living, that incorporates shelter and services for the functionally impaired or marginally socially adjusted elderly or handicapped persons, enabling them to maintain or return to a semi-independent life-style and avoid institutionalization

Residential hotel—Relatively large structure that provides private rooms and baths (not apartments), adaptable for the handicapped, with housekeeping and meal service available at commercial rates

Natural or adoptive home—The home of one's parents, usually natural parents

Other relative's home—The home of a resident's sibling, grandparent, aunt, uncle, or offspring

Friend's home—The home of someone who has befriended the resident or the resident's family

Foster family care—Serving five or fewer retarded adults in a family's own home; families are not governed by boards of directors; they collect monthly payments for the care of the residents

Developmental foster home—Similar to natural homes, foster homes, and adoptive homes, these homes should offer a living situation to a child that encourages a sense of identity and security in a homelike setting for up to three children. Placements are often made with the expressed objective that a child will remain with his developmental foster family until he or she reaches adulthood. Developmental foster home parents are trained to extend the services of the developmental center or public school program into the home environment.

Group home—Home that houses as few as two or as many as 100 developmentally disabled children or adults. Five or more handicapped persons of both sexes may live in a relatively large home (purchased, rented, or constructed), assisted by house managers or counselors and providing access to any other services (internal and external) required.

Small group home—Serving 10 or fewer retarded adults

Medium group home—Serving 11 to 20 retarded adults

Large group home—Serving 21 to 40 retarded adults

Mini-institution—Serving 41 to 80 retarded adults

Mixed group home—Serving retarded adults and former mental patients and often nonretarded people as well in group homes or rest homes

Group home for older adults—Serving only older retarded people and often nonretarded people as well in group homes or rest homes

Nursing home—Includes a variety of residential alternatives, all providing continuing medical care for anyone who needs it. The convalescent home and intermediate care facility are specially licensed nursing homes. Nursing homes are nearly always privately owned and are expected to make a profit for their owners.

Intermediate care facility—Licensed as a nursing home, making it eligible for Federal Medicaid Support (Title XIX) of The Social Security Act and its Amendments. Two classes are distinguished according to size: 15 and under, and 16 and over. The larger homes must have a nurse (licensed practical nurse) on duty at all times, whereas the smaller homes need only have one on call.

(continued)

Table 15-2. (continued)

Nursing home (continued)

Convalescent Home—A nursing home whose residents are expected to stay for a reasonably short period of time for rehabilitation before they return to the community.

The County Home—Type of nursing home whose residents are expected to stay for a reasonably short period of time for rehabilitation before they return to the community.

Boarding Home—Homes where the resident is provided room and board for a fee, but no other services are contracted. These homes house individuals of varying abilities. They are usually not classified as group or family care homes.

Hostel—Similar to residential hotel but a hostel is usually supervised and is considered transitional or temporary.

Sheltered Village—Provides a segregated, self-contained community for retarded adults and live-in staff in a cluster of buildings usually located in a rural setting.

Public Residential Facility—State institution. Until recently these were very large, typically having about 1,500 residents and occasionally having over 5,000, but today they average only about 500 residents each, and many have fewer than 50.

Private Residential Facility—A variety of privately owned and foundation-owned residential alternatives. Some of these are expensive, highly visible, multiple-treatment centers, some are largely custodial facilities, and some are communes that feature an idyllic life for handicapped and nonhandicapped co-residents.

Workshop-Dormitory—Living unit and a work training program are associated administratively and sometimes physically.

Mental Hospital—An institution for mentally ill individuals

Prison—A building, usually with cells, where convicted criminals are confined or where accused persons are held while awaiting trial.

Adapted from Pancsofar and Blackwell (1986).

Persons who are independently and competitively employed have not or no longer receive assistance related to their job outside of that made available by the employer to all employees.

Supported, Integrated Competitive Employment

This outcome offers the same advantages as those associated with nonsupported competitive employment, but is for individuals who require some degree of short- or long-term assistance to function within their job settings. The types of supports that disabled individuals might receive related to this option include job matching, modifications and placement; on-the-job training; in-service training of supervisors and coworkers; advocacy by coworkers; transportation; on-going evaluation; and follow-up.

Sheltered Employment in Integrated Settings: Enclaves

Short- or long-term employment of (usually a small group of) individuals with disabilities in local business or industry comprises this employment outcome. Employees in these positions are provided with intense training and supervision, usually with minimal payment based upon production, but below that of minimum wage standards. Enclaves may be well integrated with nonhandicapped individuals (that is, work, eat lunch, take breaks alongside nonhandicapped workers), or they may occupy a segregated area within the setting, or some combination thereof. Depending upon the extent to which they are integrated, handicapped persons in these settings benefit to varying degrees from appropriate work and social models.

Sheltered Employment in Segregated Settings

Transitional Employment.   Individuals in transitional employment are placed on a temporary basis, the intent being to afford them the option of competitive employment following evaluation and subsequent training. In this and the extended employment option following, workers earn a percentage of minimum wage.

Extended Employment.   This option may include either *sheltered employee* or *long-term work adjustment* status (Wehman et al. 1985a). Sheltered employee status has, historically, generally been considered terminal, although this is more likely a function of the numerous barriers to competitive employment and independent living that are addressed below. Persons in long-term work adjustment positions typically require great expenditures in occupational, behavioral, social, and other services to move into sheltered or extended employee status.

Work Activities Programs.   Individuals considered (by the standards of those by whom they are served) to be unemployable, or in need of prevocational skill training to advance along the continuum of employment options, can earn a token wage for work completed. Activities programs also provide numerous services and activities such as recreational activities, daily living and social skills training, and work skills development.

Although sheltered employment settings provide daily maintenance for many individuals and opportunities for some, they provide few, if any, services that could not be delivered in less restrictive settings, given adequate supports for a community-based service delivery model. Some of the disadvantages associated with sheltered settings include low wages and minimal benefits; limited opportunities for advancement because of narrow scope of jobs; limited exposure to appropriate social

models; and perpetuation of public misconceptions regarding the capabilities of persons with disabilities.

Although there are numerous drawbacks to sheltered home and work settings, it is important to note that they are far more predominant than supported service settings and that, due to fiscal and philosophic factors, they will probably remain so for some time. Therefore, while the service delivery systems are moving toward a zero reject policy of integration, it is imperative that those in less than integrated settings employ the best methods of habilitation available. The skills, instructional methods, and service delivery approaches presented in the following pages are relevant to the integration of disabled citizens into their respective communities, regardless of their current living arrangements.

Community Living Skills and Instruction

Individuals are called upon to exhibit hundreds of skills each day, whether in their homes, on a bus, doing their job, talking with their coworkers, buying groceries, or playing softball in a city recreational league. Some of these skills are more setting specific, whereas others are relevant across a variety of environments. Operating a machine in a plant, cleaning a particular office building, or using a particular type of microwave oven in one's own kitchen is an example of setting-specific skills. Social skills, such as introducing oneself to someone or asking for assistance, exemplify the latter in that they are an integral component of interactions in virtually any setting in which people are found (for example, work, home, school, shopping).

The skill domains addressed in this chapter, including domestic, consumer and mobility skills, are those that are considered crucial to maintaining one's status in the community. Employment skills, which are equally important in determining success within the community, are discussed in Chapter 13.

Best Practices in Instruction

The postschool results associated with special needs populations are best explained by the extent to which known effective teaching and transition strategies are *not* implemented. As Wehman (1990) stated, "Unfortunately, school systems either do not implement these practices or do not implement them well enough longitudinally, that is, over the duration of the students tenure in school." There are, regardless of the skill being taught or the disability or age of the person learning, a set of best practices related to the instruction of independent living skills, including teaching in integrated settings; teaching functional skills; teaching in target settings; teaching early; and teaching for generalization.

Teach in Integrated Settings

Hasazi et al. (1985) found that students who had received special education services (mentally retarded, learning disabled, behavior disordered) during school were more likely to be employed at 1 to 4 years postschool if they had received educational services through a resource program rather than through a self-contained classroom. Job retention has also been linked to integrated, chronologically age-appropriate schools (Wehman et al. 1985a).

Segregated settings provide individuals with less exposure to appropriate models, often include models of inappropriate social behavior and, by their very nature, do not afford the opportunity for reinforcement of prosocial skills in varied settings and with different people. Integrated settings, conversely, allow for imitation and reinforcement of appropriate interactional skills under natural conditions. Integrated settings should be utilized in both school and community-based programs. For ex-

ample, instruction in grocery shopping or bowling should not involve segregated activities with large groups of individuals with disabilities within otherwise integrated settings. The appropriate shopping, bowling, and social models offered by non-handicapped peers are likely to go unnoticed in large, segregated groups. Segregated groups of handicapped individuals within school and community settings are also likely to reinforce any stereotypes held by community members.

Teach Functional Skills

Functional skills are those that directly define independent living. They are the skills that are integral to one's daily existence. Nonfunctional skills are those that do not, in and of themselves, relate to specific aspects of an individuals' daily living. For example, sorting colored circles is a nonfunctional skill, whereas identifying colors on traffic lights while learning pedestrian skills is functional. Coloring coins on a worksheet is nonfunctional; selecting coins from one's pocket and buying a can of pop from a vending machine is functional.

The degree to which curricula are functional has been linked to success in the community. Participation in vocational education classes during high school and holding a part-time summer or high school job have both been linked to greater independence, as measured by employment status after existing school (Hasazi et al. 1985; Hasazi et al. 1989). Hasazi's (1985) data also indicated that there was no advantage to having participated in a work experience program over not having participated, at least with respect to postschool employment. One explanation for the apparent advantage of vocational education courses and actual employment over work experience programs in predicting future employment is that work experience programs do not provide nearly the depth of training that vocational courses do; the latter utilize direct instruction to focus on mastery of a set of skills related to a specific, community-referenced job.

The preceding data indicate that persons with disabilities benefit from having taken vocational education courses; however, students with more severe handicaps are less likely to participate in vocational education courses and summer job programs, such as those associated with the Job Training Partnership Act (JTPA). This finding is certainly not due to students' inability to benefit from such experiences. Limiting students' access to meaningful involvement in such curricula is a program decision made by significant others because of a real or perceived lack of supports; it does not necessarily reflect students' preferences or potentials.

These results reinforce the significance of providing students who have disabilities with the support services they require to be able to participate in school and postschool programs that emphasize the teaching of community-referenced competencies through functional curricula, not only as related to postschool employment, but also across all skill domains related to independent living.

Teach in Target Settings

Generally speaking, the importance of providing instruction in the setting(s) in which a skill is to be performed (that is, the target setting[s]) increases as the severity of a disability increases and as the similarity between a target setting and instructional setting decreases (Snell 1987). People labeled as severely mentally retarded, for example, are less likely to generalize dishwashing skills from one home to another than are individuals with labels of mild retardation. The degree of transfer can be expected to decrease further as the differences in the stimuli associated with dishwashing in the different residences increase. Some of these might include differences in the faucets (for example, a single hot-cold lever versus separate hot and cold handles), one sink compartment

as opposed to two, different cupboard locations, more or different distractors (for example, more noise from the street or a roommate; different wallpaper). Even skills acquired by people with mild or moderate disabilities in one setting, however, cannot be expected to transfer to a different setting. Subtle differences in lighting, distance to objects, or the height of counters might affect the transfer of the practiced skills of individuals with mild or moderate visual or physical impairments.

To increase the likelihood that persons with disabilities will be able to perform functional skills in relevant settings, instruction in those settings (that is, community-based instruction) is extremely important. In addition, instruction using stimuli that vary but that are of the same class (for example, different sink types, vending machines, lamps, fast-food restaurants), to whatever extent possible, can assist in the generalization of skills and maintenance of one's community living status. Additional benefits associated with community-based instruction are described by Wehman and colleagues (1985b) and include sampling of community reinforcers; increased awareness by nonhandicapped people of the presence and competence of people with disabilities; exposure to appropriate role models; elevated teacher-trainer expectations through observation of students' functional competencies; increased parental hope and interest through sons' or daughters' successful integrations; and improvements in curriculum selection and development through practice.

Teach Early

Dick (1985) reported the ratings of junior and senior high school special education teachers with regard to the levels of school at which community living skills should be taught. The teachers indicated that daily living skills (for example, home management, mobility) should be taught primarily in junior high (7th and 8th grades), personal-social skills in junior and early senior high (7th to 10th grades), and pre-vocational and vocational skills during early and late senior high (9th to 12th grades). Many individuals with disabilities enter school with substantial deficits in many skill areas. The general practice of delaying their instruction in functional, community-referenced skills until they are in secondary school may explain many of the poor postschool adjustments associated with having a disability. To improve on these outcomes, schools need to utilize age-appropriate, community-referenced curricula and community-based instruction in primary school and earlier.

There are countless curricula available to teach community living skills. One of the most comprehensive and functional is Brolin's (1978) Life Centered Career Education Curriculum, which consists of three broad skill domains, or curriculum areas, including daily living skills, personal-social skills, and occupational guidance and preparation skills. The three curriculum areas, along with their respective competencies and subcompetencies, are presented in Table 15-3. The curriculum is competency-based and includes a structure for easily rating students as they improve and demonstrate competencies within each domain. It consists of three phases: awareness, exploration, and preparation. All of the phases focus on the same competencies, but instruction varies depending on the goals and general grade level of the particular student(s). In this way, younger students are exposed to community living skills at earlier ages than is typical. The curriculum focuses heavily on skills that comprise independent living and has great utility in that it allows for community-based instruction, is both comprehensive and structured, and can be adapted to address the individual characteristics of students' communities.

Teach for Generalization

Although skill transfer is an instructional goal, it is also a challenge, particularly as the severity of disability increases. Al-though it is important to teach in the target setting, it may not always be possible to do so. For example, traveling to the laundromat to teach use of washers and dryers and folding clothes may not be supported by a school's budget or administration. Many teachers rely on classroom simulations to teach relevant skills. Using washers and dryers in the school to simulate the stimulus conditions at the laundromat may help in generalizing loading and unloading clothes into and from the machines and in measuring and pouring detergent. Bringing canned goods into the classroom may help in generalizing the skill of picking out those particular items in the classroom to finding them on the shelf in the grocery store. However, the degree of differences between the machines in the classroom and those in the laundromat (coin operated in the laundromat, differences in the settings, dials), their relative positions (side by side in the classroom, but separated in the laundromat), and other differences in the settings (people, noises, tables, lighting) might result in a failure to generalize skills across settings. Similarly, picking out one canned item from ten on a table or simulated grocery store shelf in the classroom is very different than finding a particular isle in the store and locating the particular item from among others that are numerous and similar. As a rule, the more similar the simulation to the target setting, the greater the likelihood that transfer will occur. Therefore, when classroom simulations are utilized in instruction, it is important to program for maximum generalization by using common physical stimuli (real cans or packages rather than drawings or worksheets); using common social stimuli (invite a local employer to come and conduct practice interviews); using a sufficient number of examples of correct responses (teaching a student different greetings); using a sufficient number of examples of stimuli that precede the response (teaching a student to throw out different types of spoiled foods); and using natural reinforcers (selecting the correct vending change in the classroom

Table 15-3. Brolin's (1978) Life Centered Education Curriculum Competencies and Subcompetencies

Curriculum Area	Competency	Subcompetencies	
Daily Living Skills	1. Managing family finances	1. Identify money and make correct change	2. Make wise expenditures
	2. Selecting, managing, and maintaining a home	6. Select adequate housing	7. Maintain a home
	3. Caring for personal needs	10. Dress appropriately	11. Exhibit proper grooming and hygiene
	4. Raising children, enriching family-living	14. Prepare for adjustment to marriage	15. Prepare for raising children (physical care)
	5. Buying and preparing food	18. Demonstrate appropriate eating skills	19. Plan balanced meals
	6. Buying and caring for clothing	24. Wash clothing	25. Iron and store clothing
	7. Engaging in civic activities	28. Generally understand local laws and government	29. Generally understand federal government
	8. Utilizing recreation and leisure	34. Participate actively in group activities	35. Know activities and available community resources
	9. Getting around the community (mobility)	40. Demonstrate knowledge of traffic rules and safety practices	41. Demonstrate knowledge and use of various means of transportation
Personal-Social Skills	10. Achieving self-awareness	43. Attain a sense of body	44. Identify interests and abilities
	11. Acquiring self-confidence	48. Express feelings of worth	49. Tell how others see him/her
	12. Achieving socially responsible behavior	53. Know character traits needed for acceptance	54. Know proper behavior in public places
	13. Maintaining good interpersonal skills	58. Know how to listen and respond	59. Know how to make and maintain friendships
	14. Achieving independence	62. Understand impact of behaviors upon others	63. Understand self-organization
	15. Achieving problem-solving skills	66. Differentiate bipolar concepts	67. Understand the need for goals
	16. Communicating adequately with others	71. Recognize emergency situations	72. Read at level needed for future goals
Occupational Guidance and Preparation	17. Knowing and exploring occupational possibilities	76. Identify the personal values met through work	77. Identify the societal values met through work
	18. Selecting and planning occupational choices	82. Identify major occupational needs	83. Identify major occupational interests
	19. Exhibiting appropriate work habits and behaviors	87. Follow directions	88. Work with others
	20. Exhibiting sufficient physical-manual skills	94. Demonstrate satisfactory balance and coordination	95. Demonstrate satisfactory manual dexterity
	21. Obtaining a specific occupational skill		
	22. Seeking, securing and maintaining employment	98. Search for a job	99. Apply for a job

Source: A noncopyrighted publication of the Council for Exceptional Children

Subcompetencies

3. Obtain and use bank and credit facilities

4. Keep basic financial records

5. Calculate and pay taxes

8. Use basic appliances and tools

9. Maintain home exterior

12. Demonstrate knowledge of physical fitness, nutrition, and weight control

13. Demonstrate knowledge of common illness prevention and treatment

16. Prepare for raising children (psychological care)

17. Practice family safety in the home

20. Purchase food

21. Prepare meals

22. Clean food preparation areas

23. Store food

26. Perform simple mending

27. Purchase clothing

30. Understand citizenship rights and responsibilities

31. Understand registration and voting procedures

32. Understand Selective Service procedures

33. Understand civil rights and responsibilities when questioned by the law

36. Understand recreational values

37. Use recreational facilities in the community

38. Plan and choose activities wisely

39. Plan vacations

42. Drive a car

45. Identify emotions

46. Identify needs

47. Understand the physical self

50. Accept praise

51. Accept criticism

52. Develop confidence in self

55. Develop respect for the rights and properties of others

56. Recognize authority and follow instructions

57. Recognize personal roles

60. Establish appropriate heterosexual relationships

61. Know how to establish close relationships

64. Develop goal seeking behavior

65. Strive toward self-actualization

68. Look at alternatives

69. Anticipate consequences

70. Know where to find good advice

73. Write at the level needed for future goals

74. Speak adequately for understanding

75. Understand the subtleties of communication

78. Identify the remunerative aspects of work

79. Understand classification of jobs into different occupational systems

80. Identify occupational opportunities available locally

81. Identify sources of occupational information

84. Identify occupational aptitudes

85. Identify requirements of appropriate and available jobs

86. Make realistic occupational choices

89. Work at a satisfactory rate

90. Accept supervision

91. Recognize the importance of attendance and punctuality

92. Meet demands for quality work

93. Demonstrate occupational safety

96. Demonstrate satisfactory stamina and endurance

97. Demonstrate satisfactory sensory discrimination

100. Interview for a job

101. Adjust to competitive standards

102. Maintain postschool occupational adjustment

earns a can of pop). These and additional concerns related to promoting generalizations are discussed in detail elsewhere (Stokes and Baer 1977; Stokes and Osnes 1986).

Domestic and Community Skills

Being able to function safely within and maintain one's residence is an important aspect of independence. Individuals who lack basic home skills are put at risk for losing their community living status (Cuvo and Davis 1981; Schalock and Lilley 1986). It is therefore important for parents, teachers, group home and support service providers, advocates, and other individuals charged with providing or organizing community living instruction and supports for persons with disabilities to be able to design, implement, and evaluate instructional programs in the areas of domestic and other community living skills.

Domestic skills are those that individuals utilize to maintain themselves within their homes and to maintain their residences and respective grounds. Steps to follow in designing and implementing instructional programs are presented below.

Assessing Present or Potential (Target) Settings

Teaching individuals home living (and other) skills begins with an ecologic inventory (Brown et al. 1979a), which involves the delineation of living environments into settings and subsettings to identify skills that are needed throughout the residence. Table 15-4 presents an inventory of domestic skills and activities that are important to community living, as referenced to the different home settings in which they are performed. Each of these settings can be further delineated, as can the respective required skills. For example, the kitchen has numerous subenvironments such as the refrigerator, the oven, and the sink. Each of these subenvironments has associated with it numerous skills. Skills that are associated with the refrigerator include cleaning, conducting an inventory of what to buy, proper food storage, and so forth.

Another way in which to assess the skills that are necessary to function within an environment is to construct a daily timeline consisting of general activities, the settings in which each occurs, and skills that are required to successfully complete each activity. Figure 15-2 depicts such a time line for domestic and employment activities associated with a typical workweek. The activities actually correspond to time segments in which certain skills are generally utilized. These skills can then be delineated into subskills. The timetable can be advantageous when scheduling skill training. Specific adjustments in the skills and order of activities are of course made, depending on settings and the individual learner. Weekend activities and exceptions to the daily routine (for example, traveling to medical or dental appointments) need also to be evaluated. The time line lends itself to assessment as well as to the planning of instruction. The importance of mobility within and between all activities is also depicted. Mobility is discussed in greater detail below.

Assessing the Learner's Skills

Assessing learners' levels of skills can be done in numerous ways. There are many instruments available that measure general competence across domestic and other independent living skill areas. The Independent Living Screening Test (Schalock 1975) measures skills in personal maintenance, clothing care, home maintenance, food preparation, time management, social behavior, community utilization, communication, and functional academics. The American Association of Mental Deficiency Adaptive Behavior Checklist (Lambert et al. 1975) is a somewhat more general instrument that is commonly used for eligibility purposes.

Table 15-4. Domestic and Home-Living Activities and Skills

Safety Skills
1. Simple first aid
2. Use of phone for emergencies (for example, fire, police, physician)
3. Avoiding hazardous substances and activities
4. Requesting assistance when necessary

General Housekeeping or Maintenance Skills
1. Dusting
2. Vacuuming
3. Mopping
4. Sweeping
5. Emptying trash in appropriate receptacle
6. Cleaning windows
7. Changing light bulbs and fuses
8. Caring for and maintaining equipment

Clothing, Care and Use
1. Sorting, washing, and drying clothes
2. Ironing
3. Folding
4. Putting clothes in appropriate storage
5. Mending
6. Selecting weather-appropriate clothes
7. Selecting color- or pattern-coordinated clothes
8. Selecting age-appropriate clothes
9. Dressing

Bathroom Activities
Personal care
1. Washing face and hands
2. Bathing and drying
3. Washing hair
4. Brushing teeth
5. Brushing hair
6. Shaving
7. Using deodorant
8. Menstrual care
9. Using the toilet

Cleaning
1. Washing tub or shower, sink
2. Scouring toilet
3. Cleaning mirror
4. Mopping
5. Storing supplies

Bedroom Activities or Skills
1. Making bed
2. Changing bedclothes regularly
3. Engaging in solitary leisure activities
4. Dressing for bed
5. Sleeping
6. Cleaning room

Kitchen Skills
Food preparation
1. Selecting appropriate foods
2. Following a recipe
3. Measuring
4. Using utensils (for example, spatula, mixing spoon)
5. Using appliances
6. Using a stove
7. Setting the table

Kitchen Organization
1. Identifying needed kitchen supplies for purchase
2. Categorizing food groups for storage (for example, freezer foods, canned goods, refrigerator foods)
3. Storing dishes, pans, utensils, and supplies

Meal planning
1. Identifying food groups
2. Planning menus of nutritious combinations of food
3. Selecting appropriate recipes

Clean-up
1. Clearing table
2. Disposing of trash
3. Storing leftovers
4. Washing and drying dishes
5. Returning dishes to appropriate storage places
6. Scouring sink and cleaning counters
7. Sweeping
8. Mopping floor

Eating
1. Using utensils (for example, spoon, fork, knife, cup)
2. Using napkin
3. Passing food dishes
4. Serving appropriate portions
5. Using table manners
6. Communicating food needs or preferences

Living Room-Family Room Activities or Skills
1. Socializing with others
2. Engaging in leisure activities such as operating and watching television, operating record player, and operating radio
3. Cleaning (listed under General Housekeeping)

Yard Care Skills
1. Grass mowing
2. Pruning
3. Shoveling snow
4. Planting
5. Weeding
6. Watering

Adapted from Wehman et al. 1985b.

Domestic activity	Rise→	Personal care→	Breakfast→	Home-to-work→ Work-to-home	Work→	Dinner→	Housekeeping→ chores	Recreation→ leisure	Retire
Home/work settings	Bedroom	Bathroom/ bedroom	Kitchen- dining room	Personal or public transportation	Place of employment	Kitchen/ dining room	All rooms/ yard	Living room/ den/yard/ own room	Bedroom/ bathroom
Sample skills	• get up (on time)	• undress • shower/bathe • make bed	• prepare food • eat • brush/floss • shave/make-up • use toilet • select clothes • dress	• leave on time/arrive • drive • clean up • cab (money use) • walk • ride, bicycle • pay fare	• perform job • socialize • take bus • self-care	• prepare food • set table • eat • clean-up	• vacuum • wash windows • launder • store foods • take out trash • recycle • inventory supplies	• operate T.V./stereo • play games (cards, board games) • socialize • read • write letters	• personal care • dressing for bed • setting alarm • sleeping

Mobility

Figure 15-2. A time line of weekly domestic and employment activities with corresponding settings and sample skills. The mobility arrows depict movement between and within activities.

Learners' skill deficits can also be assessed in relation to the ecologic inventory described previously, and even more specifically with regard to specific task analyses, which are described below. Both of these options yield more information in regard to identifying target skills. It is most beneficial to develop task analyses and use them for assessment in the target setting in which the skill will be taught.

Prioritized Skills

Skills need to be prioritized with respect to their importance to the individual's independent living status. For instance, gardening skills are not as crucial to maintaining status within the community as is personal hygiene, assuming one can or has support in acquiring groceries. Given the time it will take to teach some skills and the number of skills that there are to teach many individuals, it is important in prioritizing skills to consider the frequency with which a skill will be used, the effect it will have on the person's community status, the cost (in time and materials) of teaching the skill, and whether the skill will be maintained once instruction has been withdrawn.

Task Analyze Skills

Task analysis is the breaking down of a skill into a sequence or chain of component responses that together make up the skill. A task analysis of bed making is presented in Table 15-5. Conducting a task analysis involves actually performing the task in the target setting and writing down the steps as they are performed. In addition, the task analysis should be validated by consulting experts and written documents such as manuals (particularly regarding safe use of appliances, equipment); field testing the task analysis with experts and learners; and modifying the task analysis based on field testing (for example, estimate extraneous steps, add adaptive devices) (Cuvo and Davis 1981).

Providing Task Analytic Instruction

Task analytic instruction involves assessment or probing, the training format, and prompting procedures.

Probing. A learner's skill at performing each step in a task analysis is determined through the use of task analytic assessment in the form of probe data. Probes are typically conducted one to three times before the initial instruction session to determine the extent of the person's skill in relation to the component steps of the skill. These preintervention probes are also called a baseline. Table 15-5 includes probe instructions for a bed making task analysis. This same data collection form is used throughout instruction. Probes are typically taken before instructional sessions. This procedure allows the trainer to assess maintenance of the learned responses from one day to the next or across numerous days, depending on the frequency of sessions. Probes are also conducted on a regular (once per week or month) basis after the skill has been established until the trainer is confident that the skill has been established and is being maintained. The general sequence for conducting a probe is to

1. Set up the task.
2. Provide the initial cue, or instruction.
3. Allow a specified period for the learner to respond (for example, 5 seconds).
4. Score a plus for each step correctly completed.
5. Score a minus for an incorrect or no response within the specified time period, complete the step.
6. Deliver a prompt for the next step.

Training Format. Task-analyzed skills can be taught from beginning to end, which is referred to as simultaneous instruction or a whole task approach. Each trial involves training across all steps in the task.

Table 15-5. Task Analytic Assessment of Bed Making

Probe instructions: Place chair or bed along side, and start with partially made bed (sheet, blanket, and spread pulled down, wrinkled) and bed pushed into wall, pajamas under pillow. Give instruction: "(*Name*), make the bed." Allow 5 seconds for a response. If correct response, record (+). If incorrect response or no response, record (−) and complete the step for student, and proceed to the next step. Do not prompt or reinforce.

Teacher: _____ Student: _____ Date: _____ Environment: Home/School Bedroom Instructional Cue: _____ _____ "Make the bed" Making Partial Bed						
1. Pull bed from wall enough to walk around						
2. Place pillow and pajamas on chair, other bed, or dresser						
3. Pull top sheet with both hands to head of bed so it is straight						
4. Smooth						
5. Pull blanket with both hands to head of bed so it is straight						
6. Smooth						
7. Pull spread with both hands to head of bed so it is straight						
8. Smooth up to extra spread						
9. Grasp edge, spread both hands, and fold down from head to make a 10- to 17-inch space						
10. Smooth spread on other side						
11. Get pajamas, fold in half, and place in pillow space						
12. Get pillow, place in space, with lower edge on spread fold						
13. Smooth pillow						
14. Grasp spread edge with both hands and pull up over pillow						
15. Tuck up under pillow with edge of hand						
16. Smooth spread top and side on near side of bed						
17. Go to other side, smooth top and side						
18. Push bed back against wall						

From Wehman et al. (1985b)

Forward chaining involves teaching the first step in the task analysis to a specified criterion (for example, three correct consecutive responses with no prompting), then adding the second step such that a correct response must include both steps 1 and 2, training that to criterion, and so on. This is useful when tasks are long.

Backward chaining starts with the last step in the task analysis and trains to criterion, then adds the second to the last step. A correct response then consists of the last two steps in the task, and so on. This approach allows for task completion on every trial and is particularly useful for individuals who have yet to learn to delay gratification across longer periods of time.

Simultaneous instruction and chaining can be combined for skills that can be divided into distinct sets of steps, such as cleaning a kitchen (for example, put away food, put dishes in dishwasher, wipe table). In this format, the sets, or clusters, are individually taught using a simultaneous method and are chained together as the student acquires each cluster.

Prompting.   There are two general approaches to prompting of responses during instruction: system of least prompts and time delay.

The system of least prompts involves delivering the least intrusive prompt that results in a correct response. This continuum of least prompts includes verbal prompting (requests, instructions, questions); modeling (performing the step or task once, then requesting the learner to perform it); gestural prompting (pointing or shadowing, that is, moving hand next to, but not touching, the student's hand as the student performs a step); physical prompting (guiding the learner through the step). Also, stimulus or visual prompts (color coding, picture, or other redundant cues) may be used. Table 15-6 depicts a backward chaining procedure using the system of least prompts for teaching the bed-making task in Table 15-5. This same

prompting sequence can be utilized in either a whole task or forward chaining format.

The key components of a program format, shown in Table 15-6, include the program objective, which includes a *context* (a partially made bed), the *performance* (student will make the bed), and a *criterion* (100% accuracy for three consecutive sessions); rationale; behavior change procedure, including the *training format* (backward chaining) and description of the *prompting procedure*; data collection method for *baseline* and *intervention*; reinforcement *types* and *schedules*; criterion for success (that is, for adding additional steps); and maintenance and generalization procedures. These components are important to any task analytic instruction.

In time delay, one controlling prompt is typically used throughout the training sessions. The prompt is selected on the basis that it is the least intrusive prompt that will result in a correct response across *all* steps in the task analysis. In time delay, the initial trial of learning involves a 0-second delay, in which the initial task request (for example, "Make the bed") is made and immediately followed by a prompt (for example, verbal or model) to demonstrate the step. This is intended to reduce the chance of initial errors. Each step is subsequently prompted in this fashion during the initial session. There are two types of time delays that apply to subsequent sessions: constant and progressive.

In constant time delay sessions, a delay interval is selected as in the system of least prompts (for example, 5 seconds). The controlling prompt, such as a model of the step, is provided at the end of the interval if the student has not initiated a correct or incorrect response. In progressive time delay, the delay interval increases across training sessions, depending upon student progress (for example, from 1 second in the first two sessions to 3 seconds for session three, 4 seconds for session four, and so forth until a specified delay period is reached). An easy-to-follow overview of

Table 15-6. Program Format

Time: *7:30 a.m. at home, 10:00 a.m. at school*
Student(s): *Mike*
Name of Program: *Bed making/Partial*

Specific program objective: Given a partially made bed, the student will make the bed with 100% accuracy according to a task analysis for that skill during probe conditions for three consecutive sessions.

Rationale: Bed making is a required skill for independent or supervised community living and has been identified as a priority in the student's present home setting. Also, bed making may be useful in a vocational setting (for example, housekeeping).

Student characteristics that:

1. assist:
2. hinder:

Behavior change procedures: Up to eight trials should be conducted daily. Use backward chaining procedure; complete all steps in task analysis but the final step.

1. Give the instructional cue, "(Name), make the bed."
2. Wait 3 seconds for self-initiation of the final step in the task analysis (for example, Push bed back against wall).
3. If correctly self-initiated, record (+).
4. If incorrect or no response within 3 seconds, provide a verbal prompt (for example, "(Name), Push the bed back against the wall").
5. If correct performance follows the verbal prompt within 3 seconds, reinforce and record (V), and begin again.
6. If incorrect or no response within 3 seconds of the verbal prompt, provide a model plus the verbal prompt (for example, "(Name), push the bed back against the wall like this. Now you try.").
7. If correct performance follows the model, prompt within 3 seconds, reinforce and record (M), and begin again.
8. If incorrect or no response within 3 seconds of model, prompt, provide

physical and verbal prompt, reinforce and record (P), and begin task again.

When student has met criterion (three consecutive unprompted correct responses) on the final step in the task analysis, begin training on the next-to-last step in combination with the final step (for example, Smooth other side's top and side, then push bed back against the wall) using the same prompting procedures. Reinforcement should be delivered **only** after completion of the final step regardless of the number of steps involved in the chain. A new step should be added when criterion is met on each combination of steps.

Data collection method:

1. Baseline/Probe: Probe at onset of each session.
   a. Give instructions, "(Name), make the bed."
   b. Wait 3 seconds for response.
   c. Record (+) for correct response.
   d. Record (−) for incorrect or no response within 3 seconds and complete the step for the student.
   e. Proceed through all steps in the task analysis using these procedures.
2. Intervention: Record (+) for a correct response, or the appropriate symbol for the prompt level needed for a correct response (V, M, P). Run 1 to 9 trials per session, depending on step in task analysis being trained.

Reinforcement—type(s) and schedule(s): Social praise upon completion of each trial.

Criterion for success: Three consecutive independently corrected responses on steps trained will result in addition of a new step for training.

Maintenance and generalization procedures: Evaluate performance across settings and trainers. Maintain in his home through weekly contact with parents and provide parents with a simple checklist to evaluate performance.

From Wehman et al. (1985b)

the time delay method is provided by Schuster and Griffen (1990).

Regardless of the format or prompting procedure used in instructional programs, special attention should be given to teaching functional skills in their respective target settings, to providing realistic simulations when target settings cannot be accessed, and to using natural reinforcers, whether alone or in conjunction with supplementary rewards.

☐ Case 15-1: Teaching Microwave Cooking to an Adolescent Labeled as Severely Retarded

◻ Participant and Setting

Jenny is a 13-year-old adolescent with an educational label of severe mental retardation. Her expressive language skills are limited to some use of manual signing. Her self-care skills are good in the area of personal hygiene, partially because of the support she has received from her parents, with whom she lives. The training was conducted at their home before Jenny left for school.

◻ Rationale

Microwave ovens are relatively common in today's households. They have an advantage over conventional ovens in that they are safer; they have no hot surfaces and always shut themselves off. The likelihood of starting fires or producing toxic fumes is virtually eliminated with their use. Although prepackaged microwave food products can be expensive, many are not. They are comparable in price to their conventional oven counterparts. Learning how to cook simple, inexpensive meals in microwave ovens may assist individuals with severe disabilities to function more independently within their communities. Jenny's parents are excited to have her move into a supported living setting when she reaches adult age. They are aware that independent living skills should be established before that time to help facilitate the transition.

◻ Task Analysis

The task analysis (Table 15-7) was developed in Jenny's kitchen by the trainer, with the help of Jenny's parents. The steps in the task analysis were specifically referenced to the microwave oven in Jenny's kitchen, a common brand with digital touch controls. The two frozen microwave breakfasts selected were those that Jenny commonly eats. Because scalding steam can be released when microwaved products are unsealed, a safety component was added to the task analysis: a fork through the covering on the food tray (steps 7 and 8) before putting the tray in the oven. In addition, the task analysis included the use of potholders whenever Jenny took food out of the oven or put food into it. Even though there was no danger associated with putting cold foods into the oven, it was felt by her parents and the trainer that always using potholders would prevent any possible burns that might occur if Jenny made an error in discriminating putting in from taking out. Also, consistent use of potholders might transfer to other dangerous scenarios (for example, picking up a hot casserole or microwaved tray at the request of someone who thought it was cold).

◻ Teaching Procedure

Baseline probes on the entire task indicated that Jenny required assistance beginning with step 3, closing the freezer door after picking out a breakfast box. To provide two trials per day, two meals had to be cooked. The first meal Jenny cooked was eaten by one of her parents. The trials were conducted each day using a constant time delay procedure. The controlling prompt was a verbal prompt with physical guidance. The delay time was set at 3 seconds. During 3-second delay sessions, Jenny was provided with an initial task request, "Jenny, make your breakfast." Correct responses

Table 15-7. Task Analysis of Safe Microwave Cooking of Frozen Breakfasts

1. Open freezer.
2. Select box from door:
   —pancakes with sausage or
   —waffles
3. Close door.
4. Walk to counter by microwave oven.
5. Open box.
6. Take out tray and set on counter.
7. Get fork from drawer (close drawer).
8. Poke fork through tray covering twice (set fork down).
9. Get two pot holders from drawer (close drawer).
10. Open oven door to at least 90°.
11. Using pot holders, place tray in center of oven.
12. Place pot holders on counter.
13. Close oven door.
14. Push "cook" on oven.
15. Find cooking time on back of box.
16. Push numbers on oven.
17. Push "start" on oven.
18. Set table (separate task analysis).
19. Open oven door when timer sounds (beeps).
20. Pick up pot holders.
21. Using pot holders, take out tray and set on counter.
22. While holding tray with left hand with pot holder, pull off cover with right hand.
23. Discard cover and box in trash.
24. Using both pot holders, place tray at kitchen table.
25. Put away pot holders (close drawer).
26. Return to table and eat.

were praised. After a correct response or the delivery of a controlling prompt (for example, trainer said "Jenny, open the box" while providing the minimal physical guidance necessary to produce the response), the trainer would deliver the controlling prompt for the next response if Jenny did not initiate the response within 3 seconds. This procedure was repeated until all steps were performed or prompted. Probes were collected twice per week by cooking a third breakfast prior to the day's training session. Step 18, set table, was actually a separate task analysis of 13 steps. Setting the table while the food was cooking seemed an appropriate use of time that Jenny would otherwise have spent waiting. It also decreased the likelihood that she might leave the kitchen and not be able to hear the timer sound. These steps were taught separately from those in the cooking task analysis because the training sessions for table setting lasted longer than the cooking time.

□ **Results**

Jenny was able to reach criterion (three consecutive correct sessions of two trials each) within 12 sessions on all steps except pushing the correct numbers on the touch control (step 16). This step was trained separately by having Jenny match the numbers on enlarged copies of the instructions to those on the touch control. The size of the enlarged instructions was gradually reduced until Jenny was able to complete the step while using the actual packages.

Mobility Skills and Transportation

Orientation is the ability to establish one's position in relation to the environment. Mobility involves moving safely from one point to another (Lowenfeld 1973). Orientation and mobility training was originally developed to assist individuals with visual impairments. Mobility specialists provide training in the use of aids such as electronic canes and in travel within the community. Over the last two decades there has been a growing realization that orientation and (particularly) mobility training is appropriate for members of other disability groups as well, including individuals with multiple or severe disabilities. There has, as a result, been a significant amount of research and training in the area of mobility training. Numerous studies have demonstrated that severely disabled individuals can learn mobility skills such as street crossing (Matson 1980) and riding buses (Sowers et al. 1979).

One's mobility in the community includes movement within and between settings. Examples of mobility within a setting include movement from the bedroom to the bathroom, from a wheelchair to the toilet, from downstairs to the upstairs, from gymnasium to the locker room, or from one's work station or office to the cafeteria. Mobility between settings might include travel from home to school or work and vice versa, from the grocery store to home, from the park to a shopping mall, or from a restaurant to the theater.

Mobility can take the following forms:

1. *Ambulation within or between settings.* This category includes, primarily, walking or running. It also includes partial ambulation or movement within a setting, such as sliding or pulling oneself along, transferring oneself from a wheelchair to bed, or crawling. Ambulation can be accomplished either independently or with assistance. Forms of assistance include standard or electronic canes, crutches, prosthetic limbs or appendages, guide dogs, sighted guides, and physical adaptations (for example, railings and bars) or people who give partial physical support.

2. *Conveyance within or between settings.* Conveyance is a means of transportation in which one is carried from one place to another (Wehman et al. 1985a). This can be accomplished through the independent or assisted use of adapted or nonadapted automobiles, vans, motorcycles, scooters, bicycles and tricycles, manual and electric wheelchairs, or through being lifted or carried. Public transportation is another means of conveyance and includes buses, trains (including subways

and elevated trains), planes, elevators, escalators, and taxis.

Barriers to Mobility

Physical and Social Barriers

Legislation such as the Architectural Barriers Act of 1968, section 504 of the Rehabilitation Act of 1973 (P.L. 93-112), and subsequent 1974 amendments (P.L. 93-516) has resulted in greater access to the community by individuals with disabilities. Even though section 504 requires that federally funded programs "not discriminate against handicapped persons," it does not require access to the community at large. Still, as a result of this legislation, public awareness regarding physical barriers has increased and many improvements have been made. Many building owners in the private sector have installed ramps, widened bathroom stalls, lowered telephones and drinking fountains, and made other adaptations to assist individuals with physical disabilities. Some television networks offer closed captioned news or other programming for persons with profound hearing losses or deafness. Although such gains are encouraging, many physical barriers still remain in virtually any community. For example, steps, small bathrooms and narrow aisles and doorways typify many restaurants and other businesses. There are, in addition to these physical barriers, attitudinal barriers such as the overprotectiveness and lowered expectations of some parents and professionals toward their children and clients who happen to have handicapping conditions. Barriers to participation in normal activities are impositions on the rights of persons with disabilities to experience the same risks as do nonhandicapped individuals. Mobility within one's home and within and between different settings in the community (and between communities) is fundamental to the expression of this right to risk.

Lack of Transportation

The availability of transportation has been identified as one of the most important factors in transition planning (Bikson and Bikson 1981). Without it, employment, community-based training, generic services, and many other aspects of one's community become inaccessible. Liebert and colleagues (1990) found the availability of transportation to be a key factor in the attainment and maintenance of employment by a sample of physically disabled youth.

As important as transportation is to those making the transition to and living in the community, it is an equally crucial element in the preparation for community living of many school-aged people with disabilities. Such a simple service, though, is also one of the most difficult to obtain on any consistent basis. There are both fiscal and philosophic reasons for this. Many administrators (and many teachers, parents, and professionals) are unlikely to support programs that they do not consider integral to their respective missions. Unfortunately, community-based instruction is not part of the perceived mission of enough school personnel. For example, it is not uncommon to hear that a public school administrator has denied a special education teacher use of the school van for community-based training in banking or laundry skills because "we just can't afford 'field trips' all the time." The importance of teaching skills to some individuals in the community settings in which they will be used, such as teaching in restaurants or grocery stores those functional academics (for example, money skills) that can be utilized in those same restaurants or grocery stores, is sometimes lost in well meant but misplaced overprotectiveness or in the shuffle of an "excellence in education" program that stresses academics while overlooking individual needs. Unfortunately, although classroom-based academics allow many individuals with disabilities to be competitive and upwardly mobile

once they reach the postschool world, they are not in the best interests of all disabled individuals' futures in their communities.

Keys to Community Mobility

Resources and Supports

For individuals to receive training in mobility skills, a system of adequate resources and supports need to be in place. This is the case whether going to, coming from, or being at home, school, work or in other community environments (for example, stores, doctors' offices, recreation centers, or parks). Some of the resources and personal supports that individuals may require to achieve mobility include:

1. Adequate public and private or private nonprofit transportation services, including buses and vans equipped with lifts and seating adaptations.

2. State or local subsidies for transportation services and for conveyance and ambulation equipment (for example, vans and buses for the disabled, wheelchairs, guide dogs, prosthetics). Subsidies can be provided to individuals in the form of reimbursements for purchased services or equipment.

3. State or local equipment centers from which disabled individuals check out needed mobility aids (and other equipment such as augmentative communication devices and adapted furniture). These centers function much like a public library except that individuals keep the equipment as long as it is needed. There are very few of these; concerned individuals need to lobby for or organize them.

4. Orientation or mobility instruction.

5. Mobility assistance as needed (for example, paid or volunteer personnel who assist in transfers to and from wheelchairs or who supervise travel in the community).

6. Support from parents, advocates, volunteers, organizations, and community groups (for example, local chapters of the Association for Retarded Children, Chamber of Commerce, churches). Support may be in the form of organization of services, financial assistance, supervision, lobbying for improvements and expansion of supports and companionship.

It is important to note that some individuals may always require some form of physical assistance in their mobility, whether within or between settings. This need should not affect their places in line to receive any of the services and supports listed above. They have, as much as anyone, the right to participate in their communities, even if they are only able to engage in partial participation (Brown et al. 1979b). Partial participation can involve walking with support, touching the wheel of one's wheelchair even if not able to move it, or even laughter. These and other supports, such as those associated with the supported living models discussed earlier, should be geared to facilitate whatever level of participation an individual can accomplish.

Mobility Instruction

The development and implementation of instructional programs to assist individuals in acquiring specific mobility skills involve the same steps as those described for domestic and community skills. These are described below with specific reference to community mobility.

Assessing Present or Potential Settings. An essential aspect of mobility instruction is an ecologic inventory of the mobility skill requirements of current or potential environments as they pertain to the individual being served. These environments include present or future homes, schools, places of employment, stores, recreational facilities, one's immediate neighborhood, convey-

ances, and routes between the identified settings. The inventory should answer the following questions:

- What are the subenvironments of each setting in which the person functions?
- What are the possible modes of public and other forms of transportation between the settings?
- What are the subenvironments related to available forms of transportation?
- What mobility skills are needed in each subenvironment?
- What mobility supports are currently available in each setting?

Assessing Learner Skills. After it has been determined through the ecologic inventory what skills are needed in each environment and corresponding subenvironments, an assessment of the learner determines which skills are deficient. For example, can the learner fasten his or her seat belt? Is the learner able to move from the kitchen to the living room? Is the learner able to take a bus to work? What level of assistance is required for the individual to perform each of the skills that have been identified in the inventory?

Prioritizing the Skills. Those mobility skills that are most important to maintaining independence from more restrictive settings should be taught first. For one individual that might result in learning how to take the bus to work, whereas for someone else it may require an instructional program to teach movement within his or her residence, such as transference from bed to a wheelchair.

Task Analyze the Skills. Examples of task analyses for crossing the street and riding in an automobile are presented in Tables 15-8 and 15-9, respectively. These analyses are specific to a certain street and its subenvironments (for example, no light or signs, on-street parking) and to a specific

Table 15-8. Task Analysis with Decision Rules for Street Crossing at an Uncontrolled Intersection

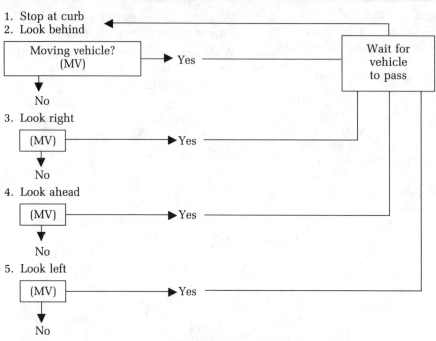

1. Stop at curb
2. Look behind

        Moving vehicle? (MV) → Yes → Wait for vehicle to pass

        No

3. Look right

        (MV) → Yes

        No

4. Look ahead

        (MV) → Yes

        No

5. Look left

        (MV) → Yes

        No

6. Walk across street quickly while watching for moving vehicles.
7. Step on curb.

model of automobile and its subenvironments (two-door, passenger side back seat, post-type lock). Task analyses should always be developed using the conditions of the real environments in which an individual functions. In addition to these, however, general case task analyses and instruction using different but similar settings and conditions (for example, streets with signs versus no signs, different levels of traffic, cars with different locks and seat belts, front seat versus back seat) can assist in the maintenance and generalization of the learned skills.

The task analysis in Table 15-8 is accompanied by a flow chart of decision rules that apply to the steps in the analysis. If a moving vehicle is observed approaching the intersection, the student is to reinitiate the sequence of looking (steps 2 to 5).

This task analysis could be changed so that the sequence would be restarted only when moving vehicles are observed to be approaching from the left or right or if a turn is indicated. This sequence will depend on the functioning level of the student, the intersection (for example, speed limit), and other factors. This particular task analysis is designed to "err" on the safe side. Such considerations exemplify the importance of tailoring the task analysis to the setting demands as well as to the characteristics of individual learners.

Providing Task Analytic Instruction. The same procedures for conducting task analytic assessment and instruction that were described previously apply whether teaching domestic, leisure, recreational, vocational, or mobility skills.

Table 15-9. Task Analysis for Entering and Riding in an Automobile

Step 1: Locate car.
Step 2: Find door handle that corresponds to riding position in car (passenger side).
Step 3: Grasp door handle with four fingers.
Step 4: Put thumb on handle button.
Step 5: Press button.
Step 6: Pull door open (until it catches in open position).
Step 7: Walk up to car seat.
Step 8: Lift left leg (bend knee) and swing it into car.
Step 9: Twist trunk to right (90°).
Step 10: Sit down on seat (bend right knee).
Step 11: Lift right leg and swing into car.
Step 12: Lean out of car.
Step 13: Grasp inside door handle (right hand).
Step 14: Pull door shut.
Step 15: Reach across body with left arm.
Step 16: Locate lock with left hand.
Step 17: Push lock down.
Step 18: Grasp left seat belt attachment (left hand).
Step 19: Grasp right seat belt attachment (right hand).
Step 20: Buckle seat belt.
Step 21: Maintain seated position throughout trip.

From Wehman et al. (1985b)

□ Case 15-2: Teaching Bus Riding Skills to a Visually Impaired Man with Challenging Behaviors

□ Participant, Rationale, and Settings

Will is a 32-year-old man who is legally blind in his left eye, with a mild impairment in his right eye. He is able to ambulate independently although his visual impairment causes him to be somewhat uncoordinated in his gross motor movement; he has difficulty in judging dis-

tances. At the time of the implementation of the mobility program, Will displayed some challenging behaviors, including intermittent verbal and physical aggression that occurred primarily when Will was having difficulties in demonstrating required or requested skills. Because his parents were apprehensive about Will's potential for aggression in frustrating situations, he had not been given instruction on how to travel independently to work each day on the bus. Gaining competence in bus riding was viewed as crucial to his being able to maintain employment status over an extended period of time because this was the most stable form of transportation available to him. He had up until that point been totally dependent on his parents for transportation. His parents understood that they could not be expected to provide transportation indefinitely.

Will was employed doing benchwork tasks in a skills-training environment. He was earning a training (that is, below minimum) wage at the time of the training, which was conducted on his bus route to and from work.

□ Task Analysis

The task analysis was developed by Will's mobility specialist trainer by riding the bus to and from Will's work site. The task analysis is presented in Table 15-10. (Notice that it is specific to his route.) A task analysis was also made and Will taught on going to work each morning. Different landmarks were used, and the order of the steps was reversed where appropriate. Other than that the task analysis and training procedure were the same. Modifications were made to accommodate his visual impairment. These included the use of landmarks large enough for Will to see while riding, a request made to the bus driver to tell him if he had the correct bus (in case he could not see the destination sign on the bus), and a request to the driver to remind him of his stop.

Table 15-10. Task Analysis: Riding and Transferring Buses from Work to Home Utilizing Landmarks

1. Select change for bus ride before leaving work.
2. Go to bus stop—stand 2 feet from curb at bus stop.
3. Motion to approaching bus.
4. When bus door opens, ask driver "Is this the Mononu bus?"
    a. If answer is "no," say "Thank you, this is not my bus" and wait for next bus (step 3).
    b. If answer is "yes," proceed to step 5.
5. Holding rail, enter bus and pay fare.
6. Say to bus driver "I need a transfer please."
7. Wait for and take transfer.
8. Say to bus driver "Would you please tell me when we get to the Buckeye bus?"
9. Thank driver.
10. Walking toward back of bus while grasping seat or overhead rail, sit in first front facing window seat in empty left row (left is facing back of bus).
    a. If there is no empty row all the way back, sit in any aisle seat.
11. Watch for landmarks on right of bus (facing forward).
    a. Walgreens
    b. McDonalds
    c. West Town Mall sign
12. When West Town Mall sign comes into view, ring bell to signal driver to stop by pushing signal button or pulling signal cord (depending on bus type).
    a. If sitting in aisle seat while next to someone, say "Excuse me" and reach up or over to signal driver.
    b. If driver says "Mononu," prepare to leave.
13. Wait for bus to stop.
14. Exit bus by back door.
    a. If sitting by window and next to someone, say "Excuse me" before standing to exit bus.
15. Repeat steps 3 to 10 except:
    4. When bus door opens, ask driver "Is this the Buckeye bus?"
    5. Holding rail, enter bus and hand driver the transfer pass.
16. Watch for landmarks on right of bus.
17. When Speedway sign comes into view, signal driver to stop.
18. Repeat steps 12a to 14 (for 12, landmark is Speedway station, and for 12b, driver will say "Buckeye").
19. Turn right after exiting bus (toward Speedway service station).
20. Walk to corner.
21. Turn left.
22. Walk to next intersection.
23. Turn right and cross street (separate task analysis).
24. Walk home (fourth house).

□ **Teaching Procedure**

Baseline analysis indicated that Will initially needed assistance on almost all of the steps in the sequence. The trainer met Will each day after work. Training began at the point when Will was leaving his work area to go home. A simultaneous instruction procedure with a progressive time delay was utilized during the training. After the initial zero-second time delay in which the trainer verbally prompted Will through each step in the task analysis, time delays progressed from 2 to 4 seconds across the training days. The controlling prompt was a combination of a verbal plus a modeling prompt. In this way the trainer would, after the specified delay period (for example, if Will did not initiate the step within 2 seconds of the last step), model the step after verbally stating the step. On step 5, for example, the trainer prompted Will by saying "Will, get on the bus like this" while modeling how to enter the bus and put the money in the fare box. Will was then prompted to "Get on, Will," and was praised (for example, "nice job!") for completion of the target step. Will was then given the specified time delay period to initiate the next response (for example, 2 seconds) before the next step was prompted, and so on through all of the steps. The procedure required that the trainer ride the bus with Will (and take the next bus home). The trainer had informed the bus company driver who regularly drove Will's routes of the basics of the training program and rationale. (Such communication is generally met with great willingness to cooperate.)

□ Results

The length of the time delay (up to 4 seconds in the latter days of training) did not seem to hinder the bus service; almost all of the delays occurred while the bus was moving. Will acquired the steps rapidly, reaching a criterion of three consecutive Monday-through-Wednesday trips (this permitted the trainer to evaluate maintenance of the skill over the weekend) with 100% accuracy on all steps (that is, no prompts were delivered and all steps were self-initiated) in less than 3 weeks. The landmarks, although helping Will to locate his stops, also served to reduce any inappropriate socializations (for example, talking to people who did not want to talk, excessive greetings) because he needed to attend to the landmarks. The bus driver and confederates of the trainer (individuals who observed Will after the trainer had faded herself from the instruction, but of whom Will was unaware) socially vali-

dated the program, reporting that Will was riding the bus independently and with only minimal occurrences of behavior that might be construed as socially questionable (some incongruent conversation). Conversational skills (including when not to converse) were targeted for subsequent instruction across relevant settings (for example, on the bus). Training on taking the bus to work was initiated after Will had reached the criterion on returning home. He reached this criterion by Wednesday of the second week of training (that is, after five days of prompts being required during training).

Transition, Collaboration, and Advocacy

It has been documented that students with disabilities are under-represented in vocational education programs during their school years (Owing and Stocking 1985). Cobb and Phelps (1983) indicated a deficit in career-related objectives in the individualized education programs (IEPs) of these students. In addition, collaboration between agencies in providing supports to make the successful transition from school to postschool employment has been found lacking (Rusch and Phelps 1987). Given that the overwhelming focus of transition planning has been on employment and that, even given this focus, the level of successful postschool work experiences of individuals with disabilities has been far less than acceptable, it is understandable that the independent living status of most members of this population is even less encouraging.

Recent legislation has mandated that transition goals be addressed in students' IEPs. One way to improve transition planning is through collaborative planning between agencies such as states' departments of vocational rehabilitation, vocational education programs, and special education and general education programs. Dick (1987) reported the efforts of a consortium of personnel from public school districts, private special education agencies, and vocational rehabilitation agencies. The teachers were given inservice training in vocational assessment terms, administration of assessment instruments, and interpretation of assessment results. As another means of collaboration, the teachers compiled a list of over 600 objectives from curricula such as Brolin's (1978), which was described previously. These were eventually compiled into a bank of objectives that contained four broad goals with a total of 24 objectives and numerous subobjectives under those. These goals are presented in Table 15-11. These goals were then used by a vocational evaluator to generate a list of vocational recommendation items that matched the language used in the bank of objectives. This list helped reduce confusion regarding the jargon employed by different professional groups. In addition, it afforded the opportunity for individuals to open a dialogue to establish future collaborative efforts such as coordinating services and delineating roles and responsibilities of teachers, evaluators, and other individuals responsible for the transition process. Table 15-12 outlines objectives and corresponding assessment instruments and available curricula related to the objectives. No evaluation of the quality of the particular assessment procedure or curriculum was offered; the list merely represented readily used or available programs. More severely disabled individuals should still be taught within the community as much as possible, and assessment of students' skills should be referenced to relevant present and future settings through ecologic inventories. The assessment, objective, and curriculum items in Table 15-12, however, are examples of a comprehensive system for identifying transition objectives and corresponding instruction.

An excellent model for developing collaboration among agencies, the community, families, and disabled individuals is that provided by Lombard (1989). Although this model is built primarily around organizing activities to assist school, agency, and other service providers and advocates to facilitate successful transitions from school to postschool employment, it is equally applicable to all areas of community functioning. The model consists of the following components, which can be viewed as a task analysis for developing a transition model in virtually any community. Each component is briefly described. Additional comments and suggestions are included.

Form a Steering Committee

A steering committee is a small group of individuals who will coordinate the formation of the transition model and form a core change team. Individuals on this committee should include representatives from school districts, agencies, and other service programs. An additional suggestion is to include highly visible community members who could stimulate publicity and garner additional support (for example, a political figure), as well as disabled persons or a parent or guardian of a disabled person.

Form a Core Change Team

This team is an expansion of the steering committee, and includes all members of the committee plus a combination of disabled individuals, their parents and guardians, rehabilitation personnel, administrators, individuals providing postsecondary services, medical personnel, vocational educators, and representatives from technical schools and colleges, social services, mental health services, and other agencies and interested parties. The function of this team is to coordinate the remaining components of the model. This coordination is vital to providing the full range of support services an individual requires to maintain status within the community. Without such collaboration, typical problems associated with uncoordinated services and

Table 15-11. Transitional Goals and Objectives

Bank of Objectives

Goal 1.0: Improve Daily Living Skills

Objectives:
1.1 Increase consumer skills and ability to handle money.
   1.1 Increase life reading skills.
   1.1 Increase life math skills.
   1.1 Improve purchasing and consumer skills.
   1.1 Improve budgeting skills.
1.2 Increase knowledge of foods and nutrition.
   1.2 Increase knowledge about food buying and planning.
   1.2 Practice food preparation.
1.3 Improve ability to maintain clothing.
1.4 Improve ability to select housing and manage a home.
   1.4 Improve ability to select housing.
   1.4 Improve ability to do home management.
1.5 Increase knowledge about community and government.
   1.5 Learn about community.
   1.5 Learn about government.
1.6 Increase awareness of leisure time and family activities.
1.7 Develop good health practices.
1.8 Improve mobility and traveling skills.

Goal 2.0: Improve Personal-Social Skills

Objectives:
2.1 Improve appearance.
2.2 Improve self-concept and awareness of emotions.
2.3 Improve verbal and written communication skills.
2.4 Improve information processing and problem solving.
2.5 Improve ability to interact with others.
2.6 Improve self-control.
2.7 Demonstrate appropriate male-female-friend social status.

Goal 3.0: Increase Prevocational Skills

Objectives:
3.1 Learn more about careers and work in preparation for jobs.
   3.1 Increase awareness about careers.
   3.1 Gather information about careers.
3.2 Develop a career plan.
3.3 Improve job-related communication skills.
   3.3 Improve job-related verbal communication.
   3.3 Improve job-related reading skills.
   3.3 Improve job-related writing skills.
3.4 Improve ability to do job-related math.
   3.4 Practice math related to jobs.
   3.4 Practice time and measurement related to jobs.
3.5 Improve perceptual motor skills related to occupations.

Goal 4.0: Increase Vocational Skills

Objectives:
4.1 Demonstrate skills needed to hunt for and acquire a job.
   4.1 Practice filling out applications.
   4.1 Demonstrate job interviewing.
   4.1 Demonstrate job hunting.
4.2 Know basics about equipment.
4.3 Improve needed job behaviors.
   4.3 Improve time on task.
   4.3 Improve following directions.
   4.3 Improve dealing with authority.
   4.3 Improve getting along with others.
   4.3 Improve accuracy of work.
   4.3 Improve job attitudes.
4.4 Learn advanced job knowledge/information.
4.5 Demonstrate ability to leave a job appropriately.

From Dick (1987)

Table 15-12. Sample of Transition Objectives with Assessment and Curriculum Materials

1.0 goal: Improve daily living skills
Objective 1.10: Increases consumer skills and ability to handle money

Assessment	Objectives	Curriculum
1.1.1 Life Reading Skills	1.1.1 Life Reading Skills	1.1.1 Life Reading Skills
Brigance Inventory of Essential Skills, section D—Functional Work Recognition	a. Read and use sale ads to locate used car, furniture, apartments, or houses for rent.	P—School Specialty Developing Everyday Reading Skills $3.25
Best Best—Reading and language arts section	b. Read and complete commonly used forms and applications.	Coping Skills—Using the Newspaper $1.95
	c. Read and interpret insurance terms.	
	d. Read newspaper for informational-consumer purposes.	
	e. Read directions on boxes.	
	f. Identify basic price labels, weights, measurements, expiration dates, and "in store" survival words.	
1.1.2 Life Math Skills	1.1.2 Life Math Skills	1.1.2 Life Math Skills
Brigance Inventory of Essential skills, section R—measurement, section S—metrics	a. Identify money and make change.	P—Weekly Reader Figure it out $2.30
	b. Know how to handle a paycheck.	Math That Pays $2.30
	c. Use the metric system related to shopping skills.	P—Janus Paychecks $3.30
	d. Interpret sale prices.	P—Publisher
	e. Interpret unit pricing of food items.	
	f. Understand monthly income including types of financial assistance.	

From Dick (1987)

Conduct Community Survey

This part of the model includes the identification of public school services and curricula, postsecondary training and employment options, and the continuum of adult support services. The support services that isolated service providers (for example, replication of services, or service voids) are likely to occur.

are integral to supported living and employment, as discussed earlier in this chapter, would be the target of such a survey. Surveys of recreation and leisure options and of supports, as well as of public transportation and supported mobility options, would also be needed. Table 15-13 is an example of a survey of public and private agencies and programs serving disabled individuals in Georgia. This survey was conducted by phone and personal interviews.

Table 15-13. Community Survey: Public and Private Agencies and Programs Serving Disabled Children, Youth, and Adults in Georgia

Agency/ Program	Responsibilities (as stated in interview)	Funding	Referred	Eligibility Requirements
Adult centered education	1. Prepare for GED 2. Teach basic reading and math (illiteracy).	State	By self or advocate	16 years and older drop-outs, age-outs
Youth detention center	1. Holding facility—detention—waiting for court date Hold up to 90 days 2. Short-term treatment • Academics • Socialization skills • Wilderness skills	State	By juvenile court system To youth services	Court assigned Juvenile
Youth Services	1. Treatment and rehabilitation 2. Alternative placement (16 years and younger) 3. 16 years and older Gainesville) • Provides on-the-job training • 6 to 8 months average on job • Probation until court sentence completed	State	By Courts, OTP, YDC To Kelly Diversified work programs (Warm Springs)	Committed by courts: 16 years and younger Committed by courts; 16 years and older drop-outs
Troubled Children Committee	1. "Trouble shooter" 2. Family intervention	State	By Youth Services	Consistent problems in schools or with court system Juvenile
JTPA	1. Private company receives up to one half of wages for placement of client. • 6 month requirement 2. Trainer—2 weeks on-the-job training	State and federal (grant programs)	By schools to companies in community	14 years and older Economic needs Handicapping condition Potential drop-out or has dropped out
Jobs for Georgia	1. 6 schools in state 2. State employee works with student (job specialist); serves as middle man between student and employer 3. Job specialist identifies 50 students; • Must place 80% • 6 months to place • Verbal contact every 2 weeks until placed	State Department of Labor	To companies in community	Graduating but not college bound
Division of Vocational Rehabilitation Services	1. Counselor works 1:1 • Sets up work experience in school setting (janitorial) • On-the-job training (e.g., florist, nursing home) 2. Work with family and school personnel 3. Teacher responsible for implementation within school setting	State and federal	By school or agencies To Athens Tech., colleges, companies in the community	16 yrs & older Disabilities

Some of the programs were identified as existing by the surveyors only after speaking to another agency or program. This survey, although not comprehensive, demonstrates what can be accomplished with little prior knowledge and with little time. The service providers were identified through the phone book or by referral from one agency or program to another, and only 1 to 2 hours per day over a 2-week-period were needed to complete the survey (including interviews). This information could also be compiled through a mailed survey. In-person interviews, however, provide exposure to the agencies or programs.

Develop Community Action Plan

A community action plan includes a plan to fill the voids in existing services (for example, mobility training, development of a home support model) by conducting training to familiarize parents with available services and how to access them, developing interagency collaboration and cooperation (for example, interagency service agreements regarding shared costs, delineation of responsibilities) and training school personnel to teach functional skills in all community living areas. Postschool service providers also need to develop these same skills.

Develop Plan for Individual Transition Process

This plan includes development of procedures for the in-school transition process, including the use of ecologic vocational surveys to identify skill strengths and deficits; the development of vocational and other transition goals (both within school and to the postschool world); the provision of instructional supports in vocational classes; and the identification of postschool follow-up procedures. This plan can easily be expanded beyond transition to employment concerns to include surveys, goals, instructional supports, and community follow-up procedures related to domestic, social, education-training, and recreation-leisure transitions.

Annual Evaluation of Transition Process

This part of the model employs follow-up of the status of students who have made the transition to the community to determine any voids in the transition process so that the difficulties can subsequently be remediated. Evaluation asks: Are the students who were transitioned under the model gainfully employed? Are they living independently at a rate comparable to that of their nondisabled peers? Are adequate supports available to maintain individuals in their jobs and homes? Is there a need for additional resources and services, what are they, and how do we expand the model to allocate and provide them?

Advocacy

When a model for collaborative transition planning is paired with functional curricula, community-based training objectives, and a system of supports to maintain the person in the community (regardless of his or her disability), postschool success rates will undoubtedly increase in the short run. There is, however, a need to provide ongoing support to individuals with disabilities to assist them in maintaining their community living status. Advocates can play a vital role by acting on behalf of disabled individuals to maintain current levels of support in some areas while establishing or increasing the level of support in others. Advocates can be just about anyone, including parents and relatives, coworkers, organization representatives, friends, service delivery personnel and professionals, other disabled persons, and the disabled person serving as self-advocate. Advocacy activities are equally varied. They can be on behalf of an individual with a disability or in the interests of disabled persons in general. Numerous types of advocacy activities are listed below.

1. Service related advocacy activities

- Communicating goals to teachers, parents, employers, and coworkers
- Coordinating services such as education or training, benefits, medical care, transportation, and recreation
- Taking an active role in transition planning, beginning as early as possible during or after the school years
- Training the individual at home, work, or in the community
- Training parents and others such as group home and apartment supervisors in such skills as performing ecologic inventories and task analytic instruction
- Delivering instruction or services related to any or all settings
- Providing emergency support related to health, transportation, and interpersonal factors

2. Politically related advocacy activities

- Demonstrating publicly on behalf of a person(s) with a disability
- Making demands
- Writing letters
- Developing newsletters and other communications
- Lobbying
- Boycotting businesses and organizations that are not accessible to or that support policies that discriminate against disabled individuals
- Litigating and providing or procuring legal advocacy
- Negotiating
- Providing model program demonstrations (Biklen 1979)

Advocates may in addition provide reinforcement to programs, politicians, teachers, and agencies for providing beneficial supports and for being advocates themselves. This reinforcement may take the form of public recognition, letters to their superiors, celebrations, and so forth.

Many advocates may lack the skills and the time to engage in all of the activities listed above. The professions, interests, and other commitments of advocates will determine the type and extent of their advocacy activities. Advocates should, however, be willing to commit whatever strengths they have in a consistent manner over some period of time, particularly if that involves forming a personal relationship with a person who happens to have a disability. Even advocates who have no skills related to the disabilities of the persons for whom they advocate can provide valuable support, whether related to daily survival (for example, grocery shopping, transportation) or given in the form of friendship.

Summary

Many individuals with disabilities require supports to maintain their independence from environments that are less than integrated settings within their respective communities. This chapter has looked at some of the barriers to community living and some solutions to overcoming those barriers. Supported living and employment models were identified as appropriate alternatives to a least restrictive environment conceptualization of community living because the latter discriminates against more severely disabled citizens by imposing a continuum-of-services approach on them. This continuum approach requires individuals to gain prerequisite skills, or be ready, before they can enjoy on any consistent basis those advantages the community has to offer. The skills that are most crucial to maintaining one's status in the community were identified, as were methods for assessing relevant settings for respective skill requirements. Task analytic assessment and instruction procedures were discussed, and teaching examples were provided. The importance of mobility to people's independence was emphasized, and instructional procedures and examples were described.

Finally, the importance of developing a collaborative transition and postschool service delivery model was stressed. Without cooperative efforts by all elements in the service planning and delivery process, service voids are likely to exist; this poses a threat to the community living status of individuals with disabilities. Advocacy was described as a means to insuring available services, as an impetus in developing needed ones, and as a service in and of itself.

Restrictive settings exist because our support resources are historically tied to restrictive settings. The redistribution of fiscal expenditures to support individuals with disabilities in community living arrangements and the formation of local transition and postschool service models, including those developed by the private sector, are considered necessary to the continued evolution of services for the disabled.

References

1. Affleck JQ, Edgar E, Levine P, Kortering L. Postschool status of students classified as mildly mentally retarded, learning disabled, or nonhandicapped: Does it get better with time? Education and Training in Mental Retardation. 25:315–324, 1990.
2. Baker BL, Seltzer GB, Seltzer MM. As Close As Possible: Community Residences for Retarded Adults. Boston, Little, Brown, 1977.
3. Biklen D. Community Imperative: A Refutation of All Arguments in Support of Deinstitutionalizing Anybody Because of Mental Retardation. Syracuse, Human Policy Press, 1979.
4. Bikson TA, Bikson TK. Functional Problems of the Visually Impaired: A Research Approach. Santa Monica, CA, Rowd Corp, 1981.
5. Brolin D. Life Centered Career Education: A Competency-Based Approach. Reston, VA, Council for Exceptional Children, 1978.
6. Brown L, Branston M, Humre-Nietupski S, Pumpian I, Certo N, Gruenwuld L. A strategy for developing chronological age appropriate and functional curricular content for severely handicapped and young adults. Journal of Special Education. 13:81–90, 1979a.
7. Brown L, Branston-McClean MB, Baumgart D, Vincent L, Falvey M, Schroder J. Using the characteristics of current and subsequent least restrictive environments in the development of curricular content for severely handicapped students. AAESPH Review. 4:407–424, 1979b.
8. Cobb RB, Phelps LA. Analyzing individualized education programs for vocational components: An exploratory study. Except Child. 50:63–66, 1983.
9. Copeland WC, Everson IA. Developing financial incentives for placement in the least restrictive alternative. In: Larkin KC, Bruininks RH. eds. Strategies for Achieving Community Integration of Developmentally Disabled Citizens. Baltimore, Paul Brookes, 1985.
10. Cuvo A, Davis P. Home living for developmentally disabled persons: Instructional design and evaluation. Exceptional Education Quarterly. 2:87–98, 1981.
11. Dick M. A comprehensive model: Vocational preparation for learning disabled and behaviorally disordered students and vocational assessment and transition objectives. Alexandria, VA, ERIC Documentation Reproduction Services (ED 265727), 1985.
12. Dick M. Translating vocational assessment information into transition objectives and instruction. Career Development of Exceptional Individuals. 10:77–84, 1987.
13. Edgar E, Levine P. A longitudinal follow-along study of graduates of special education. Unpublished manuscript. Seattle, University of Washington, 1987.
14. Fairweather JS, Shaver DM. Making the transition of postsecondary education and training. Except Child. 57:264–269, 1991.
15. Fisher AJ. Independent Living. In: Harnisch DL, Fisher AT. eds. Transition Literature in Review: Educational, Employment, and Independent Living Outcomes. Urbana-Champaign, University of Illinois, 1989.
16. Hasazi SB, Gordon LR, Roe GA. Factors associated with the employment status of handicapped youth exiting high school from 1979 to 1983. Except Child. 51:455–469, 1985.
17. Hasazi SB, Johnson RE, Hasazi JE, Gordon LR, Hull M. Employment of youth with and without handicaps following high school: Outcomes and correlates. The Journal of Special Education. 23:243–255, 1984.
18. Heal LW, Novak AR, Sigelman CK, Switzky HN. Characteristics of community residential facilities. In: Novak AR, Heal LW. eds. Integration of Developmentally Disabled Individuals into the

Community. Baltimore, Paul H. Brookes, 1980, pp 45–56.

19. Heward WL, Ovlanskey MO. Exceptional Children: An Introductory Survey of Special Education. 3rd ed. Columbus, Merrill, 1988.

20. Hill BK, Bruininks RH, Lakin KC. Characteristics of mentally retarded people in residential facilities. Health Soc Work. 2:85–95, 1983.

21. Karan O, Grantfield J, Suiter D. Supported living. Kaleidoscope. 2:1990.

22. Lakin KC, Bruininks RH. eds. Strategies for Achieving Community Integration of Developmentally Disabled Citizens. Baltimore, Paul H. Brookes, 1985.

23. Lambert N, Windmiller M, Cole L, Figueroa R. AAMD Adaptive Behavior Scale: Public School Version (1974) Version. Washington, DC, American Association on Mental Deficiency, 1975.

24. Lensink BR. Establishing programs and services in an accountable system. In: Roos P, McCann BM, Addison MR. eds. Shaping the Future: Community-Based Residential Services and Facilities for Mentally Retarded People. Baltimore, University Park Press, 1980, pp 49–66.

25. Liebert D, Lutsky L, Gottlieb A. Postsecondary experiences of young adults with severe physical disabilities. Except Child. 57:56–64, 1990.

26. Lombard R. Collaborative Community Based Transition Model: An Implementation Manual. Paper presented at 67th annual convention of the Council on Exceptional Children. San Francisco, CA, 1989.

27. Lowenfeld B. ed. The Visually Handicapped Child in School. New York, John Day, 1973.

28. Matson J. A controlled group study of pedestrian skill training for the mentally retarded. Zehairis Modification. 4:397–410, 1980.

29. Owings J, Stocking C. High school and beyond: Characteristics of high school students who identify themselves as handicapped. Washington, DC, National Center for Education Statistics, U.S. Department of Education, 1985.

30. Pancsofar E, Blackwell R. A User's Guide to Community Entry for the Severely Handicapped. Albany, State University of New York Press, 1986.

31. Racino JA, Taylor SJ. New directions in community living. Community Living for Adults. Syracuse University, The Center on Human Policy: Research and Training Center on Community Integration, 1989.

32. Rusch FR. Competitive Employment Issues and Strategies. Baltimore, Paul H. Brookes, 1986.

33. Rusch FR, Phelps LA. Secondary transition from school to work: A national priority. Except Child. 53:487–492, 1987.

34. Rusch FR, Mithaug DE, Flexer RW. Obstacles to competitive employment and traditional program options for overcoming them. In: Rusch FR. ed. Competitive Employment: Issues and Strategies. Baltimore, Paul H. Brookes, 1986.

35. Schalock R. Independent Living Screening Test. Blaine, NE, Mid-Nebraska Mental Retardation Services, 1975.

36. Schalock RL, Lilley MA. Placement for community-based mental retardation programs: How well do clients do after 8 to 10 years? American Journal of Mental Deficiency. 90:669–676, 1986.

37. Schuster JW, Griffen AK. Using time delay with task analyses. Teaching Exceptional Children. Summer:49–53, 1990.

38. Seyelman C, Bell N, Schoenrock C, Elear S, Danker-Brown P. Alternative Community Placements and Outcomes. Paper presented at the Annual meeting of the American Association On Mental Deficiency, Denver, 1978.

39. Snell ME. Systematic Instruction of Persons with Handicaps. Columbus, Merrill, 1987.

40. Sowers F, Rusch FR, Hudson C. Training a severely retarded young adult to ride the city bus to and from work. AAESPH Review. 4:15–22, 1979.

41. SRI International. The Transition Experience of Youth with Disabilities: A Report from the National Longitudinal Transition Study. Menlo Park, CA, Authors, 1989.

42. Stokes TF, Baer DM. An implicit technology of generalization. J Appl Behav Anal. 10:349–367, 1977.

43. Stokes TF, Osnes PG. Programming the generalization of children's social behavior. In Strain PS, Guralnick MJ, Walker HM. eds. Children's Social Behavior: Development and Modification. Orlando, FL, Academic Press, 1986.

44. Thompson MM. Housing for the Handicapped and Disabled: A Guide for Local Action. Washington, DC, The National Association of Housing and Redevelopment Officials, 1977.

45. Wehman P. School-to-work: Elements of successful programs. Teaching Exceptional Children. 23:40–43, 1990.

46. Wehman P, Kregel J, Barkus M. From school to work: A vocational transition model for handicapped students. Except Child 52:25–37, 1985a.

47. Wehman P, Renzaglia A, Bates P. Functional Living Skills for Moderately and Severely Handicapped Persons. Austin, Pro-Ed, 1985b.

48. Will MC. OSERS Programming for the Transition of Youth with Disabilities: Bridges from School to Working Life. Washington, DC, Office of Special Education and Rehabilitative Services, US Department of Education, 1984.

49. Wolfensberger W. The Principle of Normalization in Human Services. Toronto, National Institute on Mental Retardation, 1972.

Chapter 16
Social Security: Issues, Obstacles, and Challenges

Susan O'Mara
John Kregel

Supplemental Security Income Program Rules

Since 1980, a majority of the incentives to work outlined below have been added and liberalized under the Social Security Disability Amendments of 1980 (PL 99-265), the Employment Opportunities for Disabled Americans Act (PL 99-643), and the Omnibus Budget Reconciliation Acts of 1987 and 1989. However, the statistics are clear that, over the years, most persons added to Supplemental Security Income (SSI) and Social Security Disability Income (SSDI) disability roles remain there. Although many of the actual barriers to employment have been overcome, willingness of benefit recipients to utilize the work incentives and return to work depends in large part on their perceptions and understanding of the work incentives available to them. The system of Social Security regulations, policies, and procedures is complex and confusing.

For most supported employees and their families, mastery of the regulations and system is an unattainable goal. Many of these individuals are hesitant to return to work not only because they are unaware or unsure of the work incentive options, but also because they lack confidence in their ability to advocate for resolution of potential benefit complications caused by increased earnings. Rehabilitation professionals are in a similar dilemma, finding it difficult to provide knowledgeable and effective advocacy on behalf of persons with disabilities entering the workforce in growing numbers each year.

The SSI program is intended to provide a minimum level of income for persons who are aged, blind, or disabled and demonstrate economic need (that is, possess minimal income and resources). A basic test used by the Social Security Administration in determining whether a person is disabled for purposes of eligibility for SSI is whether he or she is engaged in substantial gainful work activity (SGA). SGA is defined as the performance of significant mental or physical duties for profit and is usually determined to be gross earnings in excess of $500.00 a month.

Before 1 July 1987, the performance of SGA after initial eligibility was established was a basis for ceasing SSI entitlement. Recognizing this severe disincentive to return to work, Congress enacted Public Law 99-643, which created special status benefits for SSI recipients under section 1619 of the Employment Opportunities for Disabled Americans Act. Public Law 99-643 established two special provision statuses known as 1619A and 1619B. Section 1619A enables individuals who continue to be disabled to receive a special SSI cash benefit in place of their regular 1611 SSI benefit when earnings exceed the $500 SGA level. If an SSI recipient continues to meet all eligibility requirements, when earnings increase to greater than $500 a month but remain lower than the break-even point, he or she automatically moves into 1619A status.

Eligibility for a 1619A cash benefit continues until earnings fall below the SGA level, at which point the person automatically moves back into 1611 status and receives a regular 1611 check, or until gross earnings exceed the break-even point, at which time the SSI cash benefit ceases.

Section 1619B of the 1987 legislation provides for continued Medicaid eligibility when a person's income is too high to qualify for an SSI cash benefit, but is not high enough to offset the loss of Medicaid. An individual is eligible for the 1619B protected Medicaid status only if the sole cause for SSI benefit cessation is increased earnings over the break-even point. A second criterion for 1619B status is that an individual's gross earnings fall below certain limits called threshold amounts. Earnings at or above the threshold amount are considered to be sufficient to replace the cost of Medicaid coverage. A final criterion for 1619B requires that an individual must need Medicaid in order to work. Compliance with this criterion is established through the individual's statements to the Social Security Administration regarding his or her use of Medicaid in the last 12 months, expected use within the next 12 months, or need for Medicaid if he or she becomes injured or ill within the next 12 months.

Section 1916B is an extremely important provision of the Social Security Act because it protects not only an individual's Medicaid coverage, but also maintains his or her eligibility to receive an SSI cash benefit in any future month that countable income falls below the allowable limits (the break-even point for 1619A and $500.00 for 1611), provided that the individual continues to meet all other eligibility requirements for SSI. Because 1619B status maintains an active SSI case standing for an indefinite period, an individual may work for several years above the allowable levels for an SSI cash benefit, then be reinstated automatically if loss of employment or reduction of earnings below the allowable levels occurs.

Because SSI is an economic need-based program, it is intended to supplement any income or resources an individual already possesses to ensure a minimum level of income. Therefore, the dollar amount of the SSI benefit received on a monthly basis varies from person to person. In January of each year Congress establishes the Federal Benefit Rate (FBR), which is the maximum dollar amount that an individual or couple can receive in SSI cash benefit on a monthly basis.

The amount of an individual's SSI payment may be reduced below the FBR level, depending on the person's earned and unearned income. The more earned or unearned income received, the greater is the reduction in the SSI payment. Not all income a person receives, however, is considered in determining the amount of the benefit. The Social Security Administration allows a $20.00 general exclusion that is subtracted from a person's income regardless of its source. In addition to the general exclusion, a $65.00 earned income disregard is subtracted from earned income. After the earned income disregard is applied, one half of the remaining earned income is counted by the Social Security Administration in adjusting the benefit amount. The remaining amounts of earned and unearned income after exclusions are combined to determine the total countable income. This total is the dollar amount of an individual's SSI benefit reduction. The following examples are simplified versions of the standardized formula used by the Social Security Administration in determining benefit reductions due to earned and unearned income.

Example 1:

Individual with earned income and unearned income (such as SSDI or Veterans benefit). Example based on a person earning $263.00 a month gross wages and receiving $225.00 SSDI.

Step 1. $225.00   Unearned income (SSDI)
         – 20.00   General exclusion
         $205.00   Countable unearned income

Step 2. $263.00   Earned income
                   (monthly gross wages)
         – 65.00   Earned income disregard
         $198.00
         ÷ 2 $1 reduction for every
                   $2 earned
         $ 99.00   Countable earned income

Step 3. $205.00   Countable unearned income
         + 99.00   Countable unearned income
         $304.00   Total countable income

Step 4. $407.00   Federal Benefit Rate
         – 304.00 Total countable income
         $103.00   SSI check

Example 2:

Individual with earned income only. Example based on a person earning $350.00 gross monthly earnings.

Step 1. $ 0.00 Unearned income

         $ 0.00 Countable unearned income

Step 2. $350.00   Earned income
         – 85.00   General exclusion and
         $265.00   earned income disregard

         $265.00
         ÷ 2 $1 reduction for every
                   $2 earned
         $132.50   Countable earned income

Step 3. $ 0.00 Countable unearned income
         + 132.50 Countable earned income
         $132.50   Total countable income

Step 4. $407.00   Federal Benefit Rate
         – 132.50 Total countable income
         $274.50   SSI check

Persons receiving an SSI benefit are subject to two separate review processes to ensure continued compliance with eligibility cri-

teria. Redeterminations are nonmedical reviews, which occur annually for persons in statuses 1611, 1619A, and 1619B. A second review process for SSI recipients is the Continuing Disability Review (CDR). The Social Security Administration is required by law to determine periodically whether a recipient continues to be disabled and therefore is eligible to continue receiving benefits.

Social Security Disability Insurance Program Rules

The SSDI benefit program authorized under Title II of the Social Security Act enables former workers who become disabled and are unable to continue working to receive monthly cash benefits and Medicare insurance. To qualify for SSDI benefits as a former worker, an individual must have insured status (that is, sufficient past work in Social Security-covered employment), be determined medically disabled, and must not be working or, if working, earning less than the SGA level. Eligibility for SSDI may also be established as a disabled adult child. A disabled adult child is an individual who is 18 years of age or older, who became totally and permanently disabled before age 22, and who is a dependent of an insured worker who is disabled, retired, or deceased.

Because the SSDI program is not based on economic need, there are no resource or unearned income limitations for eligibility as there are for SSI. The dollar amount of income support received by SSDI beneficiaries on a monthly basis is dependent on the level of contributions made to the program and therefore varies significantly from person to person. There is no provision for a gradual reduction in SSDI cash benefits as earnings increase, which is the case with the SSI program. An SSDI beneficiary receives either the full amount of the SSDI benefit in a given month or no income support at all.

Unless medical recovery is an issue, SSDI beneficiaries are entitled to a 9-month trial work period, which provides an opportunity to test work skills while maintaining their benefit. An individual may attempt to work for a trial work period of 9 months while continuing to receive full benefit checks, regardless of the level of earned income. The trial work period begins automatically in the first month that earned income is equal to or exceeds $200.00. Any subsequent months that earned income is at or above $200.00 are counted toward the 9-month limit. These months do not have to be consecutive and may accumulate over a number of years. The trial work period is exhausted when an individual has 9 months of earnings over $200.00 within a rolling 60-month period. There is only one trial work period allowed per given determination of eligibility.

When an individual has accumulated 9 months of trial work, a continuing disability review is conducted by the local Social Security Administration office. The purpose of the review is to determine whether the individual is engaging in SGA. If an individual is determined to be engaging in SGA, he or she will receive the full benefit check for an additional 3 months and then the benefit will stop. If an individual is determined not to be engaging in SGA, he or she will continue to receive the full benefit check.

At the end of the 9-month trial work period, beneficiaries immediately enter into a 36-month extended period of eligibility, provided that medical recovery is not an issue. This 36-month period begins in the month following the trial work period regardless of whether a person is determined to be engaging in SGA during the continuing disability review. The extended period of eligibility is a minimum of 36 consecutive months during which an individual may work and have SSDI benefits reinstated for each month that earned income is below $500.

Social Security Administration Title XVIII Medicare provides medical services to SSDI beneficiaries. Persons with disabilities must complete a 5-month waiting period from the month of disability onset before SSDI benefits begin. An additional 24-month waiting period after disability benefits begin is required before an individual is entitled to receive Medicare coverage.

SSDI beneficiaries who lose benefit entitlement because of SGA but continue to be disabled are eligible for extended Medicare coverage. The extended coverage is for 24 months beginning at the end of the extended period of eligibility or the last month that SSDI benefits are payable, whichever is later. In addition, recent legislation makes it possible for persons with disabilities to buy into the Medicare program once the extended Medicare coverage is exhausted. Specifically, PL 101-239, effective 1 April 1990, provides disabled beneficiaries who are not yet 65 years old and continue to be disabled, and who are no longer entitled to benefits solely because of having earnings in excess of the amount permitted, with the option of purchasing Medicare coverage after they have worked a full 48 months (9-month trial work period and 36-month extended period of eligibility) and have exhausted their extended period of Medicare eligibility.

Additional Work Incentives

Plan for Achieving Self-Support

A plan for achieving self-support (PASS) is an SSI work incentive under which persons with disabilities can set aside income or resources to be used to achieve specific, individualized vocational goals. A PASS can be established for education, vocational training, starting a business, or to purchase job coach and job support services that enable a person to work. The purpose of a PASS is to increase the individual's income-producing capacity, thus reducing reliance on government benefit support in the long run.

The income or resources used to pay for goods and services under a PASS are not counted in determining a person's eligibility for SSI or in calculating the amount of the

SSI benefit that he or she will receive. By excluding this income or resources in a PASS, the individual is able to meet the income and resources test, thereby qualifying for SSI. Likewise, an individual who already receives SSI can maintain that SSI in the same amount or even receive a larger SSI benefit by setting aside his or her income or resources in a PASS. For a PASS to be approved by the SSA, the following criteria must be met:

1. The plan must be especially designed for the individual and have a designated and feasible occupational objective.

2. A specific time frame must be established for an objective to be achieved.

3. The plan must state the sources and the amounts of income or resources to be set aside to achieve the goal.

4. The plan must state how the money set aside will be spent to achieve the goal.

Impairment-Related Work Expenses

An impairment-related work expense (IRWE) is an expense, directly related to enabling a person with a disability to work, which is incurred because of the individual's physical or mental impairments and which would not be incurred by unimpaired individuals in similar circumstances. The purpose of the IRWE work incentive is to enable individuals with disabilities to recover some of the costs of expenses to support their work incurred as a result of their disability.

The Social Security Administration's list of allowable expenditures under IRWE is extensive and includes costs of adaptive equipment or specialized devices, attendant care, special transportation costs, as well as the cost of job coach services. This work incentive applies to both SSI recipients and SSDI beneficiaries and allows for certain costs or expenses to be excluded in calculating earnings and SGA. For an SSI recipient, deducting the cost of an IRWE from monthly gross wages increases the

SSI cash payment he or she can receive. For an SSDI beneficiary, deducting an IRWE may keep monthly gross earnings below SGA, thus enabling the individual to maintain SSDI eligibility. The cost of IRWEs can also be deducted from gross earnings during initial SSI and SSDI application processes, enabling an individual to meet the SGA requirement, as well as the income test for SSI.

Subsidies

A subsidy exists when an employer pays a worker more in wages than the reasonable value of the actual services performed. To qualify as a subsidy recipient, an individual must have evidence of receiving a subsidy, such as extra support, supervision, or documentation of lower productivity when compared to unimpaired workers performing the same or similar work. In developing a subsidy the employer is requested by the Social Security Administration to submit a statement documenting the actual value of the worker's services.

Subsidies apply to both SSI recipients and SSDI beneficiaries. The dollar amount of the subsidy is subtracted from gross monthly earnings during the initial eligibility process for both SSI and SSDI, potentially reducing gross earnings below $500.00 and enabling an individual to meet the SGA requirement. Subsidies only apply to the SSI program during initial eligibility. For the SSDI program, however, subsidies are considered in ongoing SGA determinations.

Faced with the reality of extremely limited numbers of government benefit support recipients opting to return to work, the Federal government and the Social Security Administration have responded over the past 10 years with legislative and regulatory changes in the SSI and SSDI programs. The changes have been aimed at reducing the risks and costs associated with the reduction or loss of benefit support and medical services as a result of work activity. Despite efforts to negotiate a system that encourages work, significant disincentives remain in the SSDI program and, to a lesser degree, in the SSI program. Concern regarding the disincentives is readily expressed by supported employees and their families, who must consider the risk factors involved when weighing the uncertainties of success in employment against the consistent support of benefit income.

The 1619 legislative changes have virtually eliminated the disincentives to work for SSI recipients. Because work activity is no longer a consideration for cessation of SSI eligibility, a person receiving SSI is assured of an overall increase in net income as earnings increase. The ability to move freely between the 1611 and 1619A statuses as earned income fluctuates likewise provides a financial safety net in the event that employment stability is threatened. Section 1619B provides assurance that medical services under Medicaid will be protected despite the fact that cash benefits are suspended when earnings exceed the break-even point. Despite these significant improvements in the SSI program, several barriers to employment remain unaddressed.

Current Supplemental Security Income Disincentives to Employment

The SGA consideration remains a key criterion in establishing initial eligibility for SSI benefits. An individual must first prove he or she is unable to work at the SGA level to qualify for benefits. This initial emphasis on limited work capacity forces individuals to limit any current work activity to qualify and may in fact provide an inaccurate message to recipients that future earnings at the SGA level will endanger their ability to maintain SSI support.

A second concern for SSI recipients returning to work relates to the requirement of additional medical reviews precipitated by increasing earnings. Although an increase in earnings will not result in ter-

mination of SSI due to SGA, it may indirectly result in the loss of benefits due to a determination of medical recovery. Because they recognize that movement into 1619 status due to increased earnings necessitates a review of their medical files, individuals receiving SSI may choose to limit earnings to avoid further scrutiny of their disability status and a potential loss of eligibility.

Current Social Security Disability Income Disincentives to Employment

Despite the issues just addressed, the incentives for SSI recipients to engage in work far outweigh those provided to SSDI beneficiaries. The risk of reduction in overall net income is a justified concern to these individuals because SGA continues to be a primary factor not only in establishing initial eligibility, but also in maintaining eligibility after benefits are awarded.

The disincentives surrounding SGA determinations were somewhat diminished at the beginning of 1990 when the Social Security Administration implemented a change in program rules that increased the level of earnings that constitute SGA from $300.00 to $500.00 a month. This change becomes less of an accomplishment in improving the system when one considers that the $200.00 increase accounts for the growth in wages since 1980, when the SGA level was last adjusted. A second proposed rule change, which was not implemented, was a plan to index the SGA level to average wage growth in future years. The failure to implement such an index is particularly damaging given the increase in the Federal minimum wage level in April 1990 and the pending subsequent increase in 1991.

The most effective resolution to the dilemma is clearly the removal of the SGA criteria altogether. A legislative change proposed in 1989 suggested removing the

SGA disincentive by allowing SSDI beneficiaries who return to work and earn above the SGA level to be considered "disabled and working." Persons qualifying for this status, who would otherwise lose cash benefits due to SGA, would be eligible for cash and Medicaid benefits under Section 1619 of the SSI program. The formula used to adjust monthly cash benefits as earnings increase for SSI recipients would apply for persons in the disabled and working status. This proposal, intended to be a parallel to the 1619 provisions of the SSI program, was not adopted by Congress. The Medicare buy-in, a second proposal of this legislation, was adopted and provides extended medical services for SSDI beneficiaries no longer qualifying for a cash benefit.

The Social Security Administration's awareness of and concern with the problems created by lack of information or misinformation about the benefit programs and work incentives is evidenced by its growing efforts to build effective working relations with service provider organizations. One step the Social Security Administration has taken to accomplish this goal is to position work incentive liaisons in each local SSA field office across the country. These individuals serve as a primary contact for rehabilitation professionals and agencies who work with people with disabilities and are a valuable source of information regarding the work incentives. Additionally, work incentive specialists are located in each of the Social Security Administration's regional offices to coordinate outreach and public affairs activities on the work incentives.

A principal strategy of this outreach endeavor focuses on effective use of resources by working through community organizations and agencies. This requires action by the Social Security Administration to provide such organizations and agencies with the information and training they need to identify potentially eligible individuals, inform them about program requirements and benefits, and help them through the SSI application process. The Social Security Administration has established principles that lay a foundation for what managers should be doing with regard to outreach efforts on a local level. These principles speak clearly to the need for local Social Security Administration offices to accomplish the following.

- Conduct periodic training sessions for service provider organizations.
- Improve access of provider organizations to local offices and work incentive liaisons to foster cooperation.
- Set up a mechanism for getting release forms to allow advocates access to records of individuals they are assisting.
- Encourage feedback from organizations about Social Security Administration service delivery.

Developmental disabilities program leaders should be aggressive in their efforts to build a tight networking structure with the Social Security Administration to accomplish mutual goals. The local work incentive liaisons and public affairs specialists are good initial points of contact and are in a position to provide education about benefit programs, work incentives, and local outreach efforts. Educational and training efforts should be reciprocated by rehabilitation professionals to provide Social Security Administration personnel with a working knowledge of supported employment services and outcomes.

Although interagency collaboration and mutual understanding of benefit programs and employment services are critical elements, they unfortunately cannot ensure that persons with disabilities who go to work will experience smooth benefit transitions. Developmental disabilities program staff must continuously invest time and effort to advocate on behalf of the individuals they serve. Experience with benefit difficulties has demonstrated that the best results are achieved when a "preventive medicine" approach is applied as opposed to a "crisis intervention" strategy. Expending small amounts of energy to conduct periodic proactive monitoring activities will help circumvent major benefit problems. The following proactive monitoring system comprises several stages that must be performed sequentially to minimize chances of experiencing major benefit complications. It is important to work cooperatively with the Social Security Administration when rendering such advice, to guard against misinformation and to ensure up-to-date information.

1. Investigate the Client's Current Benefit Status

Before a rehabilitation professional considers placing a worker with a disability into a situation that will impact on benefit eligibility, it is essential that the professional have a firm grasp of the individual's current status. Research should be conducted to discern which benefits are received (SSI, Title II), how much money is involved, how many trial-work-period months or extended-period-of-eligibility months have already been used, and how conscientious the client or care provider has been in the past about reporting earnings. The object is to provide a complete and accurate picture of the benefit status of the individual with a disability at that particular point in time. This goal cannot be achieved unless the person's entire previous benefit-earnings history has been thoroughly assessed. Failure to perform these activities can result in some unpleasant surprises down the road.

2. Explore the Possible Effects of Future Earnings

When an employment opportunity becomes available for a person who currently receives Social Security benefits, one should carefully examine the job specifics that could affect these benefits. The pay rate, job hours, pay dates, and bonus or raise information are all necessary data. One should contact the Social Security Division Supervisor or case representative and present a "what if" scenario in which all possible outcomes are thoroughly explored. The purpose is to obtain precise information about future benefit changes that can be expected to occur, given the stated conditions. This prediction will only be as accurate as the research done on the client's past earnings' history and present benefit status; therefore it is important that this homework be done.

3. Exchange Information with Worker and Family

By this time, the rehabilitation professional is armed with complete information about how any given employment situation will affect a particular benefit recipient. This information must be shared openly with the client and family members so that informed decisions can be made. Benefit consequences must be discussed before placement, not later when irreparable benefit damage may have been done. One should never assume that the family has knowledge about the predicted course of benefit adjustment without checking with them. All benefit facts must be brought out truthfully. Valuable training time can be wasted on a placement situation if an individual feels that he or she has been mislead or ill-informed.

4. Report Earnings Correctly

Many errors can be sidestepped if employment earnings are reported in the proper manner. First and foremost, employment data must be communicated to, and received by, the appropriate person. Earnings should be reported to the current claims representative assigned to the recipient or the division supervisor. Some individuals with disabilities receive both SSI and SSDI benefits, in which case *both* divisions must be notified separately (in some states the same person is responsible for both). For SSI recipients any earnings over $85.00 a month must be reported. For SSDI beneficiaries, any months in which the recipients earn over $200 must be reported because they qualify as trial-work-period months, even if the earnings are from a sheltered workshop. To facilitate the smoothest transitions, one should relate information on start date, pay rate, pay dates, work schedule, address of employing company, and supervisor's name; report job loss immediately to hasten full benefit reinstatement; and faithfully and in a timely fashion notify the Social Security Administration of changes in pay rate, hours worked, marital status, or change in residence. *Delays will result in overpayment or underpayment.*

5. Monitor Benefit Transitions Regularly

Once initial earnings are reported, rehabilitation professionals must continue to check occasionally with division supervisors or claims representatives. It is recommended that these checkups be conducted about every 2 months. For individuals receiving an SSI cash benefit, special attention is required when an increase or decrease in earnings is experienced. SSI recipients automatically receive a cash benefit under Section 1619A when earnings increase to $500 per month. Although it is not necessary to advocate for 1619A status, monitoring an adjustment in the SSI payment because of the increased

earnings safeguards against overpayment. For SSDI recipients, a contact should be made at the conclusion of the trial work period to insure that a determination of SGA results in a timely cessation of benefits. Supported employment staff should enlist the assistance of the employee and family in this monitoring endeavor.

It is hoped that the information provided in this chapter will form a basic framework for understanding the internal workings of government benefit packages and avenues for gaining and sharing information on benefit outcomes for employees with disabilities. Assimilation of this information does not magically transform the developmental disabilities staff member into a Social Security claims representative. Successful utilization of work incentives and smooth benefit transitions ultimately depend on a cooperative effort between developmental disabilities staff, the Social Security Administration, workers with disabilities, and their families. An excellent resource for additional information is the *Red Book on Work Incentives*. This 1991 publication is available from your local Social Security office and is publication number SSA 64-030.

Chapter 17
Gerontology

Linda M. Nutt
Michael Malone

□ *Case 17-1: Helen*

Helen is a friendly and outgoing 59-year-old woman who lives with her elderly mother. Helen has been diagnosed as having mild mental retardation and experiences seizures. For the last 15 years she has been employed at a local sheltered workshop performing a variety of jobs. Although Helen concentrates on her work, her job performance and earnings are only 40% of the current rate paid to 100% performance workers in the same job. In her free time Helen likes to listen to music, watch television, and go shopping. She occasionally socializes with friends from the sheltered workshop, but considers her mother to be her best friend. Helen's mother assists her with her finances, transportation, purchases, and the acquisition of health care services. What will be Helen's future when her mother is no longer able to provide the type of support that Helen currently receives? Will Helen be able to continue a similar life-style? How will Helen meet the financial obligations of maintaining the same quality of life she currently enjoys?

□ *Case 17-2: Don*

Don is a 64-year-old who has been diagnosed as moderately mentally retarded, has limited communication skills, and demonstrates deficits in daily living skills. Don lived at home with his parents until his father passed away, at which time Don was 45 years old. After his father's death, Don's mother felt she could no longer care for Don by herself and had him admitted to a nearby institution. Prior to his move to the institution, Don was not required to assist in his own care nor was he engaged in any out-of-the-home work experiences. Don has been working as a housekeeper in the building where he lives for the past 5 years. Lately, Don has begun showing resistance when prompted to get ready to go to work. He chooses to lounge on the sofa watching the television. Numerous prompts by staff are needed to get Don to go to work. Staff who know Don believe that he wants to retire. Given that Don has made excellent progress in learning new daily living and job-related skills, should he be encouraged to maintain his current working status? To what would Don retire? What would Don's quality of life be if he remains working? If he retires?

To address the issues of "best practices" that benefit individuals such as Helen and Don, profiled above, one must begin with the seemingly simple question, "Who are Helen and Don?" Such inquiry must take on two forms: the general "who?" relative to descriptions of the population of which persons such as Helen and Don are members and the specific "who" relative to individual characteristics and needs. Comprehension of the general "who?" provides service professionals with information enabling them to understand and address issues related to the specific "who?". Indeed, failure to comprehend general population descriptions and trends relative to persons with lifelong disabilities as they enter into late life limits our ability to develop best practices in service delivery. In this chapter we attempt to provide material that will contribute to efforts to provide services to persons with lifelong disabilities as they enter into late life. Specifically, we discuss identification of the aging segment of our society who have developmental disabilities; quality of life; health care issues relevant to these persons; service provision; placement and supported living; money; regulations and legal issues; and, finally, daily activities and programs.

Demographic Profile

In the past decade, with the graying of our society, we have witnessed great change in the national population profile (Schaie and Willis 1986). Projections indicate that, as we move into the twenty-first century, the proportion of our society composed of people who have made the transition into late life will increase substantially (Blake 1981; Rice and Feldman 1983). This continued expansion in the ranks of persons within the general population who are elderly is paralleled by the growth in numbers of persons with developmental disabilities who are also aging (Lubin and Kiely 1985). Efforts to estimate the prevalence of persons with lifelong disabilities who have made the transition from mid-life to late life have been limited by both an inadequate definition of the period we call late

life and a lack of demographic and epidemiologic data on persons with developmental disabilities as they become older.

Although the definition of developmental disabilities put forth in the Developmental Disabilities Assistance and Bill of Rights Act of 1984 identifies various conditions that may impact on an individual's ability to function independently, most of what is known regarding persons with disabilities in the later years is based on persons with mental retardation. Little is known regarding service provision to those individuals with noncognitive developmental disabilities. Increases in the numbers of persons with developmental disabilities who are elderly may be attributed to a variety of factors including the shift in the population profile discussed previously, identification efforts at the state level resulting from increased awareness and attention from federal agencies, and improved health care, which has substantially extended life expectancies of persons with certain lifelong disabilities (Cotten et al. 1981; DiGiovanni 1978; Seltzer and Seltzer 1984; Thurman 1986).

To develop services for an aging population, one must determine what constitutes a transition from mid-life to late life for this group. The most widely used marker defining late life has been chronologic age. The lower limit of "old age" used by professionals has ranged from 30 years of age to 65 years of age (Segal 1977; Seltzer and Seltzer 1984; Tymchuk 1979; Thurman 1986; Walz et al. 1986). Age 60 is considered the point of transition in the Older Americans Act. Age 55 appears frequently in the literature and is consistent with many federal programs (Segal 1977). Although chronologic age, especially that of 55 years, may be useful as an arbitrary marker for entrance into "old age" for persons with extended life expectancies, it proves to be a less than adequate marker for persons who are more severely involved, have limited adaptive skills, or whose medical background is associated with a life expectancy below 55 years. As suggested by Seltzer and Krauss (1987), a more useful approach may be to identify certain life stages or functional abilities that alert one to an individual's transition to late life. A number of alternatives to chronologic age have been proposed. Thurman (1986), suggested counting back 10 years from the average life expectancy of particular subgroups to determine eligibility for services set aside for the aged, and Eisdorfer (1983) suggested four life stages:

1. Early life, when resources are invested in youth with the expectation that future societal benefits will follow

2. Mid-life, when adult workers contribute goods and services to benefit society

3. Late life, when individuals retire healthy and remain functionally independent

4. Late life, when less than healthy individuals become functionally dependent on others.

Finally, other indices of aging that have been discussed include biologic aging, which is focused on the physical aspects of aging; social aging, focused on societal expectations related to productivity and attitudes toward aging in general; and psychologic aging, focused on intellectual functioning, emotional adjustment, and individual perceptions of aging (Birren 1959; Seltzer 1985b; Thurman 1986).

Each of the foregoing approaches has its merits relative to alerting service providers to an individual's transition into late life, but no single measure of the transition period from mid-life to late life appears entirely satisfactory. The use of chronologic age as a marker is limited due to the variability of life expectancies among subgroups. Dependence on either life stage or domain-specific aging indices to determine eligibility for aging services is problematic since both rely on functional limitations in

life activities as a diagnostic marker. Given the apparent problems with each of the preceding approaches, the reliance on multiple indicators would seem to have the greatest utility to service providers. A definition including chronologic age to satisfy agency or service requirements and a number of qualifiers related to functional aspects of society and aging would be most useful. This definition should include those characteristics described in the Older Americans Act Amendments of 1987 (P.L. 100-175) and measures of the aging process relative to physical change, change in cognitive ability related to performing daily activities, emotional change, and change in social skills, any of which may impact negatively on the quality of life and longevity of an individual.

For such an approach to be considered viable, efforts must be made to collect specific demographic and epidemiologic data to guide decisions related to services appropriate for a heterogeneous group of persons with lifelong disabilities as they age. At the present time, little information of this type exists. A possible exception is for persons with mental retardation and, even with this group, examination of issues is in the early stages. A 1% to 3% prevalence rate is typically applied to figures on the general population to obtain estimates of the number of persons with lifelong disabilities in late life (Tymchuk 1979; Seltzer and Krauss 1987; Walz et al. 1986; Sison and Cotten 1989). These prevalence estimates typically refer to persons with mental retardation and differ dramatically from estimates (for example, 12% to 13%) made of the total disabled population in various states (Jacobson et al. 1985; Walz et al. 1986).

Combining prevalence rates used by the United Cerebral Palsy Association (0.3%), the Epilepsy Foundation of America (0.4%), the National Society for Children and Adults with Autism (0.032%), and the rate suggested by Baroff (1982) of 0.396% for persons with mental retardation results in a total prevalence rate of about 1%. Using this 1% prevalence estimate and population projections, reported in Rice and Feldman (1983), we get the following estimated number of persons with lifelong disabilities who are 65 or older.

Year	Prevalence Estimate
1980	258,920
1990	315,580
2000	362,520
2020	526,530
2040	672,560

Such figures should be viewed with caution because mortality rates for any given subgroup are not considered when applying prevalence rates to the general population. We do know that persons who are not severely involved and who demonstrate adaptive skills related to toileting, eating, and mobility are more likely to live longer than persons who are severely involved and have substantial deficits in adaptive skills (Eyman et al. 1989; Janicki and Jacobson 1986). In addition, it is believed that, as in the general population, the rate of disability accelerates with age after age 50 to 55 (Blake 1981; Janicki and Jacobson 1986). Increased disability may be associated with a loss of function and death (Anderson 1989; Eyman et al. 1989). Although trends may be discussed, we must not overlook the individual differences in experience, in etiology and functional ability, in gender, and in residential history.

Although the lack of specific demographic and epidemiologic data limit the extent to which professionals can obtain precise figures, reliance on inflated estimates may lead to a service system better prepared to handle the actual population expansion. Error in this direction would be preferable to error in a more conservative direction (for example, reliance on estimates derived from actual service recipients). A conservative error would result in the service system being inadequately prepared to accommodate the increasing numbers of persons with lifelong disabilities as they reach late life.

Quality of Life

The phrase "quality of life," a new buzz word in the field of mental retardation (Landesman 1986), seems on the surface to be self-defining. One's quality of life may be viewed as a function of those ingredients in one's life that enhance personal growth, independence, health, and overall happiness. Attainment of optimum quality of life is facilitated through the protection of rights and the receipt of needed services. Definition of quality of life becomes less clear, however, when service providers working with persons with lifelong disabilities in later life attempt to specify those elements that contribute to personal growth, independence, health, and happiness and how to guarantee rights and services to this group. Thus, the definition and the understanding of the concept of quality of life have become great challenges in developing best practices for service delivery to persons such as Helen and Don (profiled at the beginning of this chapter).

As discussed by Schalock and colleagues (1989), the concept of quality of life may be defined from three perspectives: social, psychologic, and social policy. From the social perspective, quality of life may be defined in terms of influences external to the individual. Such environmental influences include social welfare, standard of living, formal and informal supports, education, housing, public services, health services, safety, and leisure programming. Although not exhaustive, this list provides direction to addressing quality-of-life issues from a community standpoint.

In contrast to this perspective, the psychologic perspective of quality of life represents those things that hold personal relevance to an individual in maintaining or improving life conditions such as independence, productivity, and acceptance. These personal perceptions include satisfaction with the environmental influences discussed previously as well as general perceived happiness and well-being. An increase in one's satisfaction with personal–social resources would seem to be related to increases in life satisfaction, a sense of well-being, and feelings of personal competence.

The final perspective, noted by Schalock and coworkers (1989), from which the concept of quality of life can be understood is that of social policy. The social policy perspective relates to the documentation of needs that can be used to allocate fiscal resources. As defined by Murrel and Norris (1983), quality of life is a function of the degree to which human and environmental resources compliment one another. Best practices in service delivery cannot be developed without an understanding of either the needs of persons with lifelong disabilities as they enter into late life or the means with which to provide the services to address those stated needs.

How can service providers help elderly persons with lifelong disabilities continue to grow as individuals and maintain health and happiness in relation to the social, psychologic, and social policy perspectives? This challenge can be met in a number of ways. We must be aware of and understand the rights of older persons as fellow human beings and as recognized by law. A number of these rights have been outlined by Walker (1985):

1. Provision of services to meet habilitation needs of each person, including education, training, and care required to develop social and intellectual functioning

2. Provision of living conditions consistent with a person's age, developmental disability, and degree of involvement

3. Provision of quality medical and dental services

4. Provision of appropriate safeguards against physical and psychologic abuse or neglect

5. Provision of access to programs needed to meet individual needs

6. Provision of qualified personnel for conducting evaluations and developing program plans

7. Provision of an administrative forum for the resolution of individual problems

These rights were echoed and extended by Cotten and Spirrison (1986), who put forth a bill of rights for persons with mental retardation who are elderly. Such a bill of rights is applicable to all persons with lifelong disabilities as they enter into late life.

1. The right to an adequate standard of living, economic security, and protective work.

2. The right to humane services designed to help them reach their fullest potential.

3. The right to live as independently as they are able and wish in the community of their choice, in as normal a manner as is possible.

4. The right to an array of services that is generally available to other elderly groups.

5. The right to choose to retire. In addition, the right to retire "to something" rather than just "from something."

6. The right to participate as a member of the community, having reciprocal interdependency.

7. The right to be considered a person and not merely "elderly" or "retarded" (developmentally disabled).

8. The right to protected well-being, and to a qualified guardian, when required.

9. The right to be involved in setting one's goals and making one's decisions. The right to fail if necessary.

10. The right to a positive future, having enough involvement with life to prevent a preoccupation with death.

11. The right to be romantic, not asexual.

12. The right to sufficient activity and attention to permit continued integrity of self, individual identity, and purpose.

13. The right to an interesting environment and life-style, with an availability of sufficient mobility to provide a variety of surroundings.
14. The right to live and die with dignity.

Acknowledgment and comprehension of these rights, however, are not enough. As service providers, we must take the appropriate steps to guarantee that individual rights are respected and enforced. Although organizations advocating the rights of persons with developmental disabilities exist (for example, United Cerebral Palsy Association, American Association on Mental Retardation, Epilepsy Foundation of America, National Society for Children and Adults with Autism), a need exists for advocacy groups that focus on issues important to those persons who are aging (Sison and Cotten 1989; Tymchuk 1979; Walz et al. 1986). The basic rights that protect and enhance the quality of life of the elderly should be the same for the general population and those with developmental disabilities. We must recognize, however, that the latter group may require additional consideration to ensure they have the opportunity to experience life at its fullest. In providing such assurances we must be careful to provide a balance between the role of guardian and respect for autonomy of the individual (Howell 1988). All too often, professionals fail to ask for input from the individual with lifelong disabilities when making decisions that will affect that individual's life. We must be careful not to abuse the rights and freedoms of those persons we are intending to help. As noted previously in this chapter, individuals with lifelong disabilities who reach "old age" typically are not severely involved and have strengths in skills related to daily living. These persons have the capacity and deserve the opportunity to have input into decisions that will directly affect the quality of their life. Feelings of personal relevance and self-direction will likely be enhanced within the individual.

In addition to acknowledging, understanding, and guaranteeing the rights of older persons with lifelong disabilities, it is essential that we also be aware of the basic needs of this group. Tibbits (1979) suggested that all older persons have a need:

1. To render some socially useful service
2. To be considered a part of the community
3. To occupy increased leisure time in satisfying ways
4. To enjoy normal companionship
5. For recognition as an individual
6. For opportunity for self-expression
7. For health protection and care
8. For suitable mental stimulation [and emotional support]
9. For living arrangements and family relationships
10. For spiritual satisfactions

A primary medium through which rights and needs of older persons with lifelong disabilities are addressed is that of the support system, both formal and informal. The organization and supervision of formal and informal supports leads to increased activity on the part of the person receiving support as that person's needs are met. Increased activity level is one of two variables predictive of quality of life in nondisabled elderly persons (Osberg et al. 1987). Because persons with lifelong disabilities experience physical or mental impairments that result in life situations that are more constricted than those of persons without disabilities, the importance of the development of a strong support network becomes apparent.

Formal supports may include services related to health, vocational training, transportation, recreation or leisure, counseling, and information and referral (Segal 1978; Hamilton and Segal 1975; Tymchuk 1979). Unfortunately, such services are often underutilized by those individuals in greatest need. A number of factors may contribute to poor utilization of formal support by persons with lifelong disabilities in late life (Segal 1978). First, the level of awareness of service availability among this group is generally low. Efforts must be made to increase this awareness and to ensure positive attitudes toward accessing services once they are made known. Second, inconsistency of services across areas (for example, city, county, state) may limit access by persons in need. Such inconsistency can engender confusion and frustration that can lead to individuals "dropping out" of the service delivery system. Third, inadequate distribution of services necessarily impacts on usage by a large number of persons. Services may be inaccessible because of location; increased case loads, which creates waiting lists; and an inadequate system of identifying members of the population. Fourth, personnel who provide services are often not adequately trained to address older individuals' needs. In response to this need for trained personnel, funding has been made available such as that from the Administration on Developmental Disabilities to University Affiliated Programs for training initiatives in the area of aging and developmental disabilities.

Informal supports, in addition to formal supports, can greatly influence one's quality of life. Such support is typically provided by family and friends and includes emotional, leisure, and financial support. It is not unusual to find that persons who have developmental disabilities who are elderly have limited informal support systems. A lack of such support may contribute to feelings of loneliness (Bostwick and Foss 1981). Understandably, such feelings have a negative impact on one's quality of life. Small support systems can be high in quality and beneficial to the recipient of support but can put the recipient at greater risk when the system eventually breaks down (for example, the death of a parent).

Service providers attuned to the multifaceted nature of quality of life will be better able to develop best practices to ben-efit persons with lifelong disabilities who are aging. One must be aware of and work to protect the rights and needs of these persons. Issues related to underutilization of services and supports must be addressed. These efforts will do much to enhance the quality of life of persons with developmental disabilities as they age.

Health Care

Persons with lifelong disabilities who attain late life (by traditional markers) typically are less severely handicapped, ambulatory, do not have major physical or behavioral problems, and have adequate self-care skills (Richards 1975; Walz et al. 1986). Richards (1975) noted that death, in this group as it ages, may be related more to risk factors particular to a severe disabling condition than to the aging process itself. Even for those individuals who are not affected by such risk factors, health issues play an important role. In general, individuals with lifelong disabilities experience physiologic and physical changes associated with aging similar to those experienced by persons without lifelong disabilities.

Although there are similarities associated with aging between persons who have developmental disabilities and those who do not, age-related health changes may occur earlier in the lives of those with lifelong disabilities (Seltzer and Seltzer 1984). The most dramatic example of the early onset of an age-related health problem is the diagnosis of Alzheimer's disease in many individuals with Down's Syndrome while they are 30 to 40 years old (Wisniewski and Hill 1985).

Care Issues

There do not appear to be any "best practices" regarding the provision of health services for the developmentally disabled population. The Department of Health and Human Services [DHHS] (1987) notes that the elderly with lifelong disabilities tend to use health and medical services in three different ways. An individual who has been relatively independent all his or her life will continue to use a regular health provider but might require additional assistance from others as he or she ages. More dependent individuals, perhaps with moderate disabilities, living in a supervised living setting will most likely use generic health services but will require considerable assistance from others. As they age, they may require some highly specialized services. The last group of individuals, those with severe disabilities, have historically lived in developmental centers or nursing homes with medical personnel on staff. However, as the deinstitutionalization process continues, some individuals with the most severe disabilities are being integrated into community housing.

A national survey of facilities for individuals with developmental disabilities revealed that persons aged 63 to 74 years experienced health problems comparable to their nondisabled cohorts. High blood pressure, arthritis, and heart disease proved to be the most common ailments for both groups (Anderson 1989). Anderson (1989) also found, as did Krauss and Seltzer (1986), that individuals living in institutionalized settings are perceived to need more medical care than those living in community residences. Community residents were noted to have a greater number of unmet needs by Krauss and Seltzer (1986). However, Anderson (1989) speculates that the institutionalized group is not more medically needy but that service availability is often translated into the concept of need in developmental centers.

Alzheimer's Disease

Dementia is defined as a symptomatologic diagnosis whereby there is a loss of intellectual functioning severe enough to interfere with occupational or social functioning (American Psychiatric Association 1987).

Dementia indicates reduced functional abilities in all aspects of an individual's life. Dementia may follow a rapid, slow, or erratic course. Sometimes the dementia stops temporarily, allowing the individual to enjoy a period of stability.

Diagnosis of dementia among persons without disability normally focuses on four different areas of performance (Wisniewski and Hill 1985). Intactness of short-term memory, decrease in ability to think abstractly, inflexibility in thinking, and overall slowing of activity manifested in all areas of life are the primary areas of intellectual decline noted. Diagnosis of dementia is particularly difficult with developmentally disabled individuals. The difficulty increases as the severity of disability increases. Apathy, abrupt emotional changes, lack of care in grooming and hygiene, decreased expressive abilities, and increasing abnormalities in neurologic tests and signs have been reported in persons with Down's syndrome and Alzheimer's disease.

Many articles lead one to conclude that all persons with Down's syndrome ultimately develop Alzhemier's disease. Studiess have been conducted showing incidence rates of 24%, 30%, and 45% of the groups studied. The majority of the participants in these studies had severe or profound mental retardation and were institutionalized (Wisniewski and Hill 1985).

Persons with Down's syndrome age 30 or older should have their mental status tested at least once a year along with their physical examination. The mental status test focuses on concentration abilities, orientation, memory, and several other abilities. Intelligence tests should also be administered regularly to examine constancy of intellect. Careful observation by care givers should reveal any changes in daily living skills. Early signs of dementia require referral to specialists for further diagnosis. Locating an instrument to assess mental status for persons with developmental disabilities can be problematic. Wisniewski and Hill (1985) offer one for examination that is in the process of being standardized.

The care of an individual with developmental disabilities and Alzheimer's disease is essentially the same as for a nondisabled person. Reality orientation can provide a routine to help structure the individual's day. The goal is to encourage independence while ensuring safety of the person involved. Respite care is an important part of the treatment plan for the care givers. Participation in a support group that focuses on the families of patients with Alzheimer's disease is also helpful for many care givers.

Mental Health

Information-processing problems; associated medical, physical, or sensory disorders; an inability to express one's feelings adequately; and cultural influences lead to the development of mental health problems in individuals with mental retardation. Persons with mental retardation develop severe mental illness or difficult behaviors at a rate almost twice the rate of persons without mental retardation (Menolascino and Potter 1989).

In a recent study of mental illness in persons with retardation, Menolascino and Potter (1989) identified the major types of mental illness encountered. Of 76 elderly persons with mental retardation evaluated for 9 months in a psychiatric hospital, almost one third exhibited schizophrenic behaviors. Other diagnoses were dementia (both senile and Alzheimer's type); affective disorders such as depression; adjustment disorders such as brief reactive psychoses; personality disorders including schizoid type; and anxiety disorders (Menolascino and Potter 1989).

The major requirement in the delivery of services to elderly persons with mental retardation and mental illness is the provision of intense help (Menolascino and Potter 1989). Thoughtful care givers who allow the individuals to express themselves and who prompt them to learn new coping behaviors are an important factor in treatment.

Many treatments, in addition, include psychoactive medications. Their use has been controversial for many years (Menolascino and Potter 1989). It is important that care be taken when prescribing such drugs to elderly persons. Aging affects processes such as the absorption, transport, metabolic integration, and excretion of drugs. As a result, many drugs affect the elderly differently from the young. When psychoactive medications are combined with other medications used to treat physical ailments, the interaction of the drugs can produce unexpected side effects. In addition, psychotropic drugs sometimes produce serious side effects such as heart rhythm changes or involuntary movements as a result of tardive dyskinesia. These are only two of many possible side effects (Rinck and Calkins 1989). A recent study evaluating the use of medications by 841 older developmentally disabled persons revealed that the participants commonly took more than one psychoactive drug at a time. The type of residence where the participants lived was significant in predicting the number of drugs prescribed. Those living in settings with a medical orientation received drugs for behavioral problems more often than those living in other settings (Rinck and Calkins 1989).

Vision

Most people lose some visual function with age (DiStefano and Aston 1986). Loss of visual acuity (sharpness of image at a distance), loss of ability to focus quickly, inability to see clearly closely, sensitivity to glare, need for increased light, and difficulty seeing well at night are some of the more common difficulties encountered. Each of these occurs as a function of age. The most common causes of visual deterioration are cataracts, senile macular degeneration, diabetes mellitus, and glaucoma (DiStefano and Aston 1986). Cataracts, which cloud the lens, are the most common cause of reduced vision in elderly persons. Surgical removal is the treatment. Macular degeneration is the major cause of blindness in elderly persons. The part of the retina that allows the perception of fine detail and color deteriorates slowly. Blurring and clouding of vision are common complaints. Laser treatment can be successful as a treatment, but the condition must be diagnosed early and prompt treatment is essential. Diabetes may cause a variety of visual dysfunctions, many of which are caused by uncontrolled blood sugar levels. Prompt medical treatment is a must if any visual irregularities occur, because many of these conditions are irreversible. The final source of impairment is glaucoma. Glaucoma is not directly related to aging itself, but because the disease progresses slowly, the individual often does not realize there is a problem until serious damage has occurred. Glaucoma causes increased pressure within the eye that results in nerve damage and permanent loss of peripheral vision. The individual is left with what is commonly called tunnel vision (DiStefano and Aston 1986).

These vision problems affect the elderly regardless of disability status. However, the developmentally disabled person may not be able adequately to describe the symptoms and receive appropriate and timely treatment. It is imperative that care givers and others close to the disabled individual be attentive to the symptoms of these conditions and to the behavior of the disabled elderly individual. A person with developmental disabilities may appear to lose some functional daily living skills with no apparent cause. Visual deterioration should be suspect if behavioral changes occur in elderly disabled individuals.

Assistive devices and common sense allow those with visual problems to capitalize on their remaining vision. Magnifiers can be used for image enlargement; field-expanding devices allow those with tunnel vision to increase their mobility; large-print books are now available; and higher wattage light may be called for. Emphasizing contrasting colors of wall plates, dishes and place mats, combs and brushes, and stairs by placing contrasting tape on steps can help also. Devices such as the Kurzwell Reading Machine, which translates printed words into synthesized speech via computer and talking books, are available. Mobility training may be warranted (DiStefano and Aston 1986).

Hearing

Hearing loss is so common in elderly persons that it is rarely tested (Glass 1986). There is no evidence that older developmentally disabled individuals experience symptoms of hearing loss more frequently than nondisabled elderly individuals. Presbycusis is the term used to describe normal hearing loss due to aging. Inability to hear speech clearly, even though the enunciation and volume are adequate (speech discrimination), an increased sensitivity to certain sounds or pitch that sound specially loud (recruitment), and sounds within ones ears (tinnitus) are characteristics. Any or all of these characteristics may be present in elderly persons. Ear wax buildup, an inner ear mechanism malfunction, central nervous system changes, trauma due to loud noise, or the auditory mechanism damage due to certain drugs are the most common reasons for presbycusis (Glass 1986).

If an elderly developmentally disabled person seems to be unusually preoccupied and inattentive, his or her hearing should be evaluated (Glass 1986). The individual may not be able to express what is occurring. There are several options for the hard of hearing: a hearing aid; cochlear implants, which are expensive but may be a desirable option; and aural rehabilitation. A variety of techniques are usually used.

Devices are available to help the hearing impaired function independently and safely. Flashing lights can be attached to the telephone, doorbell, or fire alarm. Some humane societies train dogs to act as live warning systems. Closed-captioned TV, amplified telephones, and telecommunication device for the deaf (TDD) systems that use the telephone system to send and receive printed messages are available. The TDD system is being used by elderly persons with hearing impairments as well as by deaf persons (Glass 1986).

Nutrition

Physiologic changes that occur as a result of the aging process affect the way the body uses nutrients (Huber 1985). As the body ages, the proportion of lean body mass decreases, resulting in reduced energy or caloric needs. If intake is not adjusted, weight is gained. Taste is decreased; dental problems may cause food intake to be lessened; nutrients may not be absorbed efficiently; digestive disturbances become commonplace; large-bowel disorders often intensify; and conditions such as osteoporosis and vascular disease may emerge (Huber 1985).

Huber (1985) notes that these conditions are common to all elderly individuals. Nutritional status is also affected by medications taken, disease, and the individual's eating skills. Care givers and friends should be observant to weight changes and the person's ability to feed himself while maintaining a desirable weight. If physical disability encroaches upon an individual's ability to eat independently, investigation into a variety of adaptive utensils and other eating devices should be made.

Financial and Legal Issues

Recent legislative action has caused aging and developmental disabilities agencies to begin integrated planning, funding, and delivery of services for the elderly with developmental disabilities. The Developmental Disabilities Act as amended in 1987

requires more collaborative work between the developmental disabilities and aging groups. It also appropriated funds to be used in the creation of university programs that focus on training personnel to work with persons with aging and developmental disabilities.

The Older Americans Act, similarly amended in 1987, called particular attention to the needs of the older, lifelong-disabled individual. The terms disabled and severely disabled were specifically defined. The Administration on Aging was directed to develop collaborative relations with the Administration on Developmental Disabilities. This relationship encourages the mental retardation/developmentally disabled and aging networks at the state and local levels to focus on need rather than on category of recipient. The 1987 amendments specifically targeted providing developmentally disabled elderly persons access to the services offered by the Older Americans Act such as home helpers, legal services, transportation, and congregate meals (Older Americans Act as amended through December, 1988). Federally funded agencies have been directed to promote research and sponsor educational opportunities as an incentive to encourage entry to the field as a profession (Special Committee on Aging 1989). Although more options are becoming available for the elderly with developmental disabilities, the individual and the care givers must move through a maze of legal and financial choices in search of the best fit. This is not always so easy.

Braddock and colleagues (1990) found the average daily cost of maintaining an individual in an intermediate care facility for the mentally retarded (ICF/MR) was $153.54 in 1988. They also found that approximately 85% of all federal funding for residences of persons with developmental disabilities is spent on congregate (16+ bed) living settings, ICFs/MR. The costs have crept upward over the last decade despite a decrease in the number of persons living in institutional settings. As the percentage of federal expenditures has increased, the states have significantly reduced their contributions to residential care.

The Home and Community Based Services Waiver created by the Omnibus Budget Reconciliation Act of 1981 (PL 97-35) is sometimes used to enable individuals with developmental disabilities to avoid institutionalization by providing a residential exception to the Medicaid-funded ICF/MR. The cost of supporting the individual in the community under this waiver cannot be more than would be spent for the care of the individual in an ICF/MR. Because each state determines which services they will reimburse under the waiver, a lack of uniformity of services exists from state to state (Castellani 1987). Use of the waiver option for those with developmental disabilities is slowly increasing, however. Braddock et al. (1990) report that approximately 30,000 individuals with mental retardation received waiver services nationally in 1988 at a cost of $248 million dollars. This represents an increase of approximately 3,000 individuals since 1986 (Merlis 1988).

Pensions are of interest to those with a developmentally disabled family member as well to the individual. The state of New York (Ross 1989) has studied the feasibility of several pension options. They found the majority of individuals with developmental disabilities are supported by Supplemental Security Income (SSI) or Social Security Disability Income (SSDI). Although many work, they often work in low-paying, part-time jobs and do not qualify for pension benefits or in settings such as sheltered workshops that do not offer pension benefits.

A monthly paycheck is an important symbol of independence. However, because the developmentally disabled individual probably has not paid into a pension program, there are no funds to draw from (Ross 1989). Several options are possible. One Association for Retarded Citizens (ARC) Chapter in New York pays each developmentally disabled retiree a bonus of $10.00 monthly for a maximum of 24 months after retirement. Because the money is not a pension or a fringe benefit, the bonus is not considered income and does not disrupt the SSI support being received.

Sheltered workshops could charge their customers a nominal surcharge of 1% or 2% to finance their employees' retirement. This could be accomplished at the local, regional, or state level. A state-wide pension program administered by a state-wide agency or association of agencies is another option. Giving workers tax-deferred annuities as pensions is being explored; however, there is a question as to whether this plan might put the worker in an employee status and cause legal difficulties (Ross 1989). The idea of helping the developmentally disabled individual open an individual retirement account (IRA) is also under consideration. This option, however, is limited to those persons with financial resources beyond their job earnings, because SSI recipients cannot maintain over $2000.00 worth of assets without jeopardizing their need status. Some proponents feel the IRA option is the most reasonable option discussed. However, existing laws regulating IRAs would have to be modified to accommodate low-income persons with disabilities. If such an instrument were noninheritable by anyone other than the worker or his or her children, there may be an incentive to modify the existing laws.

A final option, which the state of New York is exploring, is to use a private insurance company to administer pension plans. Payroll deductions of as little as $10 per month can be deposited to a tax-free annuity account for the individual. Irregular earnings could be a problem with this option. A related area of concern is that of permanency planning. Consider the following scenario, described by Howell (1988):

> David is 75. He was the youngest of five children and lived at home with his

parents until he was 14, when first his mother and then his father died. David was a poor student and a discipline problem, and soon after his father's death, he was placed in a state residential school, where he lived for 49 years. When David was 64 he left the state school to live in a community residence, first in a group home and then later, by progressive steps, in a staffed apartment and finally his own apartment. He was visited daily by a variety of paid caregivers who provided minimal assistance to David in managing his affairs. David is illiterate and mildly retarded; both before his discharge from the state school and after, he worked diligently and successfully at a number of paid jobs. For several years he was a porter in a nursing home. His wages were always minimal, and he has no savings, retirement benefits, or pension. For the past year David has complained of mild abdominal discomforts, and also of indigestion; he has lost 30 pounds. No cause for these complaints was identified until recently, when cancer of the pancreas was diagnosed. As David became weaker and less able to take care of himself in his apartment, transfer to a nursing home was suggested. David, who has a very poor opinion of nursing homes from his personal work experience, reacted very strongly and negatively: He said that he would never go to a nursing home. The solution proposed by David is that he be readmitted to the state school he left 11 years ago, the only place that he now identifies as "home." His readmission would, of course, go against current state policy that the large state schools accept no more admissions. David, who has always been considered competent and whose competence is not now challenged, insists that he wants to go "home" to die.

How families plan for their developmentally disabled member's future is being studied. Heller and Factor (1988) found that black families expected their developmentally disabled family member to remain in the home as he or she aged, with the siblings taking over care when the parent or parents were no longer alive or able.

Black families were also less likely than white families to have made financial arrangements to maintain the developmentally disabled individual. The differences were attributed to socioeconomic rather than cultural factors.

An exploratory study of adults with developmental disabilities who live with their parents showed that the economic status of the family is a major factor in whatever long-term plans are made. In addition, the higher the adaptive functioning level of the child and the gender of the child (female), the greater likelihood there was of permanency planning. It was particularly interesting that over 50% of the parents had not made concrete plans for their child's future (Kaufman et al. 1990).

The financial and legal aspects of the life of an individual with developmental disabilities clearly are not certain. Permanency planning should be a priority, especially when one considers the likelihood that a developmentally disabled individual will outlive his or her parents. There is a host of legal issues that warrant consideration when developing permanency systems. Will the individual be able to decide and communicate his or her wishes regarding health, finances (including estates and investments), and life direction? Can the person make the decisions competently or will he or she require assistance due to the inability to conceptualize the situation and its possible outcomes? These are the issues of guardianship. Are competent developmentally disabled people giving powers of attorney to persons they trust so their wishes can be carried out in the future if they are unable to do so themselves? Wishes regarding issues such as refusal of medical treatment, resuscitation orders, advocacy desires, management of financial matters, and life direction might be specified. These are the issues confronted by the nondisabled elderly. These are the identical issues the disabled elderly should confront. An attorney knowledgeable in estates, guardianship, and powers of attorney should be consulted.

Services

Persons with developmental disabilities use formal and informal supports to create a life acceptable in activity and quality. The formal supports may be rendered by a public or a proprietary agency. Proprietary service agencies are becoming increasingly more commonplace as funding mechanisms are modified to allow public agencies to contract services. An individual who is not bound by government-sponsored financial support may choose to engage a private sector agency. The remaining discussion focuses on public service agencies, which are the backbone of the aging and developmental disabilities network. Proprietary ventures are noted specifically.

Formal Supports

The developmental disabilities and aging networks provide a multitude of services. Historically, each has served a specific group, with minimal overlap. Times are changing. Legislative action in both areas requires more collaboration among agencies. The MR/DD and aging networks are not insensitive to this pressure. Age discrimination was the impetus for establishing the aging network. Those involved in the aging system focus on creating services that are not specially geared to the elderly but are responsive to the needs of older people in general. A specific age, income status, or disability status is not the focus; the need for resources is (McDowell 1988). The Older Americans Act is one means of providing services to older persons. The funding of programs through this Act gives state and regional agencies on aging the authority to coordinate and tailor the services they offer according to identified needs (Quirk and Aravanis 1988).

Much of the current discussion on services for this population focuses on the administrative provision of the service rather than on discussion about quality, appropriateness, or rationale. Many states have conducted surveys in an attempt to determine the needs of the elderly developmentally disabled.

Seltzer and Krauss (1987) have identified three primary means of service provision for the elderly with developmental disabilities (or more specifically, mental retardation): to receive services with others who are also disabled, in an age-integrated group; to receive services with non-age-integrated groups of similarly disabled elders; or to access aging programs that primarily serve non-handicapped seniors. The state of Massachusetts conducted a survey of how the state's services were being used. They found that almost two thirds of the elderly with mental retardation received services in age-integrated, disability-segregated settings. One third received generic senior services whereas approximately 5% participated in segregated age and disability programs. The disabled persons involved were recipients of MR/DD network services (Seltzer 1988). One can only speculate about the numbers of disabled elders, unknown to the MR/DD network, using generic elder programs.

Improving access to aging programs is an area of concern for some. Referral to aging programs by interdisciplinary teams, with admission contingent on a successful trial period, is discussed as one means of incorporating elderly disabled persons in elder programs (Cotton and Spirrison 1986). Most state analyses indicate that cross-network staff training is pivotal to the success of collaborative ventures. Coordinated interagency projects, including financial sharing, are another critical area (Cotton and Spirrison 1988; Hawkins and Eklund 1990). Case management, advocacy, day services, home care, and respite services are also commonly mentioned as important services (Hawkins and Eklund 1989; 1990).

Care Givers

When services are viewed from the perspective of the care giver rather than from that of the service provider, satisfaction with services seems to be moderated by the care giver's perception of stress and his or her ability to maintain the care giver role. High levels of maladaptive behaviors are associated with more intense feelings of stress and burden by the parents. Interestingly, the age of the care giver does not seem to be related to the perception of burden (Kaufman et al. 1990) or to the assessment of the ability to perform care-giving chores. Care-giver perception of no longer being able to provide appropriate care is the impetus to access formal services (Engelhardt et al. 1988). Some of the more available services are discussed briefly.

Specialized Services

The most commonly available services are those provided by the Older Americans Act (OAA as amended through 12/88). Included are congregate meals at nutrition sites, homemaker services, advocacy, case management, legal assistance, socialization, and leisure activities through senior centers. Less commonly found, but valuable, are adult day care programs and respite care programs. These services are generally thought of as part of the aging network. Many of the same services are duplicated as part of the MR/DD network.

Case management, the organization and coordination of activities for another, has long been used in the area of developmental disabilities to assist the individual in meeting his or her obligations and receiving services as needed. The case manager may coordinate a client's day by verifying appointment times, arranging transportation to and from the appointment, briefing the client about tests to be conducted at the doctor's office, and ensuring the scheduling of transportation to pick the client up at the senior center at a specified time. Case management introduces order into the lives of those who cannot provide the order themselves. As one might imagine, this is essential in the lives of many developmentally disabled individuals. A recent trend is private case management, which is reimbursable by insurance.

Informal Supports

Informal support can be thought of as people helping each other because they care about each other. The caring is shown through economic, social, or emotional services. No formalized agreements are made between the individuals involved (Hooyman 1983). One might assume that, the larger and more active the informal support network, the less reliance an individual has on formal supports. Because the elderly with developmental disabilities typically have not married and had children, they have a smaller familial support network to rely on when they need assistance (Seltzer 1985). In fact, many of these aged individuals are outliving their parents, a relatively recent phenomenon due to increased life expectancy.

Family members are the primary informal supports for aging disabled persons living in the family home. Preliminary study indicates these individuals may receive no support from professionals and have few friends to count on for support. This is in contrast to those living in community settings. Individuals living in the community receive support from family, friends, and professionals (Krauss and Erickson 1988). Not surprisingly, the support networks (formal and informal) for the persons living in the family home are significantly smaller than for those living in community settings (Krauss and Erickson 1988). Of course, although siblings often provide much support, it is unclear whether they are willing and able to assume the role of primary resource or care giver when the parent can no longer carry on in this capacity. Kaufman and colleagues (1990) found that some aged parents have unspoken expectations that siblings will care for their disabled sibling when the parent is no longer able.

Placement Issues

In recent years, placing mentally retarded individuals in institutions has not been looked on favorably. The massive warehousing of this population through the first half of this century created such social disdain that, with the deinstitutionalization movement, the word institution itself has become negatively stereotyped. However, is the large institutional facility always an inappropriate environment for mentally retarded elderly persons? Should those individuals who are currently placed in large institutions be abruptly removed and placed in a more stimulating environment? These questions are seldom answered with a simple "yes." Before any answer may be determined with respect to a given individual, an entire set of considerations must be taken into account. These considerations include the functional ability of the aging individual, the match between the characteristics of the proposed placement option and the person's needs, and the feelings of the aging individual regarding his or her placement (Janicki et al. 1985).

Criticisms such as those relating to the abuse of civil rights, infantilization of clients by staff members, and restrictiveness of setting have some base of support (Regan 1978; Thurman 1986). Indeed, institutionalized elderly mentally retarded clients in the state of Georgia were reported to be significantly more impaired than matched community residents in the areas of social resources, mental health, and activities of daily living (Carswell and Hartig 1979). The institutionalized clients in Eyman and Widaman's (1987) study showed greater declines in adaptive behaviors than those clients living at home. Although these problems have often been generalized to be true of all institutions, impoverished environments are not necessarily a standard of these facilities today. In fact, it is possible for institutions to provide stimulating environments (for example, integrated activities, leisure programs, diverse work activities) from which clients may benefit (Cotten et al. 1981; Dickerson et al. 1979; Talkington and Chiovaro 1969).

An often neglected factor, independent of specific setting characteristics, is the desire of the client being considered for alternative placement. Clients who have been institutionalized for years develop routines, adjust to the safety of the institution, create a social network, and develop a sense of permanency and stability (Dickerson et al. 1979; Seltzer and Seltzer 1984). The disruption of a life situation caused by relocating the target individual may be severe (DiGiovanni 1978; Rago 1985; Thurman 1986). In one study, 18 of the 23 clients interviewed expressed a preference to stay in the institution (Dickerson et al. 1979). This is not to say that these elderly persons cannot or will not adjust to alternate care facilities. Indeed, evidence supports positive outcomes to this effect. However, professionals must be aware of the possibility of displacement shock and develop means to alleviate its impact (Hemming et al. 1981; O'Connor et al. 1970; Rago 1985).

Given the proper fit of all variables considered, successful outcomes of residential transitions are becoming more frequent now than in the past. In Talkington and Chiovaro's (1969) study, 105 aged mentally retarded residents were trained in a multiphase program aimed at benefiting psychosocial attributes and altering regressive trends through activity and rehabilitation. The residents were described initially as dependent and inactive. Following the training, which included increasing awareness of personal-social issues, greater participation in assorted activities, and extended independence and responsibility, residents were described as having attained competency in all areas. Twenty-seven of the residents were placed in a variety of community care facilities after completion of the program. It has also been suggested by Cotten et al. (1981) that elderly mentally retarded persons may show such positive adjustment to intermediate care facilities that they may become indistinguishable from the nonretarded elderly in these facilities. Cotten and his associates found that mentally retarded clients in these facilities required less staff time and had fewer problems overall than did the nonretarded clients.

In general, it may be said that elderly persons with mental retardation can adjust well to noninstitutional placements. This may be due in part to their past institutional experience, which prepared them for the daily routine of the community care facility (Mueller and Porter 1969; Thurman 1986; Walz et al. 1986). As Dickerson and colleagues (1978) indicated, the large institutional facility may be seen either as an aid or detriment to the functioning of the elderly mentally retarded person. Although discrepancies exist in the literature regarding the percentage of aging individuals who currently reside in institutional settings (DiGiovanni 1978; Janicki and MacEachron 1984; Richards 1975; Seltzer 1985; Seltzer and Seltzer 1984), social workers have to be prepared to adjust programming to meet the needs of elderly persons in either situation. The outcome should be highly individualized and should take into consideration a myriad of factors including the personal feelings of the individual.

As one may gather, it is difficult to disentangle the complexity of issues that relate to the quality of life for mentally retarded elderly individuals (Landesman 1986; Rosen 1986). The quality of life of these elderly persons may be enhanced through placement in the most appropriate setting. The development of proper support systems may also be considered an integral part of the concept of the quality of life. The goals of support systems are stress reduction, promotion of health benefits, and increase in general mental well-being (O'Connor 1983). Whereas the concept of support may be discussed in terms of formal and informal support, the two types are not mutually exclusive. That is, each plays a complimentary role in the life of mentally handicapped citizens who have aged.

Activities and Programs

As we have discussed in earlier sections, the majority of money spent on persons with developmental disabilities is spent within the ICF/MR setting. Certain criteria must be met for an agency to qualify for this money whether it is in a large or small community setting. A brief history will reveal the background and reasoning for the criteria used for activities conducted in ICF/MR-funded settings.

The ICFs/MR are funded through Title XIX/Medicaid of the Social Security Act. The funding itself is channeled from Medicaid through the Health Care Financing Administration (HCFA). Medicaid, having a medical orientation, takes the perspective that the individuals receiving the funding need medical or rehabilitation treatment (Merlis 1988). The treatment for developmentally disabled persons is to present them with the opportunity to acquire new knowledge and skills. The goal is that all experiences should be quality learning opportunities that are objective and measurable. Thus, the term "active treatment" was born. Active treatment means that each individual must participate in daily activities that will increase or maintain the individual's current level of functional independence.

In recent years, active treatment has been redefined to include more flexible options for older individuals who are ready to retire from work or continuous-skill-building activities. The standards focus on the wishes of the individual, his or her quality of life, and maintenance of existing skills. Rather than discuss specific activities in detail in this section, we will briefly discuss the issues associated with activities of the elderly developmentally disabled individual. Perhaps at no other time in their lives do the developmentally disabled and the nondisabled have more in common. Many persons of both groups have spent a significant period of their lives working and are looking forward to retirement. There are those who want to work forever and cannot imagine retirement. There is also the group that has never been employed but are aging and feeling the effects of the aging process.

When consulting the literature on activity and the older developmentally disabled person, there is no dominant program model. Both disability-segregated and disability-integrated programs have been used with success (Seltzer and Krauss 1987). Some fear that the developmentally disabled will be isolated as they age due to the combination of two conditions, aging and disability, often the basis of discrimination in our society. However, elderly developmentally disabled persons qualify, just as the nondisabled, for many government-sponsored services such as those funded by the Older Americans' Act.

Although hesitation and resistance may be encountered when elderly persons with mental retardation begin participating in generic senior centers, Seltzer and Krauss (1987) found general acceptance by the nonretarded seniors and senior center staff to be the norm. Good health and the age of the individual with the developmental disability were the most important factors that influenced acceptance in the generic senior centers. An important point noted by Seltzer and Krauss (1987) is that the use of generic senior centers is not desirable for all elderly individuals with lifelong disabilities. An individualized approach to this decision is recommended.

Common elements to many elder services programs are health awareness, physical exercise, independent living skills, reality orientation, counseling, nutrition, and leisure recreation activities. Additionally, some elders with disabilities may need assistance or prompting in the areas of self-help skills (Catapano et al. 1985).

One suspects that older individuals with developmental disabilities have the desire for socialization, including romance with others; participation in spiritual or religious activities; age-appropriate activities; intergenerational contact; and meaningful activities in their lives. Little investigation has been conducted with this group to identify and explore their desires. Creative approaches to obstacles will enable sensitive professionals to help them achieve their wishes.

References

1. American Psychiatric Association. Diagnostic and Statistical Manual of Mental Disorders. 3rd ed. Washington, DC, Author, 1987.
2. Anderson DJ. Healthy and institutionalized: Health and related conditions among older persons with developmental disabilities. Journal of Applied Gerontology. 8:228–241, 1989.
3. Baroff GS. Predicting the prevalence of mental retardation in individual catchment areas. Ment Retard. 20:133–135, 1982.
4. Birren JE. Principles of research on aging. In: Birren JE. ed. Handbook of Aging in the Individual. Chicago, University of Chicago Press, 1959, pp 3–42.
5. Blake R. Disabled older persons: A demographic analysis. Journal of Rehabilitation. October/November/December:19–27, 1981.
6. Bostwick DH, Foss G. Obtaining consumer input—2 strategies for identifying and ranking the problems of mentally retarded young-adults. Education and Training of the Mentally Retarded. 16:207–212, 1981.
7. Braddock D, Hemp R, Fujiura G, Bachelder L, Mitchell D. The state of the states in developmental disabilities. Baltimore, Paul H. Brookes, 1990.
8. Carswell AT, Hartig SA. Older developmentally disabled persons: A survey of impairments. Unpublished manuscript, 1979. Athens, GA, University Affiliated Program, University of Georgia.
9. Castellani PJ. The Political Economy of Developmental Disabilities. Baltimore, Paul H. Brookes, 1987.
10. Catapano PM, Levy JM, Levy PH. Day activity and vocational program services In: Janicki MP, Wisniewski HM. eds. Aging and Developmental Disabilities: Issues and Approaches. Baltimore, Paul H. Brookes, 1985, pp 305–316.
11. Cotten PD, Sison GFP, Starr S. Comparing elderly mentally retarded and non-mentally retarded individuals: Who are they? What are their needs? Gerontologist. 21:359–365, 1981.
12. Cotten PD, Spirrison CL. Development of services for elderly persons with mental retardation in a rural state. Ment Retard. 26:187–190, 1988.
13. Cotton PD, Spirrison CL. The elderly mentally retarded developmentally disabled population: A

challenge for the service delivery system. In: Brody SJ, Ruff GE. eds. Aging and Rehabilitation. New York, Springer Publishing, 1986, pp 159–189.

14. Department of Health and Human Services. Personnel for health needs for the elderly through the year 2020: Report to Congress. Washington DC: Department of Health and Human Services. Report No. 101-249. Washington, DC, U.S. Government Printing Office, 1987.

15. Dickerson M, Hamilton J, Huber R, Segal R. The aged mentally retarded client: A challenge to the community. In: Sweeney DP, Wilson TY. eds. Double Jeopardy, the Plight of the Aging and Aged Developmentally Disabled Persons in Mid-America. Ann Arbor, University of Michigan Press, 1979, pp 8–35.

16. DiGiovanni L. The elderly retarded: A little-known group. Gerontologist. 18:262–266, 1978.

17. DiStefano AF, Aston SJ. Rehabilitation for the blind and visually impaired elderly. In: Brody SJ, Ruff GE. eds. Aging and Rehabilitation: Advances in the State of the Art. New York, Springer, 1986, pp 203–218.

18. Eisdorfer C. Conceptual models of aging: The challenge of a new frontier. Am Psychol. 38:197–202, 1983.

19. Engelhardt JL, Brubaker TH, Lutzer VD. Older caregivers of adults with mental retardation: Service utilization. Ment Retard. 26:191–195, 1988.

20. Eyman RK, Call TL, White JF. Mortality of elderly mentally retarded persons in California. Journal of Applied Gerontology. 8:203–215, 1989.

21. Eyman RK, Widaman KF. Life-span development of institutionalized and community-based mentally retarded persons, revisited. American Journal of Mental Deficiency. 91:559–569, 1987.

22. Glass LE. Rehabilitation for deaf and hearing-impaired elderly. In: Brody SJ, Ruff GE. eds. Aging and Rehabilitation: Advances in the State of the Art. New York, Springer, 1986, pp 218–239.

23. Hamilton JC, Segal RM. A Consultation-Conference on Developmental Disabilities and Gerontology. Ann Arbor, University Park Press, 1975.

24. Hawkins BA, Elkund SJ. Aging and developmental disabilities: Interagency planning for an emerging population. Journal of Applied Gerontology. 8:166–174, 1989.

25. Hawkins BA, Eklund SJ. Planning processes and outcomes for an aging population with developmental disabilities. Ment Retard. 28:35–40, 1990.

26. Heller T, Factor A. Permanency planning among black and white family caregivers of older adults with mental retardation. American Association on Mental Retardation. 26:203–208, 1988.

27. Hemming H, Lavendar T, Pill R. Quality of life of mentally retarded adults transferred from large institutions to new small units. American Journal of Mental Deficiency. 86:157–169, 1981.

28. Hooyman N. Social support networks in services to the elderly. In: Whittaker JK, Garbarino J, et al. eds. Social Support Networks: Informal Helping in the Human Services. New York, Aldine, 1983.

29. Howell MC. Ethical dilemmas encountered in the care of those who are disabled and also old. Educational Gerontology. 14:439–449, 1988.

30. Huber AM. Nutrition, aging, and developmental disabilities. In: Janicki MP, Wisniewski HM. eds. Aging and Developmental Disabilities: Issues and Approaches. Baltimore, Paul H. Brookes, 1985.

31. Jacobson JW, Sutton MS, Janicki MP. Demography and characteristics of aging and aged mentally retarded persons. In: Janicki MP, Wisniewski HM. eds. Aging and Developmental Disabilities: Issues and Approaches. Baltimore, Paul H. Brookes, 1985.

32. Janicki MP, Jacobson JW. Generational trends in sensory, physical, and behavioral abilities among older mentally-retarded persons. American Journal of Mental Deficiency. 90:490–500, 1986.

33. Janicki MP, MacEachron AE. Residential, health, and social service needs of elderly developmentally disabled persons. Gerontologist. 24:128–137, 1984.

34. Janicki MP, Otis JP, Puccio PS, Rettig JH, Jacobson JW. Service needs among older developmentally disabled persons. In: Janicki MP, Wisniewski HM. eds. Aging and Developmental Disabilities: Issues and Approaches. Baltimore, Paul H. Brookes, 1985.

35. Kaufman AV, Adams JP, Campbell VA. Permanency planning by older parents who care for adult children with mental retardation. Unpublished manuscript, 1990.

36. Kaufman AV, Campbell VA, Adams JP. A lifetime of caring: Older parents who care for adult children with mental retardation. Community Alternatives: International Journal of Family Care. 2:39–54, 1990.

37. Krauss MW, Seltzer MM. Comparison of elderly and adult mentally retarded persons in community and institutional settings. American Journal of Mental Deficiency. 91:237–243, 1986.

38. Krauss MW, Erickson M. Informal support networks among aging persons with mental retardation: A pilot study. Ment Retard. 26:197–201, 1988.

39. Landesman S. Quality of life and personal life satisfaction: Definition and measurement issues. Ment Retard. 24:141–143, 1986.

40. Lubin RA, Kiely M. Epidemiology of aging in developmental disabilities. In: Janicki MP, Wisniewski HM. eds. Aging and Developmental Disabilities: Issues and Approaches. Baltimore, Paul H. Brookes, 1985, pp 95–113.

41. McDowell D. Aging and developmental disability: Personal reflections on policy for persons. Educational Gerontology. 14:465–470, 1988.

42. Menolascino FJ, Potter JF. Mental illness in the elderly mentally retarded. Journal of Applied Gerontology. 8:192–202, 1989.

43. Merlis M. Alternate delivery options and waiver programs Medicaid source book: Background data and analysis (U.S. House Committee on Energy and Commerce Prt. 100-AA). Washington, DC, U.S. Government Printing Office, 1988.

44. Mueller BJ, Porter R. Placement of adult retardates from state institutions in community care facilities. Community Ment Health J. 5:289–294, 1969.

45. Murrell SA, Norris FH. Quality of life as the criterion of need assessment and community psychology. Journal of Community Psychology. 11:88–97, 1983.

46. O'Connor G. Social support of mentally retarded persons. Ment Retard. 21:187–196, 1983.

47. O'Connor G, Justice RS, Warren N. The aged mentally retarded: Institution or community care? American Journal of Mental Deficiency. 75:354–360, 1970.

48. Older Americans Act of 1965 as Amended Through 12/88. (U.S. House of Representatives Committee Print Serial No. 101-A and U.S. Senate Special Committee on Aging Serial No. 101-B). Washington, DC, U.S. Government Printing Office, 1989.

49. Omnibus Budget Reconciliation Act of 1981, Section 2176, United States Statutes at Large, 95:812–813.

50. Osberg JS, McGinnis GE, DeJong G, Seward ML. Life satisfaction and quality of life among disabled elderly adults. Journal of Gerontology. 42:228–230, 1987.

51. Quirk DA, Aravanis SC. State partnerships to enhance the quality of life of older Americans with lifelong disabilities. Educational Gerontology. 14:431–437, 1988.

52. Rago WV. The impact of technology on the delivery of mental retardation services in the year 2000: A research perspective. In: Gaitz CM, Niederehe G, Wilson NL. eds. Psychosocial and Policy Issues. Vol. 2. New York, Springer, 1985, pp 209–218.

53. Regan J. Legal issues and advocacy. In: Rose MG, Bernstein D, Plotnick L. eds. Conference Proceedings on the Aging/Developmentally Disabled Person. College Park, University of Maryland, 1978, pp 69–85.

54. Rice PR, Feldman JF. Living longer in the United States: Demographic changes and health needs of the elderly. Health and Society. 61:362–396, 1983.

55. Richards BW. Mental retardation. In: Howells JG. ed. Modern Perspectives on the Psychiatry of Old Age. New York, Academic Press, 1975.

56. Rinck C, Calkins CF. Pattern of psychotropic medication use among older persons with developmental disabilities. Journal of Applied Gerontology. 8:215–227, 1989.

57. Rosen M. Quality of life for persons with mental retardation: A question of entitlement. Ment Retard. 24:365–366, 1986.

58. Ross DM. A Report to the New York State Developmental Disabilities Planning Council on the Feasibility of Different Pension Support Systems for New York State Residents with a Developmental Disability. Unpublished manuscript, 1989.

59. Schaie KW, Willis SL. Adult Development and Aging. 2nd ed. Boston, Little, Brown, 1986, pp 1–39.

60. Schalock RL, Keith KD, Hoffman KY, Karan OC. Quality of life: Its measurement and use. Ment Retard. 27:25–31, 1989.

61. Segal R. Trends in services for the aged mentally retarded. Ment Retard. 15:25–27, 1977.

62. Segal R. Services for the aged developmentally disabled person: A challenge to the community. In: Rose MG, Berstein D, Plotnick L. eds. Conference Proceedings on the Aging/Developmentally Disabled Person. College Park, University of Maryland, 1978, pp 5–13.

63. Seltzer MM. Informal supports for aging mentally retarded persons. American Journal of Mental Deficiency. 90:259–265, 1985a.

64. Seltzer MM. Research in social aspects of aging and developmental disabilities. In: Janicki MP, Wisniewski HM. eds. Aging and Developmental Disabilities: Issues and Approaches. Baltimore, Paul H. Brookes, 1985b, pp 161–173.

65. Seltzer MM. Structure and patterns of service utilization by elderly persons with mental retardation. Ment Retard. 26:181–185, 1988.

66. Seltzer MM, Krauss MW. Aging and mental retardation: Extending the continuum. Monographs of the American Association on Mental Deficiency. 9:25–41, 1987.

67. Seltzer MM, Seltzer GB. The elderly mentally retarded: A group in need of service. In: Getzel G, Mellor J. eds. Gerontological Social Work Practice in the Community. New York, Haworth Press, 1984.

68. Seltzer MM, Seltzer GB. The elderly mentally retarded: A group in need of service. Journal of Gerontological Social Work. 8:99–119, 1985.

69. Sison GFP, Cotten PD. The elderly mentally retarded person: Current perspectives and future directions. Journal of Applied Gerontology. 8:151–167, 1989.

70. Special Committee on Aging. Developments in Aging: Vol. 1 (Senate Sweeney DP, Wilson TY, 1979) Double Jeopardy, the Plight of Aging and Aged Developmentally Disabled Persons in Mid-America. Ann Arbor, The University of Michigan Press, 1989.

71. Talkington LW, Chiovaro SJ. An approach to programming for the aged mentally retarded. Ment Retard. 7:29–30, 1969.

72. Thurman E. Maintaining dignity in later years. In: Summers JA. ed. The Right to Grow Up: An

Introduction to Adults with Developmental Disabilities. Baltimore, Paul H. Brookes, 1986, pp 91–115.

73. Tibbits C. Can we invalidate negative stereotypes of aging? Gerontologist. 19:10–20, 1979.

74. Tymchuk AJ. The mentally retarded in later life. In: Kaplan OJ. ed. Psychopathology of Aging. New York, Academic Press, 1979, pp 197–209.

75. Walker BR. Presidential address 1985: Inalienable rights of persons with mental retardation. Ment Retard. 23:219–221, 1985.

76. Walz T, Harper D, Wilson J. The aging developmentally disabled person: A review. Gerontologist. 26:622–629, 1986.

77. Wisniewski K, Hill AL. Clinical aspects of dementia in mental retardation and developmental disabilities. In: Janicki MP, Wisniewski HM. eds. Aging and Developmental Disabilities: Issues and Approaches. Baltimore, Paul H. Brookes, 1985, pp 195–210.

Index

A

AAMR. *See* American Association on Mental Retardation
Ability/achievement discrepancy calculations, types of, 83
ABR. *See* Auditory brain-stem response
Academic skills. *See also* Learning skills
  of learning disabled, 85–86
Acoustic reflex, measurements of, 104
  sensitivity prediction from, 104
Active treatment, 293
Adaptations
  definition of, 37
  environmental, partial participation in, 37
  material
    with cerebral palsy, 37–38
    partial participation in, 37
Adaptive behavior
  definition of, 1
  measurement of, 1–2
Administration on Aging, relationship with Administration on Developmental Disabilities, 287
Administration on Developmental Disabilities, relationship with Administration on Aging, 287
Adult day care programs, 291
Advocacy, 136
  for community living, 264–265
  politically related, 265
  service related, 265
Affective and cognitive indifference, 69
  symptoms of, 69
Aged mentally retarded. *See* Elderly disabled
Aggression, noncompliance, and profanity, treatment of

defining procedures for, 76–77
  preliminary considerations, 75
  selecting variables for, 75–76
Aging. *See also* Elderly disabled
  hearing loss with, 286–287
  indices of, 279
  visual impairment with, 285–286
Alcohol abuse, 58
ALT-R. *See* Differential reinforcement, of alternative responses
Alzheimer's disease, 284–285
American Association of Mental Deficiency Adaptive Behavior Checklist, 244
American Association on Mental Retardation
  definition of mental retardation, 1, 18
  definition of mild mental retardation, 2
American Speech-Language-Hearing Association, Committee on the Communication Processes of Nonspeaking Persons, 109
Americans with Disabilities Act of 1990, 124–125, 185
Anxiety/fear, in autism, 70
Articulation disorders, 99
Articulation errors, 99
Assessment
  criterion-referenced, 154
  key resources for, 156
  norm-referenced, 154
    conditions for use, 161–162
Assessment battery
  initial, 145
  sample, 146
Assessment tools, 145–148
  behavior-specific, 146–147
  clinical evaluations, 146–147
  criterion-referenced, 146–147

S

Safety precautions
  for lifting and handling, 33
  for positioning and handling, 34
School, transition from
  to work, with mild to moderate mental
    retardation, 13–14
  to work and independent living, 131–133
Self-care. *See also* Economic self-sufficiency
  in cerebral palsy, 36–47
  with emotional impairment, 57–59
    case history, 58–59
  with learning disability, 86
  with mild to moderate mental retardation,
    4–5
    case history, 5
  with severe and profound mental
    retardation, 19
    case history, 19
Self-care skills
  dressing/grooming, 4–5
    adaptation for, 38
    assessment of, 39
  eating, 4
Self-concept, of learning disabled, 92
Self-direction
  characteristics of, 10–11
  definition of, 10
  with emotional impairment, 62
  lack of, interventions for, 62
  with mild to moderate mental retardation, 10
  with severe and profound mental
    retardation, 24–25
    case histories, 24–25
  ways to foster, 24
Self-injurious behavior
  behavior management services for, 206–227
  explanation for, 72–73
    aberrant physical process hypothesis,
      208–209
    hypotheses for, 206–210
    negative reinforcement hypothesis,
      207–208
    positive reinforcement hypothesis,
      206–207
    psychodynamic hypothesis, 210
    self-stimulation hypothesis, 208
    social reinforcement hypothesis, 207
  functional analysis of, 219–221
  punishment for, 210, 215–217
    types of, 215
  treatment of, 209
    with aversive procedures, 210–217
    based on functional analysis of
      self-injury, 219–221
    comprehensive, composite approach to,
      221–222

defining procedures for, 74
    differential reinforcement strategies for,
      218–219
    by electric shock, 214–215
    by extinction, 211
    with nonaversive procedures, 217–222
    by operant procedures, 210–222
    overcorrection for, 213–214, 216
    preliminary considerations, 72–73
    psychotropic medications for, 209
    by rearrangement of antecedent stimulus
      conditions, 217–218
    selecting variables for, 73–74
    time out from positive reinforcement
      procedure for, 212–213
Self-management, 61
  effectiveness of, 61
Self-monitoring, 89–90
Sensitivity prediction from the acoustic reflex,
    104
Service delivery, quality of, determination of, 142
Service delivery cycle, 144
  steps in, 145
Service planning and provision
  design of plan for, 145
  ecologic approach, 130–131
  family involvement in, 131
  future, implications for, 136–138
  systems approach, 130
  terminology, 129
Service providers
  challenges for, 129–131, 133–136
  future, 137–138
  competency areas for, 134
  issues for, 129–136
  roles of, 133–134
  successful, focus of training of, 28
  training of, 133–134
    comprehensive, 137
Services
  anticipated, for students exiting educational
    system, 132
  coordination among, 160–161
  that examine client outcomes, 137
Sheltered employee, 238
Shock rod, 214
Sign language, use of, with autistics, 78–79
Skill(s). *See also* Learning skills; Self-care
    skills; Social skills
  of communication, development of,
    109–110, 118
  for community living, 229
    instruction in, 238–252
  for daily living, instruction in, 240
  functional, 239
    instruction in, 239–240
  for home living, 244–245
    instruction in, 244–251

Vision training
  for deaf-blind handicapped, 116
  functional, steps in, 116–117
Visual functions, and responses, 117
Visual reinforcement audiometry, 102, 117
Vocational education
  courses, success of, 239
  definition of, 160
Vocational placement, options, 128, 137
  prior to supported employment, 184–185
Vocational rehabilitation
  eligibility for, 133
  job placement method, 26
  service options, 26–27
Vocational rehabilitation counselors, training
    of, 134
Vocational training programs, for learning
    disabled, 93

Vocational training program workshops, 184
Voice disorders, 99
VRA. *See* Visual reinforcement audiometry

W

Work
  right to, 128
  substantial gainful work activity, definition
    of, 268
  transition from school to, 131–133
    in mild to moderate mentally retarded,
      13–14
Work-activity programs, 184–185, 237
Work expenses, impairment-related, 272
Work incentives, 271–273
  plan for achieving self-support (PASS),
    271–272